REGISTERED HOMES

A LEGAL HANDBOOK

REGISTERED HOMES

A LEGAL HANDBOOK

Paul Ridout
Solicitor, Dibb Lupton Alsop

with a chapter by Philip Boyd
Barrister

JORDANS

1998

Published by
Jordan Publishing Limited
21 St Thomas Street
Bristol BS1 6JS

British Library Cataloguing-in-Publication Data
A catalogue record for this book is available from the British Library.

ISBN 0 85308 448 3

Typeset by York House Typographic Ltd
Printed by MPG Books Ltd, Bodmin, Cornwall

PREFACE

It is with a mixture of surprise and dismay that I realise that it is now more than 26 years since I first considered a legal problem concerning a registered care home. Over that period the nature and extent of the provision of social care has changed beyond all recognition. An occasional and vocational business activity has become what some may now term a mainstream business sector. The law has seen four major new pieces of legislation and numerous supplemental changes. The concept of funding for those who need and receive care has changed from domestic and familial support to provision that is mainly funded by, as opposed to provided with, public money. The demographics of an increasingly ageing and dependent population needing to use the resources of a shrinking working population have had dramatic effects in many fields. Nowhere is this more keenly felt than in the law which relates to how such provision is regulated and how it may be funded from time to time.

Against this background, it is surprising that there has been no attempt to bring together the knowledge and experience of this particular field of legal practice save in annotated publications of the principal statutes.

Many practitioners are now coming across problems in the field of residential and, indeed, domiciliary care for the first time, and there is clearly an unfilled need for them to gain some feeling for the way in which such problems are approached and solved. Simple annotations and references to particular cases are not sufficient to assist a busy practitioner facing a new field of law for the first time.

When I was first asked to consider writing this book, some five or six years ago, I was hesitant, feeling that the gap must be filled quickly by someone more suitable or able. This has not happened and the demand has remained.

It is impossible to cover such a wide topic in the greatest detail or to meet the needs of every particular situation. Within this book, I have tried to give a snapshot of the practical effect of the law as it relates to registered homes and how experience in practice has used that law to solve particular problems as they have arisen from day to day.

I have ruthlessly drawn on the experience of others and I am particularly indebted to my co-author of Chapter 11, Philip Boyd, a practising barrister in Bristol, for his patient and tireless assistance in bringing together what is very much an overview of the current position of public funding of those in care. Those who are presented with these problems on a day-to-day basis should rapidly turn to the principal legislation. The field is a veritable minefield. Often, the answer, to assist the client, may not be exactly what it seems at first and certainly not what is published by public authorities.

Many may differ from some of the suggestions that I make and some of the conclusions which I draw from legislation which has not been as fully perused by the higher courts as might be. For that matter, neither do I make apology, nor do I resent criticism. These issues deserve debate which will expose, not only that some sacred cows of construction and practice have no basis in law, but that some of the legal conclusions are a total nonsense and warrant practical solutions or statutory intervention.

The book is an attempt to assist practitioners and is set out in chapters which address particular aspects of regulation of the three principle types of homes: residential care, nursing and children's homes. Having gained experience advising both regulators and providers, I have come to appreciate that many problems arise because different participators in regulation see issues from diametrically opposed points of view. Accordingly, wherever possible, I have tried to put the issues in context from the point of view of each principal interested party and endeavoured to balance competing interests. This means that, inevitably, a degree of duplication will be found within the book. Again, no apology is made. I doubt that many will read this or any legal textbook from cover to cover. Many, of whom I am one, are exceedingly irritated to have to constantly cross-refer to different sections of a legal handbook in order to find the clues that may solve a problem. Therefore, principal areas are repeated in different chapters so as to assist readers and practitioners to grasp the point at hand without too much book-marking and back-thumbing.

The law and practice of registered homes is constantly developing. Even as we finally prepare this book for publication there is a new White Paper on what is now termed community care; there are about to be new directions on the publication of inspection reports; and there will be a heated debate upon the issue of 'the single care home'. The Registered Homes Tribunal, now itself more than 13 years old, is becoming more sophisticated and providing more comprehensive guidance when given the chance. The failure of so many appeals to come to a hearing, given the lack of available funds for home owners to fight their corner, is a matter of growing concern to many. However, of one constant principle we may remain sure, the provision of social and healthcare in the United Kingdom will remain subject to public regulation. I am convinced that no government would so mis-calculate the public mood as to feel that providers (whether public or private) should go about their business unobserved and without restraint. Regardless of how much the detail may change, the principles which have started to arise over recent years in the regulation of care will impact upon that practice as it develops.

I hope that this book will be of some assistance both to those who come to this area afresh or confused and also to those who have some experience but may feel supported and assisted by what is a collection of my experience over the last 25 years or so.

PAUL RIDOUT
February 1998

CONTENTS

TABLE OF CASES

References are to paragraph numbers; n indicates that the reference is to a footnote to the paragraph given.

TABLE OF STATUTES

References are to paragraph numbers; n indicates that the reference is to a footnote to the paragraph given.

TABLE OF STATUTORY INSTRUMENTS

References are to paragraph numbers; n indicates that the reference is to a footnote to the paragraph number given.

Chapter 1

DEVELOPMENT AND LEGISLATIVE BACKGROUND

1.1   INTRODUCTION

Over the past 50 years, demographic and social changes have increased both the importance and public awareness of establishments which provide support and care for people who are unable to care for themselves. Such establishments have developed as units operated by three distinct groups:

(1)   local authorities responsible for the administration of social services or by the National Health Service;
(2)   by voluntary organisations; or
(3)   to a very small extent, by private persons, usually those whose vocation or qualification provided an obvious link to 'care' and who for reasons of personal choice operate outside what might be loosely described as the 'State sector'.

The vast majority of all of these establishments have aimed to provide care for people, generally of advanced years, whose dependency on others has increased. Until the early 1970s, elderly persons tended to be accommodated and receive care within the family unit. Only in rare cases where there was no family unit or where the family unit was unable to provide support was the support and care of others needed.

For centuries, people of low or limited means have had to rely on local government to provide for their needs.

1.1.1   Legislative background

Legislation from the latter part of the Elizabethan era, culminating in the Poor Relief Act of 1601, had established a system through which local taxes were raised to provide relief, support and care for those who were not able to work, and facilities to improve the opportunities of re-employment for those who might be able to work.

Up to the early part of the 20th century, the legislation continued to impose a legal duty on family members to support and care for the elderly, the sick and needy within the family. That duty was supported by a parallel duty on local authorities to provide similar facilities.

Following the Beveridge Report on Social Insurance and Allied Services in 1943[1] the Government introduced revolutionary changes to social welfare and health care provision with the National Health Service legislation and the National Assistance Act 1948. A cornerstone of these legislative changes was statutory recognition that each citizen was entitled to expect free health and social welfare care. As a corollary, the legislation recognised the responsibility

---

1   1943 Cmd 6404.

upon the State and local government for that support and care in the
community. The legislative requirement on family members to provide for the
weak and sick within their family units was abolished. It has taken several
generations to see the full effect of the release of that obligation in society as a
whole; the imperative to care within the family had been transformed into a
moral responsibility.

The establishment of a mixed economy of care by the introduction of free
health and social care for all those in need tilted the development of care
establishments towards free public sector provision and away from the private
sector.

A strong family-based society, combined with support from 'free of
charge' public residential care, meant an almost non-existent market for
private care needs short of some health care needs. There was, however, a
small 'cottage industry' of providers catering for those who, for reasons of
social prejudice or affluence, chose to purchase care, rather than rely upon the
family or the state. In such circumstances, given the small numbers of units
serving a small and relatively select market, there was little need for regulation
of private residential care homes, although they were regulated to a limited
extent by the National Assistance Act 1948. Generally, private residential care
homes were seen as small businesses requiring legal support no different from
other businesses.

1.2   RECENT DEVELOPMENTS

Over the past 50 years, all this has changed. Private residential care homes now
provide the vast majority of units of care for the elderly, the chronically sick
and those unable to support themselves physically. These are operated not, as
before, by individuals driven by personal professional experience or vocational
inclination but, increasingly, by medium-sized and large professional
organisations, well capitalised and operating for profit. Groups of such homes
combine together to share management services, and larger groups seek
working capital arrangements not from traditional sources such as High Street
banks but by capital-raising exercises on the public stock exchanges.

The growth from fringe operation, through medium to substantial
cottage industry, to what has become a major sector of business, has been
rapid. It has brought with it an increasing need for regulation and a need for
the operators of such businesses to satisfy the increasingly complex
requirements in the financial, marketing and quality control aspects of their
business. Their legal advisers must also consider how the operation of a care
business relates to the law generally and how the development of the business
must comply with the developing regulatory requirements which, under
current rules, underpin every business, large or small.

1.2.1   The reasons for the change

There are three main reasons for this rapid change, as follows:

(1)   given that the majority of care homes provide for the chronically sick and
       the dependent elderly, the increase in the number of such persons and

the increase in the proportion of elderly persons generally to younger working members of the population;

(2) the actual as opposed to philosophical breakup of traditional family life and values;

(3) the changing nature of the National Health Service, increasingly seen to be a provider of the relief of acute health care needs as opposed to the needs of the chronically sick. There will be continuous debate as to whether or not the National Health Service should be expanded to meet all needs including those of the chronically sick. The reality is one of insufficient public resources to meet all needs and consequent rationing. Acute health care to meet the needs of the 'working age' population is seen by Government as a priority. That priority and the cost of maintaining dedicated care of the long-term chronically sick, whether elderly, mentally ill or otherwise afflicted, has led to inadequate resourcing and, in turn, inadequate accommodation, with no increase in capital contribution from the public sector to replace the hospital and social care accommodation.

It became widely recognised that rising numbers of elderly people and increasing life expectancy were producing a financial time bomb which, irrespective of political view, could not possibly be managed, being non-cash limited in nature, by public resources. The private sector is not ideal for the provision of general health care cover for acute health care needs. The resources and establishments required to meet a wide variety of sudden life-threatening circumstances are not compatible with running a private business which needs to operate within financial budgets and to a business plan. However, this is less of a problem in the long-term care of the chronically sick, which may include those recovering from acute medical or surgical intervention.

Accordingly, the National Health Service has increasingly welcomed private sector entrepreneurs into areas where they are well suited, such as care of the chronically sick and the elderly. It is against this background that the law of regulation of such private sector operations has developed.

1.3   THE AIMS OF THIS BOOK

This book aims to bring together:

(1) a detailed commentary on the current state of the various regulatory requirements on registered care homes;

(2) appropriate cross-references to other areas of the law which impact on the operation of registered care homes and interrelate with the regulatory requirements;

(3) explanations and examples on the operation of the regulatory framework in practice which show the problems that have arisen and the way in which they have been solved, and which may point the way towards resolving problems that may arise in the future.

However, this book does not set out to be either a definitive statement of the law as it may apply to any one situation, or an exhaustive interpretation of the relevant statutory regulations. It is principally intended to be a practitioner's handbook, giving guidance on the provisions of the law which may apply to particular circumstances, and bringing together the diverse provisions so that they may be seen as a whole, highlighting for the practitioner how examples in practice have been applied to the somewhat dry legislative language and helping to solve problems which constantly extend statutory interpretation to the limit.

1.4   TECHNICAL TERMS

A number of terms are used throughout the book to refer to statutes, regulations and case-law, as well as the institutions and authorities responsible for regulatory action or the subject of regulatory action.

1.5   WHAT IS A CARE HOME?

The essential question, of what precisely is a care home, has underpinned both the need for regulation and the need for this book. The question is complex because the types of unit which are subject to regulation as care homes under the current legislation are many and varied, and requires examination of the main problems confronting the care provider.

1.5.1   Definitions

The term 'care' and the term 'home' do not readily lend themselves to precise definition as each term has different meanings within different contexts. A dictionary definition is, therefore, not helpful.

The author's suggestion for a definition of a care home is:

> 'an establishment which looks after those who are not able to look after themselves.'

Practice guides for the care home industry have shied away from such definitions, choosing to stay with statutory definitions. The Chairman of the Centre for Policy on Ageing, in his *Introduction to Home Life – 'A Code of Practice for Residential Care'*[2] faced the dilemma thus:

> 'The two principal challenges which have faced the Working Party have been firstly, the wide range of establishments and clients covered by the legislation, and secondly, the need to address more than one audience in the same document.
>
> The legislation encompasses large homes, some of which may be part of a chain of commercial enterprises with home ownership at several removes from management, as well as small family-run homes with residents.[3] It covers the voluntary and charitable sector as well as the commercial sector. It includes homes

---

2   Centre for Policy on Ageing, 1984.
3   This would now be written as 'just one resident' (Registered Homes Amendment Act 1991).

providing specialist care for a wide variety of specific client groups, with a wide range of aims and practices, as well as homes run in a more generalist way. The legislation also covers those residential homes which provide nursing care at a level which makes it necessary for them to be registered with their Health Authority as well as with the local authority. The residents of all these homes have varying needs. Some of them are in a position to exercise a free choice about where and how to live, whilst others have little or no choice. The extent of their vulnerability, be it physical, psychological or economic, also varies, both between groups and at different periods of an individual's life, and calls for differing patterns of care. The Working Party's concern, in drawing up the Code of Practice, has been to ensure that the care provided in a home accurately reflects the stated aims and objectives of that home, and that it satisfactorily responds to the needs of the residents.'

The NAHA (now NAHAT) Yellow Book[4] covered the definition as follows:

At para 1.5:

'The Term "nursing home" as defined in the 1984 Registered Homes Act embraces a wide variety of establishments in the independent sector; they range from the small establishment providing nursing care for the elderly to large acute general hospitals. The factors common to all these establishments are:
(a) they are all in the independent health care sector
(b) nursing by registered nurses has to be provided.'

At para 1.15 (i) 'a private nursing home' is defined as:

'an independent sector nursing home including a private hospital run for profit or by charitable or similar non-profit organisation not including premises mentioned in Section 21(3) of the 1984 Act.'

The definition suggested by the author of this book is based upon the premise that the most important person in a care home is the person receiving care who is, in effect, a customer. The need for and the purpose of regulation is to protect that customer. The Court of Appeal has held that the purpose of the 1984 Act is to protect frail and vulnerable members of society.[5] Lord Justice Glidewell said:

'Of course one recognises that the Act is intended to protect those in the community who are amongst the most vulnerable.'

The law introduces regulation to intervene in the operation of activities only where it is perceived that there is a mischief which must be the subject of control. Clearly, the provision of care services is an area where it is appropriate for society to intervene to ensure a level of quality control on behalf of those in receipt of the services and to ensure that only those persons who are appropriately experienced and qualified are permitted to provide such services.

There is currently much concern about regulation generally and this concern has extended to the operation of care homes. If the primacy of the

4 *Registration and Inspection of Nursing Homes – A Handbook for Health Authorities* (National Association of Health Authorities 1985)
5 *Lyons v East Sussex County Council* (1988) 86 LGR 369, (1988) 152 JP 488 (CA).

'customer' is accepted then any proposals for deregulation will, the author suggests, be seen to be inappropriate by all those who are responsible for the purchase of care, the provision of care or the regulation of care. Tom Burgner, in his report 'The Regulation and Inspection of Social Services[6] reports that, of all those canvassed by him, only one advocated total deregulation.

1.6   WHAT IS THE PURPOSE OF REGULATION?

Regulation arises out of a perceived need to control the activities of some in their dealings with others, so as to protect those others and to ensure that society as a whole is satisfied that those in need of such protection are protected and are seen to be protected.

Whether or not there should be regulation, as a philosophical question, is beyond the scope of this book. Whether or not there should be regulation, for the purposes of this book, is a matter which is determined by the law. Regulation is, by its nature, geared to current circumstances, and therefore cannot arise out of the common law but only from statute. It is, accordingly, the supreme law-making body (in the case of the UK, Parliament) which will decide whether and to what extent there should be regulation.

Once Parliament has determined that there should be regulation, it is the purpose of the duly appointed regulator to ensure that standards within the regulated activity are maintained to an appropriate level or, in many cases, to the criteria which have been prescribed either by Parliament or those experts appointed by Parliament.

1.7   REGULATION AND CARE HOMES

The existence of regulation means that society, expressing its view through Parliament, has determined that there should be a degree of interference with the way in which particular members of society carry on their businesses or their lives. In the context of this book, this involves the operation of care homes.

The operator of the care home, ie the provider of care, will always see the regulator as a potential intruder. Disputes will frequently be concerned with arguments that the appointed regulator is over-intrusive or, indeed, that there is no need for interference. Whilst understandable, such arguments have no place within a system of regulation. Any change can be achieved by democratic means with a view to political change and thus change of the law. There can never be an argument justifying resistance to the actions of regulators, acting within the law and in accordance with a law that is in force.

It is, however, not the business of the regulator to:

(1)   operate or manage the operation of the regulated business (ie the care home) or direct the owner as to such operation; or

---

6   Department of Health, 1990.

(2) give detailed advice to the owner as to how the regulated business should operate.

If an owner is in need of such detailed input from the regulator or is so incapable of operating the care home business as to require the intervention of the regulator in the interest of those receiving care, then it is suggested that the owner is not fit to continue to carry on such a business. It must be a pre-requisite of continuing to carry on a regulated business that the owner has sufficient resources, experience, know-how and ability to conduct the business.

The regulator should appreciate that there may be many different ways of achieving the goal of acceptable standards. Those standards will at some point be defined within the regulatory legislation, either in great detail or in general terms. The powers of the regulator will be similarly prescribed. Parliament, in fixing a scheme of regulation, will have attempted to strike an appropriate balance between the need to oversee areas of concern, ie care home operation, and the need to allow private sector entrepreneurs to operate as they see fit in order to run their business successfully and profitably.

1.7.1 The scheme for regulation

In the current scheme for regulation of care homes set out in the Registered Homes Act ('the 1984 Act') and subordinate legislation, standards have been adopted by reference to general description rather than specific prescription (Burgner concludes in his report[7] that greater national bench marking of standards is required).

In broad terms, the standards to be met are standards of adequacy, ie sufficiency and suitability, and the regulatory scheme does not yet prescribe in detail what constitutes minimum standards. This will be ascertained from an understanding of the business of the operation of care homes and from experience and practice in the field. A regulator, taking the position and expressing the view of a responsible member of society, will expect anyone who aspires to operate a care home to understand basic care practice and the basic requirements for operating a care home business in the 1990s. Later in this book, under the definition of a 'fit person' to operate a care home, this will be discussed in greater detail.

Major business decisions will be taken by the care home owner. The regulator cannot and should not intervene in the course of the decision making. However, the care home owner should be aware of the scrutiny of the regulator. If the decision is so bad as to suggest that standards will fall below the prescribed level of adequacy, then the regulator will intervene. A prudent care home owner will ensure that he understands the views of the regulator before he makes major decisions, for example the employment of senior staff.

It is wrong for the regulator to seek to vet the appointment of staff or to approve major decisions. The owner may not expect detailed advice about a particular decision but he may expect and will no doubt receive advice as to the

---

7   *The Regulation and Inspection of Social Services* (Department of Health, 1990).

general view taken by the regulator. The owner may not be bound by that view, but he will ignore it at his peril.

1.7.2   The purpose of regulation

The purpose of regulation in relation to the registration of care homes falls into three categories:

(1)   to control entry to the care home business;
(2)   to observe the conduct of care home businesses;
(3)   to determine when and how quickly an owner shall be barred from the care home business.

1.7.3   Self-regulation

The suggestion is often raised that care home owners should be subject to 'self-regulation'.

Good care home owners do regulate their own businesses. They visit at anti-social hours; install effective quality assurance programmes; monitor and appraise the performance of staff and so-called 'outcomes' of the business by canvassing those in care and their relatives as to their views on the service provided.

Quality assurance is maintained by trade associations, particularly the Registered Nursing Home Association and the British Federation of Care Home Proprietors. These organisations have done pioneering work in improving standards by establishing themselves as specialist bodies to which entry may be gained only if the standards established by the Associations concerned are met, irrespective of the standards required for simple registration.

Care home owners may also devise their own methods of self-regulation or take on nationally accredited systems of regulation such as ISO 9002. However, the author suggests that, while self-regulation or industry-organised regulation is welcome and necessary, it can never be a substitute for regulation by an externally state-controlled body.

Self-regulation may be nothing more than business common sense combined with the regulation of the market place. The business entrepreneur trying to ensure that he maintains and enhances his position in the market place will want to offer a service that satisfies customers and potential customers. Even externally accredited quality assurance schemes achieve little more than identifying whether a business has met the standards which it has set for itself. However, if regulation is determined merely by the continued willingness of an operator to be regulated, then it cannot meet the demand expressed by society, and enacted by Parliament, that there should be objective external regulation. The role of regulators of care homes is not as advisers to or partners with care home owners but, in a sense, as custodians of the public conscience.

Without doubt, self-regulation would remain even if statutory regulation were to be abolished (both Burgner in 'The Regulation and Inspection of

Social Services'[8] and Day, Klein and Redmayne in 'Why Regulate'[9] firmly reject self-regulation as an alternative to statutory registration and inspection). However, as long as statutory regulation remains, forms of self-regulation, welcome as they are, cannot be regarded as substitutes.

1.8 CLASSIFICATION OF CARE HOMES

There are a wide variety of care homes, and if one adopts the author's definition of care home, it is obvious that differing facilities, accommodation, staff experience and skill will be required as the needs of those who require support change.

Much of the development of the care home business, and the regulation of that business, has been bedevilled by what many see as artificial distinctions. These are sometimes preserved, with respect to certain professional bodies, by representation of the sectional interests of particular professions or those with skills akin to professional qualifications. Terms that have become legal terms of art, for example 'nursing home' and 'residential care', will, in effect, be used to describe many activities which might well be regarded differently in the public perception.

For example, few people would regard a large privately operated acute service hospital, or a medical general practitioner's day surgery unit, or the treatment rooms of dentists and physiotherapists who use certain laser equipment as nursing homes. However, all of these are classified as nursing homes, within the statutory definitions.

However, the statutory definitions cause some concern over which establishment should be regulated and which should not. If a unit cannot be classified within the ambit of the statutory wording, it will not be regulated at all, irrespective of whether it ought to be. The following comment, made to the author by a registration officer: 'My concern is that the unit does not appear to be registered with any authority', is thus inappropriate, as that situation may well apply, and in that event the unit is outside regulation.

1.8.1 Types of care home

This book deals with three types of care home:

(1) residential care homes (sometimes known as 'rest homes'), which provide social residential care, falling short of health care;
(2) nursing homes, which provide health care on a residential or non-residential basis;
(3) children's homes, which come in various types largely determined by the status of the organisation operating the business, ie public sector, charitable or private.

There are detailed provisions concerned with avoiding double registration, particularly where the residential care of children is concerned. Somewhat

---

8   Department of Health, 1990.
9   The Policy Press in association with Joseph Rowntree Foundation, 1996.

paradoxically, there are also provisions which have been construed so as to enable homes to register with more than one authority, creating the so called dual-registered home, which will be considered in some detail at para **3.18**. Despite the views of some commentators, there would appear to be no reason why a particular unit for the supply of care should not register with all the various regulatory authorities so as to be able to provide the entire range of care, should the owners choose to do so.

The vast majority of care homes are established to provide care for those who cannot care for themselves in their advancing years.

1.8.2   The distinction between residential care and nursing homes

The need for and advantages of dual-registered homes, ie those which provide both residential care and nursing care, itself exemplifies the difficulty in making the distinction between the two types of home.

It is suggested that the distinctions which exist have been caused as a result of the timing and speed of regulation of different types of homes throughout the history of regulation. The unfortunate consequence for the owner who has to meet registration requirements, whilst facing the changing day-to-day care needs of individual clients, is that any mistake may expose him and his senior staff to prosecution under the law or disciplinary action from the professional bodies.

The distinction between 'residential care homes' and 'nursing homes' is an artificial one. The distinction between 'nursing homes' and 'mental nursing homes' is particularly artificial, for there will be few nursing homes whose owners can say, hand on heart, that they do not have in their care at least one person suffering from a condition which might be described as a mental disorder.[10]

The problem of nursing patients in residential care homes or providing institutional nursing care for those who are perceived to need social care in residential care homes, has been the subject of heated argument. The reality of such disputes is that the classification of residential homes is wholly artificial and whilst it is easy to identify individual cases where the needs and care supplied fall clearly into a bracket which might loosely be described as 'nursing' or 'residential/personal', a large number of elderly people who need support because they are not able to look after themselves are impossible to categorise on a permanent basis as falling into one type of care or the other.

The facilities provided and the qualifications of staff in the different types of residential homes are usually similar. In homes which provide nursing care, a relatively small proportion of staff are qualified nurses. The majority of tasks are routine, performed by staff who do not have nursing qualifications. In dual-registered homes, some nursing staff are present. There would be no sense in suggesting that qualified nurses should not be permitted to care for patients identified as residents or in suggesting that they are acting illegally if they work in other registered homes which are similar but are classified differently.

---

10   Different definitions in the Registered Homes Act 1984, s 21 and s 22.

The different classification of the two types of home, staffed by people with differing training, combined with different regulation carried out by different regulatory bodies, is likely to preserve the distinction between residential care and nursing homes.

The needs of people who are unable to look after themselves will change from time to time. Those needs may increase or decrease depending on variable factors such as the weather, the season or illness. Health care may be required, which may improve the client's condition so that only personal care is then needed, although these needs may change again with, perhaps, the onset of seasonal influenza. To burden the providers of care and those in need of care with a legal obstacle course seems odd, but the distinctions remain and will be identified later in this book.

1.9   HISTORY OF REGULATION

Regulation of nursing homes and residential care homes came together in the Registered Homes Act 1984 and the two types of home are generally regarded as being merely different manifestations of the same idea. However, the common perception of the need for regulation of the two types of home has developed on differing scales and this can be clearly shown in an examination of the history of the regulatory statutes.

Nursing Homes	*Residential Care Homes*
Nursing Homes Registration Act 1927	National Assistance Act 1948
Public Health Act 1936 (sections 186 and 187)	
Nursing Homes Amendment Act 1963	
Nursing Homes Act 1975	
Health Services Act 1980	Residential Homes Act 1980
Health and Social Services Administration Act 1983	
Registered Homes Act 1984	Registered Homes Act 1984

Whereas society perceived the need to regulate the delivery of health care as early as 1927, residential care homes were not regulated for another 21 years and it was 53 years later before a statute, designed specifically to regulate the delivery of so-called personal or social care on a residential basis, was introduced.

1.9.1   The National Assistance Act 1948

The National Assistance Act 1948 first provided for the regulation of residential accommodation for those in need, although the underlying principle of that legislation was that those in need would receive care from local authorities providing their own accommodation. By s 26 of Pt III of that Act, the source of the modern community care purchasing power, local authorities were entitled to purchase private sector social (but not health) care as an alternative to provision from within their own facilities. Certain limited offences were provided in relation to the conduct of such homes and the commission of such offences restricted future contracting with the local authority.

All of this was in the context of limited as opposed to the current extensive regulation. It was also set against a background where clients perceived that they would not purchase care themselves from a home but would receive care through provision made by the local authority, whether from its own resources or by local authority purchase from a private provider. The logic of exclusion of providers who had committed offences under the 1948 scheme is clear. Many feel that the logic of continuing that exclusion into the post-1993 'Care in the Community' scheme is not so clear.

1.9.2   The Nursing Homes Act 1975

Until 1975, regulation of health care premises operated privately was controlled by county councils and not by health care authorities, despite the fact that county councils had no function in the provision of health care. The Nursing Homes Act 1975 consolidated the existing legislation, then to be found in the appropriate sections of the Public Health Act 1936 and the amending legislation (most importantly the 1963 Act). The 1975 Act introduced the requirement that a reasonable proportion of staff on duty in nursing homes should be qualified nurses. It also introduced the new idea that health care premises should be regulated by the Secretary of State, acting through Area Health Authorities, as they then were,[11] so that the regulation of provision of health care in the private sector should be carried out by those responsible for providing health care in the public sector.

1.9.3   The changes of the early 1980s – a 'Golden Age'

The change to District Health Authorities in 1980 resulted in the transfer of the regulation of private health care to those new authorities and this has been continued by retaining that function within the health purchasing unit (the Health Authority), now securing, as opposed to providing, health care under the National Health Service and Community Care Act 1990, as amended by the Health Authorities Act 1995.

The demographic changes discussed earlier in this chapter will be seen as resulting in the development of increasingly sophisticated legislation, throughout the 1980s, starting with the enactment of the Residential Homes Act 1980 (the first detailed regulation of residential care) and the Health Services Act 1980, which significantly advanced and refined regulation of private nursing homes.

---

11   Subsequently, District Health Authorities under the Health Services Act 1980 and now Health Authorities under the Health Authorities Act 1995.

These legislative changes were responding to demographic changes, in particular, to acknowledge the notion that able family members (other than spouses or parents of young children) were no longer either legally or morally obliged to care for less able family members, with the introduction of universal entitlement to state welfare support. Many people may consider the explosion in the development and proliferation of care homes to be inextricably linked to the introduction of universal access to 100 per cent payment of care home fees by central government. Despite the removal of the legal imperative and the erosion of the moral imperative to care for the elderly and sick within the family, the changes could not have been implemented while traditional values prevailed and without the financial resources to meet the cost.

The introduction of support by way of social security benefit payments for residential boarders, including those in nursing homes and residential care homes, in the late 1970s, opened up an opportunity for families who were either unable to find alternative placement for dependants in need or, if able, severely financially restricted, to obtain the support needed. The potential market for the private provision of residential care was vastly increased, at a stroke.

The early 1980s were truly golden days for care home owners. The Department of Health and Social Security, as it then was, provided Supplementary Benefit payments to meet the full cost of residential care wherever that was supplied, and in homes selected by the patient or resident. Care home fees to be reimbursed were only limited to an amount which coincided with the local norm. Families released both from the legal and moral imperative of caring for the sick and the needy within the domestic environment saw a true advantage, as did the care home owner. The obligation, financially and physically taxing, to care for the elderly could be avoided. Personal cash resources could be released and, better still, such limited cash resources as were available to the elderly would not, subject to certain limits, be required to be employed in paying for residential care, ie benefit was not dependent on zero assets and assets were not depleted below certain levels.

The market for care homes exploded. Care homes could be filled overnight at basic standards and at fees that would show a profit and which could be adjusted on a regular basis to continue to show profits as expenditure rose with inflation and as a result of increasing demand.

Obviously, this could not continue, and on 11 April 1985, the government effectively capped the residential care and nursing home fees which would be met by social security benefit and brought about a change of dramatic proportions in the operation of nursing and residential and nursing homes.

The issue will be considered in greater detail in Chapter 11, which deals with funding of care home placements by third parties.

1.9.4 The Registered Homes Act 1984

The 1984 Act is often described as a watershed although, save for the introduction of the Registered Homes Tribunal and the urgent procedure for the cancellation of registration, the Act is more a consolidation of separate statutory provisions rather than ground-breaking legislation

1.9.5   The late 1980s and the 1990s – the end of the 'Golden Age'

What was truly a watershed, in early 1985, and coinciding with the introduction of the 1984 Act, was the combination of:

(1)   greater awareness in local authority social services' departments and District Health Authorities of the obligation to regulate and, in consequence, the gradual development of teams which were not only required to regulate but did regulate; and
(2)   the dramatic capping of social security benefit.

Increased regulation would lead inevitably to increased costs and capping would lead to decreased income.

The culmination of the effect of these two factors came in 1989, coinciding with the collapse of the property boom of the late 1980s. Care home owners were met with slumping capital values, and increased financial requirements derived both from expenditure required as a result of proper regulation and reductions in income as a result of capping.

Within a decade, residential care homes and nursing homes had come from relative obscurity through a Golden Age, where they appeared to be money printing machines, to a position where, for many, businesses were no longer viable.

The change of emphasis for publicly funded patients and residents from 1 April 1993 (pursuant to the delayed introduction of the financial reforms of Pt III of the National Health Service Community Care Act 1990) completed the dramatic transformation. With those changes, apparently, although not absolutely, entitlement for all to free residential and nursing care was abolished. Entitlement was not only rationed, but rationed by a local authority. Such rationing is by reference to both individual and, possibly, local authority resources.[12] All such care and entitlement was subject to the pre-entry qualification of assessment.[13]

For many, this was seen as a reversion to the pre-1948 situation where provision by the local authority had been only the final safety net, under the Poor Laws of 1927 and 1930. However, in 1993, as opposed to the period of 1601–1948, there was no legal requirement upon more able family members to provide care for their less able relatives except upon spouses and upon parents in relation to their children.[14]

1.10   SCOPE OF THIS BOOK

1.10.1   England and Wales

This book addresses the law and procedure as it applies in England and Wales.

---

12   Cf *R v Gloucestershire County Council and another ex parte Barry* [1997] 2 WLR 459, HL; *R v Sefton Metropolitan Borough Council, ex parte Help the Aged* (1997) *The Times*, 23 August (CA).
13   See National Health Service and Community Care Act 1990.
14   See National Assistance Act 1948, s 42.

1.10.2 Scotland

The legislation which applies to Scotland is drafted in similar terms, although it is enforced through different authorities (ie Health Boards) and is subject to appeal through the ordinary legal system compared with the specialist system in England and Wales.

1.10.3 Northern Ireland

In the province of Northern Ireland, a Tribunal system has been introduced. Furthermore, there have been updating orders introducing provisions in relation to the regulation of residential care and nursing homes in Northern Ireland. These are broadly similar to those which are discussed in this book. Detailed consideration of the Northern Ireland provisions is beyond the scope of this book.

1.10.4 Other jurisdictions

Although this book does not apply specifically to other jurisdictions, the examples of the application of regulatory law in the private health and social care field may prove useful to other jurisdictions either for establishing or interpreting their own similar provisions. Necessarily, such provisions are tailored to meet particular local and national expectations, and standards cannot be expected to be identical or even similar in jurisdictions with different histories and attitudes to such sensitive issues as the provision of social welfare and health care.

1.11 SOURCES OF LAW

1.11.1 Common law

Regulation is not known to the common law except insofar as its origins derive from the need for the Crown to regulate its subjects in all matters. However, common law principles will remain of importance in interpreting and enforcing the law of regulation as it applies to a particular area from time to time.

1.11.2 Statutes

Any regulator subordinate to Parliament must be able to point to a statutory source for the power of regulation. If no such source exists or if the source does not permit an exercise of authority in the way or to the extent to which it purports to have been made, then insofar as the regulator attempts to state that a rule has the force of law, it will be overturned. That does not necessarily mean that a rule that does not have the binding force of law is to be disregarded, but merely that it may not be quoted ipso facto, as justification for subsequent decisions. By way of example, in relation to the question as to whether or not valid conditions of registration may be imposed, interpretation of the statutes shows:

(1) in relation to residential care homes and nursing homes, no conditions

may have the force of law, unless relating specifically to subject matter made the particular subject of registration by the 1984 Act;

(2)   in relation to registered children's homes, regulators have wide powers to impose, as conditions of registration, anything they believe to be appropriate;

(3)   in Northern Ireland, Health Boards have a similar wide power in relation to residential care and nursing homes as that which local authorities enjoy in relation to registered children's homes in England and Wales.[15]

Anyone who is to have lawful authority to make regulations must be appointed by Act of Parliament, which will also make provision as to the extent that such power may be delegated.

Examination of the legislation shows a clear distinction between Parliament appointing the Secretary of State to make regulations (Parliament not being able to deal in sufficient detail given resources and time) and appointing Registration Authorities (being social services, local authorities, or Health Authorities) to implement and administer the regulation of care homes as created by the statutes enacted by Parliament and the regulations made by the Secretary of State.

1.11.3   Regulations

Chapter 2 examines the nature and powers of those involved in the regulation of care homes. In relation to the regulation of nursing homes, all regulation is done by the Secretary of State or in the name of the Secretary of State by the appropriate Health Authority. As the Health Authority is acting in the name of the Secretary of State, it follows that the Secretary of State has power to and sometimes does direct the Health Authority to follow his instructions in a particular matter.

In relation to residential care homes, local authorities derive their power directly from Parliament (contrast Pt I and Pt II of the Registered Homes Act 1984). Rule-making powers are reserved to the Secretary of State, but local authorities are, by separate legislation, required to act under the general guidance of the Secretary of State, words less limiting than 'directions'.[16] The extent to which Health Authorities are required to act under the general guidance of the Secretary of State, as opposed to having regard to that guidance, is a more difficult issue.

The matter will be examined in more detail towards the end of this chapter. However, it is suggested that, whilst Health Authorities are clearly not obliged to follow the guidance, as opposed to directions, of the Secretary of State to the letter, they are required to pay proper heed and attention to general guidance, and are obliged to make decisions on their own in the appropriate context having considered all the issues, including such guidance, without regarding themselves as bound by the letter of such general guidance. The Secretary of State cannot anticipate every set of facts which might arise and

---

15   Registered Homes Act 1984, s 5(3) and s 29(2); Children Act 1989, Sch 6, para 2; *Warwickshire County Council v McSweeney* (unreported) 8 December 1988, Roch J.

16   Local Authority Social Services Act 1970, s 7(1).

the concept of general guidance leaves open a discretion to act appropriately in the circumstances.

1.11.4 Case-law

The courts usually avoid giving guidance on general principles in particular cases because the application of legal principle will vary from one case to another. Where there is a departure, then what is said may be regarded only as being of persuasive authority, for example *Lyons v East Sussex County Council*,[17] where the Court of Appeal was asked to give guidance about the vexed question of procedures for an application for the urgent cancellation of a registration certificate for a residential care home. Having declined to do so, the Court then expressed views about the advantages of combining an application for urgent procedure with a notice seeking cancellation by the longer and so called 'ordinary' method. In the course of the judgment, the view was expressed that it matters not which procedure is started first. This was not germane to the dispute and clearly 'obiter dictum'. The author suggests, with respect, that the Court was drawn into error and overlooked the sharp distinction (as will be argued in Chapter 9 on cancellation) between the immediate nature of urgent cancellation and the suspended nature of ordinary cancellation. In the author's submission, it may make a great deal of difference as to whether or not the urgent procedure is initiated before or after the completion of the ordinary procedure. If the ordinary procedure is not completed, it may be halted if the effect of the urgent cancellation is to bring the registration to an end and then there no longer exists any subject matter upon which a local authority or Tribunal decision could be based. A different result will follow if the urgent cancellation order is only suspensory in nature.

Care must be taken to ensure that the relevant case-law authority is in fact binding upon the court or Tribunal considering the issue. Whether or not a decision is binding or merely persuasive will be of crucial importance to those who have to decide a future case.

1.11.5 Registered Homes Tribunal cases

Since the institution of the Registered Homes Tribunal in January 1985, there have been nearly 330 cases. These make interesting, illuminating and, in some instances, amusing reading for students of the practice of the regulation of care homes.

Few of the cases that have come before Tribunals have concentrated upon legal issues or issues of principle. The vast majority of such cases are exercises in the application of the principles of the law of regulation of care homes to particular facts and circumstances, which will not be repeated. The peculiarity of such cases to their own facts and the constitution of the Tribunal in having a majority of non-legally qualified expert practitioners to determine all issues, including issues of law, means that the decisions of Tribunals should be

---

17 (1988) 86 LGR 369; (1988) 152 JP 488 (CA).

approached with caution and should be regarded, at the highest, as mildly persuasive. It would be dangerous to regard such decisions as being in any way binding upon future Tribunals.

Furthermore, the practice and procedure of care home management and operation can change and develop over the years. Tribunals must be astute to keep their thinking up to date and it would be wholly wrong, in principle, to regard themselves as bound by decisions on particular facts set in an historic context when considering a modern case. Circumstances can change due to the advance of technology, changes in custom and practice, changes in the availability of numbers or qualifications of particular grades of staff and, generally, in relation to what is regarded as acceptable conduct in relation to the care of the sick, the frail and the vulnerable.

Such cases are instructive for care home owners and regulators as regards the conduct of future investigations and provide a useful background to an explanation of the principles of regulation. However, in common with all trials and enquiries where particular facts are investigated, it has to be accepted that the decisions will be influenced by the impression made by the presentation of evidence and the performance of witnesses upon the individual Tribunal. To seek to draw rules of principle from such circumstances is dangerous and will lead the practitioner into error.

1.11.6   Guidance

The practice of care home regulation is fraught with difficulty caused by the introduction of so-called guidelines, rules, 'local' regulations and 'requirements'. These are usually issued, by or on behalf of bodies who appear to have the force of law, to those who are not students of the finer points of constitutional law. It is important to appreciate that such pronouncements do not have the force of law unless they can be shown to derive from statutory or delegated statutory authority.

Such guidance is issued in practice:

(1)   by central government through one of the Departments of State;
(2)   through national organisations, ie organised groupings of regulators or organised groupings of care providers;
(3)   by individual local regulators or local providers.

1.11.7   Departmental guidance

Health Authorities receive regular advice and guidance from the Department of Health in Health Circulars and Guidance Notes. Where such guidance does not take the form of a legal direction, it should not be regarded as binding. Such guidance should not be disregarded and must be carefully considered. Where a view of the law is expressed, it should be taken as no more than a view, which, like any legal opinion, may not necessarily be correct.

Health Authorities act in the name of the Secretary of State. Local authorities are autonomous, but are subject to the general guidance of the Secretary of State.[18] Such guidance will broadly fall into two areas:

---

18   Local Authority Social Services Act 1970, s 7(1).

(1) general guidance on interpretation of the law and the implementation of procedures for enforcement of the law;

(2) guidance as to the implementation of good care practice.

It is suggested that general guidance about the interpretation of the law and procedure is nothing more than the Government's expression of its view, by way of assistance, to advise the authorities as to the way in which they go about the business of enforcing the regulatory provisions. Such guidance will be issued by seasoned and able lawyers and civil servants and, as with any guidance or advice, merits serious consideration by those who are required to act in the field. It is, however, by no means certain that such guidance will be correct and reliance upon the guidance can never lead to the conclusion that actions based upon it will necessarily be right. Interpretation of the law is a matter for the Tribunal and, ultimately, the court. Any and all lawyers or civil servants or others seeking to interpret without the authority to make final decisions are no more than advisers.

In some cases, guidance given by the Department can be shown to be wrong, and in some circumstances this had been criticised by the courts. In the late 1980s, a health circular was issued suggesting to authorities that when an owner whose registration had been cancelled sought to appeal to the Tribunal, the authorities should write to the owner telling him that, in exercising the right of appeal, he was required to state briefly why he was appealing. Nothing could be further from the correct position. Such a prospective appellant has an appeal as a matter of right. He is not required to give reasons for exercising the appeal, and, indeed, the burden of proof in establishing the reasons and justification for the decision to cancel lies upon the authority. That circular was not only misleading, but dangerously wrong. However, where the Department seeks to give guidance as to general issues of care practice, and which practices it would like to see encouraged, which discouraged, and which abolished, then the author would suggest that the strength of the persuasive power of the circular is significantly increased.

Much assistance, in this field, can be drawn from a recent decision involving the registration of child minders, *London Borough of Sutton v Ann Davis*.[19] This, the so-called 'right to smack' case, is very instructive on the relative force to be given by local authorities, in making pragmatic decisions on registration, to general guidance issued by the Department of Health in the 'Blue Book'.[20] Wilson J. said:

> 'What is abundantly clear is that the guidance in the Blue Book, whether in relation to smacking or anything else, is not intended to be applied so strictly that, if an application for registration is in conflict with part of it, there should automatically be a finding of unfitness.'

Whilst, as a matter of law, the local authority was bound to follow the guidance,[21] that guidance itself had to be construed strictly to see if it bore the prescriptive effect contended by the local authority.

---

19 [1994] 2 WLR 721, Wilson J.
20 *The Children Act 1989 Guidance and Regulations* Vol 2 (HMSO, January 1995).
21 Local Authority Social Services Act 1970, s 7(1).

1.11.8   National and local guidance

Local authorities, public health authorities, organisations representing
regulatory authorities, and care home owners associations frequently issue so-
called 'guidelines', relating, generally, to the operation and management of
care homes and to appropriate practices for personal and nursing care.

From time to time, these 'guidelines' are elevated by individual
practitioners to the status of binding rules and regulations. They are never so.
At the highest, they represent the collected wisdom in a particular field of
practice, of those whose experience has been accumulated and is then
published for the assistance of others already the field or who may wish to
enter. The value of the guidance is dependent upon the credibility of the
authors of the guidelines and whether or not their views coincide with
generally established customs and practice throughout England and Wales.

It is not the function of local authorities, or public health authorities, by
the publication of guidelines or otherwise, to supplant the Secretary of State's
rule-making function. Regulatory authorities may wish to influence the
development of care within their jurisdiction. That aim is to be applauded.
However, the authority must remember that its purpose is to regulate the
establishment of care homes, and not to seek to dictate the way in which those
care homes are managed.

Care home owners should resist introducing requirements which,
although given as 'requirements' through guidelines, do not have the force of
law unless it can be shown that those 'requirements' accord with nationally
recognised practice, and that to operate without them would be to operate
below a standard which might be regarded objectively as adequate, ie sufficient
and suitable.

Care home owners, however, should also be aware that such guidance is
the accumulated wisdom of specialists in the area of care home regulation and
should not be treated lightly. At the highest, the guidance may reflect modern
thinking on minimum standards. At the lowest, the guidance may represent
constructive ideas about how to provide better care and better service and how
to enhance the position in the market of the particular care business.

New facilities which are not strictly requirements will, with the passage of
time, become standard so as to make a care home without them inadequate.
Examples include:

(1)   hydraulic shaft lifts for premises built on more than one floor;
(2)   low surface temperature radiators;
(3)   temperature controlled valves on all hot water systems.

That is not to say that the absence of any of these facilities indicates that a care
home is unfit to operate. However, these facilities have been introduced
gradually over the last 10 years, and have been seen as constructive
innovations. New purpose-built homes will rarely not have them and homes
without them will compete poorly in the market. It is perhaps inevitable, if it
has not already happened, that homes that do not have these facilities will not
only be less well regarded by potential customers, but will also be inadequate to
continue in operation.

There are two further features to note in relation to local guidelines.

(1)   It is important to establish whether the guidelines have the force of policy from the appropriate public authority, or trade association. Frequently, such guidance is published almost as an aide-mémoire by officers of the particular organisations. However, the guidelines may be seen as having more force if they have been considered, debated and formally adopted as policy by the organisation concerned.

(2)   In the changing world of purchase of community care services (since 1 April 1993), it is a commercial fact of life that local authorities and Health Authorities are increasingly purchasers of care services. It is inevitable that a purchaser of care services is likely to be dissuaded from purchasing from those who do not adhere to the same standards of care as appeal to the purchaser, albeit in the form of its registration unit. This is simply another example of the effect of market forces.

Regulators must be careful not to overstate requirements. The purchasing divisions of the local authority may be dissuaded from purchasing care from all available providers, if some are perceived not to meet a standard of excellence which excludes registration requirements. It would be unhealthy, in the author's submission, if there were a situation where a local authority, in effect, declined to purchase from a unit which was regarded as fit for registration by the registration unit. Surely, the watchword should be that, if the home is fit to be registered, it is fit to operate and thus fit to deal with any purchasers in the market place, including the local and public authorities. Purchasers must be free to select care services which are more attractive, but that freedom of choice should not be distorted by a misguided belief as to levels of adequacy of services or facilities.

Home owners must be astute to observe when newly published guidelines (particularly where these are adopted formally by a local authority), step beyond the line of currently acceptable standards of practice. With the importance of such guidelines in the minds of local authority and public health purchasers, it may be that the courts will be asked to subject such guidelines to judicial review, based upon the effect that they will have upon purchasing decisions. It would, it is suggested, be unreasonable to set standards which could not be met by homes recognised by the regulatory authority as fit to remain registered, and thus, in effect, to reduce the possibilities of business for such homes, whilst not seeking openly to cancel the registration. The author would suggest that any home which is fit to be registered is fit to be used by a local authority, and if fitness is in question, then the issue of regulation should be addressed.

1.11.9   Policies

Inevitably, and quite correctly, local authorities, whether exercising regulatory powers, purchasing powers or general powers in relation to the conduct of professional practice within their location, will publish and seek to implement policies.

However, such policies, whether propounding guidelines, or general policies about the provision of care, or the number or location or size of units of care, must not be elevated into rules of law unless there is authority in the statute providing for regulation, or some other statute, for such policies to become rules of law.

Authorities are required to register and issue a certificate of registration in relation to a residential care or nursing home upon receipt of an application.[22] However, when exercising other discretions in relation to regulation, for example the imposition of conditions of registration, the authority may take into account any matters material to the decision, including their own policies, so long as they are not capricious and seriously consider each case.[23] Decisions must not be fettered or constrained by fixed policy as opposed to law.

Local authorities should also appreciate that, whilst argument about whether or not policies may be taken into account may be interesting, it is inevitably slightly arcane.

Whilst the decision-making power may take into account the local policy, if the source of decision-making authority changes, for example to the Tribunal, then it is for the Tribunal or alternative decision-maker to take into account the material that it considers appropriate, ie the Tribunal may take into account the authority's policy but may also take into account its own experience.

A policy is likely to have less effect on the Tribunal than it will upon a registration authority, and a local authority may find that it has wasted time and money, and, indeed, may have its policy criticised if the Tribunal finds that the policy is not justified, and does not justify the decision made, as occurred in the *Humphreys* case.[24] Considerable argument was deployed in trying to prevent the Tribunal from considering the policy issues, particularly by the owner, Humphreys, but the court permitted the Tribunal to consider the issue – a policy that prevented the development or extension of new care homes in the Isle of Wight beyond a fixed number. The Tribunal had no difficulty at all finding that it would not espouse the local authority policy and would grant Mr Humphreys the registration to which he was otherwise entitled.

Local authorities should exercise extreme caution when basing decisions on matters of policy, and in the author's view only rarely, if ever, should a decision be based purely upon policy. Policy will rarely be enshrined in the binding rules of law and it is the duty of the regulatory authority to implement those rules, not further to advance rule-making by attempting to give force to policies which cannot be the subject matter of law.

It may be that those who have to exercise a discretion conferred by statute, will formulate policies as to how such a discretion should be exercised, but consistency and fairness will need to be shown. However, each case must be heard and no case should be determined by reference to the policy alone.

'There are on the one hand cases where a tribunal in the honest exercise of its discretion has adopted a policy, and, without refusing to hear an applicant, intimates to him what its policy is, and that after hearing him it will in accordance with its policy decide against him, unless there is something exceptional in his case. I think Counsel for the applicants would admit that, if the policy has been adopted for reasons which the tribunal may legitimately entertain, no objection

22 Registered Homes Act 1984, s 5(2) and s 23(4).
23 *Isle of Wight County Council v Humphreys* [1992] COD 308, Hutchison J.
24 Ibid.

could be taken to such a course. On the other hand there are cases where a tribunal has passed a rule, or come to a determination, not to hear any application of a particular character by whomsoever made. There is a wide distinction to be drawn between these two claims.'
(per Bankus LJ in *R v Port of London Authority ex parte Kyroch Ltd*)[25]
'The general rule is that anyone who has to exercise a statutory discretion must not "shut his ears to an application". ....
I do not think there is any great difference between a policy and a rule. There may be cases where an officer or Authority ought to listen to a substantial argument reasonably presented urging a change of policy. What the Authority must not do is to refuse to listen at all. But a Ministry or large Authority may have had to deal already with a multitude of similar applications and then they will almost certainly have evolved a policy so precise that it could well be called a rule. There can be no objection to that, provided the Authority is always willing to listen to anyone with something new to say – of course I do not mean to say that there need be an oral hearing.'
(per Lord Reid in *British Oxygen Co v Minister of Technology* (HL))[26]
'The authority must not act capriciously but within "the rules of reason and justice, not according to private opinion. ... according to law and not humour. It is to be, not arbitrary, vague and fanciful, but legal and regular.' These well known words. ... come from the speech of Lord Halsbury LC in *Sharpe v Wakefield* [1891] AC 173 at 179. If as appears to be the case here, the authority has determined upon a general policy they must state it publicly for the information of all concerned and must, despite their policy, apply their minds properly to the circumstances of each individual case in order to decide whether the policy should be applied in that particular case or whether there are grounds for reaching a decision at variance with the policy.'
(per Hutchison J, possibly *obiter dicta*, in *Isle of Wight County Council v Humphreys*)[27]

The principal sources of the current law, insofar as the same are to be found in statute, regulations or guidance are listed in paras **1.11.10** to **1.11.13** below.

1.11.10 Important statutes

(1) *Registered Homes Act 1984 ('the 1984 Act')*
This consolidating statute governs the regulatory requirements of residential care homes and nursing homes. Residential care homes are the subject of Pt I of the 1984 Act and nursing homes are the subject of Pt II.
(2) *Children Act 1989 ('the 1989 Act')*
This important statute provides a unified code of the law as it relates to issues affecting children and deals with issues relating to residential accommodation and the care of children.
> Part VI provides for community homes operated by local authorities;
> Part VII for voluntary homes operated by voluntary organisations;
> Part VIII for registered children's homes;
> Part XI for private arrangements for the fostering of children; and

---

25   [1919] 1 KB 176.
26   [1971] AC 610 at 624, 625.
27   [1992] COD 308.

Part X for registering child minding and day care services for young children.

(3) *Local Authority Social Services Act 1970*
This provides the background for the statutory provision by local authorities of social services.

(4) *Nurses, Midwives and Health Visitors Act 1979*
This sets out the modern code for the regulation of the professionals within the nursing sector. Previous regulation was made under the Nurses Act 1957. It is instructive and may still be necessary for interpreting certain provisions of the 1984 Act, despite the repeal of the 1957 Nurses Act.

(5) *National Health Service Act 1977*
The 1984 Act provides for regulation of nursing homes, by the Secretary of State for Health. The National Health Service Act 1977 provides for the delegation of certain of those powers, by the Secretary of State, to District Health Authorities, and this delegation includes the function of registration and inspecting and supervising regulatory action in relation to nursing homes.

(6) *Misuse of Drugs Act 1971*
This statute contains important provisions as to the storage, recording of use and destruction of drugs which may only be obtained and used on prescription and subject to sanction. All nursing homes and residential care homes will have day-to-day regular interaction with drugs which are only available on the prescription of a registered medical practitioner. Misuse of such drugs can contravene the provisions of this legislation, which is more widely known in the criminal context of drug misuse.

(7) *Fire Precautions Act 1961*
This Act is mentioned for completeness because it does not apply to residential care homes and nursing homes save for the provisions of sections which are of general application. This statute, which provides for statutory fire certificates for certain types of buildings which may be prescribed by central government, has never been extended to health care premises in the private sector.

The scheme of the Registered Homes Act 1984 and the Children Act 1989 is examined and explained in greater detail in Chapter 4.

1.11.11 Important regulations

(1) *Residential Care Homes Regulations 1984,*[28] as amended
These are the regulations which apply to the registration and operation of residential care homes by local authority registration authorities. The amendments since 1984 are relatively minor, and deal mostly with increases in registration and other regulatory fees.

(2) *Nursing Homes and Mental Nursing Homes Regulations 1984*[29]
These regulations govern registration, inspection and operation of

---

28   SI 1984/1345.
29   SI 1984/1578.

nursing homes and mental nursing homes and are the equivalent regulations, in relation to those homes, to the Residential Care Home Regulations 1984 for residential care homes. Amendments have been similarly sparse and, generally, relate to changes in fee structures for registration and regulatory activity.

(3) *National Health Service (Functions of Health Authorities and Administration Arrangements) Regulations 1996*[30]

These are important regulations which are changed and updated on each occasion that there is a reorganisation in relation to the National Health Service. These are the authority for the delegation, by the Secretary of State, of National Health Service functions to subordinate authorities. They are, for authorities, the important source of power for carrying out each and every act that they do in relation to the registration and inspection of nursing homes, and, particularly, in relation to the cancellation of registration, whether by urgent or ordinary procedure.

(4) *Nurses, Midwives and Health Visitors (Parts of the Register) Order 1993*[31]

Regulations made under the Nurses, Midwives and Health Visitors Act 1979, these prescribe the registration of nurses and identify parts of the register in respect of which particular nurses are required to be registered in order to practice in particular fields. Whilst not determinative of a particular staffing notice, this would be of extreme importance in determining issues on staffing levels and conditions as to staffing in registered nursing homes.

(5) *Children (Secure Accommodation) Regulations 1991*[32] and *Children's Homes Regulations 1991*[33]

These regulations apply to registered children's homes and are the equivalent of regulations made in respect of residential care homes and nursing homes under the 1984 Act. Much of the statutory scheme for children's homes is to be found within Schs 5, 6, 8 and 9 to the Children Act 1989.

1.11.12   Important guidance

Each and every Health Authority and local authority is likely to have published its own guidance as to the registration and inspection of residential care homes, nursing homes and, possibly, children's homes in its area or for which it has responsibility. Detailed discussion of the individual guidelines of approximately 200 Health Authorities and all County Councils, London Boroughs and Metropolitan Borough Councils throughout the UK is beyond the scope of this book.

The practitioner should approach consideration of individual guidelines with caution. However, certain national guidelines do exist. In relation to

---

30   SI 1996/708.
31   SI 1993/588.
32   SI 1991/1505.
33   SI 1991/1506.

residential care homes, the handbook *Home Life*[34] was published before the implementation of the 1984 Act and is still regarded as an original bible for the basic principles of the ethics of care home practice. It is a good starting point but, having been published during the course of 1984 and not having been the subject of review, the author would suggest that it needs to be approached with some caution. By way of example, *Home Life* is particularly unhelpful in relation to staffing levels in residential care homes; Annex 5, which deals with staffing levels, omits to deal with staffing levels in homes for the frail elderly, which is the largest proportion of registered residential care homes, in the author's experience. Staffing levels for specialist homes can certainly be considered under these provisions, but standard residential care homes for the standard client appear to have been omitted.

Home Life has now been supplemented by *A Better Home Life*[35] but this has yet to achieve the universal acceptance which its predecessor enjoyed.

In relation to nursing homes, there is the well-established guidance to Health Authorities issued by the National Association of Health Authorities, as it was in 1984 (now the National Association of Health Authorities and Trusts), supplemented by a helpful Memorandum in 1988 and further supplemented recently by handbooks in relation to the care of the terminally ill in registered nursing homes. Clearly, the NAHAT Yellow Book guidelines have drawn on the accumulating experience of registration officers in nursing homes and mental nursing homes throughout the UK, but caution must be exercised. The NAHAT guidelines are still guidelines, and not set in stone, and are written from the point of view of the inspecting public authority officers. Each case still falls to be determined on its own merits. In Registered Homes Tribunal Decision No 61 *Reid Smith v Bristol and Weston Health Authority*, which concerned room sizes, a size of room which was smaller than both Health Authority guidelines and NAHAT guidelines was found to be acceptable and adequate by a Tribunal. In the author's submission, the NAHAT guidelines should be approached, as written by those drawn from one side of the regulatory spectrum, with the same caution with which one would approach guidelines issued by a care home or nursing home trade association.

1.11.13   Department of Health Guidance in relation to the operation of the Children Act 1989

This guidance (published in 10 volumes known by their colours, eg the Blue Book) has more force than either of the guidelines mentioned before as it is issued by the Department of Health as general guidance to local authorities as to the way in which they should discharge their duties under the Children Act 1989. It therefore falls within s 7 of the Local Authority Social Services Act 1970 and is general guidance in accordance with which local authorities must act.

The instructive judgment in *London Borough of Sutton v Davis*[36] made it clear that, despite its origin from central government, the Blue Book remains

---

34   *Introduction to Home Life – 'A Code of Practice for Residential Care'* (Centre for Policy on Ageing, 1984).
35   Centre for Policy on Ageing, 1996.
36   [1994] 1 FLR 737, Wilson J.

guidance, and whilst the local authority were required to act generally in accordance with that guidance, it was not to be substituted for or regarded as fettering their discretion on individual cases. Accordingly, in that case, a council policy said to be derived from non-corporal punishment policies set out in the Blue Book was held not be absolutely binding. Each child minder is to be regarded on that person's merits and not disqualified because the child minder declines, in an individual case, to follow the policy of guidance of a local authority, even if that policy or guidance finds, as its source, the guidance issued by central government.

Chapter 2

THE PARTICIPANTS IN THE OPERATION OF A REGISTERED CARE HOME

2.1 INTRODUCTION

This chapter examines each of the participants in the operation of a registered care home and how each inter-relates with the others in their regulation.

2.2 THE PARTICIPANTS

The participants are as follows:

(1) **The Client**: the person in receipt of care; sometimes known as resident, patient or service user;
(2) **Parliament**: as law maker;
(3) **Central Government**: the executive force which implements the legislation;
(4) **The Regulatory Authority**: the authority to which Parliament, via central government, has delegated the day-to-day functions of effecting and overseeing regulation;
(5) **The Home Owner**: the proprietor of the business of care regulated by the regulatory authority upon the direction of central government in accordance with the wishes of Parliament, ie the party responsible for ensuring that the business meets the required regulatory standard.
In many cases, the home owner will manage the care home, but in large organisations it will delegate such functions to the home manager;
(6) **The Home Manager**: the person responsible for the day-to-day operation of the care home (who may or may not be qualified or experienced in the delivery of care) but who is answerable to the home owner for ensuring that the home is managed to the required regulatory standard.

2.3 THE CLIENT

The client is the most important participant in the business of care. It is the client's needs which the regulatory system is designed to protect. Whether the client is satisfied with the service or whether (since in many cases the client is not in a position to express a full and informed opinion) objective observers are satisfied that the service delivery is adequate will determine:

(1) whether the business of care in question succeeds or fails; and
(2) whether or not regulatory action is required.

Section 1(1) of the Children Act 1989 provides:

'Where a court determines any question with respect to—

(a)   the upbringing of a child; or
(b)   the administration of a child's property or the application of any income
      arising from it,
      the child's welfare shall be the courts' paramount consideration.'

No such provision is to be found in the 1984 Act insofar as it relates either to
the care of children or adults. Nevertheless, it is established law that the
purpose of regulation is the protection of frail and vulnerable members of
society.[1]

It is thus a reasonable proposition that for any registration authority,
Tribunal, court, or indeed professional adviser determining issues relating to
the regulation of registered care homes, any decision should consider, as an
issue of paramount importance, the interest of clients or potential clients.

This may suggest that, when in doubt, decisions should tend to favour
cancellation of registration in order to protect the client where there is doubt
about the welfare or safety of patients. However, experience has shown that for
the frail client, particularly the elderly client, moving location is traumatic and
may be against their best interests unless absolutely required.

An authority considering cancellation of registration and faced with
evidence which entitles it to exercise its discretion to cancel will consider the
effect of the cancellation upon the clients.[2]

Cancellation is always discretionary. Despite the view of the Tribunal in
Zaman v Lancashire County Council[3] (which suggests that an authority, having
found evidence which suggested an owner or a business to be unfit, was obliged
to decline the registration), it is suggested that an authority must always have a
true discretion in considering the option to cancel or refuse registration.

Zaman's case does not sit well with the decision of the High Court in *Avon
County Council v Lang.*[4] In *Lang's* case, both the authority and the Court were
satisfied that accommodation used by an elderly lady was inadequate for
general purposes. However, the lady concerned had occupied the particular
room for a considerable period of time and it was not in her interest that she
should be required to move. As her accommodation in that room, in effect,
required an increase in registration, the Court held that her interests overrode
general policy conditions in relation to the size of rooms.

The relationship of the client with the other participants in the operation
of the care home can be divided into:

(1)   the relationship between the client and those responsible for the day-to-
      day operation of the home;
(2)   the relationship between the client and those responsible for the
      regulation of the home, namely Parliament, central government and the
      local authority.

---

1   *Lyons v East Sussex County Council* (1988) 86 LGR 369; (1988) 152 JP 488 (CA).
2   'Discretion to Cancel', Registered Homes Act 1984, ss 10, 25, 28, 59.
3   Registered Homes Tribunal decision No 103.
4   [1990] COD 365.

2.3.1 Relationship with care home owner and manager

The relationship between the client and the home owner, in the home owner's capacity as business proprietor, is the contractual relationship identifying the basis upon which the client occupies accommodation in the home.

2.3.2 The contractual relationship

Historically, the relationship between client and home owner has been one of contract. The question of contract and the funding of registered care home placements are the subject of Chapter 11.

The rights of the client and the obligations of the home owner have usually been set out in a written agreement. Historically, such agreements have tended to be short and covered basic principles, with no detailed provision for service level. Much will be left to individual interpretation of appropriate standards of care, or be left to be implied into the contract as terms that would be agreed between the parties, as a matter of commercial efficacy.

The advent of community care contracting via local authorities and Health Authorities has resulted in more detailed provisions for service level. These have developed throughout the 1990s, especially since 1 April 1993, which saw the implementation of the new 'Care in the Community' Scheme.

Whether or not there should be detailed service level provision in contracts is a matter of ongoing debate. Some local authorities and, indeed, some associations representing particular client groups have advanced the proposition that the service level needs to be defined precisely, so that clients and those representing and supporting clients can understand what is expected. In many cases, the attempt to find such service levels does nothing more than reduce to writing what are basically adequate standards of care.

The difficulty for both home owner and client is that the contract of care is not a commercial contract, in the true sense of the word, but an understanding whereby one will care for the other 24 hours a day and 7 days a week, in a domestic environment. That proposition, it is suggested, leads to the conclusion that there must be a degree of flexibility. Both parties to the contract will require flexibility if it is to work smoothly and in their mutual interest. To prescribe minimum standards for facilities is likely to be restrictive and may be embarrassing to one party or the other. A better course is to provide detailed service guidance as to the facilities available and provide that facilities must be made available for individual clients according to need. The need for flexibility increases as the level of dependency and requirement for care increases.

The essence of a contract for care, therefore, is that the home owner is required to provide whatever care is required as and when needed. To pay too much attention to service level provisions is to confuse care home services with hotel services.

2.3.3 The problem of fees

The lack of sophistication in business methods within the care home business and the uniformity of the weekly fee produced by capping social welfare benefit, have deflected attention from the issue that in many businesses it would be regular practice that different levels of service attract different fees.

With greater sophistication and more detailed contracting, fees will, inevitably, be geared to the service level provided. This may happen in a way which will not be in the interests of individual clients.

If the service level is set out in detail then the home owner will expect increased charges should the service level increase, and inevitably, if the charge cannot be met the client may be required to vacate. Required services should be not expected to be supplied free of charge, but home owners would be in breach of regulatory standards if they let clients stay without providing adequate care.

Furthermore, detailed service level provisions, as part of a contract, are snares for the unwary home owner. Specific provisions as to, for example, times of day for care provision will inevitably lead to allegations of breach of contract which could disrupt the cash flow of the care home business if used to justify withholding payment of fees.

Care home businesses are not vastly profitable. One of their advantages is the regular generation of cash, rarely affected by bad debt or delayed debt, so that all working capital is employed on a virtually guaranteed revolving basis. Detailed service level provisions which lead individual clients or their supporters to seek refunds or withhold payments would not be in the interests of clients within a care home, as a whole.

The clients are not prisoners. Their remedy, if dissatisfied, is to seek alternative accommodation or to complain, ultimately to the regulatory authority, who may take action which will result in the closure of the home.

2.3.4   The Community Care Scheme

The advent of the Community Care Scheme has seen a change in contracting arrangements:

(1)   contracts are now seen to be very important. Previously, they were incidental to the acceptance of the provision of total care for a fee;
(2)   contracts made with local authorities or Health Authorities are contracts not with the client but for the client.

In some cases, the client may be a party to the contract, in order to acknowledge and accept the contract, or to agree that part of the fee should be directed, as the client's contribution, direct to the care home owner rather than to the local authority. However, the responsibility for payment of the fee to the owner and responsibility for the provision of the service to the local authority are obligations as between local authority and care home owner. The client, in these circumstances often described as 'service user', is incidental to the contractual agreement.

Local government, as purchaser, arranges the provision of the care service by the owner for the client. This is a change from the previous central government funded support of care contracts, where the client sought care provision, contracted provision and claimed grant support from central government to assist with payment of fees.

Even where the client has a direct contract with the home owner, the client will not have the same power to cancel the contract or relocate. Such steps will require the intervention and support of the local authority.

A practical effect of the change is that whereas the home owner, under the previous regime, had a variety of contractual relationships with each and every client, it is likely that, for those homes who provide services for local authority or Health Authority sponsored clients, the multiplicity of client contracts will have been replaced by one relationship with one client, ie the local authority, whether that is reflected in a block contract or a series of contracts.

Any disturbance of the contractual relationship will have a more immediate impact and the local authority will have the power of purchaser in addition to the power of regulator. The client will cease to have the power of contracting purchaser and, whilst remaining the subject of the contract of care, will be in the position of a party dependent upon a patron or sponsor.

The client's rights as against the sponsoring local authority may or may not be spelt out in any detail in the contract, but the client's power to leave the care home must be seen as diminished where the position of client is altered to sponsored client as opposed to contracting party.

2.3.5 Relationship with local authority

The client's relationship with the local authority, as a purchaser, is one of the benefits of the exercise of the power (sometimes duty) of the authority to provide accommodation.[5] The relationship between client and local authority, as regulator, is essentially one of ultimate quality control. The client and those who support the client, whether they be friends, relatives or professional supporters, for example charity or social workers, will know that the continued ability of the home owner to carry out his business is dependant upon continued registration.

2.3.6 Complaints procedure

As a matter of good practice, every care home owner is required to have and to publish a complaints procedure. That procedure should provide for the effective referral by the client of complaints to objective parties. In large homes, complaints should be referred in the first instance to the home manager and thereafter to the owner. Many homes arrange for outside counsellors to be available to receive and investigate complaints and report to the owners on the substance of complaints and action which may be required. Ultimately, the client should know that he may complain to the regulatory authority. A recent direction by way of general guidance to local authorities by the Department of Health, requires that all residential care home owners be required to include, within their complaints procedure, full details of the name, address and telephone number of the local authority for the purpose of receiving complaints.

The 1984 Residential Care Homes Regulations[6] require the owner to make arrangements (suitable to the number, age, sex and condition of residents) for persons authorised by the regulatory authority or the Secretary of State to interview residents in private.

---

5 See National Assistance Act 1948, s 21 as amended by National Health Service and Community Care Act 1990.

6 SI 1984/1345; see reg 10(1)(o).

In relation to nursing homes, the requirement for disclosure of contact information in relation to the regulatory authority, ie the Health Authority, is recognised by owners and trade associations alike as a proper and required part of a complaints procedure.

The 1984 Nursing Homes Regulations provide similar provisions requiring owners to make available facilities for clients to receive visitors in private or for persons authorised to interview patients in private at the home.[7] In relation to mental nursing homes (see Chapter 7 on inspection), the statutory inspector is entitled to seek unimpeded interviews and examinations of patients.[8]

The Children's (Secure Accommodation) Regulations 1991 and the Children's Homes Regulations 1991[9] provide that there must be provision for private meetings between children and a variety of people with a proper interest in their welfare,[10] and such homes are required to have private telephone facilities for children.[11]

Accordingly, as a result both of law and practice, the relationship between the client and the regulatory authority leaves open clear lines of communication for the clients to communicate their concerns direct to the regulatory authority and thus to involve the regulatory authority in quality control issues.

2.3.7   Relationship with Parliament and central government

The client will have a relationship with Parliament or central government only to the extent that opinion as to the effectiveness of the operation of the regulatory scheme may prompt amendment of executive regulations and directions made by central government, and thus changes to the regulatory framework as prescribed by Parliament.

2.4   PARLIAMENT

Parliament creates the law of regulation by statute. The law of regulation is repealed and changed by statute. Furthermore, the powers will be circumscribed by the wording of statutes or by appropriately passed subordinate legislation. Accordingly, while regulators frequently appear to those who they are required to regulate, or even to those for whose protection the regulation is designed, to be powerful in themselves, their power is always limited and circumscribed.

Having observed that Parliament can appoint those who make regulations and implement the provisions of regulations, it is important to remember that the delegate cannot sub-delegate his authority unless specifically authorised or required so to do.[12] The Latin maxim which is used to reflect this principle is:

---

7   SI 1984/1578; see reg 12(1)(r) and (t).
8   See Registered Homes Act 1984, s 35.
9   SI 1991/1505 and SI 1991/1506.
10   See Children's Homes Regulations 1991, reg 7(3).
11   Ibid, reg 7(5).
12   See, for example National Health Service Act 1977, s 13 and s 14.

'*Delegatus delegare non potest*'. The principle is that an agent cannot sub-delegate his appointment, except to the extent he is authorised so to do by his principal. This is a general principle of English law and it applies in the field of public administration as it applies in private sector agency law.

The relevant statutes were outlined in Chapter 1. They are the Registered Homes Act 1984, the Children Act 1989 and the National Health Service Act 1977. Part I of the 1984 Act, in relation to residential care homes, combines the statutory regulatory rules with the authority of the Secretary of State to make rules, and the authority of the registration authority to enforce the rules. Part II of the 1984 Act, in relation to nursing homes, merely prescribes the statutory framework of regulation and designates the Secretary of State both as rule maker and enforcer.

As Parliament cannot be involved in monitoring detail about good practice in the operation of care homes, so the Secretary of State cannot be responsible for day-to-day decisions. Accordingly, by s 13 and s 14 of the 1977 Act, the Secretary of State may delegate functions under the 1977 Act to Health Authorities.

The regulations currently in force are the National Health Service (Functions of Health Authorities and Administration Arrangements) Regulations 1996.[13] The regulations are amended frequently, with changes in procedures for the administration of the National Health Service, the latest amendment being required as a result of the reorganisation of the National Health Service and the integration of District Health Authorities and Regional Health Authorities into new Health Authorities, with effect from 1 April 1996.

2.4.1   Parliament's relationship with other participants

(1)   *The client*
      The relationship with the client is indirect. Parliament reacts to changes of demand from clients and concerns expressed by or on behalf of clients by adjusting the statutory framework of regulation.

(2)   *Central government*
      The link between statute passed by Parliament and central government is the crucial link of authority for any action to implement or enforce the regulatory requirements.

(3)   *Local government*
      Local government derives its authority to act in the regulatory scheme either directly from Parliament (as in Pt I of the 1984 Act), or from central government, by the delegation of power from the Secretary of State, to the extent that this is permitted by Parliament.

(4)   *Home owner/manager*
      There is no direct relationship between Parliament and a home owner or manager. The position is similar to the position of the client. Parliament, in providing the framework of regulation, takes account of the perceptions of society as to the need for and the extent of regulation, guided by evidence as to the conduct of home owners and the need to

---

13   SI 1996/708.

ensure a plentiful supply of care homes, in order to enable those in need and able to purchase to choose appropriate care.

2.5   CENTRAL GOVERNMENT

The function of central government is to act as an executive to implement the requirements of statute enacted by Parliament. Most legislation will be introduced at the behest of the Government of the day which will be seeking powers to implement policies that it has formulated, thus seeking the seal of legal approval before taking steps to implement changes in policy.

The function of central government, through the Secretary of State, will be to work up a detailed framework of regulation to expand upon the basic framework created by statute. Its aim is to ensure that the rules so promulgated are enforced by delegating decisions as to day-to-day implementation and regulation, to bodies (currently local authorities and Health Authorities) who are sufficiently able and well-resourced, to ensure that the law is observed and enforced.

Central government and practitioners advising in the care business need to look to statutes to identify the regulation-making power of the Secretary of State. A variety of Secretaries of State may make regulations in relation to care. Principally, this is likely to be done by the Secretary for State for Health, or possibly the Secretary of State for the Environment, but other Secretaries of State have the power. Any one of Her Majesty's principal Secretaries of State may exercise the power conferred on a Secretary of State by Parliament.

When construing such regulations, those responsible must also ensure that the regulations are actually within the limits prescribed by the relevant statute and are not made unreasonably, taking into account the power granted and the mischief against which the regulations are aimed. It will, however, be only in rare cases that the exercise of power granted by Parliament to the Secretary of State will be said to be unreasonable.

Whether or not regulations are ultra vires, either because they go beyond the powers granted or because they are unreasonable, is a matter to be considered by any court or tribunal considering those regulations and which is required to make a decision regarding the legal position of parties before that court or tribunal in relation to the implementation of those regulations. Tribunals are, however, enjoined that they should only make decisions as to the unreasonableness or legality of regulations to the extent that such a decision is required to determine the issue before them.[14]

The Secretary of State has power from Parliament to make regulations:

(1)   in relation to residential care homes, pursuant to ss 5, 8, 16, 17 and 57 of and Sch 2 to the 1984 Act;
(2)   pursuant to ss 21, 23, 26, 27, 29, 35, 56 of and Sch 2 to the 1948 Act;
(3)   in relation to the implementation of nursing home registration by Health Authorities, pursuant to s 13 and s 14 of the 1977 Act;

---

14   A decision of the House of Lords in *Chief Adjudication Officer v Foster* [1993] 1 All ER 705.

(4) in relation to registered children's homes, under ss 62, 63, 64, 104 of and Schs 4, 5 and 6 to the 1989 Act.

As has already been seen, implementation of registration is delegated directly by Parliament to local authorities in respect of residential care homes and registered children's homes.

In relation to the implementation of regulations concerning nursing homes, power is vested by Parliament in the Secretary of State and delegated by the Secretary of State to the Health Authority.[15]

With regard to residential care homes, registered children's homes and nursing homes, the power of making regulations is delegated to the Secretary of State. In exercising his power to delegate implementation of nursing home regulations to Health Authorities, the Secretary of State has repeatedly, since 1982, excluded from the delegation of regulation-making power, the power to make regulations, ie there is no authority for the proposition that the Secretary of State has delegated to Health Authorities powers that would give the force of law to local requirements, guidelines or rules.[16]

Local authorities are required to act under the general guidance of the Secretary of State.[17] However, if the Secretary of State requires social services authorities to publish guidelines as to the implementation of their duties and regulation of registered residential care homes and registered children's homes, such guidance is no more than a reflection of the considered view of the authority. The authority will have complied with the guidance by issuing guidelines. Those guidelines are not thereby converted into regulations.

Central government, through the Secretary of State, has power to promulgate rules and policies. Those responsible for operating or seeking to operate registered care homes have to recognise that they operate in a regulated arena. Irrespective of personal views, a disinclination on the part of home owners to follow the policies, practices and procedures which the Secretary of State is empowered by Parliament to regulate, suggests unfitness to continue to operate. The ultimate arbiter of practice must surely be the Secretary of State, in whom the rule-making power is vested. Moreover, a disinclination to follow rules set out in regulations may well amount to a criminal offence.

2.5.1 Funding

The issue of funding in this context is the function of central government in providing funds for the purchase of care by those in need, who are unable to meet the financial requirements of the care home from their own resources. The history of the development of care homes, as has been seen, is closely identified with the debate as to whether or not funds for the purchase of health care and social welfare should come exclusively from private individuals, or from central government, or be funded by local government.

---

15   See National Health Service (Functions of Authorities and Administration Arrangements) Regulations 1996.
16   Ibid, reg 4(2).
17   See Local Authority Social Services Act 1970, s 7(1).

Central government is required to ensure that, for each and every citizen, there is a proper health care service provided free.[18] Local government has traditionally been charged with providing residential accommodation and other welfare services for those in need within its area, to the extent that such services do not amount to health care requirements.[19] The power to provide residential accommodation has been made an obligation where central government so directs. Such powers and obligations have, since their inception, included the power to purchase services from the private sector where not available from public sector resources.[20] This power was extended so that local authorities may purchase health care services with effect from 1 April 1993.[21]

Prior to 1 April 1993 and thereafter, in respect of those who were entitled to and in receipt of residential and nursing care home care prior to that date, central government made available means tested grants for all those in need of such care. Such budgets were not in any way cash or resource limited. The amount of such grants, whilst unlimited when first conceived, were cash limited (from April 1985) to a statutory maximum, adjusted from time to time to take account of inflation.

Central government perceived a need to limit cash expenditure in the support of care home placement and this was effected by switching the obligation from one of central government to each and every citizen in need, to an obligation on the part of local government to each citizen who may be assessed as being in need by local government. This remains the case, notwithstanding the availability of means tested and non-means tested welfare benefits to the sick, disabled and needy, which continue beyond 1 April 1993, for those who may not be assessed by a local authority as in need or may not seek such assessment.

The detail of funding care home placement of registered homes will be discussed in greater depth in Chapter 11.

Central government has two distinct roles:

(1) determining the detail of regulation;
(2) providing funds to support the provision of care to individuals, either directly to such individuals or by funding or providing facilities for revenue raising for those who are responsible for such care.

2.5.2   Relationship with clients

The relationship between client and central government is remote but experience as to the conduct of care homes shows that criticism, whether negative or positive, of the operation of care homes will filter through to

---

18   See National Health Service Act 1977, s 1.
19   See, for example National Assistance Act 1948, Pt III and Chronically Sick and Disabled Persons Act 1970.
20   See, for example National Assistance Act 1948, s 26.
21   See amendments to National Assistance Act 1948, Pt III, s 21 by National Health Service and Community Care Act 1990.

central government and, to that extent, the client will have an indirect influence upon the way in which central government exercises its role in promulgating regulations.

Further, the increasing or decreasing needs of clients for funds to meet their care requirements means that the client is ultimately dependent on central government to provide sufficient such funds. As clients are electors, shortfalls in funds are likely to be reflected at the ballot box, with adverse consequences for central government.

2.5.3 Relationship with local authorities and Health Authorities (local government)

Local government looks to central government, as a regulator, to set the detailed regulations within the context of which local government is required to implement regulation of care homes. In relation to the regulation of nursing homes, all power is delegated by central government to local regulators (ie Health Authorities) who also act in the name of central government as they carry out the process of implementation and enforcement of the regulation of such homes.

In relation to the regulation of residential care homes, in addition to implementing the regulations set by central government, local government must have regard to general guidance issued by central government. With regard to funding, local government is not entitled to look to central government for the provision of funds specifically to support the provision of any care that local government may purchase. Subject to specific exceptions, for example, the special transitional grant made by central government to local government to assist with the transfer of responsibility for residential community care, from 1 April 1993, local government must look to its own resources to meet its obligations as a purchaser and provider.

Where local government decides to purchase care, whether local authority or Health Authority, it should be aware of the extent of its powers and the limitation on those powers imposed by Parliament or central government. There is always the vexed question as to whether or not a purchasing power includes a power to pay part of monies incurred by clients. The better view is that such local purchasing authorities must purchase as a whole, in the case of local authorities seeking reimbursement from clients but not seeking to pay, by way of 'top up', a shortfall in fees left after the main portion has been discharged by the client or third parties.

2.5.4 Relationship with care home owners and managers

The relationship between central government and care home owners/ managers is, as with central government's relationship with clients, remote. Central government sets the framework and, to a certain extent, provides funds available for the purchase of services, reacting to the demands of society by the amendment of the regulatory regime. Having created the general regulation scheme, as permitted by Parliament and, in relation to nursing homes, having delegated the implementation of the regulatory scheme to the Health Authority, central government is not directly responsible or accountable to home owners, nor are home owners entitled to leap frog local government regulators and deal directly with central government, otherwise than by way of political lobbying.

2.6 LOCAL GOVERNMENT

In considering the position of local government, it is right to begin by considering those organs of local government which may be concerned in the delivery of care:

(1) social services authorities (in the appropriate context this will mean County Councils or Unitary Authorities, Metropolitan Borough Councils and London Boroughs);
(2) Health Authorities;
(3) National Health Service Trusts.

2.6.1 Social services authorities

Social services authorities have roles as both:

(1) regulators of care homes;
(2) purchasers of care supplied within care homes and, since 1 April 1993, nursing homes.

2.6.2 Health Authorities

Health Authorities have two functions in the context of registered homes:

(1) most importantly, to implement the regulation of registered nursing homes, at the direction of the Secretary of State, in accordance with the power delegated by Parliament[22] (Health Authorities have no power to make regulations in relation to the conduct of nursing homes);
(2) on behalf of the Secretary of State, to commission, ie purchase, care for those in need within their jurisdiction. Accordingly, to the extent that NHS facilities may not be available to the Health Authority, the Health Authority may purchase health care from private sector providers operating registered care homes.

2.6.3 NHS Trusts

NHS Trusts (the creation of the National Health Service and Community Care Act 1990) are created, in broad terms, to own or provide hospital buildings and facilities and manage services conducted from such buildings and facilities. As such, they are described as the providers of services, as opposed to the purchasers of services. NHS Trusts are not concerned with the regulation of registered care homes, or the purchase of care for patients. NHS Trusts, as a part of their own diversification of service, may seek to make available facilities equivalent to registered care home facilities or to purchase, so as to enhance their own facilities, registered care home placements, so as to be able to fulfil

---

22 See National Health Service Act 1977, s 13 and s 14.

the requirements of purchasers attracted to the services of the Trust. Also, NHS Trusts, organised to provide community services, may well see the need to purchase, in block or individually, nursing home placements, to fulfil the requirements of their own private or NHS purchasers for care needs.

The care home owner dealing with an NHS Trust will be making arrangements for the provision of a facility for the Trust, rather than the provision of care for an individual.

2.6.4 Social services authorities and Health Authorities as regulators

Social services authorities acquire their power to regulate residential care homes from Pt I of the 1984 Act and to regulate registered children's homes from Pt VIII of the 1989 Act.

Health Authorities acquire their regulatory powers under the direction and authority of central government, ie the Secretary of State, under the National Health Service (Functions of Health Authorities and Administration Arrangements) Regulations 1996[23] (as amended from time to time) made pursuant to s 13 and s 14 of the National Health Service Act 1977, implementing the powers granted to the Secretary of State by Parliament in Pt II of the Registered Homes Act 1984.

Both local authorities and Health Authorities are subject to review by the courts by way of judicial review and the more judicial the nature of the decision which authorities are making, the more likely it is that they will be challenged in the courts successfully, if the decision is shown to be unreasonable or perverse. Conversely, the more administrative the nature of the decision, the less likely the courts are to interfere.

In order to succeed, an applicant for judicial review must show that a local authority has acted unlawfully, including perversely, ie acted in such a way that no reasonable authority could have acted.[24]

It is unlawful for an authority to fetter itself in the way it exercises its powers, in advance of an individual decision. It is not unlawful, where otherwise permitted by the regulatory statute, to have regard to its own views, policies and requirements in making the decision, so long as the decision is not pre-determined by the policy.[25] The power of public authorities to bind themselves by pre-determined policy is discussed in Chapter 1.

Even if the authority has not fettered its discretion, it may still be subject to judicial review if its decision is shown to be perverse in the sense that it was a decision that no reasonable authority could make. There is no recourse to judicial review simply because the applicant considers the decision should have been made otherwise. The applicant must show that the decision is so unreasonable as to be perverse and thus beyond the powers of the authority, for an authority is not considered to have power to act perversely. Similarly, a local authority must make a decision in accordance with the powers granted to

---

23   SI 1996/708.
24   *Associated Provincial Picture Houses v Wednesbury Corporation* [1948] 1 KB 223.
25   See, for example *Isle of Wight County Council v Humphreys* [1992] COD 308; *Ismail v Birmingham City Council* (unreported) 29 October 1992, McPherson J.

it, taking into account the matters which it is required to take into account and permitted to take into account. An authority does not have a personality or a moral conscience, nor may it adopt the moral conscience or subjective concerns of the majority of the authority or of a committee of the authority.[26]

2.6.5 Social services authorities and Health Authorities as purchasers

Apart from their role as regulators, these local authorities have the function, of purchasing care. Whether or not such care can be purchased and whether or not contracts for purchase are valid once again requires an analysis as to whether or not the ability to purchase is within the powers of the authority. The ability must be seen to be within the powers of the authority not merely as a matter of principle, but in the individual case. If the exercise of the power to purchase goes beyond the purchase of care for an individual, but involves a block contract over a period of time, then it needs to be shown that the authority not only had the power to purchase, but also exercised that power taking into account all relevant circumstances. Both the contract must be *intra vires* and the actual contact must only have been concluded after due consideration taking into account all relevant matters and not taking into account irrelevant matters.

Social services authorities have powers and obligations to provide and purchase care pursuant to the National Assistance Act 1948, Pt III. Health Authorities have powers and obligations to make arrangements with third parties for the provision of health care services pursuant to s 23 of the National Health Service Act 1977.

The widening of social services authorities' powers to purchase health care, with effect from 1 April 1993, and the consequent implementation of Government policy that residential care home and nursing home placement should be purchased through the local authority (whether or not health care) has led to consideration of whether or not potential or existing arrangements for the purchase of health care from the private sector by Health Authorities are or remain valid.

2.6.6 Regulator/purchaser – conflict

There is an inevitable conflict between the position of regulator and purchaser, in which many local authorities and Health Authorities find themselves placed.

The power to purchase is in itself an effective regulator. Should the power to purchase be withdrawn without regulatory powers being taken to cancel registration, the same effect may have been achieved.

Information obtained as a regulator, it is submitted, is obtained in a relationship of confidence. Should that information be communicated to the recipient in his role as a purchaser or would that be improper?

Should the purchaser restrict purchase because a regulated home which

---

26   See *R v Somerset County Council ex parte Fewings* (Laws J) [1994] COD 338.

meets the test of the regulator does not meet superficial tests imposed by the purchaser and which are not imposed by the standards of regulation? Will the market purchasing power of the local authority supersede, as a regulator, the rules set in place by Parliament for limiting the scope of regulation?

There have always been difficulties about the extent to which regulators should publicise or make available, whether or not others have a legitimate interest, information obtained in the course of regulation. As a general principle, confidential information imported in a special relationship (eg solicitor and client) may only be used for the intended purpose. The enforced inspection of care homes is likely to be found to be such a relationship. This dilemma and conflict must be heightened where, albeit through different departments, purchaser and regulator are housed within the same authority.

Local authorities should approach these difficulties with great caution.

2.6.7   Local authority's relationship with other participants

The client
The local authority will relate to the client as a regulator:

(1)   at arm's length, by seeking to ensure that facilities available to the client in any care home meet adequate standards;
(2)   subjectively and directly with the client, by being available to discuss complaints or concerns either as a result of action initiated by the client or by the authority.

The local authority will relate to the client as purchaser where the local authority, in proper exercise of its powers, sponsors the client by purchasing the appropriate care for the client, wherever that care may be situated.

Parliament
The relationship between local government and Parliament will be entirely circumscribed by the statutes enacted in relation to regulation and purchasing powers.

Parliament has provided direct regulatory roles for local authorities in the registration of residential care homes and registered children's homes, through Pt I of the 1984 Act and Pt VIII of the 1989 Act.

Parliament has provided direct power for local authorities to purchase residential and other social welfare services and health care services, pursuant to the National Assistance Act 1948, as amended by the National Health Service and Community Care Act 1990, Pt III.

2.7   CARE HOME OWNER

The home owner is the person who carries on the business of the care home, providing care for those in need – the residents/clients.

2.7.1   Problems of definition

The legislation (the 1984 Act and the 1989 Act) gives little assistance in determining what is meant by 'carrying on'. The author would suggest that the term 'carry on' carries with it the usual meaning ascribed in law, namely that 'carry on' indicates that the person is entitled to ownership and profit and is expected to bear losses. Insofar as the business undertakes responsibility, the person 'carrying on' the business is the one who undertakes responsibility for the business liabilities. The person carrying on the business is clearly the person responsible to the regulators for compliance with regulatory requirements.

The person carrying on the business is the person registered. The person carrying on the business is the person who, on loss of registration, will lose the business. Therefore, it is suggested that the person carrying on the business is the business owner as opposed to the person having day-to-day management of the business from time to time.

'Carry on' is defined in the *Concise Oxford Dictionary*, 1991 edition (as a second meaning) as 'engage in business'. How much activity may be needed to constitute 'carrying on' will be a matter of fact and degree in each case.

2.7.2   Registration

Registration is restricted to the person carrying on the business (see the discussion on this in relation to registration of a manager at para **2.8.1** below). The authorities are:

(1)   section 2 of the 1984 Act:

> 'If a person carries on a residential care home without being registered under this Act in respect of it he shall be guilty of an offence.'

(2)   section 23(1) of the 1984 Act:

> 'Any person who carries on a nursing home or a mental nursing home without being registered under this part of this Act in respect of that home shall be guilty of an offence.'

(3)   section 63(10) of the 1989 Act:

> 'Where any child is at any time cared for and accommodated in a children's home which is not a registered children's home, the person carrying on the home shall be—
>
> (a)   guilty of an offence; and
> (b)   liable to a fine not exceeding level 5 on the standard scale,
>
> unless he has a reasonable excuse.'

Registration offences will be dealt with later, but it will be observed that offences under the 1984 Act in relation to carrying on a business are absolute, while offences under the 1989 Act are qualified, in the sense that a reasonable excuse may avoid criminal liability.

2.7.3   Duties

The care home owner owes duties:

(1)   to clients, to provide a sufficient and adequate standard of care according to their needs, insofar as commitments are made over and above

adequate standards as defined by the regulatory authorities, in accordance with contractual commitments asked and given, including ensuring that the home complies with the regulatory requirements;

(2) to the regulatory authority, to comply with the requirements of regulations.

The consequences of breach of the duties are, however, different. Consequences of a breach of duty to a client (or an extended client if the contract is made with a local authority acting as a purchaser) will give rise to financial consequences, including consequences arising out of termination of contract.

Consequences of a breach of an obligation to the regulatory authority may lead, ultimately, to the loss of registration and thus, in effect, the loss of the licence (registration) to carry on the business.

2.7.4 Rights

The reverse of duties is often seen as rights and the care home owner enjoys rights. To be a care home owner, he must have secured acceptance as being fit to operate a care home, in accordance with the standards of the regulatory authority. That acceptance is signified in the Certificate of Registration granted pursuant to ss 5 or 23 of the 1984 Act and sub-para 7 of para 1 of Sch 6 to the 1989 Act. In the latter case, in relation to registered children's home applications, the application is granted and is followed simply by notification to that effect from the authority, whereas in relation to residential care homes and nursing homes, the application is granted and the authority is obliged to issue a Certificate of Registration.

Armed with the Certificate of Registration or formal notification of registration of a registered children's home, the home owner is entitled to trade, to 'carry on' the business of running the home. He has thus been admitted to a privileged sector entitled to carry on a regulated business and this will give him the advantage of a market place in which only those who have been objectively tested and have reached a satisfactory standard are permitted to carry on the business.

The process of regulation must be seen against the background that admission to the right to trade is a privilege not accorded to all and, accordingly, is subject to review and cancellation, should standards anticipated at the time of registration not be maintained.

2.7.5 Relationship with other parties

Clients

The home owner is in direct relationship with the client. In traditional care home management, the client is the customer of the care home owner. Their relationship is defined by contract, usually supplemented by a review as to the supply of adequate and proper standards of care, from time to time.

In the modern 'community care' context, the relationship, often described as one of service performance, may be one of contract but may be one limited to an obligation on the part of the owner to supply services to a standard agreed with a third party, ie the local authority or other sponsor.

It is suggested that this relationship is nothing more than an extension of the former relationship where relatives contracted as sponsors for the person in care so that the person in care was not a contracting party, but was entitled to receive the benefit of the contract negotiated and maintained on his or her behalf by a third party.

Parliament
The home owner is in no direct relationship with Parliament, but his ability to carry on the business is circumscribed by changes in the regulatory structure specified by statutes enacted or amended from time to time by Parliament.

Central government
The home owner is not in direct relationship with central government but insofar as central government, through the Secretary of State, reviews and amends the detailed provisions of regulation, which impact upon the direct operation of care homes or particular classes of care homes, then the home owner operates subject to a licence which is subject to the changing rules of regulation or deregulation as decided by central government in accordance with the brief outlined by Parliament. If the rules are changed (by proper process) the home owner cannot complain even if his interests are seriously adversely affected. He may, however, test the validity of the process. If defective, the change will be of no effect.

Local government
The home owner is in direct relationship with local government:

(1)   as a regulator;
(2)   as a supplier of services to local government acting as a purchaser.

The care home owner will be involved in an intimate day-to-day relationship with local government acting as regulator. Local government is the manifestation of the power of regulation for the individual care home owner.

Whilst the power of local government is entirely circumscribed by the rules of regulation established by Parliament and developed by central government, it will be local government acting within those limits which implements the rules of regulation and ensures that standards are maintained.

With regard to local government acting as purchaser of services, for all purposes, the owner will be in a contractual relationship with the local authority as with any other client/customer. The practical differences are greater comfort on credit risk and the need to ensure that the local authority has acted within its powers.

2.8   THE MANAGER

Whatever may be his relationship with other participants in the operation of a care home business, it is suggested that the manager will always be the servant or agent of the care home owner. He may have a position of independence or individual responsibility, but his relationship with the care home owner will be circumscribed by a contract requiring him to provide services (ie an independent contractor) or a contract of service, making him the employee of the home owner.

The manager, as will be seen in the next section, may be required to be registered with the local authority in respect of residential care homes, but not in relation to registered nursing homes or registered children's homes. The home owner's relationship with the manager will always be one of control of the manager in the proper conduct of the care home business.

There may arise a conflict for the manager if the care home owner requires the manager to operate in such a way as is outside proper standards of care or in breach of conditions of registration or, if a registered manager, in circumstances that may put his registration, as a manager carrying on the care home business, in jeopardy.

Be that as it may, it is suggested that the relationship of appointment between owner and manager is such that such a conflict can only be resolved by the manager, by resigning from his appointment. The care home owner, being the business proprietor, is entitled to expect compliance with instructions and the only route for those who believe those instructions to be flawed is resignation and possibly the pursuance of a claim for damages for breach of contract, or (if employed) constructive dismissal, being unfair and/ or wrongful.

To require a care home manager to act in such a way as to contravene rules of good practice, conditions of registration or to endanger his own Certificate of Registration, must surely be seen as conduct entitling the manager to determine his contract either by way of fundamental breach, so as to entitle determination of a contract for services, or such fundamental breach as to amount to constructive dismissal from a contract of employment.

2.8.1 Who is the manager?

The 'manager' of a care home may have a number of meanings. The 'manager' may be a term of art used to describe a person responsible for the whole of the operation of a care home, or one or more divisions of the care home business. A manager, as has been indicated in the previous section, will operate either under a contract for services or a contract of service and will, in effect, be the servant or agent of the care home owner.

Managers may be individuals or limited companies. Frequently, care home owners who lack the ability, knowledge or time to conduct the business will appoint managers to have control of the business on a day-to-day basis, reporting regularly to their principals.

An interesting question can arise as to whether or not such managers are indeed carrying on the business and whether they require to be registered. As has been suggested, 'carrying on a business' involves acknowledgment of ownership of and responsibility for the business rather than conducting a business on the behalf of another so that the other person is undertaking the commercial risk. It is suggested that a manager acting for a fee and supported by working capital provided by an owner cannot be described as carrying on the business. If that is so, then such managers, whatever the terms of their agreement, cannot seek registration and should not be registered.

Managers in such positions, who seek or accept registration, should understand that such acceptance involves accepting that they are business proprietors responsible for the actions of the business. They may thus be found to hold themselves out as principals and become liable for business debts.

From a regulatory point of view, a manager who seeks or accepts registration accepts that loss of that registration for failure to meet standards will bear the consequence that the manager and not just the owner will be stigmatised by responsibility for the proven inadequacy of service.

A manager who is not carrying on the business but seeks or obtains registration, should be careful to establish that he has, from his principal, sufficient means, at all times, to fulfil properly the obligations of management, supported by an appropriate contract of indemnity for business liability.

Managers should proceed with care. Registration cannot be resigned and once adopted may carry tremendous risk. This is the more so where managers conduct business providing management services to a number of owners in a number of centres. The essence of such arrangements is that the business risk is taken by the business owner and the executive function is carried out by the manager. The executive function cannot be carried out without sufficient resources and the manager needs to know that he can resign if resources are withheld or are not available to meet proper standards. An unregistered manager can always resign, subject only to the terms of his contract of engagement.

2.8.2   What is a manager?

No definition is provided in the 1984 Act. Many local authorities, in their guidelines, make a mistake in equating management with control of care. The author would suggest that a manager is a person who is vested with power to direct and control the business on a day-to-day basis, making all decisions which may be relevant to day-to-day control of the business, as opposed to medium or long-term strategic development of the business. The manager may or may not be synonymous with the person in charge of care.

If the above definition is correct, the manager will assume business control. He may be a skilled and experienced carer or nurse, although it is not necessary that he be so. If such skills and experience are not present, the manager must procure for his principal such skills by appointing suitably qualified and experienced persons to deliver and manage care, subject to his direction and control, as a business manager.

In exactly the same way, a business owner who lacks experience or skill in the particular field of delivery of care must either acquire those skills, dispose of the business, or appoint sufficiently experienced and qualified staff to supply the care skills needed.

In relation to the operation of a registered nursing home, there must be a qualified person in charge and that person in charge must be a nurse possessing appropriate qualifications, which may be made a condition of registration, or a registered medical practitioner.[27] It is not necessary that the qualified person in charge be the manager. The requirement is that 'the home

---

27   See s 25(1)(f) and s 25(2) of the 1984 Act.

is or will be in the charge of a person who is either a registered medical practitioner or a qualified nurse or in the case of a maternity home, a registered midwife'.

There is a clear distinction, in the author's view, between business ownership, business management and the assumption through appointment of taking charge of a nursing home. Being 'in charge' can be distinguished from management of business by being limited to the assumption of responsibility for care. If 'in charge' were to equal 'manage', every nursing home would have to be under the effective business control of a doctor or nurse. The fact that that is not the practice suggests that it is not the law.

Owners and managers must appreciate that, if the person in charge or in charge of care in residential or registered children's homes are not business proprietors or appointed managers, then their appointment or replacement is vital to the continued operation of the home. The absence of such a person in charge of care will inevitably lead to consideration as to whether the registration should be cancelled and, in appropriate circumstances (ie if no experienced carer or nurse is available), may lead to the inevitable conclusion that there will be a serious risk to life, health or well-being, entitling the registration authority to apply for urgent cancellation.

Cancellation or urgent cancellation does not necessarily carry with it the stigma of bad behaviour, simply the recognition of an inability to carry on the business in a proper way or, in the case of urgent cancellation, without what is perceived objectively as a serious risk to clients' health and safety.

2.8.3   Residential care home management

In the case of residential care homes, it is provided by s 3 of the 1984 Act that a manager may be required to be registered. As will be examined in later chapters, this provision is probably meaningless.

Section 3 reads as follows:

> 'Where the manager or intended manager of a residential care home is not in control of it (whether as owner or otherwise) both the manager or intended manager and the person in control are to be treated as carrying on or intending to carry on the home and accordingly as requiring to be registered under this part of this Act.'

Thus, it will be seen that the requirement for registration as a manager is a situation which puts that manager in the position of being deemed to be 'carrying on' the home. As already argued, the person 'carrying on' the home is a person who has ownership and has assumed the risk for the conduct of the business.

What is curious about s 3 is that a manager (who according to the author's definition would have assumed direction and control on a day-to-day basis) must not be in control if registration is to be required; but registration is required for a manager not in control, as well as for the person in control. It is suggested that the person in control (whether as owner or otherwise) must be equated with the business owner.

A person who is in control but who is not carrying on the business is not required to be registered either by s 2 or s 3 of the 1984 Act. However, curiously, a person not in control is required to be registered.

The obvious answer of differentiating ownership from management control is avoided by the words in parentheses, '(whether as owner or otherwise)', included in the section. It would seem that practitioners can reasonably safely ignore s 3 as an abberation by Parliament which has been ill-thought out and which has little meaning.

A manager who is not in control, although casually described as a manager, will not in reality be a manager at all and, accordingly, not require registration. Any other view would mean that any person having departmental responsibility short of control of the business would have to register along with the business owner, whereas a business manager who had control would not be required to register.

Owners are not required to register managers, and managers whose registration, if at all valid, is separate from the owner and thus not threatening to the business if lost or not obtained, will be well advised to avoid registration, in view of the difficulties.

2.8.4 Duties and rights

The duties and rights of the care home manager will be circumscribed, in the contract of employment or appointment, by the business owner. The care home manager, who holds professional responsibilities, will owe duties in respect of conduct of management and discharge of duties at a professional level to the relevant professional body (eg the United Kingdom Central Council for Nursing and Midwifery, if a nurse) as well as to the business owner under the appointment or contract of employment.

If the two come into conflict, a care home manager must appreciate that his own status will be affected unless he procures proper performance of adequate standards by the business owner or, as previously suggested, resigns. This, of course, only applies in extreme cases.

The care home manager will not be directly responsible or accountable to clients, except insofar as his own acts or omissions in the discharge or non-discharge of his duties impact directly upon such clients, or if he holds himself out to be a principal.

The care home owner will be vicariously responsible for employees and, possibly in some cases, those appointed as managers pursuant to an appointment to perform services.

The care home manager has no direct relationship with Parliament or central government, except insofar as enactments and regulations may impact upon the owner's ability and obligation to provide what is seen, in contemporary terms, to be an adequate service for clients in a care home.

The care home manager has no direct relationship with local authorities, except to the limited extent that he or she may be required to be registered.

The care home manager will, whether a manager or not, have professional responsibilities, if a member of a recognised profession, for conduct towards clients in the performance of duties as manager of the care home for the business owner.

Managers left in control of care homes on a day-to-day basis are in an invidious position whether or not it is found that they are required to be registered. They should be astute to understand the capacity and financial strength of the business owner who appoints them and to recognise that, with their ability to supply a proper service entirely circumscribed by the means and resources of their appointor or employer, their ability to provide proper service and to maintain their own professional reputation is entirely in the hands of others.

Managers should not be quick to resign and risk the future of business owners or the clients in care. However, they do need to be aware that, with the business dependent upon the owner's resources as opposed to their own, but on their skills and not those of the owner, there is a long-term professional risk, the consequences of which may outlast mishaps in the particular care home venture at any one time.

Chapter 3

REGISTRATION AND CONDITIONS OF REGISTRATION

3.1 INTRODUCTION

It is often assumed, wrongly, that an obligation to register arises as a matter of course. The concept of registration, which is the essence of regulation, finds no place in the common law. Accordingly, registration is necessary only if the law requires it and such a requirement can be introduced only through primary legislation. If a particular operation can be shown to fall outside the restrictive wording of the legislation prescribing registration, then that operation may be conducted without the assistance or interference of the regulator.

This chapter will address the following issues:

(1) what is registration?
(2) how long does the registration endure?
(3) different types of registration;
(4) conditions of registration;
(5) the consequences of registration;
(6) criminal offences that arise directly out of registration or non-registration;
(7) the difference between the requirements of registration and the observation of guidance or practice.

The scheme of the legislation affecting the registration of the various types of care homes will be addressed in Chapter 4.

3.2 WHAT IS REGISTRATION?

Registration is the act which concludes the process of evaluating a registerable care home business. This consists of, first, recording registration in a permanent record and, second, the issue of a certificate. The certificate shows that the business concerned has passed the appropriate tests and the registration authority is satisfied that it may conduct a care home business, according to the conditions prescribed by law.

In relation to residential care homes, s 5(2) of the 1984 Act requires that 'the registration authority shall register the applicant in respect of the home named in the application and issue to him a certificate of registration'.

With regard to nursing homes, s 23(4) of the 1984 Act provides that the Secretary of State (upon whose behalf Health Authorities act) shall 'register the applicant in respect of the home named in the application and shall issue to the applicant a certificate of registration'.

3.2.1   Children's homes – a special case

In relation to children's homes, s 63(11) of the Children Act 1989 introduces Sch 6, which provides that an application for registration shall be made by the person carrying on or intending to carry on the home to the local authority in which the home is to be situated.

Crucially, para 1(4) of Sch 6 provides that a local authority shall grant the application either unconditionally or subject to such conditions as it thinks fit if it is satisfied that the application complies with prescribed requirements and such other requirements, if any, as appear to it to be appropriate. The authority, therefore, has an unfettered discretion as regards registration and if the authority is not satisfied it must refuse registration (see para 1(8) of Sch 6 to the 1989 Act).

Accordingly, in respect of children's homes there is a different basis for considering the application. Only if the applicant has satisfied the authority on all counts is he entitled to expect to be registered.

Curiously, if an application has not been granted within 12 months, it is deemed to be refused and the applicant has a right of appeal. This is indeed curious for, although with residential care and nursing homes the onus of justifying refusal of registration lies clearly upon the authority, the position would appear to be the reverse in relation to children's homes. It appears to be for the applicant to discharge the burden of proving that he should be registered. This presents an appellant whose application has been deemed to be refused with the difficulty of mounting an appeal without knowing the reason for refusal of the application, while having, in effect, to present before the Registered Homes Tribunal all conceivable evidence about the operation of the home.

If this interpretation is correct then it serves as a significant disincentive to applicants to register children's homes, or submit an application, if there is any degree of resistance from the relevant local authority.

3.2.2   Voluntary children's homes

In relation to voluntary homes in respect of which regulations are made under s 64 of the Children Act 1989, and where an application for registration is made directly to the Secretary of State, the Secretary of State has a completely unfettered discretion to grant or to refuse applications as he thinks fit, or to grant an application subject to such conditions as he considers appropriate.

It will be seen, therefore, that the burden of establishing registration of voluntary children's homes or registered children's homes is significantly greater on applicants than in relation to residential care homes and nursing homes.

3.3   THE REGISTER

3.3.1   Contents of the register

In relation to residential care homes, reg 7 of the 1984 Residential Care Homes Regulations provides that registers kept by an authority shall contain the particulars set out in Sch 3. That information is as follows:

(1)   the full name and address of the person registered in respect of the home and, where both the manager and person in control of the home are registered, their full names and addresses;

(2)   where the person registered is a company, society, association or other body or firm, the address of its registered office or principal office and the full names and addresses of the directors or other persons responsible for the management of that body, or the partners of the firm;

(3)   the name, address and telephone number of the home and in the case of a small home, if different, the name, address, and telephone number of the person to whom enquiries are to be made;

(4)   the number, sex and categories of residents (excluding persons registered or persons employed at the home and their relatives) indicating the various categories by reference to the following code:

    (i)   old age (not falling within any other category) – I;

    (ii)   mental disorder other than mental handicap past or present – MP;

    (iii)   mental handicap – MH;

    (iv)   alcohol dependence, past or present – AA;

    (v)   drug dependence, past or present – D;

    (vi)   physical disablement – PH;

    (vii)   add if the resident is:

        (a)   over 65 years of age (but not within the category of old age) – E;

        (b)   a child – C;

(5)   the date of registration and the issue of the certificate of registration where applicable, or the date of any cancellation of registration;

(6)   the details of any conditions imposed on registration and of any addition to those conditions or variation thereof;

(7)   whether the certificate of registration issued relates to a small home.

The importance of this obligation is emphasised by s 7 of the 1984 Act which provides:

> 'The register kept by a registration authority for the purpose of this part of the Act should be available for inspection at all reasonable times and any person inspecting such register shall be entitled to make copies of entries in the register on payment of such reasonable fee as the registration authority may determine.'

3.3.2   Local authority obligations

Authorities responsible for registration are, therefore, under specific obligations:

(1)   to maintain detailed registers;

(2)   to update such registers on a regular basis;

(3)   to have such registers available for inspection by the public (apparently without charge);

(4)   to permit copies to be taken upon payment of reasonable fees.

It is interesting to note that no charge may be made for permitting inspection and it is suggested that the reasonableness of the fee for copying must relate to the cost to the authority of making the copies, so that no fee would be chargeable to a person who makes handwritten copies.

The obligation to record the numbers and categories of residents will not cause the same difficulties as arise with the registration of nursing homes, since categorisation is not specified in Sch 3 to the 1984 Nursing Homes Regulations or elsewhere. However, with the increasing diversification of care homes and the possibility of overlap between categories within the same unit, authorities wishing to discharge their obligations regarding a proper standard of care will need to think carefully about the correct registration of categories and numbers of particular categories. With a clear statutory obligation to register successful applicants combined with an obligation to make registered particulars available to the public, it must surely be held, should the case arise, that this statutory obligation gives rise to a private right to compensation, should there be reliance upon information in the register, which is, subsequently, found to be inaccurate.

3.3.3   Equitable registration

A Tribunal, in the case of *Moustafa v London Borough of Ealing*[1] found little difficulty in holding that there was no concept of equitable registration. Registration, being a statutory concept, involved physical steps of registration in a permanent record followed by the compulsory issue of a certificate and it could not be argued that a person was registered (and thus subject to regulation) if the registration process had not been so concluded.

This is one of the many puzzling differences between residential care homes and nursing homes, for the purposes of registration. No provision requires the Health Authority or the Secretary of State to maintain registers of nursing homes or to permit such registers to be inspected by the public. The reason may be that the carrying on of the nursing home entails management and care service by medical and/or nursing professionals, whose obligations are imposed by separate regulation and who are responsible to either the General Medical Council or the United Kingdom Central Council for Nursing and Midwifery.

3.3.4   Registration certificate

The definition of a registration followed by issue of a certificate of registration requires the registration authority to make a permanent registered record of registration. Common sense suggests that a similar record should be made of variations in that registration or of cancellation of the registration. It will not be in every case that a registration authority manages to recover cancelled registration certificates and without a formal record of the registration process, ambiguity and potential abuse can occur.

The issue of the registration certificate is a compulsory obligation upon the registration authority once registration has occurred. The registered owner must display that certificate in a conspicuous place in the particular home (see s 5(6) and s 23(6) of the 1984 Act). Failing to be registered when carrying on a home and failing to display the certificate of registration can amount to two separate criminal offences.

---

1   Registered Homes Tribunal decision No 153.

Given the two separate stages of registration, a difficult question could arise for the person who had evidence of his registration by the authority, thus permitting him to trade, but who had failed to receive from the authority a certificate of registration. Such circumstances suggest that owners should demand the issue of a certificate immediately upon registration and not rely upon assurances from registration authority officers.

Whilst s 18 of the 1984 Act might provide a defence to a registered owner from whom a certificate of registration was being withheld, in the case of a residential care home, no such defence exists for a nursing home owner.

3.4 THE PURPOSES OF REGISTRATION

Registration serves a number of purposes:

(1) Registration entitles the care home owner to carry on the home and to carry it on in such way as he thinks appropriate, subject to the continuing supervision of the registration authority and to such legal restrictions as may be imposed to derogate from the grant of permission.

(2) Registration signifies to the public in general, and to anyone wishing to purchase care services from a particular care home, that that home has passed a test which satisfies the authorities that it will be sufficiently well run for the authority's standards to be maintained. Continuing registration signifies that those standards are continuing to be maintained.

(3) Registration of a care home is essential to its business viability. It is extremely valuable to both care providers and users, bringing with it opportunities and restrictions for the home owner, and obligations and risks for the registration authority.

(4) Registration of a care home is essential to its commercial viability. Whilst registration applies to the business, operating within a building, because that business cannot operate without registration the value of the building will be significantly down-graded without it, which will have financial consequences for owners, lenders, investors and patients (the purchase and sale of care homes will be considered in detail in Chapter 7). For anyone involved in investing in a care home business, registration of the business is as important an issue as any in assessing the value of the business. Registration, free from any restrictions or conditions, will increase the value of the business.

3.5 CONSEQUENCES OF REGISTRATION FOR THE CARE HOME OWNER

3.5.1 Positive effects

For the care home owner, registration can bring positive effects. That owner will be permitted to operate within a defined area of business activity, competing in what may be a very substantial market. Registration is a prize, to be valued and preserved. If lost, monies invested or monies borrowed may be at risk. Registration is the start to a successful business to be built out of goodwill and satisfied clients. That goodwill will, however, be dependent upon continued registration.

3.5.2   Negative effects

For the care home owner, registration can also bring some negative effects. Whilst granting permission to trade, registration may also restrict that trade, not only by the constraints of good practice but by those conditions of registration which derogate from the grant of the registration. In *Warwickshire County Council v McSweeney*,[2] Roch J saw registration as a matter of right, once excluding factors were satisfied. In ruling that registration authorities and Registered Homes Tribunals could only impose conditions for which provision was made by the 1984 Act, Roch J held that the grant of registration, which was a matter of right, could only be the subject of derogation to the extent permitted by Parliament ie by reference to those matters specifically provided by statute.

3.6   REGISTRATION CONDITIONS

Registration conditions must deal with the number of persons to be accommodated and may deal with the categories of person to be accommodated (distinguishing between categories imposed by conditions of registration and categories recorded in the register by the registration authority of a residential care home, which may be different). In relation to nursing homes, there are conditions as to the qualifications of a nurse in charge of a home and of the number of nurses to be on duty in the nursing home from time to time.

In relation to children's homes registered under the Children Act 1989, authorities may impose such conditions as they consider appropriate, without restriction. It is interesting to note that, in relation to residential care homes and nursing homes operating in Northern Ireland, a similar wide-ranging ability to impose conditions is introduced by primary legislation. It may be that this is a pointer to the future, but if it is, one must approach such expectations with caution, given current populist views about deregulation, and the undoubted fact that the Secretary of State has power to make regulations as to further conditions for residential care and nursing homes, but has declined to exercise that power. A simple solution would be a brief statutory instrument allowing authorities full latitude in the imposition of conditions.

Breach of conditions of registration constitutes a criminal offence. This is a restriction on the licensed trade and requires careful attention, particularly prior to registration. An owner who accepts onerous conditions as the price of obtaining registration will live to regret it and may find such registration to be commercially non-viable. Numbers of clients clearly restrict the ability to trade, categories of clients may be a matter of personal choice for business conduct,

---

2   (Unreported) 8 December 1988.

but in relation to nursing homes, the numbers of nurses will have a direct impact upon the most important expense incurred by any nursing home business, namely employees. An obligation to employ staff beyond an economic level may be, in effect, as damaging to the value of registration as loss of that registration.

A conviction for breach of conditions of registration (as with any conviction under the 1984 Act) operates as an automatic, inflexible, unappealable, non-time limited ban on dealing with the principal customer for community care, namely local authorities (see s 26(1)(e) of the National Assistance Act 1948).

3.7 REGISTRATION AUTHORITY

In discharging its functions as to registration, the authority is fulfilling an important regulatory role delegated to it by Parliament, either directly in the case of residential care homes, or via the Secretary of State for Health in the case of nursing homes. Regulation by means of registration is not a matter of choice, but an obligation which the authority is required to fulfil in accordance with the rules that are laid down.

An authority must take the duty of regulation seriously. Whilst it seems clear in relation to residential care and nursing homes, as opposed to children's homes, that the authority has an obligation to register as a primary duty, it is also clear that the authority has a statutory discretion to refuse registration if not satisfied in relation to the matters specified in s 9 and s 25 of the 1984 Act.

By granting registration, the authority will be determining that the applicant is an appropriate person to conduct the particular business of the care or nursing home and supplying to that applicant a valuable asset. The underlying purpose of regulation, as provided in the 1984 Act, is the protection of vulnerable members of society (see the decision of the Court of Appeal in *Lyons & Anor v East Sussex County Council*),[3] so that in addition to conferring a valuable licence for trade, the authority, by the fact of registration, is representing to the public in general and in particular to those vulnerable members of society whose duty it is to protect that this particular operator of a particular care home is an appropriate person to whom they may turn for care.

3.7.1 Positive duties

The duty of registration provides the authority with a positive opportunity to screen applicants who aspire to conduct these restricted businesses and thus, through such screening, to ensure that only those properly qualified and suitably experienced and appropriately motivated are placed in the position of securing the valuable licence. Registration is personal to the particular applicant; sub-licensing is not permitted, nor is assignment. Also, the authority has the opportunity to weed out those who are inappropriate.

---

3   (1988) 152 JP 488; (1988) 86 LGR 369.

Prior to registration, the applicant having no right to trade, the authority is in a positive position to control entrance to the business of care. Once registered, notwithstanding the regulatory powers of the authority to intervene, it will be much more difficult for steps to be taken if it is perceived that a mistake has been made. The consequence of registration for the authority is that it has and will be seen as having endorsed an applicant to run a care home business.

If the authority has doubts, those doubts should be satisfied prior to registration and if those doubts are matters upon which the authority is entitled to exercise its discretion to refuse registration, then an authority should exclude those about whom there are such doubts.

3.7.2   Negative duties

There is an on-going obligation on the authority to inspect, so as to remain assured that the registration the applicant has obtained is still appropriate. This is a not an insubstantial burden.

The public is entitled to expect that a home which is registered with the authority is regarded by the authority as being fit to continue in operation and a place to which they may entrust themselves and their relatives for care. By granting registration, the authority has issued a valuable licence upon which the owner and others, for example mortgage lenders, will rely. The authority may risk a claim for damages if its actions have an adverse affect upon those relying upon the validity of registration, although probably not if those actions are conducted in the course of the registration process (as opposed to ancillary to the registration process) and are not done with malice (see *Martine v South East Kent Health Authority*)[4]. On the other hand, an authority may have a duty to those accommodated in a home or who may decide to become accommodated in a home in relation to the registration and continued registration of that home.

Even where an authority exercises regulatory powers for the protection of a vulnerable group of citizens, it will not owe a duty of care to those citizens. This is a matter of public policy. Officers should not have to look over their shoulders (fearing litigation) when exercising those powers and discretions. Policy should not open the floodgates to claims against public bodies.[5] Generally, public authorities do not owe a duty of care to private citizens arising out of the exercise of regulatory powers unless it can be shown that breach of a statutory public duty cleary gives a private right to claim damages. Given recent developments, it is unlikely that such a right will be implied (in relation to regulatory action or inaction) unless expressly stated.

However, the authority is not protected where it owes a duty of care (as a matter of general principle) or is vicariously responsible for the actions of an employee or agent who has or assumes a duty of care. Authority staff who

---

4   (1993) *The Times*, 8 March.
5   See *Martine v South East Kent Health Authority* (1993) *The Times*, 8 March; *M (A Minor) v Newham LBC*; *X (Minors) v Bedfordshire County Council* [1995] 2 FLR 276.

assume a voluntary duty of care (perhaps by providing advice – gratuitous or paid) may make their employers liable under *Hedley Byrne v Heller* principles. A special relationship may be found to have arisen. Surely such a relationship must arise where a registration officer gives relevant advice which is followed.[6]

A comparison of the position, duties and powers of authorities as community care purchasers with their position as regulators, will be addressed in Chapter 11, but the dilemma created by those different roles is well illustrated by the prospect of an authority who declines to purchase community care services from a care home owner registered by its own regulatory department, upon the ground that the facilities of such a registered home do not meet that particular authority's own requirements as a purchaser.

Whilst the authority clearly has a right to purchase services of a standard which it considers to be appropriate, that decision, combined with a decision to permit the registered home to remain registered, whilst not a breach of the duty of care which the authority may owe to those residents within the registered, but allegedly unsatisfactory, home, might be seen as an unreasonable or perverse discharge of the authority's public duty. Such conduct might be subject to judicial review. If the registered home remains fit to be registered, then the authority will need to consider carefully all the implications of declining to purchase places from a home the suitability of which it continues to acknowledge. Equally, an authority will be examined severely as to continuing to purchase care after it has made a decision to cancel registration. That would demonstrate inconsistency. Either the regulatory decision was bad or the decision to purchase is unreasonable or perverse.

3.8 THE PUBLIC

Registration simply advises the public at large that a particular owner is considered suitable by the registration authority to conduct business of a particular type of care home. A member of the public would still wish to make sensible investigations before making a decision to purchase care, but that decision may be based on the fact that the appropriate authority has decided that the home under consideration is operating at the standard required for registration and has continued and continues to meet that standard up until the time when the purchase decision is being made. Registration, therefore, assists the would-be purchaser of care in the selection process by indicating that a business has been selected as one which operates in a suitable and satisfactory manner.

Registration, therefore, is not a tiresome technicality, but a vital and valuable foundation for important decisions which have to be made by all those concerned in the delivery of residential care.

---

6   See *Welton v North Cornwall County Council* [1997] 1 WLR 570 (CA).

3.9   HOW DOES REGISTRATION OCCUR?

Registration occurs by the recording of the appropriate details on approved applications for registration in the appropriate register, followed by the issue of the appropriate certificate (Chapter 5 will examine the application for registration in some detail).

The time-scale of applications, whilst under the control of the authority, is dictated, to a large extent, by the speed and accuracy with which an applicant prepares and submits an application form. There are formalities to be observed, and authorities must consider all relevant material and certain minimum material prescribed by the appropriate regulations, namely the Residential Care Home Regulations 1984, the Nursing Home and Mental Nursing Home Regulations 1984 and the Children's Homes Regulations 1991.

With regard to registered children's homes, an authority has complete discretion as to whether or not to grant registration. In relation to residential care and nursing homes, the relevant registration authorities have an obligation to register, but that obligation only arises in the context of considering an application containing prescribed information and having given proper consideration as to whether or not the authority should exercise its discretion to refuse registration. No authority may reasonably be expected to consider that important exercise of discretion unless it has received full and complete information necessary to enable it to make that decision. It may be suggested that an authority is going beyond the legitimate bounds of its interest by requesting further information from an applicant. An applicant who takes such a stance will have only himself to blame if the authority is then slower than he would wish or possibly declines to accept his application, being dissatisfied as to lack of information.

An authority is bound to process an application for registration but if that application is incomplete, the authority may properly decline to proceed and thus not be obliged to make a decision from which an appeal may lie.

An applicant should also bear in mind that an authority will consider the issue of fitness as a potential care home operator in the light of the manner in which the application is conducted. This may be particularly important in relation to the application for registration of children's homes, where there is no automatic right to registration. It is likely that an authority may decline registration merely where it is not satisfied with aspects or some particular aspect of the application which is presented to them.

Registration will thus occur more swiftly and more effectively if applicants show a positive approach to the registration process, seeking to persuade by the supply of sufficient information rather than demanding registration as of right, whilst refusing to make available material that may be relevant.

3.10   RIGHT TO REFUSE REGISTRATION

The right to refuse registration is introduced by the permissive word 'may', to be found in s 9 and s 25 of the 1984 Act. In *Zaman v Lancashire County Council*,[7]

---

7   Registered Homes Tribunal decision No 103.

the Registered Homes Tribunal held, somewhat curiously, that the word should be read as directory and not permissive, as it could not have been envisaged that if an authority were satisfied that an applicant was an unfit person, the authority would have a discretion as to whether or not to refuse registration. It is submitted, with respect, that this view is simplistic and indeed wrong. A whole variety of matters may arise in the course of an application for registration. If the application is for the registration of an existing home, then there will be existing residents within the home whose interests will need to be considered (see *Avon County Council v Lang*).[8] Circumstances in relation to the operation of the home, the location of the home or the identity of the prospective transferee of the business might give some cause for concern, but might not be of such weight as to compel an authority to consider that it should reject an application, looking at the circumstances as a whole. It might be able to regulate by condition or it might consider that the overall interests of those concerned justified a decision not to exercise its discretion to refuse registration. It is submitted that if Parliament had intended to direct registration authorities to refuse registration, they would have legislated accordingly and would not have implied a discretion, time and time again, in relation to many of the authority's obligations. Parliament has not shrunk from imposing a directory obligation in circumstances, for example the number of persons to be accommodated or kept in a particular home (see s 5 and s 29 of the 1984 Act) where, clearly, the authority is required to limit those numbers.

In a particular case, it may well be that the evidence which satisfies the authority that a particular application falls within one of the groups where refusal of registration is permitted, is so overwhelming that no reasonable authority could fail to exercise discretion. This does not mean that each and every time evidence which does not support an application is substantiated, the application is bound to be refused. The preferred construction is that if no matters indicating refusal exist, then there is an obligation in favour of the applicant to register, but if such material as would justify refusal is indicated, then the authority should exercise its discretion taking into account all relevant matters.

Section 10 and s 28 of the 1984 Act, which deal with the discretion to cancel registration, both give the authority a discretion. It surely cannot be argued that, upon the appearance of any material which might justify the removal of the licence to trade, the authority is bound to so act.

3.11 TYPES OF REGISTRATION

The classes of care home, for the purposes of this book, are:

(1) Residential Care Homes;
(2) Nursing Homes;
(3) Mental Nursing Homes;
(4) Registered Children's Homes;

---

8 [1990] COD 365.

(5)   Voluntary Children's Homes.

It is clear that registration is not required unless the home can be classified into a type for which registration is prescribed by statute. Careful examination of the appropriate statutory provisions is required. They may be overlapping and, in the case of a children's home, an application for registration as a residential care or nursing home may preclude the need for the more stringent registration process.

Owners will need to consider very carefully not only whether registration is required but if so, what the most appropriate type of registration may be or whether more than one classification of registration may apply. The issue of dual registration will be considered, but perhaps this should more appropriately be regarded as multiple registration. The term itself is misleading in that many think it provides for a separate classification of home. In fact, it is merely shorthand, with no statutory definition, to indicate a home which has achieved registration with more than one registering authority, ie a dual-registered home is a home with two or more registration certificates which are not inter-dependent.

Section 1(5)(a) of the 1984 Act provides that registration is not required in respect of an establishment used or intended to be used solely as a nursing home or mental nursing home. It should be noted that, whilst registration is not required, it does not mean that it may not be conferred and great emphasis should be placed upon the word 'solely'. If the home is used as a residential care home as well as a nursing home or mental nursing home, then registration under Pt I may be required. Part II of the Act, which deals with nursing homes, approaches the matter, as we shall see, by a comprehensive definition of nursing home, which does not include a residential care home. Section 4 of the 1984 Act, however, permits those who are registered as owners of a nursing home, but require registration as a small home, ie one accommodating less than four residents (which did not require registration prior to April 1993), to register not as a small home for residential care, but as a 'full' residential care home.

The answer is that the two registrations are entirely separate. Registration is of an individual to carry on the business of the care home from particular premises. Registration is not of rooms and facilities, but of individuals. Against that background, it is appropriate to consider the individual classifications.

3.12   RESIDENTIAL CARE HOMES

The starting point is s 2 of the 1984 Act, which provides that it is an offence to carry on a residential care home without being registered. 'Residential care home' is defined in s 2(1).

The legislation then proceeds to indicate certain types of home which would fall within the definition set out in s 1(1), but which are not required to be registered. This must be contrasted with the requirement in relation to nursing homes in Pt II, where the definition of a nursing home excludes certain types of home, which may lead to the conclusion that such homes are not registerable, rather than a potentially registerable home, where the owner is not obliged to seek registration.

The distinction may have very important ramifications in the field of social welfare benefits. In many cases, the opportunity for a person accommodated in a care home to seek social welfare benefit will be linked to the registration of that home under the Registered Homes Act 1984. If the home is excluded from registration, then it will not be registerable and residents in that home may not have access to certain benefits, for example Income Support or the provision of residential accommodation under Pt III of the National Assistance Act 1948, but, on the other hand, may have entitlement to benefits such as Housing Benefit. If the home is registerable, but it is not mandatory for it to be registered, then the residents may claim certain benefits by seeking a voluntary registration, which would not be available if the possibility of registration were excluded.

3.12.1   Definition

The definition of a residential care home is as follows:

> 'Subject to the following provisions of this section, registration under this part of the Act is required in respect of any establishment which provides or is intended to provide, whether for reward or not, residential accommodation with both board and personal care for persons in need of personal care by reason of old age, disablement, past or present dependence on alcohol or drugs, or past or present mental disorder.'[9]

Unless those criteria are fulfilled, registration is not required but, it is suggested, may be sought.

For such an important definition, it is surprising that there is little attempt by the Act to define any of the key words.

3.12.2   'Establishment'

The *Concise Oxford Dictionary*, 1991 edition, suggests this means 'a business organisation or public institution; a place of business; a residence; the staff or equipment of an organisation; a household or any organised body permanently maintained for a purpose'. This expression is wide enough to include any physical construction or grouping of people. In considering whether or not a unit is an establishment, it is important to look critically and laterally and not to be diverted by an approach which may be simplistic. Prior to 1 April 1993, registration was not required at all for so-called 'small' homes which accommodated less than three persons. Nonetheless, such homes, subject to conditions as to staffing, were still able to qualify for their residents to claim social security benefit payments (all such homes are now required to be registered, the transitional 'amnesty' period having long expired).

The opportunity to provide care without regulation attracted those who knew that they would not be likely to penetrate the screen of the registration process. In a number of cases, proprietors ran several so-called 'small' homes providing care for reasonably large numbers of persons, which were in slightly different locations, so as to justify the suggestion that they were operating a group of small homes as opposed to one residential care home. Careful

---

9   Registered Homes Act 1984, s 1.

investigation revealed factors such as common entrance doors, linking internal doors, common services and staff working at more than one of the homes.

Clearly, the appropriate course of action for a registration authority is to look at the business unit as a whole and decide if it constitutes an establishment and only permit non-registration (now only in very limited cases) or multiple registration for small homes if it can be shown clearly that each 'establishment' is a separate free-standing unit operating for the care of its own residents with its own staff. Any inter-linking which cannot be shown to be independent is likely to indicate one establishment rather than a series of establishments.

The expression 'establishment' is quite clearly sufficient to identify something that is less than the whole of a building. Registration is of units, ie establishments and not of rooms, but unsatisfactory accommodation can be excluded by careful definition, by registration authorities, of what constitutes the establishment.

Whilst it is customary to describe the home merely by reference to its title, possibly combined with its address, there is no reason why a certificate should not contain greater detail if, for a particular reason, owners and registration authorities, or registration authorities on their own, consider that an otherwise acceptable establishment is adjacent to areas which would not be suitable for inclusion within a registered care home.

It is possible for two physically separate establishments to exist on one site.[10] In *Harrison v Cornwall County Council*,[11] the conclusion was that a house and lodge within the same grounds should be regarded as one establishment.

3.12.3 'Provides or is intended to provide'

The possibility of future provision is clearly intended to cover two circumstances:

(1) circumstances in which the home is not yet operational; thus it might be suggested that, with no provision of care, it was inappropriate for registration. Given that the criminal offence is carrying on a residential care home as opposed to proposing to carry on a residential care home, this is probably an excess of caution on the part of the draughtsman and it is difficult to see how the business of the residential care home can exist so that one can be said to be carrying on such a business whilst having only the intention to provide as opposed to actually providing. The distinction between the 'definition' of 'residential care home' and the careful description of the offence in s 2 may be of great importance.

(2) interestingly, this provision may prevent an abuse, where upon inspection of what is believed to be an unregistered residential care home, no residents and no care is found. Perhaps in anticipation of a raid, the residents have been taken on a trip, or perhaps all the residents are away attending day centre training or taking a holiday. Under those

---

10 Registered Homes Tribunal decision No 109, *Moorhouse v Derbyshire County Council*.
11 Registered Homes Tribunal decision No 146; (1991) *The Times*, 15 May; 11 BMLR 21, 90 LGR 81.

circumstances, an owner faced with prosecution might argue that the prosecuting authority had failed to prove that he was providing the elements of a residential care home. It would not be so easy to argue that they had failed to prove intent to make that provision if matters ancillary to care were all in place when the inspection took place.

3.12.4 'Whether for reward or not'

This makes it quite clear that registration is required, both by private 'for profit' business entrepreneurs and for charities and voluntary organisations. Registration looks to the nature of the business being considered, not whether it is operated for a profit, or even for the payment of fees. Charitable homes run, perhaps by a religious order, without making any charge to its residents, would still require registration.

These words are often used to support the proposition, which has found much favour with the Registered Homes Tribunal, that lack of financial viability or the lack of financial ability to purchase equipment or facilities are not to be regarded as grounds to justify a failure to provide what is otherwise seen as appropriate facilities for care.

3.12.5 'Residential accommodation'

The prime element of the service to be provided is that residents should reside at the home. Upon this construction, it is suggested, and this is widely accepted, that a day centre which provides no sleeping facilities or accommodation for its clients, requires no registration. Of course, this may not be a bar to registration should it be sought. It may also be observed that if operators separate the provision of residential accommodation on site from the supply of board and personal care (disturbing as that might seem), it may be that neither unit would require registration. Anyone considering that course should proceed with great caution to ensure that they provide two clearly separate establishments.

3.12.6 'Board'

In essence, this is taken to mean that food and drink should be supplied. The *Concise Oxford Dictionary*, 1991 edition, defines board, inter alia, as 'provision of regular meals, usually with accommodation'. Other definitions include 'food served at table'; 'daily meals provided in a lodging or boarding house according to stipulation'; and 'the supply of daily provisions'. In the case of *Otter v Norman*,[12] the House of Lords found that the provision of a daily continental breakfast constituted board for the purpose of determining whether or not an accommodation arrangement fell within the protecting provisions of the Rent Act 1977. Perhaps that decision should be regarded with caution as the mischief at which the legislation was aimed was quite different to that which created regulation of care.

The question must essentially be one of fact, but as the necessity to register may have important consequences for winning welfare benefit payments, it

---

12 [1989] AC 129.

should not be dismissed. For example, it should be considered carefully whether or not the supply of food in an uncooked form can constitute board; whether an irregular supply of meals constitutes board; whether food and drink can still be regarded as board if they are purchased from shop facilities, whether or not managed by a landlord, from the resident's own money and not incorporated within a single rent or accommodation payment.

It is suggested that the correct definition should be the provision of such food and drink upon a regular basis as is sufficient to sustain and nourish the resident, the payment for which is included within the accommodation charge which is payable at the same inclusive rate, irrespective of the consumption of food and drink.

The concept of a residential care home is not of a unit where the residents select whether or not they eat at the unit or purchase food from the unit or indeed use personal care available, but rather of a unit that supplies the needs of the residents because of their vulnerable condition. Selectivity in relation to board and personal care indicates a degree of ability to choose whether and when to be sustained by food and personal care to the extent that both could be declined. Any suggestion that a resident might decline personal care, or an owner accommodates those in need, but does not provide the care needed simply because it was not requested and separately paid for, would be alien to the concept of a residential care home. On the other hand, it would be surprising if an owner could avoid regulation by making meals and personal care optional.

The solution seems to be a reversion to the words 'provides or intends to provide' for, if regular meals and personal care are provided to some but not others, then registration is required and this slightly odd practice will come under the scrutiny of the authority. Furthermore, if facilities exist to provide regular meals to residents but extra charges are made or no guarantee of food is provided, then it is likely to be argued that it is an establishment from which it is intended to provide board.

However, it is submitted that the provision of an establishment without food, combined with facilities to purchase food, would not be registerable or that, possibly, the supply of uncooked food and drink at a charge additional to the accommodation charge might well avoid the need for registration.

3.12.7 'Personal care'

Section 20(1) of the 1984 Act defines personal care:

> 'Personal care means care which includes assistance with bodily functions where such assistance is required.'

In *Harrison v Cornwall County Council*,[13] Kennedy J found, somewhat curiously, that that definition operated to exclude any personal care which did not involve assistance with bodily functions. The Court of Appeal had little difficulty in reversing that decision and it is submitted that the definition does little to assist. Care would have been limited to 'assistance with bodily functions' had it not been for the saving words 'where such assistance is

---

13   (1991) 11 BMLR 21, 90 LGR 81.

required'. Clearly, care where no such assistance was required was embraced by the definition. It is submitted that this broad expression should be interpreted as widely as possible so as to require registration of the greatest variety of potential care units. It is submitted that the word 'care' means little more than 'attention' and, proceeded by the word 'personal', directs the word 'attention' to the individual person, as opposed to property, insofar as that can be separated from the person. In effect, any establishment where the residents require assistance with daily living, whether that assistance be by way of physical support, mental support or otherwise, seems sufficient to require establishment to seek registration, provided it also supplies both residential accommodation and board.

The courts are highly unlikely, when construing legislation which is established to protect vulnerable members of society, to welcome artificial distinctions which might prevent some vulnerable persons having the benefit of regulation over those who provide their care and support.

3.12.8 'For persons in need of personal care by reason of old age, disablement, past or present dependence on alcohol or drugs or past or present mental disorder'

The effect of this passage is to limit the requirement of registration for those who provide care for those in need by reference to the specific causes of the requirement for care. If the care is not provided for those whose needs may be categorised within the statutory classes, then registration is not required. For example, one will note that there is no provision for registration for those in need of personal care by reason of youth. Under the 1984 Act and its predecessor, the Residential Homes Act 1980, there was no requirement to register a children's home; such registration did not occur until the implementation of the appropriate part of the Children Act 1989. However, homes for disabled children are registrable, although guidance issued by HM Government under the Children Act 1989[14] suggests that authorities should register such homes under the 1984 Act, unless more than three children are accommodated but only three or fewer are disabled. That is guidance which authorities must follow.[15] What happens, if, preferring the 1984 Act regime, an applicant insists upon his right to be registered as requiring accommodation in a residential care home?

We may think that 'old age' is a simple term to define, but it may be difficult to decide exactly what age may be described as old. In most cases, difficulties will be resolved by the all-embracing term 'disablement', which may be defined simply as deprivation of the ability to carry on normal life. That in turn begs the question as to what, in extreme cases, may be regarded as a normal pattern of life. Dependence on alcohol, drugs or past or present mental disorder are easier to identify.

Lest it be thought that these phrases will necessarily embrace all potential types of home, one should consider the concept of so-called 'mother and baby' homes. These homes provide counselling and support for young women in

---

14 *The Children Act 1989 Guidance and Regulations*, Vol 4, HMSO.
15 Local Authority Social Services Act 1970, s 7.

coping with the emotional difficulties presented by motherhood. The purpose of such homes is to counsel, advise and support such women to enable them to integrate into the community with their babies. It would be harsh to describe them as disabled or as suffering from past or present mental disorder. Their difficulties may lie simply in immaturity or inexperience. Such homes will very often involve reliance upon public services for medicine, nursing and maternity expertise. Thus, it is suggested it is inappropriate that they be registered as nursing or maternity homes, despite the suggestion to that effect in the relevant Department of Health circular, which many perceive as being outdated.

It is submitted that there is a valid argument that such a home is not registerable as a residential care home and may not, for the reasons indicated, be appropriate for registration as a nursing or maternity home, as its purpose is to provide social welfare rather than medical or nursing support. Registration as a children's home would only arise to the extent that children were accommodated and that would not include children who were residing with their own parents, so only if the young mothers were under the age of 18 (the definition of 'child' under the Children Act 1989) would consideration of registration arise. As it is likely that the policy of such homes would be to incorporate the accommodation of all mothers, irrespective of age, so that children, as defined, would be accommodated with those who were not children, it is possible that such a home would not be properly registered under any of the established models.

Doubtless, other examples do arise and will arise, and the need to examine closely the basis for demanding registration remains.

3.12.9   Residential care homes excluded from the requirement for registration

Many in this category are excluded simply because registration is required elsewhere:

(1)   nursing homes or mental nursing homes registerable under Pt II of the 1984 Act;
(2)   hospitals as defined in the National Health Service Act 1977 and maintained by Act of Parliament. Hospitals not so maintained would be registerable as nursing homes;
(3)   hospitals as defined by the Mental Health Act 1983 are subject to separate regulation;
(4)   community homes, voluntary homes or children's homes registrable within the Children Act 1989;
(5)   schools as defined in the Education Act 1944, with one important exception: a school is only registrable as a children's home if it provides accommodation for more than three children for more than 295 days in any year, ie 42 weeks, significantly more than the total number of weeks in normal boarding school terms throughout a year;
(6)   educational establishments to which the Secretary of State has made maintenance grants under the Education Act 1944, but only for the period of 12 months after the date of making the payment;
(7)   small homes which provide care only for relatives or staff of the owner;

(8)   universities, university colleges, schools or halls of residence;
(9)   establishments managed or provided by government department or local
        authority or any authority or body constituted by an Act of Parliament or
        incorporated by Royal Charter.

In all cases, the clear intention of the Act is to exclude establishments from
multiple regulation or to exclude from the requirement to register
establishments which are in fact themselves conducted by public authorities,
or by Government as part of a publicly provided service. In this way, residential
care homes carried on by a local authority pursuant to Pt III of the National
Assistance Act 1948, are not required to be registered and units which provide
what would normally be recognised as personal social care, but with the
provision being made by a National Health Service Trust constituted under the
National Health Service and Community Care Act 1990, or other public
bodies, will not require registration. However, different rules concerning
funding of publicly funded care, from time to time, may encourage such
establishments, even if not required to register, to seek registration.

The registration authority may be less than pleased, but unless one can
construe lack of requirement for registration as a restriction on application to
register, it is difficult to see how the registration authority can refuse to
entertain such applications. Such registration may not of itself guarantee
payment of benefits provided by social welfare funds to the residents in such
units, but it may open a door which would otherwise be closed.

3.12.10   Small homes

A 'small home' is a residential care home providing care for fewer than four
persons, excluding the persons carrying on the home or employed there and
relatives of those persons. Prior to 1 April 1993, a small home, as defined, did
not require registration.

On and after 1 April 1993, a small home is required to be registered unless
the only persons for whom it provides, or intends to provide, care are the
persons who carry on the home or their employees or relatives. Different rules
apply to small homes insofar as they apply for registration and are subject to
inspection and the regulatory process.

The effect of this amendment is that all establishments, other than those
not required to register, which fit into the definition of a residential care
home, require registration. Some requirements of registration are relaxed for
'small homes' but, in essence, 'small homes' are smaller residential care homes
subject to the same rules of regulation as their larger counterparts.

3.12.11   Managers

A manager of a residential care home is, under certain circumstances,
required to register, in addition to the owner, as the person who is carrying on
the residential care home. Provision for registration of managers is to be found
in s 3 of the 1984 Act. This section is one of the most obscure in meaning and
defies interpretation to such an extent that it may, possibly, be meaningless.

The section reads:

> 'Where the manager or intended manager of a residential care home is not in
> control of it (whether as owner or otherwise) both the manager or intended

manager and the person in control are to be treated as carrying on or intending to carry on the home and accordingly as requiring to be registered under this part of this Act.'

It is clear that the position of manager does not carry with it an obligation to register arising out of the position itself, but only because the manager (if he fits other criteria) is deemed to be carrying on the residential care home, a function which a manager clearly does not do. This creates difficulties in interpretation because to bracket the manager with the business owner, ie the person carrying on the business, is to increase the inference that a manager who should seek registration must have a degree of control of the business akin to ownership.

Once again, it is to be noted that it is the manager who is required to be registered and not that the owner is required to register a manager.

As the registerable manager is to be treated as carrying on the business, then it is he who is liable for prosecution for carrying on the business of the residential care home without being registered, rather than the person who is carrying on the business.

3.12.12 Type of manager to be registered

A manager who is not in control of the home (whether as owner or otherwise) is the type of manager who is to be registered. The section might be capable of definition if the words in brackets had not been included, for it would then have been possible to draw a clear distinction between a business proprietor and a business manager. However, it is quite clear that control can be effected otherwise than by ownership. Accordingly, the registrable manager is a person who may fit the description of manager but is not in control of the business, either because he owns the business or because he does not own the business. It is suggested that the concept of a manager who is not in control is, in fact, a contradiction in terms. The section speaks of a manager of a residential care home and, accordingly, it clearly does not speak about a manager of a division of the residential care home.

One would anticipate that the section would have in mind requiring registration where a manager was appointed to run a home on a day-to-day basis with the registered owner being absent and taking little interest in those daily decisions. A person could not be described as managing a residential care home if, in fact, that person defers to a registered owner who controls the operation of the home.

The principal definition of control in the *Concise Oxford Dictionary*, 1991 edition, is 'the power of directing or command'. The primary definition of 'manager' in the same Dictionary is 'a person controlling or administering a business or part of a business'.

It would seem that Parliament has prescribed that managers, appointed by absentee owners to take total control of the business, do not require registration, but that managers not in control, who perhaps merely take the title of manager, may find themselves liable to prosecution because they do not seek separate registration at their own expense. Non-controlling managers should take particular care in the negotiation of their job description. If this interpretation is correct, then registered owners and their managers should give very careful thought as to whether or not they should seek registration of an individual as a manager.

No such provision exists in relation to nursing homes. No assistance is provided by the 1984 Nursing Homes Regulations, and, indeed, this may add to the confusion. Schedule 1 identifies information to be supplied to the authority by an applicant. Separate requirements are made for the manager who is not in control of the home and for an application by a person in control of the home, but no provision is made for the supply of company information by a company applying to be a manager. It is suggested by some that this indicates that the manager of a residential care home cannot be a limited company, but many respectable companies are set up in business just to manage residential care homes and take that burden away from the registered owner.

Clearly, a manager manages on behalf of the business and thus is operating in an agency function and not carrying on the business. It cannot be right to suggest that primary legislation is to be interpreted by regulations made pursuant to powers derived out of the same legislation. Power to make rules as to the information to be supplied on an application for registration is provided by s 16(1)(k) of the 1984 Act. Those rules cannot, it is suggested, change the category of persons who are required to apply, but merely define the material which those applicants are required to supply.

It is no answer to suggest that the manager should seek registration as a person carrying on the business because he is in control of the business. Clearly, someone who is in control of the business is not ipso facto carrying on the business and s 3 tells us that only managers who are not in control of the business (whether as owner or otherwise) are deemed to be as carrying on the business.

The author suggests that the section is a nonsense and that any person who can properly be described as the manager of a residential care home will also appropriately be described as having control of the business.

Lest it be thought that this leaves a massive loophole for the absentee registered owner to leave a home to be managed by those not subject to control by the authority, it should be remembered that registration carries with it the obligation to comply with the provisions of the 1984 Act and to provide adequate facilities and services for the persons accommodated and receiving board and personal care. Persons registered are required either to provide such facilities and services by themselves or by properly appointed staff, who are seen to carry out the services and functions appropriately. The author's submission is that the concept of a registered manager is redundant, for even if the manager is registered, the registered owner will bear the responsibility for inadequate management of the service. It will be no answer to a proposal to cancel registration on the basis of inadequate management by a registered manager, to blame the registered manager. The owner would be expected to discipline or possibly dismiss the registered manager. Exactly the same situation applies in the case of a manager delegated to take control of a home who, in accordance with these submissions, was not registered because he was not required to be registered.

The purpose of registration is that the authority, on behalf of the public, know to whom they may look to ensure performance of statutory obligations and the delivery of a proper service. From an owner's point of view, the requirement to register a manager which will almost inevitably leave the registration authority dealing with the manager rather than the owner, taking the registered owner out of control of the business and leaving that control in the hands of someone who is not the business proprietor (and in terms of legislation cannot 'ex hypothesi:' be in control of the business).

3.13   NURSING HOMES

Once again, the requirement of registration is personal to the business proprietor. It is a criminal offence to carry on the business of a nursing home without being registered (see s 23(1) of the 1984 Act).

Nursing homes embrace a far broader group of businesses than might at first be thought. As mentioned in the passage dealing with residential care homes, there is a difference in statutory approach. Nursing homes are defined by s 21 of the 1984 Act, but the section goes on to exclude certain types of premises from the definition of nursing home. 'Nursing home' being a legal term of art created by the legislation, businesses excluded from the definition of nursing home clearly cannot be registered as such and, accordingly, there is no room for the alternative of optional registration which may exist in relation to residential care homes.

The corollary is that registration authorities must be careful not to register as nursing homes premises that are not nursing homes, for that would be to fail to comply with their statutory duty. Persons dealing with businesses registered as nursing homes will expect them to be nursing homes as defined in the 1984 Act and are entitled to complain or possibly seek compensation if misled into dealing with premises which are clearly not a nursing home by the fact of non-registration.

An example would be a private medical insurance company who only undertook to discharge fees payable by patients at an establishment if that establishment were registered as a nursing home. If, upon examination, the premises were found to have been registered although clearly not a nursing home and thus excluded from registration, that private medical insurance company would, it is submitted, have a right to seek redress against the erring registration authority.

Nursing homes fall into three broad categories (excluding mental nursing homes which will be dealt with in para **3.14**.

(1)   residential nursing homes;
(2)   maternity homes;
(3)   units providing surgical and medical services which do not necessarily include nursing.

3.13.1   Residential nursing homes

These are defined as 'any premises used or intended to be used for the reception of and the provision of nursing for persons suffering from any sickness, injury or infirmity'.

3.13.2 'Premises'

This, it is suggested, means any form of building. As with the definition of establishment in relation to residential care homes, registration authorities can and should take care to define the premises in respect of which registration is granted and in respect of which a certificate is issued to the registered owner. The registration will attach to premises as defined and not to individual rooms or sections within those premises.

Whilst the registered owner will have a duty to provide adequate accommodation facilities to all who enter the premises for care, it will not be possible for the registration authority to indicate specific uses for particular rooms as a condition of registration. The authority's remedy is to regulate by reference to a quality assessment of the standard of facilities and care supplied, rather than relying upon conditions of registration. If the authority considers that particular areas of the proposed premises are unfit to be used as any part of a nursing home then the registration should seek to exclude the part or parts considered to be unsuitable.

3.13.3 'Nursing'

The key to the identification of a residential nursing home is the provision of 'nursing'. It is the provision of nursing as opposed to the provision of personal care which differentiates a registerable nursing home from a registerable residential care home. Those considering this problem should not feel artificially restricted by pre-conceptions as to what constitutes a residential nursing home. Any premises providing nursing care are registerable so that all private hospitals, private medical treatment centres where nursing is provided and units which provide only day facilities, as opposed to units which provide residential facilities or both day and residential facilities, are included within the definition and registration will apply equally to all of these.

The editor of Sweet & Maxwell's *Encyclopedia of Social Services and Child Care Law*,[16] in his note on this section, refers to the well-known definition from *Principles and Practice of Nursing*:[17]

> 'nursing is primarily helping people (sick or well) in the performance of those activities contributing to health or its recovery (or to a peaceful death) that they would perform unaided if they had the necessary strength, will or knowledge. It is likewise the unique contribution of nursing to help people to be independent of such assistance as soon as possible.'

However, as the editor of the *Encyclopedia* suggests, this definition really provides no assistance in drawing a distinction between nursing care and personal care.

The matter will become of very grave importance in considering whether or not a person carrying on a business which is not registered as a nursing home may properly be prosecuted, for to do so it must be established beyond all reasonable doubt that nursing, as opposed to personal or other care, has

---

16   Sweet & Maxwell, 1993.
17   Virginia Henderson and Gladys Nite *Principles and Practice of Nursing* 6th edn (1978).

been conducted on the premises. This may be of less importance if there is cooperation between prosecution authorities, but if a Health Authority seeks to prosecute a party for carrying on a nursing home without being registered, they will fail unless they can establish that the care being supplied may clearly be established as nursing care. Paradoxically, to establish that the persons in residence are failing to receive nursing care, is to ensure that the prosecution will fail. It is no offence to fail to provide nursing care for those in need of nursing care within a residential care home, but it is an offence to provide nursing care for those in need of nursing care in a residential care home unless that home is also registered as a nursing home. Even Gilbert and Sullivan might have been proud of this result. The Henderson/Nite definition, it is suggested, is really quite unhelpful.

The author would suggest that the only correct definition of nursing is those functions of care which may only be properly carried out by a qualified nurse. There is clearly a huge overlap between personal care and the care provided for a patient in a nursing home. Many of the tasks performed, usually by unqualified staff, in a nursing home will mirror exactly the tasks performed in a residential care home. It is submitted that in a nursing home, the patient's medical treatment requirements and the patient's dependency will be such that care cannot properly be delivered without the intervention on a regular basis of a qualified nurse.

It is beyond the scope of this book to enquire into the full range of the duties of a qualified nurse. However, a professional nurse is accountable not only to the employer, but also to the patient. Duties relating to the planning, delivery, recording and administration of nursing care will evolve over time. Current practices may be ascertained by reference to the practice guidance of the United Kingdom Central Council for Nursing and Midwifery. Among the tasks to be carried out by qualified nurses will be tasks involving the control and administration of drugs and medicines, the administration of injections and other invasive medical techniques and the general supervision and training of unqualified staff. Where the dependency needs of a resident or client are low, then in many cases their needs may be fulfilled by staff without professional qualifications. As those dependency levels increase, then proper management will require the supervision, knowledge and experience that go with professional nursing qualifications.

Each individual case will turn upon its facts and almost certainly require the calling of expert evidence. Qualified nurses would be best able to identify when care is properly characterised as nursing care rather than personal care. Experience shows that, typically, where nursing care is required and not supplied, or required and supplied poorly, or ineffectively or insufficiently regularly (as with a residential care home, depending upon the necessarily irregular visits of members of the community nursing service), then the condition of the resident/client deteriorates. It will be rare indeed to find nursing care being provided other than by qualified nurses. More common is to find qualified nurses employed in residential care homes who, because of their professional qualifications, proceed to deliver nursing care in the interests of their employers or themselves if they are owners, rather than seeking either proper registration as a nursing home for the particular premises, or the discharge of the particular patient to premises which are registered to provide the right level of care, ie nursing care to meet the growing dependency.

When considering whether or not to prosecute an allegedly unregistered owner, it is always necessary to consider not what are the patient/client needs, but what is the care that can be shown to be delivered. A residential care home failing to provide care for a patient who needs nursing home care cannot be prosecuted for operating a nursing home, but may be prosecuted after appropriate notice for failing to provide adequate services and facilities for residents within the home.

3.13.4 'Sickness, injury or infirmity'

The words 'sickness, injury or infirmity' are sufficiently wide to embrace any form of illness. Unlike residential care homes, this broad categorisation makes it unnecessary for registration authorities to seek to categorise patients. It is suggested that artificial characterisation of patients is not only unnecessary but unhelpful and may be positively dangerous.

If such categorisation is carried out for the right purpose, ie to limit the category of patient who may be received into a home or remain in a home, so that it becomes a condition of registration, then the authority considering such a step needs to consider whether or not it is really appropriate to restrict admissions of sick people. Further, given that the remedy for breach of condition of registration is prosecution, it needs to consider just how practical it would be to establish on the criminal standard of proof that one patient is actually in a category different to that specified upon the registration certificate.

Once admitted to a nursing home, both the owners of the home and the qualified nursing staff owe a duty to the patient to provide proper care. Failure to deliver that care may lead to:

(1)   proposals to cancel registration;
(2)   consideration of prosecution of the home for the provision of inadequate services and facilities;
(3)   consideration of professional complaint about the nurses concerned to the United Kingdom Central Council for Nursing and Midwifery.

The owners and nurses must have or acquire appropriate facilities for every patient or, if those facilities are not available, must discharge the patient. It is never an excuse to plead that services could not reasonably have been provided, for whatever reason.

3.13.5   Maternity homes

Such homes are now rare indeed. Such homes are defined as 'premises used or intended to be used for the reception of pregnant women or of women immediately after child birth'.

Several provisions in the 1984 Act make it clear that the essential requirement of a registered maternity home is the provision of registered midwives. For the sake of completeness, it is suggested that the 'mother and baby' homes referred to in the section on residential care homes are not properly registered as maternity homes for, although they will receive women who may be pregnant, those women will in most cases leave the home for delivery of their babies elsewhere and although women will be admitted or readmitted relatively quickly after the birth, they will usually be admitted only under circumstances where the medical complications of childbirth have been solved or such complications as continue will be resolved by the attentions of the community midwifery service.

Registered nursing homes have as a common theme the provision of care for those who are sick or require medical or nursing intervention. Premises whose rationale is to provide care other than medical care and need to seek medical or nursing care from outside services, including the public or community services, are, it is suggested, not appropriately registrable as nursing homes.

3.13.6   Premises providing surgical services without nursing

A number of services of a surgical nature require the premises from which they are conducted to be registered as a nursing home. It should be remembered that if nursing care is associated with any of these, then the premises are registerable as a registered nursing home in any event. This third category will arise only where there is no nursing care and, in many cases, there may be an overlap. The services in question are:

(1)   the carrying out of surgical procedures under anaesthesia;
(2)   the termination of pregnancies;
(3)   endoscopy;
(4)   haemodialysis and peritoneal dialysis;
(5)   treatment by specially controlled techniques.

The latter requires some further comment. Specially controlled techniques means such techniques as may be specified by regulations made by the Secretary of State. Particular cases will require reference to those regulations, but in essence specially controlled techniques means services making use of laser equipment, for example cosmetic surgery, dentistry, acupuncture and physiotherapy.

Curiously, if the laser equipment is used otherwise than at specific premises registration is not required. Thus the peripatetic physiotherapist who visits patients in their own homes requires no registration, but the dentist using a class 4 laser drill in his own surgery commits a criminal offence unless he registers his premises.

3.13.7   Premises excluded from registration as nursing home

Various premises are excluded from the definition of nursing home and are thus excluded from the possibility of registration:

> 'NHS hospitals or premises maintained or controlled by Government departments, local authorities or bodies instituted by special Act of Parliament or incorporated by Royal Charter.'

This, it is suggested, means that a nursing home is a term essentially to be attached to a business operated for profit in the private sector or by a genuinely independent charitable or voluntary organisation. If establishments owned or controlled by Government departments or local authorities seek to register as nursing homes, those applications should be rejected upon the basis that the premises cannot constitute a nursing home as a matter of legal definition.

There seems to be no logical reason why, in the case of residential care homes, registration should simply be excused, whereas in the case of registered nursing homes registration should not be permitted. In both cases, public authorities will face the difficulty created by independent inspection and regulation and the prospect that, if their standards were not upgraded upon what is sometimes described as a level playing field with private sector operated homes, then the registration, even if sought voluntarily, could be refused or cancelled.

One might ask why anyone should seek registration and voluntarily become subject to an intrusive system of regulation. The answer will most likely be financial. The opportunity to seek social welfare benefits for residents within the home may be dependent upon the home being registered.

Community care contracts are restricted to contracts with proprietors of the homes that are registered. Public authorities seeking to increase the scope of public funds available to them to meet their responsibilities may consider that the obligations of registration, particularly if they are controlled within the same organisation, may be a worthwhile burden.

Health Authorities acting on behalf of the Secretary of State should, upon the arguments advanced here, have little difficulty rejecting such applications. Local authorities dealing with applications for residential care homes who wish to be registered, although not required so to do, may need to look very critically at the reasons entitling them to exercise their discretion to refuse registration if they perceive that the application for registration is conceived simply for financial motives. This problem will be highlighted if the applicant for registration is the same authority as is charged with regulating the process of registration. Here is surely a problem that needs to be addressed.

3.13.8 Exclusion of mental nursing home from registration as nursing home

This is excluded because it is a separate term of art and will form the subject of the separate registration title which will be considered next. However, note that this exclusion clearly establishes a 'mental nursing home' as distinguished from a 'nursing home'.[18]

3.13.9 Exclusion of sanatorium from registration as nursing home

A sanatorium, provided it is at a school or educational establishment and used or intended to be used solely by persons in attendance at or members of the staff of that school or establishment or members of their families, is excluded from registration.

---

18 See Registered Health Tribunal decision No 296, *ALM Medical Services Ltd v South Lancashire Health Authority*.

Once again, there is a clear exclusion to avoid duplication of regulation. The purpose seems clear. Registration under whatever legislation should be directed to the principal purpose of the establishment concerned and ancillary services should not require separate registration. There will, however, be cases at the borderline. Where the establishment concerned is providing permanent residential care for chronically sick persons who also require education, then it may well not be right to regard the extensive medical facilities within such an establishment as a sanatorium provided at a school. It may be better to regard the establishment as a school provided at a private hospital which will be designated as a nursing home. All the circumstances will have to be taken into account, but registration authorities should not, it is suggested, decline to register permanent health care facilities merely upon the basis that they are exclusively or even extensively linked to education.

It is suggested that the test in these cases is to look at the dominant purpose of the establishment, although in the case of a school combined with a hospital that may not be an easy task. If one cannot be seen to be subordinate to the other it may be that double registration is a requirement.

3.13.10 Exclusion of first aid room from registration as nursing home

This applies to any first aid or treatment room provided at factory premises, at premises to which the Offices, Shops and Railway Premises Act 1963 applies or at a sports ground, showground or place of public entertainment. Once again, it is quite clear that where premises are subject to regulation under other legislation, then the intention is to avoid a double registration or regulation requirement.

Naturally, each case needs to be regarded on its own facts. The creation of a leisure centre which includes health care, sports and entertainment facilities will not necessarily mean that the health care facilities do not require registration under the 1984 Act. In the author's view, such an exclusion would only apply if the medical treatment facilities can be shown to be only used in relation to the dominant purpose of the premises and ancillary thereto. If patients attend the centre otherwise than as a result of medical needs which occur as a result of use or enjoyment of the dominant purpose of the premises, then the question of registration will need to be considered very carefully. A sports clinic providing sports injury related treatment and therapy generally to members of the public and which would otherwise qualify for registration as a nursing home may well be required to register if it can be seen as operating a separate business and not a business related to treating by way of first aid injuries which occur to users of other facilities on site.

3.13.11 Other medical premises excluded from registration as a nursing home

This refers to any premises used or intended to be used wholly or mainly:

(1) by a medical practitioner for the purpose of consultations with his patients;

(2) by a dental practitioner or chiropodist for the purpose of treating his patients;

(3)   for the provision of occupational health facilities

unless they are used or intended to be used for the provision of treatment by specially controlled techniques and not excepted by regulations made by the Secretary of State.[19]

By this provision, the mischief of requiring doctors and dentists to register their premises as nursing homes is avoided unless specially controlled techniques are in use. Thus a dentist who practices with conventional equipment will not be required to register, but a dentist who supplements his equipment with laser equipment will be required to register the premises.

An interesting distinction between medical practitioners, on the one hand, and dental practitioners and chiropodists, on the other, is to be noted. The premises for dental practitioners and chiropodists are excluded if they are used wholly or mainly for treatment purposes. In the case of medical practitioners, the dominant use must be for consultation. With the increasing development of day surgery units this may need some attention.

Clearly, a private hospital, providing day surgery only, requires to register as a nursing home. Equally clearly, a doctor's consulting room from which he conducts occasional operations of a minor surgical nature or endoscopy or haemo- or peritoneal- dialysis will not require registration. However, if the registerable aspect of the business becomes dominant so that the main purpose of the premises can no longer be described as for consultation purposes, then registration will be required.

The legislation is a re-enactment going back over many decades. The modern practice of doctors combining together in health centres and, possibly, building an extension to provide day surgery facilities will cause difficulties. The author's view is that if the day surgery unit is a separate unit staffed and operated on a basis dedicated to surgery, then that unit will require registration. It is difficult to see how such a surgical unit could operate without separate reception facilities, separate waiting and preparation facilities and post-operative care facilities. The kind of surgery which must take place in a dedicated theatre cannot take place in what most would recognise as a doctor's consulting room. It would be wholly artificial to suggest that if such a unit were built as an extension to a conventional doctor's surgery, then it did not require registration, but if it were freestanding on a green field site registration would be required.

The issue is one which needs to be readdressed by Parliament, but in the meantime, registration authorities and their officers should appreciate that the duties delegated by the Secretary of State to the Health Authority will include registration of these units which the law requires and it is not a matter for the discretion of the authority as to whether they pursue registration applications. Registration is not optional and if premises are registrable, then they are required to be registered. No reasonable authority could exercise a discretion not to take action against the owners of premises which require to be registered and who decline to register.

---

19   Registered Homes Act 1984, s 21(3)(e) and (g).

3.13.12   The exclusion of any premises used or intended to be used wholly or mainly as a private dwelling from registration as a nursing home

This seemingly innocuous provision may give rise to very considerable difficulties. Many small private nursing homes either were or bear the characteristics of private residential dwelling houses. Many would suggest that the best quality residential nursing homes retain the character of a private home and avoid 'institutionalisation'. Clearly, individual cases will be decided upon their individual facts and Health Authority inspectors will have full power to inspect any premises in respect of which they reasonably believe the business of a nursing home may be carried on without registration. In many cases, the decision will be clear, for an inspection of the premises that reveals hospital-style beds and medical-type facilities situated within the facade of a normal residential dwelling house will clearly not fall within the definition of use or intended use as a private dwelling. However, matters may not always be so clear; a qualified nurse may decide to receive into her own home one or more persons who require nursing care and provide that care in that house without the introduction of furniture or equipment which might normally be associated with a more substantial medical or nursing establishment. If the inspectors find what appears to be a private residential dwelling house, furnished and equipped as such but whose residents include lodgers who are dependent on, and possibly in receipt of, care services from qualified nurses, it will clearly be arguable that those premises are, in fact, a nursing home.

Consideration would be given as to whether such a unit should be registered as a residential care home on the basis that nursing care incorporating the lower level of care described as personal care. But that might be successfully resisted by evidence that the care provided was nursing and not personal.

Consideration might be given as to whether or not the nurse concerned was breaking the terms of her own professional conduct under the rules set out by the United Kingdom Central Council for Nursing and Midwifery but such a course would be fraught with difficulty and would not provide any short-term answers to what would be a difficult situation.

It may be that the courts would construe the legislation on the basis that Parliament intended such a situation to be permitted, provided the qualified nurse concerned could properly supply the care without so converting her home as to take herself and the premises outside a use where an objective observer would conclude that the dominant use was that of a private dwelling. In any event, registration authorities will have great difficulty in ascertaining the existence of such units where there will necessarily be no external signs of the provision of nursing care.

3.13.13   The exclusion of any other premises excepted from that definition by regulations made by the Secretary of State from registration as a nursing home

At the time of writing, no such regulations have been brought into effect.

3.14   MENTAL NURSING HOME

A mental nursing home is defined by s 22(1) of the 1984 Act. 'Mental nursing home' means:

> 'premises used or intended to be used for the reception of and the provision of nursing or other medical treatment (including care, habilitation and rehabilitation under medical supervision) for one, or more, mentally disordered patients (meaning persons suffering, or appearing to be suffering, from mental disorder), whether exclusively or in common with other persons.'

The purpose of a mental nursing home is clearly extended so that, looking at the type of care provided, one is not restricted to defining such care by reference to nursing but also by other forms of medical treatment which may not include nursing.

The exclusions from the definition of 'mental nursing home' are, in essence, mental hospitals and similar institutions provided by public authorities or managed by Government departments; health service hospitals within the meaning of the National Health Service Act 1977; accommodation provided by a local authority and used as a hospital under the provisions of the National Health Service Act 1977; but not accommodation provided by private sector or voluntary sector operators.

Thus a mental nursing home will embrace any privately operated mental care business, whether or not the care is provided on a residential basis or day visiting basis, where care is supplied for one or more mentally disordered patients. Nursing homes are not mental nursing homes. Each is a separate class of registrable health care business. To qualify premises for registration in this category the patients need not be mentally disordered, but merely 'appear to be mentally disordered'. One may well ask whether or not all residential nursing homes should be registered as mental nursing homes – given that many patients will have both mental and physical needs. Certainly, artificial distinctions between the mentally ill and mentally infirm would not seem to be as conclusive as some argue.

3.14.1   'Whether exclusively or in common'

It is clear that a registered nursing home coming within the definition discussed earlier may not receive and care for mentally disordered persons, but that a registered mental nursing home so registered because it provides care for a small number of mentally disordered persons may also receive into care patients who are not suffering from mental disorders. The clear proposition following from this analysis of the statute is that all nursing homes which care for both mentally disordered patients and physically frail patients should register as mental nursing homes. There is no obligation or need to affect dual registration, as the mental nursing home registration will suffice. The difficulty is that this does not reflect what occurs in practice or what is generally accepted to be the right approach to long-term care for the elderly mentally frail.

By para 47 of Circular No HC(81/8) issued by the Department of Health and Social Security in 1981, advice but no direction was given to District Health Authorities.

'private nursing homes catering for elderly people may often accommodate some people who are mentally confused, but this need not necessarily involve registration as a mental nursing home. In such cases the authority will need to keep under consideration the number of such patients and the seriousness of their conditions. Where the possibility of additional registration as a mental nursing home arises this should be fully discussed with those responsible for the home.'

With respect, it is difficult to see how such advice could possibly be given in the context of the statutory wording. For the reasons given, registration under those circumstances should be as a mental nursing home, in place of general nursing home registration and not in addition thereto. Furthermore, the clear wording indicating a requirement to register as a mental nursing home for premises caring for one or more mentally disordered persons, which will include persons who may simply appear to suffer from a mental disorder, cannot possibly permit either an owner or a registration authority to register and allow the continued registration of a home as other than a mental nursing home if even one of the patients appears to be suffering from a mental disorder.

It has become common for Health Authorities to register general nursing homes to provide care for categories of patients which may include the psychogeriatric or the elderly mentally ill or the elderly severely mentally infirm. These are known as EMI homes or ESMI homes. The author has argued for many years that such registrations are wholly misconceived. If the registration authority identifies patients as being within a category 'elderly mentally ill' how can it possibly have come to the conclusion that they are not persons who at least appear to be suffering from a mental disorder?

The difficulty has arisen because a very large number of elderly persons who are properly cared for within a general nursing home context and have received care in that context over a number of years are necessarily regarded as confused whether or not suffering from a condition known as Alzheimer's Disease or Dementia, but would not be regarded as appropriately placed within a mental nursing home as that expression is perceived by the public. It is submitted that this cannot excuse incorrect registration practice. The author suggests that authorities' attitudes to the requirements to staff mental nursing homes have led to an incorrect approach to the registration of such units. A large number of authorities expect the nursing staff at registered mental nursing homes to consist predominantly of and to be led by registered mental nurses, ie nurses now registered in Pts 3 and 5 of the register maintained pursuant to the Nurses, Midwives and Health Visitors Act 1979 by the United Kingdom Central Council for Nursing and Midwifery. Many argue that the skills acquired by such nurses working in the largest centres of employment, ie mental hospitals for the treatment, care and secure custody of mental offenders, are not suited by way of training or experience to care for the moderately confused elderly, who may receive perfectly appropriate care from registered general nurses with relatively limited mental nursing special experience. No two cases are alike and, of course, the requirements of the patients will determine the necessity for individual evaluation of the experience and qualification of nurse staffing establishments.

A recent decision of the Registered Homes Tribunal[20] that an authority cannot require, as a condition of registration, that a mental nurse be in charge of a nursing home not registered as a mental nursing home, highlights the issue. A sound basis of registration in accordance with the 1984 Act will avoid the difficulties perceived in securing proper staffing establishments for such homes.

It is submitted that registration authorities should not fall into the trap of effecting and maintaining registrations which are inappropriate, as a means of seeking to provide correct regulation, where the right course would be to register correctly in accordance with the 1984 Act and then to tailor the facilities, staffing and services to meet the individual needs of the patient group proposed to be accommodated. In these cases, registration authorities would no doubt wish to look very carefully at the applicant's proposals as to the type of patients to be accommodated and, contrary to the author's general submissions as to open categorisation, to seek to limit the type of mentally confused or disordered patients who may be received into a mental nursing home beyond simple separation between patients required to be maintained under the Mental Health Act 1983 and other patients.

Given the recent re-emphasis by the Registered Homes Tribunal that 'mental nursing homes' are specifically excluded from the definition of 'nursing homes'[21] so that it is inappropriate, inter alia, to require, as a condition of registration, that registered mental nurses be employed in or take charge of nursing in such homes, there would appear to be little room for registration as a nursing home of units providing care to any patient with mental confusion – other than the mildest case of 'elderly forgetfulness'.[22] If the care of one patient who appears to be suffering from mental disorder[23] requires such care to be in a mental nursing home registered as such (as is clear), then there can be very few units which do not require 'mental nursing' registration. The distinction between 'elderly mentally ill' and 'elderly mentally infirm' (at least for legal purposes of categorisation of care homes registered under the 1984 Act) would seem artificial and possibly illusory if argued to be a distinction of substance rather than semantics.

Perhaps a mildly mentally confused person is more appropriately placed in a residential care home for the presently mentally disordered.

3.15 CHILDREN'S HOMES

No child may be provided with accommodation in a children's home unless the home is registered with the local authority (see s 63(1) of the Children Act 1989).

---

20 Registered Homes Tribunal decision No 296, *ALM Medical Services Ltd v South Lancashire Health Authority*.
21 Ibid.
22 The author's non-technical expression.
23 Registered Homes Act 1984, s 22.

3.15.1   Definition

A children's home is defined as:

'(a) A home which provides or usually provides or is intended to provide care and
     accommodation wholly or mainly for more than three children at any one
     time; but

(b) does not include a home which is exempted by or under any of the following
    provisions of the Section or by regulations made for the purpose of this
    Section.'[24]

It is interesting to note that the draughtsman has not thought fit to include the
concept of board and has limited service to 'care and accommodation'.
However, the author suggests that a child (defined by the Children Act as a
person under the age of 18) cannot really be considered to be in receipt of
appropriate care unless that care includes board.

Children receiving care in any home, whether care and accommodation
are provided by parents or those in loco parentis or by relatives, are not
deemed to be cared for and accommodated in a children's home. The home
is not a children's home if it is a 'Community Home' as defined in the Act
(essentially a home for children operated by the local authority and beyond
the scope of this book) a Voluntary Home (a home run by charitable
organisations and registered with the Secretary of State); a Residential Care
Home, Nursing Home or Mental Nursing Home (but note that a 'small home'
may be registrable, if disabled children are accommodated, as a small home
but not as a children's home, where registration only applies where more than
three children are accommodated at one time); a Health Service Hospital;
homes provided and equipped by the Secretary of State or a school subject to
an important exception.

The Burgner[25] Report has recommended that the exception for non-
registration of children's homes caring for less than four children, should be
abolished. This has a simplistic attraction. However, there are ramifications for
child care in a wider context. It may be that the exclusion was intended to
dovetail with the maximum number usually permitted for a private foster-
parent. Fostering works on a system of exclusion of the undesirable and
post-operative notification rather than pre-operative registration. Non-
registration of private foster-parents avoided the need to consider whether or
not such 'parents' were in fact operating in loco parentis and thus exempt
from registration in any event. If a foster parent is not in loco parentis – and
thus required to register – will there be double regulatory requirements? If
such 'parents' are in loco parentis, how easy will regulation be? Is the private
fostering arrangement to be abolished? All these questions will provoke
interesting debate. However, it is not now correct to say care of three or less
children is not subject to a form of regulation.

To avoid duplication of registration, a school is not to be regarded as a
registerable children's home unless it provides accommodation for more than
three children for more than 295 days in any year and is not approved as a

---

24   Children Act 1989, s 63(3).
25   *The Regulation and Inspection of Social Services* (Department of Health, 1990).

school supplying special educational needs under the Education Act 1993. The limit is a little over 42 weeks' care in each year (perhaps eight to nine weeks longer than expected boarding school term provision). This is more sensible than the previous limitation on numbers as it clearly excludes usual boarding school provision except where that provision is extended to provide accommodation during holidays.

The expression 'home' is defined by s 63(9) to include any institution but the definition of the word 'institution' may itself cause difficulties as it is not defined in the Act and the 'interpretation' s 105 gives no further assistance with the word 'home'. However, the definition may be of little impact as the real test would seem to be the provision of 'care' and 'accommodation'.

Certain homes are excluded by order of the Secretary of State, including:

(1)   holiday homes;
(2)   bail hostels;
(3)   homes for trainee professional footballers under 18 years.

Clearly, the exclusions are to avoid 'over-regulation' and duplication of public resources in child care. The most interesting is the exclusion of the 'holiday home' (one in which the child is accommodated for less than 28 days in any year). The practicality of the exclusion is clear but 28 days is a long time in the life of a child. Interestingly, it has not been suggested that such an exclusion should be extended to adult homes.

A dilemma may arise for those who wish to operate a home for physically disabled or mentally disordered children. As a matter of law, registration may be under Pt I of the 1984 Act or Pt VIII of the 1989 Act. There are distinct differences in the registration process and one form of regulation may be seen as preferable to another.

Guidance to local authorities on implementation of the 1989 Act suggests that some such homes should be registered as children's homes and some as residential care homes: local authorities are required to act in accordance with such guidance[26] *but* that guidance does not bind applicants nor those who hear appeals, for example magistrates and Registered Home Tribunals.[27]

Surely, the applicant should be able to select a form of registration, where more than one path is available. The 1984 Act gives a right to expect registration which is not repeated by Pt VIII of the 1989 Act.

3.16 VOLUNTARY HOMES

Voluntary homes are one of a variety of forms of accommodation into which a voluntary organisation must place or maintain a child to comply with s 59 of the 1989 Act. Such homes, as has already been indicated, are registrable not with local authorities but with the Secretary of State for Health. The registration of such homes has not, at the date of writing, been delegated by

---

26   Local Authority Social Services Act 1970, s 7(1).
27   *London Borough of Sutton v Davis* [1994] 1 FLR 737.

the Secretary of State to any local authority and such of these homes as do exist are regulated through central government and not local authorities.

3.16.1   Definition

A voluntary home is somewhat unhelpfully defined by s 60(3) of the 1989 Act as a home or other institution providing care and accommodation for children which is carried on by a voluntary organisation. It does not include nursing homes, mental nursing homes, residential care homes (other than small homes), schools, health service hospitals, community homes, homes or institutions maintained by the Secretary of State (presumably because he could not act as regulator and maintainer at the same time) or homes exempted by regulations. No exemptions are yet made.

Thus the character of the home and its registrability are here determined by the nature of the person carrying on the home. A 'voluntary organisation' is defined by s 105 of the 1989 Act as a body (other than a public or local authority) whose activities are not carried on for profit.

Non profit-making bodies, therefore, seem to have the option of registering as children's homes with the local authority or as voluntary homes with the Secretary of State for Health. Enquiries made of the Department of Health have suggested that, if applications are made for the registration with the Secretary of State of homes which are perceived to be registrable children's homes, the Secretary of State will decline to accept such applications and refer the applicants to the local authority for registration as children's homes under Pt VIII of the 1989 Act. Quite what is the purpose of maintaining a distinction between registrable voluntary homes and registrable children's homes, under these circumstances, is not clear. Such a course is legally permitted because the Secretary of State has a complete discretion on registration.

3.17   CONDITIONS OF REGISTRATION

Conditions of registration must be distinguished immediately from so-called requirements of the registration authority or local rules or guidance promulgated by the registration authority for the assistance both of owners in considering whether or not to apply for registration and how to conduct care homes once registered and for the assistance of registration officers in more easily understanding the tasks which face them in day-to-day registration and inspection of residential care and nursing homes. Such requirements, rules and guidance will be examined in the next section but, in general, are to be regarded as evidence of the views of the authority as to good practice but not as set in stone so as to be enforceable in their own right.

Conditions of registration are quite different. If a matter is a condition of registration, it is enforceable irrespective of its merit simply by reason of having been made a condition of registration. A proposal to make a condition or to vary a condition must be taken seriously. Proof of breach of a condition of registration will lead to a criminal conviction. The proprietor subject to prosecution will not have the opportunity to argue whether or not the condition is justified.

3.17.1 Flexibility of conditions

Homes registered within the province of Northern Ireland (whether they be residential care homes or nursing homes) are subject to such conditions of registration as the local registration authority or health board may consider appropriate.[28] Homes registered in England and Wales may only be subject to conditions of registration covering matters for which there is provision in the statute. The authority for this is the decision of Roch J in the case of *Warwickshire County Council v McSweeney*.[29] The registration authority was sympathetic to Mrs McSweeney's application for registration as a residential care home. However, the character of her husband, Mr McSweeney, was such that the registration authority considered that he was not a fit person to be in any way concerned in carrying on a residential care home. Upon that ground, in due course, the authority refused to register Mrs McSweeney. The Registered Homes Tribunal had sympathy for Mrs McSweeney and tried to assist. Relying on the power which appeared to lie under s 15(6) of the 1984 Act, the Tribunal allowed Mrs McSweeney's appeal, but imposed a condition that Mr McSweeney should not be allowed to come within a specific radius of several miles from the proposed residential care home.

Section 15(6) provided:

'A tribunal shall also have power on an appeal against a decision or order:

(a) to vary any condition for the time being in force in respect of the home to which the appeal relates by virtue of this part of this Act;
(b) to direct that any such condition shall cease to have effect; or
(c) to direct that any such condition as it thinks fit shall have effect in respect of the home.'

The Tribunal recognised the force of the argument that there were limits to the conditions which might be imposed by the registration authority and saw those limits expanded by sub-paras (a) and (b) of subs 6. However, it felt that the general power given by sub-para (c) entitled the Tribunal to go beyond matters that might have been the subject of a decision by the registration authority and impose conditions of a wide ranging nature based upon their own specialist experience of the operation of such care homes.

Roch J had little difficulty rejecting this proposition. He expressed the view that any conditions imposed by a registration authority or Tribunal were a derogation from the clear right of an applicant to registration. Given that there were clear limits upon the conditions of registration which might be imposed by the registration authority, Roch J held that the Registered Homes Tribunal, acting on appeal to review the decision of that authority, could not have powers greater than the authority acting at first instance and, accordingly, the Tribunal had misdirected itself in taking on a wider jurisdiction to impose wide ranging conditions not anticipated by the legislation.

Whilst heralded at first by some representatives of home owners as a welcome curb on the powers of authorities and Tribunals, this case has rapidly been seen by all concerned in registration issues to be unhelpful. Clearly,

---

28 Registered Homes (Northern Ireland) Order 1992, SI 1992/3204.
29 (Unreported) 8 December 1988.

owners need to consider very carefully before consenting to conditions of registration and disagreement about conditions of registration can lead to costly and unacceptable delays. Equally clearly, if conditions of registration are to be enforced through the criminal courts, they must be prepared carefully and with such certainty that owners who are required to obey the terms of such a condition know exactly where the line is drawn. No doubt, authorities in Northern Ireland and authorities dealing with children's homes address those issues very carefully and their experience will be invaluable. It should not be beyond the capability of a draughtsman acting on behalf of a regulatory authority to draft a condition in such a way that it is clear to those who are required to obey the restriction and those who are required to enforce the restriction when a breach has occurred.

The difficulty with the decision in *McSweeney*, which, it is submitted, is absolutely right as a matter of law, is that it does not assist authorities and Tribunals to help applicants for registration, or owners whose registration has run into regulatory difficulties, to adjust their applications or improve their performance. Many disputes which arise both at the time of registration and during the operation of a care home relate to specific issues. A power to impose specifically enforceable conditions to address the issue which is providing difficulty would, in many cases, enable authorities and Tribunals to grant applications or avoid cancellation of registration, but the restriction on the ability to be creative and imaginative with conditions leaves such authorities and Tribunals with no option but to register or allow the owner to remain registered without immediately enforceable regulatory provisions or to cancel registration without giving the proprietor the opportunity to prove that he can improve performance by reference to rules that are clearly defined. The loss of flexibility in conditions of registration in England and Wales has, on many occasions, proved an impassable stumbling block to negotiations to resolve difficulties between registration authorities and owners of such homes.

3.17.2 Permissible conditions of registration

In relation to residential care homes, such conditions are limited to:

(1) conditions as to the number of persons to be accommodated;
(2) a discretion as to the category of persons to be accommodated.

In relation to nursing homes, the conditions are limited to:

(1) a condition as to the number of persons to be accommodated ('kept');
(2) a discretion as to the category of persons to be accommodated ('kept');
(3) a discretion as to the qualifications of the nurse in charge of a nursing home, should the nursing home be in the charge of a nurse rather than a medical doctor;
(4) a condition as to the number of nurses to be on duty at particular times.

There is provision for the Secretary of State to make further regulations as to conditions to be imposed in respect of nursing homes but not, curiously, residential homes, but at the time of writing, no such regulations have been either prepared or introduced.

3.17.3 Numbers and categories

It is proposed to deal with these two items together as they are common conditions to both residential care and nursing homes. In relation to residential care homes, the authority is s 5(3) of the 1984 Act:

> 'It shall be a condition of the registration of any person in respect of a residential care home that the number of persons for whom residential accommodation with both board and personal care is provided in the home at any one time (excluding persons carrying on or employed at the home and their relatives) does not exceed such number as may be specified in the certificate of registration; and the registration may also be subject to such other conditions (to be specified in the certificate) as the registration authority consider appropriate for regulating the age, sex or category of persons who may be received in the home.'

In relation to nursing homes, the authority is s 29(1) and (2) of the 1984 Act:

> '(1) It shall be a condition of the registration of any person in respect of a nursing home or mental nursing home that the number of persons kept at any time in the home (excluding persons carrying on or employed in the home together with their families) does not exceed such number as may be specified in the certificate of registration.
>
> (2) Without prejudice to sub-section (1) above, any such registration may be affected subject to such conditions (to be specified in the certificate of registration) as the Secretary of State may consider appropriate for regulating the age, sex or other category of persons who may be received in the home in question.'

It will be seen that the provisions effectively mirror one another and thus legal precedents in relation to residential care homes may be taken to apply to nursing homes and vice versa.

3.17.4 The condition as to numbers

The condition as to numbers is a mandatory requirement so that the registration authority is obliged to limit numbers in a home. Section 5(3) is carefully drafted and clearly refers to the number of persons accommodated in the home to receive board and personal care, ie there is a link to the registration requirement.

A study of s 29(1) shows the difference. Here, the limited number is not defined by reference to those accommodated to receive nursing care or other care as may require registration, but rather the limit is on the number of persons to be kept in the home. Once again, one suspects that little thought was given by the Parliamentary draughtsman to expansion in the field, for it is difficult to see how effective conditions as to numbers can be imposed upon those who supply services to an growing number of patients, for example surgeons, dentists and others using specially controlled techniques, and doctors carrying out dialysis or endoscopy.

A matter of great interest arises in relation to those homes which are registered both as nursing homes and residential care homes. Clearly, the registration authority for residential care homes is limited to registering the number of persons who will, in effect, be receiving personal care, but can 'persons kept' not be defined to include all those receiving care within the premises irrespective of whether that care is to be defined as nursing or personal? Under those circumstances, it is arguable that, in relation to a dual registered home, the Health Authority has jurisdiction to limit the total number of persons within the home and not just the number of persons in respect of whom it is proposed to provide nursing care. This issue will be addressed further in para **3.18** below.

The matter also becomes of importance if the proprietors of the nursing home seek to justify the accommodation over and above their registered numbers for patients who may be described as guests not receiving any care, or may be described as those receiving personal care but not requiring registration under Pt I. Before the compulsory registration of small homes, this was of some significance and, in one unreported case, a magistrates' court declined an invitation to acquit a defendant prosecuted for exceeding permitted registered numbers, even if it were to be established that the persons concerned were in receipt of personal care and not nursing care and, being only two in number, would not require registration under Pt I. The magistrates took the view that the expression 'persons kept' embraced all persons at the home irrespective of the level of care.

It is submitted that this view was quite correct and that the argument could be extended to entitle the Health Authority to regulate not just the number of nursing patients and those accommodated to receive personal care, but all others excluding the owners, their staff and their relatives received into the home on any basis. Such persons can properly be described as 'persons kept'. The rationale for such a view might well be that, in relation to the care of sick persons, the Health Authority has a legitimate interest to regulate the number of other persons who may be accommodated within the same premises and whose presence, to a greater or lesser extent, may impact upon those who may properly be described as patients in care in the home.

3.17.5   The condition as to categories

Conditions as to category of patient have caused difficulty. First, such a condition is not required. It is suggested that registration authorities should approach imposing such conditions, as a matter of discretion, with great caution and only act if both such a condition is required and can be imposed in such a way as to be clearly understood.

Schedule 3 to the 1984 Residential Care Home Regulations requires the registration authority to record in the register the number, sex and categories of residents, such categories being indicated by a code. There being no statutory obligation to impose a condition in that regard, but there being an obligation upon an applicant for registration to supply that information,[30] it is submitted that this requirement for a record within the register is simply a requirement to record the categories of resident for whom the applicant indicates that he proposes to care. The register will then record the applicant's intentions, which may be useful both to members of the public and in subsequent enforcement provisions, but does not in itself give such registered

---

30   See Residential Care Home Regulations 1984 (SI 1984/1345), Sch 1.

particulars the character of an enforceable condition of registration. The requirement, contained in delegated legislation, to register particulars about the registered residential care home, or to require information, can never supplant the discretion to impose a condition of registration for which provision is made in primary legislation.

Similar arguments relate to the imposition of a discretionary condition as to age, sex and categories of patient within a nursing home save that, in relation to nursing homes, the argument is enhanced by the lack of provision to record particulars of age, sex or category in the register. Similar requirements are made of an applicant to supply such information upon his application for registration (see para 10 of Sch 2 to the Nursing Homes and Mental Nursing Homes Regulations 1984).

The restriction on the type of resident or patient who may be accommodated is thus confined to classification by way of age, sex or other category. Registration authorities, it is suggested, would do well to have regard to classification by reference to age and sex because such matters are relatively straightforward. The words 'other category' have been troublesome. At least one chairman of a Registered Homes Tribunal has raised the issue as to whether it is possible to interpret the word 'category' so as to be sure what Parliament intended. What is clear is that if categorisation is to take place as a condition of registration, it must be drafted in such a way as to be clearly understandable. Given that this is a restriction upon the owner's ability to use his business assets, the restriction must be clearly justifiable if it is to be sustained where the owner makes strong representations to the contrary before the authority and before a Registered Homes Tribunal, if there is an appeal.

It is quite impossible to limit the possibilities of groups who might form a category, although it is suggested that it would be too restrictive to interpret these words 'ejusdem generis' with age and sex. Conditions which are difficult to interpret and which may inhibit a owner without enabling the authority to regulate effectively in the event of a perceived breach should be avoided. This may arise even in relation to 'age'. It is suggested that authorities should stick clearly to 'x years old', and not seek to define age by reference to other factors which may be moveable. The frequently found phrase 'above pensionable age' gives rise to a considerable number of possible interpretations. Private pension schemes allow participants to take benefits at a variety of ages and past differences in State pensionable age as between men and women have given rise to a number of legal difficulties in a number of areas. Phrases such as 'elderly' should be avoided because of their imprecision. Artificial distinctions created more in the mind of registration authorities than in reality should also be avoided. Debates such as the difference between 'chronically sick elderly' and 'medical geriatric' should be avoided at all costs.

If it is decided to categorise patients or residents, authorities should take into account the advice of the High Court in *Avon County Council v Lang*[31] that one of the factors to be taken into account in regulation is the interests of patients or residents accommodated in the home. If one views a registered care

---

31 [1990] COD 365.

home as, in effect, a home rather than a temporary residential institution, an authority needs to take care before imposing conditions that may require an owner to evict an individual resident because their condition or their age has changed so as to contravene regulation. Such a condition should not be enforced unless there is a clear reason. If a nursing home caring for some children with severe learning difficulties has its conditions limited, so that it is unlawful to retain such children in such accommodation beyond a certain age, say 20, authorities should bear in mind that such children, upon attaining that age, may still retain the characteristics of children. They should consider whether it is not right for the authority and those responsible in a relationship of guardianship for the child and the home to debate each case constructively, in order to determine whether the placement is still correct, rather than force a change which may be against the interests of the particular patient, simply on the grounds of an artificial rule.

Authorities may seek to overcome this problem by making individual waivers as to conditions of registration. Owners should not regard that as a safe practice. There is no authority within the 1984 Act for the registration authority to undertake not to take action in respect of a breach of a condition of registration. Section 18 may provide some comfort for residential care home proprietors in the case of a sudden change of mind but cannot prevent revocation of permission or justify a permanent waiver or exception. No such provision exists for nursing homes. The matter will always be within the discretion of the authority but that discretion will always be subject to review. It is suggested that it would be ultra vires the registration authority to permit or promise to fetter its discretion in regulation in a manner not permitted by statute or regulations made thereunder.

3.17.6   Conditions relating to part of 'a home'

Another issue which will arise is whether or not a condition as to category of patient or resident may be imposed in respect of part of any home as opposed to the whole home and whether it will be necessary to create artificially different homes to cater for different categories of resident. This argument often develops in relation to the use of parts of residential care homes or nursing homes which provide good facilities but which would not be accessible or suitable for patients or residents with particular physical difficulties. The course of choice should be not to seek to regulate by conditions of registration, but to rely upon the enforcement provisions within the 1984 Act and the 1984 Residential Care Homes Regulations and the 1984 Nursing Homes Regulations as they apply to residential care and nursing homes and which provide, in relation to residential care homes, that each resident should be provided with such accommodation and space by day and night as is reasonable and that the person registered shall make such adaptations and provide such facilities as are necessary for residents who are, inter alia, physically handicapped (see reg 10(1)(b) and (e) of the Residential Care Homes Regulations 1984). In relation to nursing homes, the owner is required to provide for each patient in the home adequate accommodate and space, including day room facilities (see reg 12(1)(b) of the Nursing Homes and Mental Nursing Homes Regulations 1984). Accommodating residents or patients in parts of a home not suitable to their needs would clearly contravene such regulations and would be subject to correction and, if necessary, enforcement by prosecution.

Both the appropriate statutory provisions as to condition of registration speak of conditions in relation to 'the home'. There is no specific authority on the point, but it seems to the author that, for this purpose, 'the home' should be interpreted to mean parts of the home so that if a registration authority wishes to restrict use of a particular part of the home, perhaps an upper floor where there is a difficult flight of stairs to negotiate, then it should be possible to impose a condition of registration restricting the category of patient who may occupy such accommodation. However, any such condition must be drafted clearly so as to be beyond doubt in its meaning. Words such as 'ambulant' cause more difficulties than they solve. Restrictive conditions such as 'able to walk unaided' may, in fact, restrict from occupation of the room those for whom the room may provide good accommodation, but who need a walking stick or perhaps assistance from the care worker.

The guiding principle, it is suggested, should be that conditions of registration should not be imposed, given the existence of other methods of enforcement against a particular practice, unless they are both understandable and necessary in all the circumstances.

3.17.7 Conditions in relation to nursing homes

In relation to registered nursing homes, there are two separate matters which may be made conditions of registration and which arise out of the opportunities for regulation provided to the registration authority by s 25 of the 1984 Act. These relate to conditions:

(1) as to the qualifications of a qualified nurse who is to be in charge of a nursing home; and

(2) as to the number of nurses possessing particular qualifications who are to be on duty in the home at particular times.[32]

These matters are grounds upon which the Health Authority may refuse to register an applicant or, read into s 28 of the 1984 Act, grounds upon which registration may be cancelled. In relation to the qualifications of a nurse in charge, the matter is to be identified by reference to a notice served upon the owner and, in relation to the number of nurses to be on duty, is referred to as a condition. As breach of their provisions could lead to refusal of registration or cancellation of registration, it would be odd if such matters could not be elevated to the status of a condition of registration and enforceable by prosecution for breach. Both are matters which can clearly be drafted with certainty and both are central to core issues in relation to operating a registered nursing home. It is standard practice with registration authorities who wish to make conditions of registration about nursing qualifications or nurse numbers to incorporate such material, to the extent that such may become a condition of registration.

It is suggested that if Parliament has identified matters which are so grave

---

32 Registered Homes Act 1984, s 25(1)(f), (g), (2), (3).

that they can lead to a challenge to the creation or continuation of registration, then Parliament must have intended that such matters should be classified as conditions of registration rather than statements of good practice in relation to registration. If that were not so there would be no need for such provisions to be introduced into this part of the primary legislation relating to the provision of adequate staff in both residential care and nursing homes (see reg 10(1)(a) of the Residential Care Homes Regulations 1984 and reg 12(1)(a) of the Nursing Homes and Mental Nursing Homes Regulations 1984).

Following a notice served under regs 15 and 20 respectively of the relevant Regulations, an owner may be prosecuted for continued failure to meet standards. The only reason for Parliament to have drawn such attention to these particular issues must be, it is argued, because Parliament had intended such items to achieve the status of a condition of registration.

3.17.8   Qualifications of the nurse in charge

The matter in respect of which the Health Authority may act to refuse or cancel registration is said to be:[33]

> 'that the home is not, or will not be, in the charge of a person who is either a registered medical practitioner or a qualified nurse or, in the case of a maternity home, a registered midwife.'

Section 25(2) provides:

> 'in sub-section (1) above qualified nurse in relation to a home, nurse possessing such qualifications as may be specified in a notice served by the Secretary of State on the person carrying on or proposing to carry on the home.'

By a Direction made by the Secretary of State in September 1984, shortly before the 1984 Act came into force, Health Authorities were directed that any notice specifying the qualification of a nurse in charge should specify that that nurse should be a nurse whose qualifications comprised registration in Pts I, III, V and VII of the Nurses, Midwives, and Health Visitors (Parts of the Register) Order 1993.[34] In essence, the qualification is required to be that of a registered as opposed to enrolled nurse, as the expression was formerly understood, now perhaps better expressed as the difference between a first level registered and a second level registered nurse. There are detailed differences between such qualifications, but the substance of the difference is that, in relation to the nursing care of patients, second level nurses are required to work under the direction of a first level nurse.

It will be observed that the condition may only be imposed if the home is not to be in the charge of a registered medical practitioner. Many authorities do not bother to address this particular issue which, while it may be a condition of registration, is certainly not a mandatory condition of registration.

With regard to specialist homes, the authority may wish to specify specialist qualifications. Among such homes would be specialist homes caring for sick children or for the mentally ill. The author's observations in relation to

---

33   Registered Homes Act 1984, s 25(1)(f).
34   SI 1993/588.

the registration of mental nursing homes and the actual type of patients accommodated from home to home in such establishments may usefully be readdressed. Clearly, an authority cannot require as a condition of registration that a nurse possess qualifications *not* required (or perhaps permitted) for the particular type of nursing home or mental nursing home.[35]

Nurses may qualify and maintain their qualification in a particular specialist part of the register but experience may give them the ability to practice with distinction in other areas. Many nurses who qualify as mental nurses devote their lives to caring for the generally sick elderly and may be regarded as equally competent to play a leading role in a general nursing home without having to work under the supervision of a General Nurse, ie a first level nurse registered in Pt 1 of the register. Authorities may feel that it is sensible to retain flexibility and, subject to following the direction of the Secretary of State, that a nurse in charge must be a first level nurse, not seek to distinguish further between disciplines, relying upon the general regulatory scheme to prevent an abuse in a particular case. The urgent procedure, which may be invoked without warning or notice to the proprietor, to vary a condition of registration, is always an ultimate safeguard for an authority should an unexpected difficulty arise.

Artificial restrictions as to the qualifications of the nurse in charge may be unduly restrictive in enabling an owner to appoint the right person to be in charge, particularly if there is a change of senior appointment, as frequently occurs, during the period of conduct of the nursing home. Once again, it is suggested that the authority should take into account its overall regulatory powers and not seek artificially to restrict by condition matters which may not be appropriate in each in every case.

3.17.9 Numbers of nurses

A condition of registration with regard to staffing is of great importance both to an authority for effective control over quality of care, by ensuring adequate numbers of qualified nurses employed, and for an owner, as the costs of labour and, in particular, the costs of qualified labour are significantly the highest expenditure within the overall budget of a registered nursing home. It is estimated that staff costs represent somewhere between 45% and 60% of turnover of a nursing home. On current pay rates, the annual cost of employing one extra qualified first level nurse (RGN) over a period of 24 hours is approximately £76,000. What appear to be relatively minor adjustments to staffing levels can make enormous differences. Experienced owners will say that the important issue about staffing is to ensure that the staffing is right. Under-staffing is wholly unacceptable, but over-staffing is counter-productive.

Section 25(1)(g) authorises registration authorities to refuse or cancel registration if satisfied:

> 'that the condition mentioned in sub-section (3) below is not or will not be fulfilled in relation to the whole home.'

---

35 See Registered Homes Tribunal decision No 296, *ALM Medical Services Ltd v South Lancashire Health Authority*.

Sub-section (3) reads:

> 'the condition referred to in sub-section (1) above is that such numbers of nurses possessing such qualifications and in the case of a maternity home such number of registered midwives as may be specified in a notice served by the Secretary of State on the person carrying on or proposing to carry on the home are on duty in the home at such times as may be specified.'

Sub-section (4) provides:

> 'in preparing any notice under sub-section (2) or (3) above, the Secretary of State shall have regard to the class and in the case of a notice under sub-section (3) above, the number of patients for whom nursing care is or is to be provided in the home.'

Sub-section (4) seems to add little to a common sense approach to best practice in nursing homes for, in determining the numbers of nurses on duty and the qualifications of the nurse in charge, one could hardly imagine that any reasonable authority considering the issue would not have regard to the type of patient (it is suggested that 'class' should be interpreted as type or category) and the number of patients concerned. A Registered Homes Tribunal has held that s 25(1)(f) entitles an authority to take into account dependency levels or prospective dependency levels of patients when considering the imposition of such a condition.

There is no clear mandatory requirement to impose a staffing condition. Therefore, it is wrong for authorities to assert that they are bound to impose such a condition and it is suggested that, this being a discretionary matter, the authority should approach each case by first considering whether they feel it necessary to impose staffing conditions (the Tribunal held in favour of the appellant and proceeded to fix no such condition[36]). Responsible owners will themselves wish to ensure that the staffing levels in their nursing homes meet the needs of patients. The nursing staff levels prescribed by any condition which the authority seeks to impose can only be regarded as a minimum. The owner has an overriding obligation to provide adequate professional, technical and ancillary staff for the patients, having regard to their age, sex and category (see reg 12(1)(a) of the Nursing Homes and Mental Nursing Homes Regulations 1984). Therefore, if patient care requires staff over and above the staff required by the staffing condition, it is no defence to an allegation of inadequate staff for the particular patients for an owner to point to the staffing condition and claim to be in compliance. An owner must have sufficient nursing experience or have engaged nurses with sufficient experience to know when it is necessary to increase staffing levels.

3.17.10   Flexibility of qualifications of nurses

The imposition of the staffing condition may be seen as artificially restrictive. Such a condition will restrict reduction of staff levels (although this would only rarely be of relevance), should patient dependencies decrease significantly.

---

36   Registered Homes Tribunal decision No 306, *Takare Homes Ltd v North Staffordshire Health Authority.*

Insofar as qualifications of nurses are specified, it removes from the owner the flexibility to appoint nurses of appropriate experience and skill merely because their qualifications do not match the conditions of registration. This is not a trivial point. If nursing and staff conditions require the appointment of first level nurses, then any default will lead to the commission of a criminal offence. It may very well be that the best nurses available to fill gaps in a working shift may not be of the qualification prescribed by the staffing condition. A distinction is drawn between a nurse leading a particular shift and a nurse in charge of the nursing home. The nurse in charge is usually defined as a senior nurse responsible for the planning and implementation of nursing care, but not necessarily in charge of each and every shift – what is sometimes described as a 'hands on' basis. It may well be that there are second level (enrolled) nurses who have worked in the nursing home for many, many years and are very well known to the patients and know the conditions and requirements of the patients. If a shift which is normally to be lead by a first level (registered) nurse is suddenly the subject of a vacancy, it may very well be better that the experienced second level nurse leads the shift, subject to having recourse to a first level (registered) nurse should he or she feel that such a degree of support and supervision is needed. The alternative would be to appoint, on an ad hoc basis, to fill the gap, a first level nurse unknown to the patients and who had no knowledge of the home, but was appointed via a nursing agency to meet the crisis in hand. Many would consider that that situation, which may actually be caused by an artificially restrictive staffing condition, would be less advantageous to patient care than arranging for the appointment of the experienced second level (enrolled) nurse.

3.17.11 Prosecution for breach of a condition

Any breach, at any moment of the day, of an effective staffing condition amounts to a criminal offence which may be prosecuted and, hence, neither the owner nor the authority is in a position to issue a legal waiver. It will be remembered that, in relation to prosecution, there are no statutory defences available with regard to the owners of nursing homes, as there are for the owners of residential care homes, to claim mistake or reliance upon information supplied by a third party. It would be open to an authority to prosecute an owner even if a concession had been granted by one of the authority's officers, if the authority felt that the officer had acted in error. A magistrates' court might express its disapproval of this course of conduct in the penalty imposed or by giving a discharge (conditional or unconditional), but would be in no position, assuming the offence to have been proved, not to convict.

3.17.12 The authority's jurisdiction

If the authority decides to impose a condition as to staffing, it is important that it considers the limits on its jurisdiction. The condition may have force as a condition (as opposed to guidance or a statement of the authority's views) only to the extent that it covers matters provided for within the statute. A firm expression of the authority's view on sufficiency and suitability of staff (effectively signalling the content of a pre-prosecution warning) may well be more efficacious. One can question whether or not authorities would ever use the draconian power to prosecute an otherwise acceptable home because of a momentary lapse in staffing levels which may have a reasonable explanation. The material items are: (a) numbers; (b) nurses; (c) qualifications; (d) on-duty in the home; (e) times. Numbers should cause no difficulty, but the draughtsman should remember that this means numbers of nurses and not numbers of hours which are to be worked by particular nurses or groups of nurses. All too frequently, one sees proposed conditions speaking in terms of the numbers of hours interpreted into the number of whole-time equivalent qualified nurses with the slightly absurd proposition that a condition of registration be that, say, 8.269 qualified nurses are employed during each week. Such a provision does not meet the statutory requirements, although it may be completely in accordance with the way in which nursing establishments are formulated in hospitals run under the National Health Service and possibly elsewhere.

3.17.13   The meaning of 'nurse'

'Nurse' is a term which has caused some considerable debate. There are two schools of thought. The one, to which the author subscribes, is that the word 'nurse', being a protected term, the use of which is restricted by the provisions of other legislation (the Nurses, Midwives and Health Visitors Act 1979, replacing the Nurses Act 1957), can only refer to qualified nurses. An examination of nursing legislation is beyond the scope of this book. Suffice to say, that, under the Nurses Act 1957, it was a criminal offence for anyone to describe themselves as a nurse without being qualified as such. The Nurses, Midwives and Health Visitors Act 1979 changes the position and it is now a criminal offence to hold oneself out as a nurse possessing particular qualifications without possessing those qualifications. Given that, in order to practice as a nurse, it is necessary to obtain one or other of the types of qualifications prescribed by that legislation, to use the title 'nurse' must infer that some qualifications are involved. This surely leads to the conclusion that a person who uses the name 'nurse' has committed a criminal offence. At the very least, it calls for a definition of the word 'nurse' which would surely be taken by an ordinary person in the street to mean someone with qualifications and/or experience rather than someone employed 'ad hoc' in a particular capacity. It does suggest to the author that the title nurse is protected and that if the word 'nurse' is used in legislation in the context of the control of the supply of qualified nursing care, then it must be right to construe that word as referring to qualified nurses, rather than unqualified persons.

The contrary argument is that 'nurse' should be read to mean 'any person of any background or experience (including no health care experience whatsoever) who happens to be engaged in direct care tasks at a particular time'. Those who propound this theory are forced to conclude that if there is a shortage of unqualified nursing staff on a particular shift and the owner decides to redirect gardening or maintenance staff to work in direct care, then for that time and upon that shift, those gardeners and maintenance people are properly described as nurses. The author suggests that, if that were right, it would be a very surprising conclusion.

Failure to include non-qualified nursing assistants within the expression 'nurse' does not leave a gap in the regulation. The owner who provides inadequate staff is still at risk of a proposal to cancel registration. An alternative submission is that 'nurse' (while inferring some qualification or experience) cannot be limited to those possessing a full 'nursing' qualification. The difficulty with this 'half-way' home is the point at which 'nursing' experience in a so-called nursing care assistant is sufficient to meet that definition. The establishment of this would tax any prosecutor. As a matter of practice, nursing homes all employ a significant number of carers on the rota who would not meet any definition of 'experienced qualification'.

It is quite clear that the expression 'nurse' would not include those engaged in domestic cleaning, catering, maintenance or gardening tasks or those engaged in office work. All of such members of staff are equally vital to a proper and complete staffing establishment and if not present in appropriate numbers, would still require the intervention of the regulatory authority.

No such provision exists in relation to residential care homes, where nurses are not to be employed, and the submission that 'nurse' must mean qualified nurse is supported by the proposition that this provision is unique to the registration of nursing homes as opposed to other care homes, and must surely relate to what distinguishes nursing homes from other care homes, ie the provision of nursing care which, if to be properly so described, must be delivered by qualified nurses. Further, the reference to 'qualified midwives', in relation to maternity homes, suggests that the condition is to be concerned with qualification rather than lack of qualification.

Furthermore, the inclusion of the words 'possessing such qualifications' suggests that all nurses comprised in the staffing condition should have qualifications. The statute does not use words such as 'such qualifications (if any)'. Therefore, it is suggested that it would be an inappropriate exercise of the authority's discretion in relation to the imposition of conditions to impose a condition in relation to nurses stating that the nurses should be nurses who possess no qualifications.

3.17.14   Statute and the meaning of 'nurse'

If one looks at the history of legislation, one sees a clear concentration on the need to regulate numbers of qualified nurses as opposed to other care workers.

Section 4(1)(d)(ii) of the Nursing Homes Act 1975 made a ground for refusal of registration that 'there ... will not be a proper proportion of qualified nurses among the persons having the superintendence of and employed in the nursing of the patients in the home'. 'Qualified nurses' were defined as Registered General Nurses or Registered Nurses of other disciplines where patient care could properly be provided by such other disciplines. That definition of 'qualified nurse' was repealed by the Nurses Midwives and Health Visitors Act 1979. The consequences of the changes in the system of registration of qualified nurses flowed through into nursing home legislation.

Section 4(1)(d) and (e) of the 1975 Act were replaced by para 3 of Sch 4 to the Health Services Act 1980 (which contained revisions to the 1979 Act).

Those changes introduced the current law – now s 25(1)(d), (e), (2) and (3) of
the 1984 Act. The essence of the change was to give the Secretary of State
powers (exercised through Health Authorities) to prescribe the numbers and
qualifications of nurses. This change coincided with a change in the system of
admitting nurses to professional qualification and of the recording of such
professional qualifications. The change also bestowed a power to be flexible
about nursing qualifications, replacing a fixed regime.

It is submitted that, as there is doubt about the construction of the section,
it is difficult to see how it can have been intended to replace provisions which
deal with sufficiency of qualified nurses with provisions covering powers to
prescribe numbers of qualified nurses and other care workers. The expression
'nurse' has a long tradition of being held as a protective term to describe a
carer having a professional qualification in nursing. It would have been very
easy to provide, within the power, a power to prescribe numbers of care
workers, ie nursing auxiliaries. Other workers are just as important in the
overall picture of care. Why have a power to prescribe numbers of care workers
but not domestics or caterers? The word 'nurse' has always been used in statute
in this field in the context of a qualified nurse and it is submitted that it should
continue to be so interpreted.

3.17.15   The Registered Homes Tribunal and the meaning of 'nurse'

The alternative view impressed the Tribunal in *Uter v Bath District Health
Authority*.[37] This decision, with respect, is barely persuasive. The Tribunal only
expressed a 'tentative view' and that only after having legal submissions in
private. It is hard to see how this matter could be properly resolved without the
Tribunal being assisted by some expert evidence on professional nursing
practice and the views of the United Kingdom Central Council for Nursing and
Midwifery as to the propriety of the use of the word 'nurse'. In expressing this
view, the Tribunal was minded to find that 'nurses', who might include those
without qualifications, were 'by definition trained and wholly and exclusively
engaged in nursing'. If they were 'nurses carrying out nursing duties', surely
this raises the question rather than providing an answer. Also, the Tribunal
found that 'many duties' included 'making tea' but 'not catering or laundry'.
As no evidence was received, that finding seems wholly unconvincing.

In any event, a settlement was reached. The Tribunal approved a
condition including 'nursing care assistants' – it is not clear how that differs
from care assistants or whether the Tribunal would have approved a condition
referring to 'care assistants'. The author suggests that this tentative view is
unhelpful in resolving this difficult issue.

The Tribunal did decide, in *Takare Homes Ltd v North Staffordshire Health
Authority*[38] that 'unqualified care assistants' fall outside the scope of 'nurses'.
Although the *ratio* of this case limits its application to those clearly

---

37   Registered Homes Tribunal decision No 237.
38   Registered Homes Tribunal decision No 306.

'unqualified', the difficulties of equating qualification with experience and then trying to identify suitable eligibility criteria raise all the issues canvassed and earlier.

3.17.16 The meaning of 'on duty'

The nurses, to be incorporated within the staffing condition, must be 'on duty in the home'. The expression 'on duty' is capable of more than one definition, but it is suggested that the right interpretation is on duty caring for patients as opposed to on duty in some other capacity. Thus it is inappropriate to formulate, as a staffing condition, calculations as to hours of work by week or by year which incorporate holidays and sick leave, which are times when the nurses are not on duty. The question may very well be highlighted by the consideration of the position of the person in charge, or matron, who is often said to be to some degree supernumerary to the staffing establishment. The expression 'supernumerary' is taken to mean that that person is not engaged in direct patient care. Many would suggest that it is quite inappropriate for a matron to be wholly supernumerary except in a very large nursing home as the matron may, in order to most effectively carry out her duties, need to work on duty in patient care from time to time. To the extent that the expression 'supernumerary' indicates that the matron is not to be rostered to be on duty in patient care, then it is suggested that it is an inappropriate provision to be regarded as part of an enforceable condition of registration.

It should be re-enforced that these arguments are addressed to the issue of the drafting and enforceability of staffing requirements as a condition of registration. The matters which are criticised are very often very proper matters to be drawn into account in formulating a wide ranging staffing establishment policy. We are here concerned with the legal issues relating to the enforcement of provisions which are up-graded so as to be characterised as conditions of registration.

3.17.17 The meaning of 'at such times'

The expression 'at such times' may not be without its difficulties. The sensible course is to prescribe particular hours during which numbers of nurses are to be on duty. Expressions such as 'day time' and 'at night' are not helpful and probably unenforceable. The draughtsman would also wish to consider whether or not there should be an overlap in duty times to ensure that qualified nurses who are comprised within the condition of registration have sufficient time to report to their colleagues to whom they are handing over shift duties.

3.17.18 The number of nurses and the number of patients

A frequent mistake in the drafting of such conditions is to identify the number of nurses to be on duty in respect of the maximum number of patients to be accommodated or 'kept' in the home. Given that the condition is to be construed as one subject to criminal sanction, such drafting can lead to the defence that unless the home is full, a staffing condition does have effect. Nurses will be engaged in accordance with the number of patients actually accommodated rather than the number of patients who may be accommodated. A sensible proprietor would not engage nurses for 30 patients if only accommodating 20, nor does the 1984 Act require him so to act. This difficulty may be overcome simply by the introduction of a staffing chart or matrix indicating the numbers of nurses to be on duty by reference to the number of patients in the home. A very common practice is for the matrix to show differing numbers by reference to blocks of 5 patients. No bench marks are satisfactory, but a regulator must, at some point, draw a line if he wishes to regulate by something that requires such precision as a condition of registration. If he wishes to enforce effectively, he must ensure that in setting the benchmark he is acting within the strict legal authority of his statutory powers.

3.17.19   Enchancing prospects for prosecution

Those who fear that the argument restricting the condition of registration to the number of qualified nurses may impede the proper regulatory process, may improve their position significantly by incorporating within the staffing notice a separate statement as to the authority's views about the adequacy of numbers of ancillary staff which can clearly extend beyond nursing assistants to domestic staff, catering staff, gardeners and maintenance men.

Whilst not a condition of registration, if an authority was minded to prosecute for the failure to supply adequate numbers of staff, and precede that with the necessary prosecution warning notice, then, if that notice coincided with the authority's views on staffing expressed either at the time of registration or by subsequent notice, this could only strengthen the authority's position in persuading magistrates that there had been a failure to supply adequate staff. The fact that the owner had known and not objected to the authority's views on adequacy at an earlier time, would be seen, it is thought, as most persuasive.

3.18   DUAL REGISTRATION

It has already been suggested that this term might be better described as 'multiple registration'. In effect, the term is a loose one, adopted by practitioners and 'dual registration' does not exist. The expression 'dual registration' means, in practice, that the premises or establishment concerned are registered with different registration authorities in different capacities. The standard registration would be as to a residential care home with the local County or Metropolitan Borough Council or unitary authority or London Borough and, as to nursing registration, with the local Health Authority.

Dual registration, if achieved, may have significant advantages both for the home owner and for patients and residents. The home owner will be able to widen the type of persons whom he may seek to attract to purchase care within his home and be freed from the worry that may occur should patients' dependencies vary and it be suggested that particular patients are no longer appropriate to be accommodated. Necessarily, the owner must engage and maintain a staffing establishment which is sufficiently flexible to meet changing needs. Patients and residents may be comforted to know, if accommodated in such a home, that they will not necessarily be required to move should their care requirements change.

Dual registration consists of two separate registrations; a dual registration should not be regarded as a unified registration and owners, residents, patients and authorities will have in mind that the type of care required for those in need of personal care and those in need of nursing care will be quite distinct. Those responsible for operating and regulating such homes must ensure that all 'clients' of the home receive appropriate care and that those in need of personal care are not encouraged towards higher dependency by nursing-style institutionalisation, or that those in need of such higher dependency care are not neglected by over-emphasis on the lower care needs of the so-called residents.

The philosophy of dual registration is that there should be a seamless service within care as dependency varies. The aim, it is suggested, should be to achieve a service which enables 'clients' to continue to receive their appropriate care needs without even moving as between rooms. Movement between rooms may be as distressing for 'clients' as movement between one building and another or one care home unit and another. In determining whether or not to register, each registration authority will apply its own criteria against the material which it is required to take into account under the 1984 Act and determine whether or not to register and if so, upon what conditions. If appropriate facilities and services exist, there is no reason why one home should not be fully registered by two separate authorities so that within the overall maximum number of persons to be accommodated in the home, there may be total flexibility.

Suggestions that there need to be separate staff for separate types of client are not well-founded, as a matter of law and in practice. One will often find that care assistants engaged in residential care, other than the most senior positions, are little different from nursing assistants and nursing auxiliaries engaged in nursing homes, both of whom will conduct broadly equivalent tasks. The number of qualified nurses to be on duty may be regulated by condition and this may be entirely flexible, according to the number of nursing patients.

Any suggestion that the owner would then be able to, in effect, double up the number of 'clients' by reason of two certificates, can be dismissed immediately. Such an owner is required to provide adequate and suitable accommodation for all. Regulation 10 of the Residential Care Home Regulations 1984 and reg 12 of the Nursing Homes and Mental Nursing Homes Regulations 1984 make that quite clear. An operator which accommodated patients in an overcrowded situation would soon find itself subject to stringent regulation. Any warning which was not heeded would result in prosecution and, probably, in some variation of condition by means of an application for an emergency cancellation or variation of condition order, under s 11 or s 30 of the 1984 Act. Overcrowding would, inevitably, lead to a suggestion of serious risk to the health, safety and welfare of patients or residents.

Whilst in relation to the residential care home, the registration authority can only limit the number of persons to be accommodated to receive personal care (see s 5(3) of the 1984 Act), if the words 'persons kept' in s 29 of the 1984

Act are given the interpretation suggested by the author, then the Health Authority can, by condition of registration, as opposed to other regulatory practices, limit the total number of persons, so that a registration in respect of a dual registered home might read:

> 'to accommodate x persons for the provision of personal and/or nursing care provided that the total number of persons kept in the home at any one time, excluding the person registered and their employees together with their families, shall not at any time exceed x.'

Part II of the 1984 Act (nursing homes) contains no reference to residential care homes registered under Pt I and there is nothing contained within s 29 that can be argued to have any effect upon the registration of the same premises as a residential care home. Part I assists the argument by s 1(3), which provides 'registration under this Part of this Act does not affect any requirement to register under Part II of this Act' and s 1(5)(a) which removes the requirement from registration establishments used or intended to be used solely as a nursing home or a mental nursing home.

It thus follows that premises, to be used as a nursing home as well as a residential care home, may not only be registered under Pt I of the Registered Homes Act 1984 but also should be so registered.

It will be recalled that any distinction between a residential care home and nursing home, for registration purposes, concentrates on the nature of the care delivered, ie whether that care is personal care or nursing care (contrast s 11 and s 21 of the 1984 Act).

3.19 DURATION OF REGISTRATION

Registration is personal to the registered owner. There is no machinery or provision for the transfer of a registration certificate from one owner to another. Registration does not run from year to year, but is continuous, until the registration is cancelled. Nor can a certificate of registration be issued on a temporary basis or for a probationary period.

Retiring owners and owners in difficulties sometimes offer to surrender their registration. There is no procedure whereby registration may be surrendered, or such surrender may be accepted. Such invitation should be treated as a request by the owner for cancellation of registration and the termination of the registration should be recorded as a cancellation in the register. If an owner seeks to surrender a registration in order to avoid regulatory action, particularly after a proposal to cancel registration has been issued by a registration authority, the authority should have no difficulty in rejecting such a request. There may be reasons why the authority wishes to establish the correctness of its decision to cancel registration in order that the matter be one of public record. Should the owner seek to make a further application in the same or another area, or should the owner have other registered care homes, the registration authorities would benefit from the knowledge that cancellation proceedings had been concluded.

In respect of residential care homes, there is one slight exception which provides for the situation where a single owner dies. Under those circumstances, for a period of 4 weeks only, his personal representatives or his widow may continue to carry on the business of the residential care home without being registered. Under any other circumstances of transfer, any person who carries on the business of a residential care or nursing home without being registered is committing a criminal offence and may expect to be prosecuted. This point will be explored further in Chapter 7, dealing with the purchase and sale of registered homes.

3.20 STANDARDS, RECOMMENDATIONS AND GUIDELINES

Circulars of guidance issued to Health Authorities, prior to the implementation of the 1984 Act and following the publication of the Handbook on the registration and inspection of nursing homes, by what is now the NHS Confederation (formerly the National Association of Health Authorities and Trusts), suggested to Health Authorities that they should all seek to formulate and publish their own guidelines in relation to the registration and inspection of nursing homes. Such guidance to Health Authorities was not in the form of a Direction by the Secretary of State and, although not binding on them, was guidance which they were required to take into account. Most authorities have taken steps to publish their own so-called guidelines, which may be termed as guidelines or guidance, recommendations or standards.

The status of such guidance has caused considerable difficulty, but there can be no doubt about the position. Such material is nothing more than guidance and as such constitutes the collected experience and wisdom of those responsible for the administration of the registration and inspection of nursing homes within a particular Health Authority or, in the case of the NHS Confederation nationally. It cannot be elevated to the status of binding conditions. Even guidance issued by the NHS Confederation cannot be regarded as binding.

Some may suggest that the guidance to NHS authorities was an invitation to 'set standards'. It may have been. It may be a good thing if those with experience express their views on contemporary standards but, in the absence of legal authority, it is wrong for *any* would-be standard-setter to suggest that his views are advanced into binding rules.

The best that can be said is that this collected experience needs to be viewed objectively and if it represents an overwhelming consensus on what amounts to good practice in a particular field, then it will be regarded as highly persuasive to those who are required to solve a dispute relating to registration.

Rule-making power is delegated by Parliament to the Secretary of State. The power to make rules is to be found in ss 16, 26 and 27 of the 1984 Act.

In relation to residential care homes, a power to make regulations delegated by Parliament to the Secretary of State (see s 16(1)) is to be contrasted with the delegation of responsibility for registration to 'the registration authority' (see, by way of example, ss 5, 9, 10, 11, 12, 13, 14 and 15).

In respect of the registration of nursing homes, the situation is different. All powers have been delegated to the Secretary of State. This needs to be read in conjunction with ss 13 and 14 of the National Health Service Act 1977, which requires the Secretary of State both to delegate his functions in relation to the registration and inspection of nursing homes to Health Authorities. Thus, the functions in relation to registration and inspection of nursing homes are delegated by Parliamentary authority to Health Authorities.

Parliament has not permitted the Secretary of State to delegate his regulation-making powers. The regulations which deal with such delegation, currently the National Health Service (Functions of Health Authorities and Administration Arrangements) Regulations 1996 provide by reg 4(2) that nothing in the Regulations shall operate so as to delegate any regulation or rule-making powers which have been delegated by Parliament to the Secretary of State.

3.20.1 Guidelines and policies

So-called guidelines are, in effect, expressions of policy on the part of individual public authorities. Expressions of policy must always be approached with caution. Whilst policies are important and unavoidable in the proper administration of public authority duties, where public authorities are vested with a discretion in relation to particular functions, they must never fetter themselves in advance as to the way in which they will exercise that function.

Public authorities may have regard to policies in making particular decisions, but if the evidence shows that, rather than making an individual decision as to how to exercise a discretion, a public authority has made the decision regarding itself as bound by a pre-existing policy, then that decision will usually be found to be invalid in an application to the courts for judicial review and the appropriate prerogative order will be made.

3.20.2 The applicability and enforceability of guidelines

A substantive argument that so-called guidelines are not binding does not carry with it the corollary, often sought by home owners, that the guidelines may be disregarded. Guidelines, being collected wisdom, are extremely valuable in helping individual officers of registration authorities, home owners and Registered Homes Tribunals in their deliberations on matters of difficulty. In considering any matter concerning registration, the authority must take into account, in addition to its own guidance:

(1)   the individual facts and circumstances relating to the particular home;
(2)   such representations as the home owner may wish to make;
(3)   any national guidance on relevant material;
(4)   the guidance issued by other authorities.

Finally, in considering such matters, an authority must take careful advice to ensure that such proposals as it intends to make are not only appropriate as a matter of practice, but do not contravene any rights of the registered owner enshrined in the 1984 Act or the regulations made by the Secretary of State thereunder. If the legislation, primary or delegated, provides a right or restricts the ability of the authority to regulate, the authority may not regulate against such provisions, even in the case where it feels that good practice may indicate the need for such regulation. An example would, clearly, be seeking to introduce, as conditions of registration, material for which no provision is made in the 1984 Act and the validity of which has been expressly disapproved.[39]

Disputes about the applicability or enforceability of guidelines will always be resolved relatively easily if both sides recognise the true status of such guidelines, ie helpful guidance but not determinative of any issues and not binding in each and every set of circumstances.[40] There can be no substitute for the proposition that 'each and every case must be determined by careful reference to its own facts and circumstances'.

3.21   THE EFFECT OF CHANGE OF OWNERSHIP

If there is a change of ownership in the party carrying on the business, the registrations cannot be transferred and the new purchaser will require a new certificate. While the legislature intended that the transfer of care home businesses should be an opportunity for reappraisal, registration authorities should not take advantage of the position. Whilst home owners must expect re-registration to be an occasion for objective review of standards and facilities in a care home, they are entitled to expect that the authorities will not seek artificially to change ground rules or upgrade standards above that which could reasonably be expected. It would be wrong for an authority to seek to impose changes in respect of the operation of a care home unless it was satisfied that a proposal to vary conditions of registration or cancel registration would be sustained, if such matters were advanced to the decision-making committee of its own authority or to a Registered Homes Tribunal.

Such decisions will be made taking into account the interests of the residents or patients within the particular home.[41] The interests of those residents or patients will, it is submitted, be exactly the same whether or not the home is continuing under existing ownership.

3.21.1   An intransigent authority

A prospective vendor and purchaser will say that arguments as to the merits or demerits of an authority's position in considering an application for registration on transfer of ownership are all very well, but if, in practical terms, registration cannot be achieved without compliance with the authority's requirements, the authority is, in effect, in a position to force its will.

The more likely scenario, to the disadvantage of a prospective vendor, is that the purchaser will seek to take advantage of the position to reduce the price. A remedy, although unwieldy, is to stipulate in the terms of the contract for sale that, if the registration authority proposes to refuse registration or only

---

39   *Warwickshire County Council v McSweeney* (unreported) 8 December 1988.
40   See Registered Homes Tribunal decision No 61, *Reid Smith v Bristol and Weston Health Authority.*
41   *Avon County Council v Lang* [1990] COD 305.

to grant registration subject to conditions which are unsatisfactory and materially different from conditions imposed in respect of the current registration, then the purchaser shall appeal in respect of such unsatisfactory matters to the Registered Homes Tribunal and completion of the transaction shall be postponed until the Registered Homes Tribunal decision is known. Terms can be agreed as to the funding of the appeal and assistance by the prospective vendor in the conduct of the appeal. Knowledge by the authority that it will have to face the Tribunal, which might have dissuaded it from seeking to enforce its aims against an existing owner, may and often does have exactly the same effect in relation to a transfer of ownership.

The purchaser may perceive a commercial advantage in seeking to conclude earlier at a lower price and the vendor may be desperate. By the time this stage is reached, the business may be in a delicate balance, as residents or patients or staff destabilise as a result of news of the prospective transfer having been leaked – this being unavoidable if an appeal to a Tribunal by a prospective purchaser is to proceed.

In those circumstances, the prospective vendor will continue to carry on the care home business pending the decision of the Tribunal and the decision of the Tribunal would trigger optional clauses within the contract leading to completion, completion at a reduced or enhanced price, or recission of the contract with a return of any deposit paid.

3.21.2   Who may carry on the business?

The only person who may carry on the business is the person who is registered to carry on the business, so that no other party is acting lawfully if they purport to carry on the business unless they are doing so as agent for a registered person. There is no provision for temporary registration or conditional registration.

3.21.3   Insolvency managers

The position of insolvency managers, such as Liquidators, Trustees in Bankruptcy and Receivers, is interesting. Where such managers, for example Receivers or Administrative Receivers, as a result of their appointment, act as agent on behalf of the registered person (most Receivers act on behalf of the borrower, whose lender has appointed the Receiver), then it seems that such Receivers may trade in the name of the original registered person. If, however, the Receiver, for example a court-appointed Receiver or Liquidator or Trustee in Bankruptcy, takes over a business in his own right and carries it on his own account, perhaps pending sale, then that insolvency manager needs to be registered as carrying on the business.

As a corollary, if the registered person is unable to carry on the business they may be held as no longer 'fit' and, accordingly, their registration may be cancelled – albeit that, in terms of professional care, there has been no criticism of their conduct.[42] An insolvency manager needs to be aware of this potential registration gap.

---

42   Registered Homes Tribunal decision No 289, *Oldfield v Stockport Health Commission.*

Whilst the registration authorities will often welcome the arrival of an insolvency manager, which may bring certainty into what may have been a difficult situation, taking into account, especially, the interests of the vulnerable residents, the authority should not feel itself compelled to register the insolvency manager. Normal criteria should apply. That manager will be seeking to sell the registered care home business in the relatively short term. Just as a new purchaser-at-arm's-length will complain if new terms for services or facilities are required shortly after registration, so an insolvency manager is entitled to say to a registration authority that, if they have registered him to carry on the business, perhaps at short notice, then that registration effects a representation by the authority that the business was fit to be operated at the date of change of registration in the name of the insolvency manager and that the authority is not in a good position to seek to suggest that there are material flaws in the business when the insolvency manager comes to effect a sale in his own name.

Authorities should recognise that they are under no more obligation to an insolvency manager than to any other transferee, except that their duty to take into account the interest of the residents may entitle them to overlook matters which might be of greater concern in a transaction at arm's length.

The duty to have a regard to the interest of the residents is important, but it is not paramount and cannot be used as an excuse by any applicant for registration or the owner to avoid the consequences of registration. The very purpose of registration is to protect vulnerable patients and residents in care and it cannot be right that, in any situation where regulatory action might result in those patients or residents having to leave an unsatisfactory home, the action should fail because it is suggested that residents might be better served by remaining, albeit in unsatisfactory circumstances or facilities. A line must be drawn if the establishment, premises or persons concerned in the operation of the premises are considered not to be fit to carry on such a registered care home business; then the registration authority should not feel coerced or dissuaded from taking appropriate action.[43]

3.21.4   Difficulties in effecting a transfer of registration

Difficulties in effecting a transfer of registration might be met on suitable commercial terms by a purchaser and vendor agreeing that the purchaser should carry on the business on behalf of the vendor pending the resolution of difficulties; and suitable agreement as to division of receipts, expenses and profits. Equally, the purchaser might be persuaded to pay the purchase price pending registration difficulties being resolved, or to lodge the purchase money in a secure account, with the vendor continuing to carry on the business pending resolution of outstanding difficulties, including a prospective appeal to the Registered Homes Tribunal. Whilst such courses are possible, it is suggested that they are not practical in a commercial sense, in that prospective transferees of the business and those who support them by providing loan finance are unlikely to wish to see their capital placed at risk or even taken out

---

43   *Harrison v Cornwall County Council* (1991) 11 BMLR 21, 90 LGR 81 (CA).

of their control unless they are satisfied that the ultimate result will be a satisfactory registration.

An exception to this rule is where registered care home business is carried on by a limited company. The person carrying on the business is then the limited company and if there is a transfer of ownership of the shares in the company giving rise to the opportunity to appoint new directors of the company, then there will have been no change in the identity of the person carrying on the care home business and no need to apply for a new registration certificate. Such a course commends itself to vendors and many owners are advised, as is considered in detail in Chapter 6, to so arrange their affairs so that the business of the registered care home is conducted through a limited company with the principal assets remaining in individual ownership. Whilst the registration authority is not able to veto changes of ownership in the shares in a particular company, a purchaser taking that course would be wise at least to have consultations with the authority. Change of ownership will be regarded as a material change of circumstance and if the new executives in charge of the operation of the company were perceived, on good grounds, to be unfit persons to be concerned in the conduct of a registered care home business, then there can be little doubt that the authority would be expected to exercise its discretionary power to propose cancellation of the registration, particularly in circumstances where such ownership had been acquired without prior consultation.

On the other hand, those prospective owners who have a tried and tested reputation in operating care homes and are sure that no serious criticism can be made of their fitness to carry on the particular business, may use this route as a quick and secure means by which to acquire new businesses. Any registration authority who sought to cancel the registration of an existing care home owner on the basis that there had been a change of shareholding and executive direction into the hands of persons who were manifestly fit, experienced and able in the conduct of the business would find such proposal to cancel doomed to failure.

3.21.5 The contract

Parties to the transaction inevitably require a contract, even if that contract is only effected very shortly before completion of the transaction. In preparation of the contract, very careful attention must be given to the necessity of effecting satisfactory registration in the name of the purchaser.

A vendor may be anxious to achieve contractual commitment, but given that most prospective purchasers will be borrowing money to fund the acquisition and no properly advised lender will advance funds, irrespective of contractual terms, until registration difficulties have been completely overcome, a vendor may find himself in a dangerous and exposed position if he has exchanged contracts to sell a home to a party who is not in a position to complete, because funds which are dependent upon registration are not available. The apparent security of an exchange of contracts may be of no real advantage to a vendor unless completion is secured. What exchange of contracts will secure is that the vendor will not be able to deal elsewhere and thus a vendor who, in haste, executes an ill-considered contract may find himself having effectively granted a timeless option to the purchaser from which extraction may prove both time-consuming and costly.

If such a contract is to be entered, both parties must consider effective machinery to bring the contractual obligation to an end and secure the return of a deposit to the purchaser unless satisfactory registration is effected within a reasonable time.

The purchaser should beware. Registration itself is not a sufficient contractual condition. The registration must be satisfactory to the purchaser and those funding the purchaser. The purchaser will need to ensure that registration and the consequent issue of the certificate in the name of the purchaser is the trigger which removes any condition precedant to completion. A proposal to register subject to conditions is unsatisfactory, as Registered Homes Tribunal litigation about the subject matter of the conditions may for last many months. From a purchaser's point of view, there is no substitute for the condition precedent to completion being the fact that the purchaser has been registered and has received the certificate.

3.21.6   The importance of the certificate

There appears to be no inextricable link between the issue of the certificate and the fact that the registered person is carrying on the business. The registration authority may issue a registration certificate to a prospective purchaser notwithstanding that completion has not then been affected. Naturally, authorities will not wish a multiplicity of certificates in relation to the sale of a registered care home and may require evidence that the property and business has been or is about to be transferred into the name of the prospective purchaser before releasing the certificate.

In practice, matters are resolved by the authority advising that registration has taken place and that the registration certificate is available for collection from their offices on the day of completion, upon satisfactory evidence (usually confirmation from the vendor's solicitors) that completion has taken place and title to the business is now vested in the purchaser. This will enable the purchaser or the purchaser's solicitors to collect the certificate of registration shortly after completion, or it may be that an authority would release the certificate of registration either to the purchaser's solicitors or the vendor's solicitors upon a satisfactory solicitors' undertaking that they will not personally release the certificate to the purchaser until the business transfer has been completed.

The importance of such certificate may lead a purchaser to conclude that he does not wish to be contractually bound in any way until he knows that he is in a position to complete. The sale of a registered care home business is a sensitive issue. Patients, residents and staff are often disaffected if it is known that the owners are proposing to sell the home. At the very least, referring agencies may cease to recommend new patients while there is a lack of certainty as to the continuation of ownership and some residents and patients, or their relatives, may actually seek to remove from the home in fear of changes in terms and conditions of occupancy or caring facilities accompanying either a transfer of ownership or anticipated transfer of ownership. Nursing staff, particularly qualified nursing staff, may feel that they do not wish to be subject to a compulsory change of employer and may seek alternative employment. The greater the delay surrounding the proposed transfer, the more likely these fears are to crystallise and damage the underlying business.

If the purchaser has made proper investigations and received representations or, possibly, contractual conditions as to levels of occupancy or business generation, then a slump in business pending contract completion may be disappointing and that disappointment may culminate in a claim that the contract should be terminated as a result of breach of contractual warranties or conditions or pre-contractual representations. It may lead to a claim for damages even where there have been no such warranties or conditions. The purchaser will say that the vendor is not delivering at completion the business which the purchaser contracted to purchase.

For these reasons, a prudent vendor, anxious to keep the prospective transfer secret, is often well advised to insist that there be no interval before contractual completion and that he will take the chance of failure in negotiations by waiting until the purchaser is truly in a position to complete, having not only completed investigations and secured registration, but also secured the satisfactory release of funds from his own resources or the resources of a lender.

Given the various uncertainties surrounding the transfer of a registered care home business, it is strongly recommended that both parties give active consideration to there being no contractual commitment in force until both sides know that they are ready to proceed to completion.

It will be seen that the personal non-transferable certificate of registration, which adds so much value to the registered care home business, is a matter which cannot safely be ignored by prospective purchasers or their solicitors and the purchaser's difficulties in obtaining such registration cannot safely be ignored by prospective vendors.

The transfer of a registered care home business is much more than simply property sale and purchase. It is a business transfer with considerable value dependant upon the successful management of 'registration' on transfer. Ignoring the idiosyncrasies of registered care home registration places the parties to the transaction in jeopardy and their professional advisers in default of their professional obligations and duties of care.

Chapter 4

REGULATION

4.1   INTRODUCTION

The practitioner, in a case of involving a registered care home problem, will need to look in detail at the provisions of the appropriate Acts and regulations. Those in a position of power may often believe that they have the ability to make or enforce rules of their own choosing. However, both the regulator and the regulated should be aware of the limits of the power of regulation, which may be ascertained from its originating statute. No matter how much a local authority inspector may feel that a particular view is correct in practice, there must be justification within primary legislation for enforcing a particular rule.

Statute thus prescribes the fact of regulation and its ambit. The statute prescribes that specific rule-making power should be delegated to the Secretary of State. The statute prescribes who shall be responsible for enforcement and the limit of their powers of enforcement. In relation to registered nursing homes, the statute (the Registered Homes Act 1984) must be read together with s 13 of the National Health Service Act 1977 and s 14 of the Health Authorities Act 1995, which provide for the delegation of regulation and enforcement powers from the Secretary of State to individual Health Authorities. In both such cases, it is quite clear that the rule-making power is reserved to the Secretary of State. Guidelines, requirements, rules or local regulations in relation to the registration, inspection and conduct of registered care homes, whilst of great interest and of some persuasive value as to local practices, can never be seen to take upon the force of law. If local regulators purport to enforce such guidelines or other material as rules of law, they may find that they are in error.

The ambit of regulation of care homes is to be found within the Registered Homes Act 1984 and the Children Act 1989. This chapter examines the statutory legal basis for regulation of each type of home and, thereafter, the constitution of the appeal tribunal and the provisions for the creation of offences and supplementary matters. The chapter will be divided as follows – residential care homes, nursing homes, community homes, voluntary homes, registered children's homes, regulation of fostering, child minding and day-care for children, the Registered Homes Tribunal and, finally, miscellaneous statutory provisions. The purpose of this chapter is to give an overview of the law of regulation and not to deal with particular and precise implications of the legislation in practice. These matters are dealt with in detail in other chapters.

4.2　RESIDENTIAL CARE HOMES

The law is to be found in Pt I of the Registered Homes Act 1984 and the Residential Care Homes Regulations 1984, as amended. The Regulations themselves are made pursuant to s 16 of the 1984 Act, which provides that it is the Secretary of State who may make regulations and, in detail, the matters as to which the regulations may relate. Those considering the validity of particular regulations will wish to view those regulations carefully against the matters which are permitted as part of their content. Further regulation-making powers are to be found in other sections of the 1984 Act:

(1)　section 5(1) – fees payable on application;
(2)　section 8(1) – amount of annual fee to be paid;
(3)　section 17(4) – regulations as to the identity of inspectors and the frequency of inspection;
(4)　section 57(2) and Schedule 2 – provisions for transitional matters – savings to protect established positions upon the coming into force of the Act).

All substantial matters relating to the conduct of residential care homes dealt with in s 16. The content of the regulation will be discussed after an examination of the structure of Pt I of the 1984 Act.

4.2.1　Registration requirement

These provisions are to be found in ss 1 to 4 of the 1984 Act. Section 1 sets out in detail the requirement for registration and exclusions from the requirement for registration. Section 2 provides for a criminal offence, for failing to observe requirements of registration. Section 3 deals with the registration of managers not being persons in control of the home and s 4 deals with the position of registration of a small home when the home is registered as a nursing home and, under those circumstances, is permitted to register not as a small home but as a full sized residential home.

4.2.2　Registration procedures

Section 5 sets out the requirements in respect of an application for registration and the powers of the registration authority in respect of that application. It must be read together with s 9.

Section 6 provides for the position when a registered proprietor dies. It gives authority for the home to be carried on for four weeks from death. Given the delays in obtaining probate or letters of administration of an estate, four weeks will seem a very short time. Those advising personal representatives will need to be alert both to an emergency application for a grant of probate or letters of administration and, thereafter, an emergency application for re-registration prior to the conclusion of the four-week suspension period.

Section 7 provides for public right of access to registration registers. It is of interest to note that neither s 6 nor s 7 are reproduced in relation to the registration of nursing homes.

4.2.3 Registration fees

Section 8 provides for the payment of annual fees for registration and the provision in relation to a small home (by s 8(A)) of the requirement to make an annual return.

The annual fee is to be distinguished from the registration fee paid upon initial registration. The regulations provide for different fees for initial registration, registration on transfer of ownership and annual so-called 'renewal of registration'. The annual fee is payable by reference to the number of beds and may be waived in relation to a small home. Some authorities have suggested erroneously that the payment of an annual fee makes registration a matter which is reviewable on an annual basis. That is not correct. However, non-payment of the annual fee is a ground for cancellation of the registration, which is itself subject to appeal. If the only issue were non-payment of an annual fee, it is difficult to imagine that, eventual, albeit late, payment would not result in cancellation being avoided, even if it were by the allowing of an appeal.

4.2.4 Refusal and cancellation of registration

The centrepiece of Pt I of the 1984 Act, which is of vital importance to all registered owners, is contained in s 9 to s 15 of the Act. This sets out the framework for refusal of registration or cancellation of registration or variation of conditions of registration, as well as the structure of the administrative and judicial process in place to review such a decision. The decision is, in all cases, the decision of the registration authority, but is subject to appeal to the Registered Homes Tribunal.

First, s 9 sets out the grounds upon which a registration authority may refuse registration and these are incorporated into and supplemented by s 10 in relation to providing the grounds for cancellation of registration.

Sections 11 to 15 provide the framework for the decision-making process. Section 11 provides for the extraordinary emergency cancellation procedure – made simply by application to a magistrate without the need to notify the owner. Section 12 provides for the ordinary procedure in relation to an application for registration, followed by s 13, which outlines the applicant or owner's right to make representations, s 14, which outlines the decision, power and process for the registration authority and s 15, which deals with the right of appeal.

The framework of the process is as follows:

(1) initial proposal from the registration authority; followed by
(2) the right for the applicant/owner to make representations to the registration authority about its proposal; followed by
(3) having considered those representations in the context of the proposal, the duty of the authority to make a decision (not a decision to endorse the proposal but a decision taking into account the representations);
(4) following the decision of the authority (which concludes the authority's participation as a decision maker), an appeal to a Registered Homes Tribunal.

It is worth nothing here the important distinction between this process and the s 11 process. In the ss 12 to 15 procedure, the matter is not resolved until the appeal process is completed by the decision of the Tribunal. In relation to the s 11 procedure, the process is completed and the operating home ceases to operate lawfully with the magistrate's order, the home must cease to operate pending appeal, whereas in the procedure that might be described as 'ordinary' procedure, the home continues to operate pending appeal.

4.2.5   Inspection

Compulsory inspection of registered care homes is an intrusion on the normal rights of property of the owner. The right for the registration authority to inspect is prescribed by s 17 of the 1984 Act and inspectors must be aware of the extent and limit of their powers. If suspicious as to the commission of a criminal offence, inspectors should consider the impact of the Police and Criminal Evidence Act 1984 and the Codes of Practice thereunder.

4.2.6   Offences

Section 18 provides a statutory defence to prosecution for offences under the 1984 Act for those whom admit the facts but seek to say that the offence was due to a mistake or reliance on information supplied, or default by another person, or matters beyond their control.

Where another is blamed for the commission of the offence, seven days' notice of that defence must be given to the prosecutor so that the prosecutor may investigate, similarly to an alibi defence in criminal proceedings.

4.2.7   Definitions

Section 19 provides definitions of relatives which are relevant to the definition of small homes to be found in s 1(4) and (4)(a); conditions as to numbers of persons who may be accommodated in the home (s 5(3)); and the identity of those who may carry on the home following the death of the proprietor (s 6). Section 20 provides definitions of 'disablement' 'personal care', 'prescribed' 'registration authority' and 'small home'.

These definitions may be regarded as less than helpful, particularly the all-important definition of 'personal care', which has been rendered virtually ineffectual by the decision of the Court of Appeal in *Harrison v Cornwall County Council*.[1] A definition which is not exhaustive is hardly of assistance to those who construe the statute.

4.2.8   The Residential Care Homes Regulations 1984[2]

Regulations 2 and 2(a) prescribe, by reference to Sch 1 to the 1984 Regulations the information and documents required to be supplied, as a minimum, for an application for registration. Regulations 3 and 5 prescribe the registration fees

---

1   (1991) 11 BMLR 21, 90 LGR 81.
2   SI 1984/1345.

payable upon registration and the annual fees to be paid. Regulation 4 provides for a time-limit for registration, which will scarcely be of relevance this long after the Act's coming into force and the regulations being made. Homes registered under the Residential Homes Act 1980 remain registered without further application. Homes not registered as in operation prior to the Residential Homes Act 1980 are required to make an application for registration within six months. This will only apply to the relatively rare cases of people who were not required to be registered under the 1980 Act, but were required to be registered under the 1984 Act.

The obligation to register small homes from 1 April 1993 has led to a number of amendments to the legislation specifying differences between registration and regulatory requirements for small homes, as opposed to full sized residential care homes. These need to be studied by specific reference to the regulations and especially the schedules, as they will be of great importance in practice.

Regulation 6 sets out the records which an owner of a residential home is required to keep and makes certain specific exceptions in the case of a small home. As opposed to registered nursing homes, very detailed records are required to be kept. It may be argued with some force that matters not referred to in reg 6 of or Sch 2 to the 1984 Regulations are not records which the home is required to keep. Similar arguments cannot be made in relation to registered nursing homes, where the prescribed records are not set forth in such detail. It will be argued that professional nurses should be required to keep, in relation to the operation of a registered nursing home, those records which are required in relation to the proper professional delivery of nursing care.

Regulation 7 provides the registers that are required to be kept by the registration authority and the information which is thus available to the public. As was discussed in Chapter 3, it is interesting to note the difference between the wealth of information prescribed to be kept by a registration authority, having regard to the type and category of persons accommodated within the home, as distinct from specific regulatory and restrictive conditions of registration limiting the type of resident who may be accommodated.

In general, the conduct of homes is covered by regs 8 to 12, which encompass the duty to consult with the fire authority, general provisions as to the conduct of the home and detailed provisions as to facilities and services to be made available, visits to residents in the home and religious observance.

It is interesting to observe that whilst reg 20, providing for the commission of a criminal offence as a result of breach of the regulations, only prescribes breach of regs 10 and 11 as giving rise to a potential offence. Regulations 8, 9 and 12 carry with them no criminal sanction, at least under the 1984 Act. That is perhaps surprising given that reg 8 requires consultation with the fire authority and, among other items, reg 9 forbids corporal punishment for children within a residential care home.

Regulations 13, 14, 15 and 16 make provisions with regard to the registered owner being required to notify the registration authority and certain other public authorities as to incidents within the home.

Regulation 13 requires notification of the arrival of a child in the home. Regulation 14 requires notification of death, outbreak of disease, absence of a child, and any event which affects the well being of a resident, or any theft, burglary or fire. Where children are accommodated, their parents or those in loco parentis must also be informed. Whilst it might be thought, on a brief examination, that this overlaps with the provisions of the Children Act 1989 in relation to registered children's homes, it will be remembered that registration as a residential care home avoids the need to register as a registered children's home, so that a situation will not arise where a home is registered or registerable under two separate statutory disciplines.

Regulation 15 requires notice to be given of the absence of the registered owner or registered manager. It will be noted that, where there is not a registered manager, even though senior staff may be appointed to executive care functions within the home, absence of the registered owner for more than four weeks still requires to be notified.

Regulation 16 requires notice to be given to parents and those in loco parentis prior to terminating accommodation for a child. Regulation 17 provides that all residents shall be advised of a proper complaints procedure and that that complaints procedure should include details of the name and address of the registration authority so that complaints or lack of satisfaction with the way in which complaints are handled may be referred to the registration authority.

Regulation 18 requires a registration authority to inspect every home, other than a small home, not less than twice in each year. Lest it be thought that this matter is of great concern, it will be remembered that the requirement to inspect on a number of occasions is not *less* than twice, rather than *more* than twice. Registration authorities may inspect as often as they think it appropriate. However, they must inspect every home no matter how good they believe it to be, in accordance with this regulation, at least twice in each year.

Regulation 19 makes provision for the situation where the person in control of the home is not also its manager. That person must visit the home at least once by himself or by his agent, and if by an agent, must arrange for a report to be given to the registered person in control as to the conduct of the home.

Regulation 20 provides for prosecution of persons registered for breaches of certain provisions of the regulations. The scheme for this must be followed by a registration authority prior to and in the course of bringing such a prosecution. At this stage, it is sufficient to draw attention to the fact that only the breach of certain regulations (6, 10, 11, 13, 14, 15, 16 and 19) give rise to commission of an offence which may be prosecutable. No offence may be prosecutable unless, prior to prosecution, there shall have been served a notice on the person registered which specifies the matter which is the subject of complaint, what action is to be taken and the period within which the action must be taken. Breach of the appropriate regulations after the expiry of the period specified in the notice is what constitutes an offence.

The preparation and service of such a notice is thus fundamentally important, from a technical point of view, if a prosecution is to be effective. Regulation 21 gives assistance as to the form of notices and the method for service, ie by hand, by post, by registered mail, or by recorded delivery. Warning of prosecution is sufficiently served if sent to the person registered addressed to him at the home.

Regulation 22 provides that compliance by one registered person with the provisions of the regulations is sufficient to effect compliance by all persons registered, ie if the registered manager complies with the regulations, the registered owner is deemed not to be in default.

Regulation 23 relates to appeals under the 1980 Residential Homes Act and is of little importance.

Regulation 24 exempts from registration, as a small home under Part I of the 1984 Act, accommodation provided by foster parents for a child pursuant to various provisions of the Children Act 1989. It should be noted that the exclusion of the need to register is restricted to particular types of homes and, although of passing academic interest, must be regulated by reference to s 14B of the 1984 Act, which does not on the face of it appear to be one of the sections under which the 1984 Regulations are made. However, given that registration for such accommodation for more than three children is required under the Children Act 1989, this potential gap is probably not of great relevance.

Regulation 25 provides for the making of annual returns in respect of small homes. The information required to be given, every year, is the information set out in Sch 4 to the 1984 Regulations. This provision is intended to dovetail with reg 18 requiring registration authorities to inspect homes, other than small homes, not less than twice each year. Clearly, an authority can inspect a small home as often as it wishes to do so, but it is not required to inspect at all. Given this exemption, it is natural that the Secretary of State should have required such homes to provide a regular flow of information to the authorities, covering the sort of material that would be checked on routine inspections of a residential care home. The matters required to be included with an annual return, in accordance with reg 25, are basic information as to the home, those who run the home, those who own the home, and those who receive care within the home.

Small homes may be inspected under s 17 of the 1984 Act, for they are still within the definition of residential care homes to be found in s 1(1) of that Act. The extension of the regulatory system to small homes was intended to bring them within the requirement of registration, save to the extent specifically excluded by the 1984 Act.

Disclosure of criminal convictions is a topic which is discussed in detail in Chapter 5, but it is worth emphasising that there is an ongoing obligation upon the small home owner to disclose criminal convictions not previously disclosed. This would clearly include criminal convictions obtained during the period to which the return relates, ie the period from first application or last return up to the date of the new return. The returns are made retrospectively so that the authority keeps its information bank up to date.

4.3 NURSING HOMES

Here again, the scheme of the Act is not set out in any logical order, but provides a broadly similar framework of registration to that of residential care homes. Whilst there is overlapping and much that is similar between the regulatory system for nursing homes and residential care homes, there are essential differences. It must never be assumed that a procedure for the one home is exactly equivalent to the other.

4.3.1 Definitions

Section 21 and s 22 of the 1984 Act set out detailed definitions of two types of home – a nursing home and a mental nursing home. The distinctions were examined in detail in Chapter 3. In relation to the definition of a nursing home, certain establishments are identified as not being a nursing home so that registration is impermissible as opposed to not required.

The basic provisions as to registration and regulation of nursing homes are to be found in s 23 and s 24 of the 1984 Act. Section 23 sets down the procedure and the obligations of the applicant and the registration authority in relation to the registration of a nursing home. It should be read closely with s 25, which gives to the registration authority discretion to refuse registration. It will be seen from s 23(4) that, subject to the discretion to refuse a registration arising under s 25, registration is a matter of obligation placed upon the Secretary of State and not a matter of wide ranging discretion.

Section 23 provides for two criminal offences:

(1) carrying on a nursing home without being registered;
(2) failing to keep affixed in a conspicuous place the certificate of registration.

Section 24 introduces a new type of offence. This is not carrying on a nursing home or mental nursing home without being registered, but *appearing* to carry on such a home without being registered. The section was enacted to meet the mischief that was perceived at the time when the 1984 Act was being considered, ie of those who were seeking to widen their franchise to the business of operating the recently registerable residential care home, sometimes known as 'rest homes', but were attaching to the premises the style or trading name of 'nursing home'. Carrying on a nursing home involves the supply of nursing care in the classic sense, but calling a home for those in need of care a nursing home and only supplying personal care did not, prior to s 24, constitute any offence. Section 24 meets a clear abuse and it is the author's experience that since this loop-hole was plugged, there has been a sharp decline in those seeking to pass off non-nursing establishments as nursing homes and thus prosecutions under this section are rare.

It is interesting to note that, save in relation to mental nursing homes, the statutory authority for inspection of nursing homes is not to be found as a matter of primary legislation, but as a matter of delegated legislation authorised pursuant to s 27(d) of the 1984 Act. Thus the Secretary of State may make regulations with respect to entry into and inspection of premises used or reasonably believed to be used as nursing homes.

4.3.2 Conditions of registration

Section 29 of the 1984 Act provides for those conditions of registration which may be imposed and be incorporated within the certificate. It will be remembered that s 25 (which provides grounds for refusal of registration) anticipates certain conditions of registration relating to numbers of qualified nurses and the qualifications of a nurse in charge. Those conditions, although not normally to be expected to be incorporated within the certificate of registration, are nonetheless conditions of registration.

4.3.3   Governing regulations

Section 26 and s 27 of the 1984 Act make provision for the Secretary of State to make regulations as to the conduct of nursing homes and mental nursing homes and in relation to other matters relating to such homes. These sections correspond to s 16 of the 1984 Act, in relation to residential care homes, and form the essential statutory authority for the regulations which are made. Once again, these must be studied to ensure that the regulations actually address the issues. Some other provisions of the 1984 Act also entitle the Secretary of State to make regulations. Regulation-making power is not delegated to Health Authorities, being specifically exempted by reg 4 of the National Health Service (Functions of Authorities and Administration Arrangements) Regulations 1996. Other regulation-making sections are:

(1)   section 21(4) – regulations as to specially controlled surgical techniques, ie lasers;
(2)   section 23(3)(b) – application for registration;
(3)   section 29(3)(a) – variation of conditions;
(4)   section 29(3)(b) – additional conditions of registration (not yet effected);
(5)   section 35(3) – regulations in relation to mental nursing homes which were previously registered as hospitals and for inspection of mental nursing homes (mental nursing homes were, prior to 1 November 1960, registered as hospitals under the Lunacy Act 1890);
(6)   Schedule 2, para 41 – transitional regulations in relation to homes registered prior to the 1984 Act coming into force.

4.3.4   General registration requirements

Sections 25, 28, 30, 31, 32, 33 and 34 of the 1984 Act should be read together. Section 25, which must be read together with s 28, provides a list of the grounds upon which an authority may refuse or, alternatively, cancel registration. All matters which would entitle an authority to refuse registration also entitle the authority to cancel registration. Such steps are taken at the discretion of the authority.

Section 30 mirrors the emergency cancellation of registration procedure in respect of residential care homes, to be found in s 11. Application to a magistrate may be made without notice to the owner if there is perceived to be a serious risk to the life, health or well being of patients.

Sections 31 to 34 re-introduce the system for dealing with applications for registration, variations in registration conditions and cancellation of registration, where the circumstances are not deemed to be so serious as to justify the use of the emergency procedure under s 30. The procedure is the same:

(1)   proposal by the registration authority (s 31);
(2)   representations by the applicant/owner (s 32);

(3)   decision by the Secretary of State, ie Health Authority (s 33);

(4)   appeal to Registered Homes Tribunal (s 34).

Similarly, it will be observed that decisions of the Secretary of State or Health Authority to register subject only to agreed conditions, or decisions of the magistrate to cancel, by the urgent procedure, take immediate effect. Other decisions are subject to a longer process of examination. The purpose of the Act is the same as with residential care homes. First, the authority advances its proposals, supported by reasons. Second, the owner has an opportunity to make representations to put his side orally or in writing and, thereafter, the authority makes a decision, once again not rubber stamping the proposal, but reflecting upon the basis of what the owner or applicant has said.

Appeals to Tribunals must be brought within 28 days and it is worth stressing here, as elsewhere, that there appears to be a trap for the unwary practitioner in that there is no opportunity to extend the time for appeal. Appeals lodged out of time or withdrawn without proper consideration leave the appellant without remedy, save, possibly, against his advisors.

4.3.5   Special provisions for mental nursing homes

Section 35 and s 36 include special provisions in relation to mental nursing homes. These provide for inspection of such homes and extended rights to inspectors. Section 36 provides, in relation to homes registered to receive patients liable to be detained under the Mental Health Act 1983, that registration shall continue, notwithstanding cancellation, until 2 months from the date of cancellation or until all patients have been removed, whichever is the sooner; or in the case of death of a sole proprietor, until whichever shall be the sooner of two months from the death, the time when all patients have ceased to be liable to be detained under the Mental Health Act 1983 or the time when another person has been registered.

It should be noted that 2 months from the disabling event is the maximum period over which the registration is continued and it is interesting to note that this continuation is provided only in the very limited cases of registered mental nursing homes registered to care for those who are secure patients under the Mental Health legislation. The reason is clear. Other patients are entitled to leave a registered nursing home of their own volition. Secured patients are not so entitled. The effect of cancellation or death in relation to a nursing home registration certificate is that the home ceases to be registered and secure patients are no longer correctly detained. In principle, such secure patients, without s 36 of the 1984 Act, would be entitled to vacate the premises in which they have been accommodated, upon cancellation or death.

In practice, the authorities are kept closely advised of developments in relation to premises registered to care for patients detained under the Mental Health Act 1983 and would ensure the removal of those patients to other secure accommodation rather more rapidly than the maximum time limit provided by the Act. Certain provisions of the Mental Health Act 1983, which apply to patients detained in registered mental nursing homes, were carried forward into the 1984 Act by s 38 of the 1984 Act.

4.3.6 Christian Science homes

The Secretary of State or Health Authority are, by s 37 of the 1984 Act, entitled to grant exemption from registration for homes carried on in accordance with the practice and principles of the body known as The Church of Christ Scientist. It should be noted that this is a discretionary exemption and not one which the Secretary of State is bound to grant and one which can be revoked at any time, if the Secretary of State is dissatisfied with the way in which the home is operated.

4.4 NURSING HOMES AND MENTAL NURSING HOMES REGULATIONS 1984 (AS AMENDED)

4.4.1 Medical treatment

Regulations 2 and 3 define the various terms of art to be used in the Regulations. Regulation 3 contains the one and only categorisation of specially controlled techniques of medicine or surgery which trigger the obligation to register as a nursing home. The crucial equipment is a laser product, described as a class 3b or class 4 laser. Chapter 3 deals with registration and identifies the consequences for medical practitioners who use such equipment in terms of being required to register as a nursing home.

These provisions should be read together with reg 13, which provides that the person registered should ensure that any treatment by specially controlled techniques in a nursing home is carried out only by a person who is or who is acting in accordance the directions of a medical practitioner or a dentist. Failure to comply with reg 13 is a criminal offence, which may be prosecuted and is not subject to the warning notice procedure, (similar, but by no means identical to that discussed under reg 20 of the Residential Care Homes Regulations 1984), before a prosecution can be brought.

What amounts to acting in accordance with the directions of a medical practitioner or a dentist may cause some difficulties, given the growth in sophistication of equipment and the manpower resources objective of delegating relatively simple tasks to a wider range of professionals.

4.4.2 Definition of 'adequate'

'Adequate' is defined in reg 2 as meaning 'sufficient and suitable'. Many advocates and commentators have questioned whether or not the definition adds anything to the original word.

The *Concise Oxford Dictionary*, 1990 edition, has the following primary definitions:

(1) adequate – sufficient, satisfactory;
(2) sufficient – sufficing, adequate, enough;
(3) suitable – well fitted for the purpose, appropriate.

However, it may be important to note that 'satisfactory' as a definition of 'adequate' is excluded by the statutory definition of the term.

4.4.3   The process of registration

The process of registration is covered by regs 4, 5 and 6. Regulation 4 identifies the form of application and, through Schs 1 and 2, identifies the minimum information required to be supplied by an applicant. This, of course, does not mean that registration authorities may not require further information, but does mean that an applicant may not even begin to consider his application as well founded until that information has been supplied. The authority may require such other information as may be reasonably required.

Regulation 5 provides for annual fees, the original registration fee being provided by reg 4(1). Regulation 6 deals with the variation of conditions of registration. Regulation 6 sits unhappily, as subordinate legislation, with the scheme introduced by ss 31 to 34 of the 1984 Act, which clearly provide for variation of conditions of registration to be introduced by the 'proposal, representation and decision' process, leading to a Registered Homes Tribunal appeal; or, if an emergency, under the urgent procedure under s 30 of the 1984 Act.

The 1984 Regulations were, in effect, a replacement for the similar Nursing Homes and Mental Nursing Homes Regulations 1981 and the author suggests that, to the extent that a separate and less protected system for changing conditions of registration seems to be imposed by the regulations, that must stand as secondary to the regulatory framework under the 1984 Act, ie the primary legislation.

It is interesting to note that, where the condition of registration as to numbers is to be reduced, then (and there is no corresponding provision for residential care homes) the Health Authority must specify that the original maximum shall be retained for so long as patients accommodated at the home at the date of variation remain accommodated there.

4.4.4   Conduct of the home

Regulation 7 specifies the records which must be kept at a nursing home. Reference is made to Sch 4, but it should be noted that the records to be kept in accordance with Sch 4 are only described as included within those required to be kept. Unlike residential care homes, the requirement for records is more general than specific and the owner is required to ensure that records, in order to comply with reg 6, are kept in a form that is appropriate.

Regulation 8 requires notification of death of patients to the Health Authority within 24 hours. Regulation 9 requires notice to be given of the absence of the person in charge and, indeed, of the person registered if that absence is to last longer than four weeks. Further, the person registered or the person in charge are required to give notice within one week of their return.

Regulation 10 is the authority for the inspection of nursing homes, as opposed to mental nursing homes. Breach of reg 10 gives rise to a variety of offences. Serious issues arise in relation to the restrictions on inspection of clinical records by medical officers in the employment of the Crown (see reg 10(3)). Regulation 11 requires that there be a minimum of two inspections each year, in similar terms to inspections of residential care homes.

Regulation 12, probably the best-known regulation, provides for the standards of facilities and services. This will frequently be the foundation for a pre-prosecution warning under reg 15 and, indeed, a subsequent prosecution. Prosecutors and defendants will need to study the precise wording of the various sub-paragraphs in reg 12(1), bearing in mind that the standard is universally described as 'adequate' and that the criminal burden of proof requires proof beyond all reasonable doubt.

Regulation 14 relates to transitional provisions. Regulation 15 sets out the offences which may be committed pursuant to these regulations. These offences can be divided into those which are instantly prosecutable and those offences which may only be prosecuted after a 'Warning Notice'.

4.4.5 Offences meriting immediate prosecution

The following offences merit immediate prosecution:

(1)   refusal to allow inspectors to inspect premises or records (reg 10(1));
(2)   any offence committed whilst a s 30 application is pending (hardly likely, as these are usually brought without notice to the owner);
(3)   failure to have treatment by specially controlled techniques carried out by or in accordance with the directions of a medical practitioner or dentist (reg 13).

4.4.6 Offences which are not prosecutable prior to the service of the notice under reg 15(4)

The following offences are not prosecutable prior to the service of the notice under reg 15(4):

(1)   keeping and retaining records (reg 7 or Sch 4);
(2)   failing to give notice of absence of person in charge or person registered, or notice of death (regs 8 and 9);
(3)   failure to furnish information required to be furnished in relation to an inspection (reg 10(2)). Contrast this with reg 10(1);
(4)   failure to comply with the requirement to provide adequate services and facilities (reg 12). Interestingly, the reg 12 breaches exclude, as a prosecutable breach, consultation with the fire authorities, which mirrors the residential care home regulations.

The prosecution warning notice has to specify:

(1)   the regulation said to be breached;
(2)   the respect in which the breach has occurred;
(3)   the action required to remedy the breach;
(4)   the period within which action should be taken.

Curiously, it is not clear whether prosecution can be brought in relation to activity or inactivity prior to the expiry of the warning period. This contrasts with reg 20 of the Residential Care Homes Regulations 1984.

4.5 COMMUNITY HOMES

Community homes are homes provided by local authorities, alone or in conjunction with voluntary organisations, to provide care and accommodation or services in relation to welfare of children who may or may not be looked after by the local authority. Being at least controlled by the local authority, such homes are not subject to registration, but they are subject to the ultimate control of the Secretary of State. As opposed to an obligation to register, it is the duty of local authorities, alone or together with other local authorities, to ensure that homes are available to look after children. Such obligations arise under s 53 of the Children Act 1989.

If such homes are not provided by the local authority alone, they may be provided by a voluntary organisation, but in that case, agreements must be made either that the home is managed by the local authority or that the local authority agrees that the home be under the control of the voluntary organisation. Homes that are controlled by local authorities are designated 'controlled community homes'. Homes controlled by voluntary organisations are designated as 'assisted community homes'.

Section 54 of the Children Act 1989 entitles the Secretary of State to intervene to direct that premises are not be used as a community home, if dissatisfied with the way in which they are operated, and to revoke the instruments of management. Disputes relating to the management of controlled or assisted community homes are referred to the Secretary of State, who is to determine those disputes. The Secretary of State's power to intervene is quite clearly retained, even though the instruments of management may provide that either the local authority or the voluntary organisation can make decisions to determine issues in relation to a dispute.[3] The only exception is that the Secretary of State may not intervene with the power to determine disputes, where this is reserved to a Bishop or other ecclesiastical denominational authority.

Voluntary organisations may not cease to provide controlled or assisted community homes without giving to the Secretary of State two years' notice of their intention so to do.[4] If they are not able to continue providing the home during the whole of the two-year period, then an additional notice must be given at the time of serving notice of termination to that effect. The Secretary of State may then intervene to revoke the home's establishment or to require the local authority in whose area the home is situated to take over the running of the home.

4.5.1   Compensation

Section 58 of the Children Act 1989 provides for the payment of compensation by voluntary organisations. The purpose of compensation is to reimburse to the public purse, public monies invested in providing the community home facility. Such compensation is calculated and agreed by reference to sale proceeds, or in default of agreement, determined by the Secretary of State. Compensation is paid at or after sale or other disposal.

Clearly, the intention of the legislation is to ensure that public funds invested in creating public facilities are not re-directed into other facilities, whether or not for a beneficial charitable purpose, at the discretion of those responsible for managing a voluntary organisation, as opposed to those

---

3   Children Act 1989, s 55(4).
4   Ibid, s 57.

responsible for public funds generally. Voluntary organisations are defined, for the purposes of the Children Act 1989, as bodies whose activities are carried on not for profit, other than public or local authorities.[5]

4.6 VOLUNTARY HOMES

Voluntary homes are homes provided by voluntary organisations and are one of the options available to a voluntary organisation for the provision of accommodation for children. They are regulated by Pt VII of the 1989 Act, being ss 59 to 62.

4.6.1 Registration requirements

Section 59(1) of the Children Act 1989 provides that voluntary organisations providing accommodation for children must do so in voluntary homes, community homes or registered children's homes. Section 60 of the Children Act 1989 provides for the registration and regulation of voluntary homes. Section 61 and s 62 provide, respectively, for the obligations of voluntary organisations and local authorities in relation to the provision of accommodation for children. Voluntary homes shall not be carried on unless registered with the Secretary of State.[6]

4.6.2 Definition

A voluntary home means any home or other institution providing care and accommodation for children carried on by a voluntary organisation.[7] A voluntary home does not include:

(1) a nursing home, mental nursing home or residential care home (but may include a small home);
(2) a school;
(3) a health service hospital;
(4) a community home;
(5) homes provided and equipped through the Secretary of State;
(6) homes exempted by regulations made by the Secretary of State.

4.6.3 Regulation

Schedule 5 to the Children Act 1989 provides regulations and a regulatory framework in relation to the registration of voluntary homes. Part I of Sch 5 deals with the registration of voluntary homes, providing the regulatory framework and Pt II provides for the making of regulations as to voluntary homes. In essence, Pt I enacts a regulatory framework similar to that found within Pts I and II of the 1984 Act in relation to residential care and nursing homes.

---

5 Children Act 1989, s 105(1).
6 Ibid, s 60(1).
7 Ibid, s 60(3).

Paragraph 1 of Sch 5 provides for an application to be made. Paragraph 2 provides for the options available to the Secretary of State in dealing with an application made for registration of a voluntary home, and also provides for variations and conditions of registration. It should be noted that the Secretary of State retains a total discretion as to the nature and application of conditions to voluntary homes, which are not limited in extent, as they are with residential homes and nursing homes.

Paragraph 1(3) provides that the Secretary of State may cancel the registration of a voluntary home. Paragraph 1(5) provides it is an offence to carry on a voluntary home without being registered, or if registered, in breach of a condition of registration. Paragraph 1(6) provides for penalties for operating a home. Paragraph 1(7) provides for notice to a local authority that a voluntary home registration has been cancelled (clearly necessary as the local authority may have children placed in such a home, will have a responsibility to other local authorities in respect of children placed in the home and will have responsibility to re-accommodate children placed in the home in respect of which registration has been cancelled).

Paragraph 2 establishes a procedure whereby the Secretary of State is required to give notice of a proposal to grant or refuse or cancel registration in respect of a voluntary home. Paragraphs 3, 4 and 5 provide a similar procedure to that provided by ss 12 to 15 and ss 31 to 34 of the 1984 Act, ie proposal, followed by applicant/owner representations, followed by decision, followed by appeal to the Registered Homes Tribunal.

Paragraph 6 provides for particulars in respect of voluntary homes, giving such details as are prescribed by regulation to be delivered to the Secretary of State by the owners of the voluntary homes on a regular basis. Failure to do so is an offence and penalties are prescribed.

Part II, incorporating para 7 of Sch 5 to the Children Act 1989, is equivalent to ss 16, 26 and 27 of the 1984 Act, which lay out the nature of the regulations which the Secretary of State may make in relation to the conduct of voluntary homes. These are all-embracing but, once again, those concerned with the enforcement of such regulations will need to study the precise limits of the regulation-making power. At the time of writing, the Secretary of State has not made regulations specifically as to the conduct of voluntary homes, other than the Children's Homes Regulations 1991.[8] Regulations have been made as to the placing of children in homes, being the Arrangements for the Placement of Children (General) Regulations 1991.[9] Such regulations as have been made pursuant to s 59(2) and (3) of the Children Act 1989 would seem to suffice, irrespective of any reference to Sch 6 of the 1989 Act. The Children's Homes Regulations 1991 are regulations made under all the appropriate provisions of the Children Act 1989 in relation to homes, whether they be community homes, registered children's homes or voluntary homes and include regulations made under Sch 5, paras 1, 6 and 7, as well as Sch 6, which deals with the statutory regulation of registered children's homes.

---

8   SI 1991/1506.
9   SI 1991/890.

4.7 REGISTERED CHILDREN'S HOMES

The law relating to the registration of children's homes is to be found in Pt VIII of the Children Act 1989, being ss 63, 64 and 65, supplemented by Sch 6 to the Act and supported by regulations made under various provisions of the Act, namely the Children's Homes Regulations 1991.

Section 63 of the 1989 Act imposes the restriction on caring for children unless the accommodation is registered as a children's home. The provisions carefully avoid overlapping between voluntary homes, community homes, residential care homes, health service hospitals, nursing homes and schools.

4.7.1 Definition

In essence, a children's home is a home providing care and accommodation for more than three children at one time, which is not otherwise registerable under the Children Act or other legislation. Anyone caring for and accommodating a child in a home without being registered is guilty of an offence.

4.7.2 Regulation

A detailed regulatory framework is introduced by Sch 6. Section 64 provides general background to the duties of persons carrying on children's homes, in relation to the welfare of children who may be accommodated in those homes, and whose duty it is to consult with various other people concerned in the welfare of the child. Section 64(4) imposes an obligation on local authorities to inspect children's homes and visit children accommodated in children's homes from time to time in the same way that they have obligations, under s 62 of the Children Act 1989, in relation to voluntary homes.

Section 65 of the 1989 Act provides that persons disqualified from private child fostering shall not carry on or be concerned in the management or have a financial interest in a children's home unless the fact of disqualification has been disclosed to the responsible authority (the registration authority) and the consent of the authority has been obtained. It is an offence to employ anyone who has been so disqualified.

Where an authority refuses to give its consent to a person to be concerned or interested in the carrying on of a children's home or employed in such capacity as a result of such disqualification, there is a right to appeal to the Registered Homes Tribunal. Failing to comply with these provisions amounts to an offence.

4.7.3 Disqualification from Caring for Children Regulations 1991[10]

Disqualification from fostering is specified in regulations made under s 68 of the Children Act 1989, the Disqualification from Caring for Children

---

10 SI 1991/2094.

Regulations 1991. In essence, persons are disqualified from fostering children if:

(1)   a child of which the applicant is a parent has been the subject of a care order under the Act;
(2)   a variety of orders have been made under the Act, or former or similar legislation, removing the care of a child from the applicant;
(3)   orders have been made removing a child from care of the applicant under the Adoption Acts or under the former Foster Children Acts;
(4)   the applicant has been convicted of criminal offences in relation to children, as specified in the regulations;
(5)   the applicant has been concerned in the management of a home removed from the register of voluntary homes;
(6)   the applicant has had an application to register a voluntary home refused;
(7)   the applicant has had an application to register a children's home refused;
(8)   the applicant was concerned in the operation of a children's home which has been removed from the register;
(9)   the applicant has been the subject of an order prohibiting him from being involved in private fostering;
(10) the applicant has been refused registration or had registration cancelled in respect of nurseries, day care or child-minding.

4.7.4   The Children Act 1989, Sch 6

Schedule 6 to the Children Act 1989 introduces a registration scheme in Pt I, and regulation-making power under Pt II, in exactly the same way as the scheme introduced under Sch 5 in respect of voluntary homes.

Paragraph 1 sets out the requirement for an application for registration and the procedure which should be adopted by the local authority in considering such an application.

Paragraph 2 provides for the imposition of conditions upon registration and there is a general discretion upon a local authority as to the conditions of registration which they may impose, ie no artificial restrictions are to exist under Part I and Part II of the 1984 Act in relation to residential care homes and nursing homes.

Paragraph 3 provides for an annual review of registration. Here, there is a complete distinction between registered children's homes and other forms of children's homes. It has been seen, that certificates are perpetual. Registration certificates for children's homes are perpetual, but are subject to review and only continue if the registering local authority is satisfied that the home should continue to be registered. If it is not so satisfied, then the registration is to be cancelled.

4.7.5   Cancellation of registration

It will be observed that the obligation on the authority is to be satisfied that the home continues to be satisfactory. The onus of proof is upon the applicant to show continued suitability. In the absence of satisfaction (which could mean in the absence of objective evidence provided by the owner to satisfy the local authority, there is (apparently) an obligation to cancel.

Paragraph 4 provides for cancellation of registration. Unusually, the person carrying on the home may apply to have the registration cancelled. The authority may cancel the home if it has ceased to be a registerable school establishment or if it is satisfied, on annual review, that those concerned in carrying on the home have been convicted of criminal offences.

Paragraphs 5, 6, 7 and 8 of Sch 6 to the Children Act 1989 repeat the normal procedure in relation to applications for registration, or decisions as to variation of condition or cancellation of registration:

(1)   para 5 – proposal;
(2)   para 6 – representations by the registered owner;
(3)   para 7 – independent decision of the local authority;
(4)   para 8 – appeal to the Registered Homes Tribunal.

The well-known procedure in relation to cancellation of registration, paras 5 to 8 inclusive, does not lie particularly well with the authority's apparent duty on annual review to cancel unless satisfied that the registration should continue; for under para 5(5), the authority, having made a proposal to cancel registration, is required to give reasons. This does not sit well with the apparent obligation to cancel if the authority are not satisfied, ie if the registered owner has not convinced the authority that his registration should continue. Clarification of this issue has been attempted by the Registered Homes Tribunal in the recent cases of *Paul Hett v Gwynedd County Council*[11] and *Bryn Alyn Community Ltd v Clwyd County Council*[12] (although these cases related to first registration upon the implementation of the Children Act 1989).

Paragraph 9 provides a prohibition on renewing applications for registration, following refusal or cancellation, for 6 months beginning with the date of notification of refusal or the date of cancellation of registration, ie in the case of cancellation, the date of issue of the decision of the local authority or the Registered Homes Tribunal, if an appeal has taken place. Curiously, the power to cancel registration, by the urgent application to a magistrate, seen in the case of residential care homes and nursing homes under ss 11 and 30 of the 1984 Act, has not been introduced into the scheme effecting registration of children's homes. Perhaps the regular annual review, not a feature of the registration of residential care homes and nursing homes, and the need to retain security of accommodation for children, combined with the extensive powers under other parts of the Children Act 1989 to take emergency action to protect children at risk, make this unnecessary.

Part II of the Regulations, by reg 10, prescribes the type of regulations that the Secretary of State may make. A variety of regulations have been made and these include the Children's Home Regulations 1991,[13] the Review of Children's Cases Regulations 1991,[14] the Arrangements for Placement of

---

11   Registered Homes Tribunal decision No 214.
12   Registered Homes Tribunal decision No 231.
13   SI 1991/1506.
14   SI 1991/895.

Children (General) Regulations 1991[15] and the Representations Procedure (Children) Regulations 1991.[16]

4.7.6   Children's Home Regulations 1991

These regulations are intended to cover community homes, registered voluntary homes and registered children's homes. Part I provides an exhaustive definition and, in reg 3, a helpful guide to indicate which parts of the regulations apply to which types of homes. Parts II and III, relating to the conduct and administration of children's homes, apply to all homes, but the other homes have particular regulations tailored to them.

Regulation 3(2) provides that accommodation provided for children for holiday purposes for less than 28 days at a time is excluded from regulation. On that basis, holiday activity centres, that many might consider appropriate for regulation, are taken out of regulation, at least under the Children Act 1989.

Part II (regs 4 to 14) relates to the conduct of children's homes. Generally, these provisions may be compared with the sections, outlined above, dealing with the conduct of residential care and nursing homes. The drafting style is different, but the content is similar. Regulation 4 requires a register of children's homes to be kept, including information as required in Sch 1, ie information as to the purpose and function of children's homes. Regulation 5 requires that the person carrying on the home (described as the 'responsible authority') shall ensure sufficient staffing. Regulation 6 provides that the person registered shall provide suitable accommodation.

Regulation 7 goes on to provide further definition about suitability of accommodation, but interestingly, whilst the word 'adequate' is not used universally, the words 'adequate', 'suitable' and 'sufficient' are to be found frequently in the individual regulations so that, in essence, there is not a great movement away from the general standard of adequacy prescribed in relation to residential care homes and nursing homes.

Regulation 8 makes specific provisions as to control and discipline. Regulation 9 makes arrangements as to the storage of medicinal products. Regulation 10 deals with the provision of employment opportunities for children (ie those 18 or under) who are above compulsory school age, ie 16. Regulation 11 makes provisions for religious observance. Regulation 12 makes provisions for proper and adequate food to be provided. Regulation 13 provides for the purchase of suitable clothing.

Regulation 14 deals with arrangements to notify the local fire authorities of accommodation and facilities at registered children's homes and the expected adequate precautions in relation to fire risks, means of escape, detecting and extinguishing fire, etc.

Part III of the Regulations, applying to all types of children's homes, deals with administrative matters in relation to children's homes. Regulation 15 requires the maintenance of records, including the information as specified in Sch 2 to the Regulations, and provides that that information should be treated as confidential and shall be retained for the surprisingly long period of 75 years

---

15   SI 1991/890.
16   SI 1991/894.

from the date of birth of the child or 15 years from the date of his death, if he dies before attaining the age of 18. Regulation 16 provides that home owners should provide access to records to a guardian ad litem, ie an official guardian appointed in accordance with the provisions of the Children Act 1989, to look after the interests of children in litigation. Regulation 17 provides for further records to be kept, these records to be kept only for 15 years, except for menus, which are to be kept for only one year.

Regulation 18 requires the Regulations themselves and guidance given by the Secretary of State, under s 7 of the Local Authority Social Services Act 1970, to be kept at the home and made available to staff, children, parents, guardians and other relevant people. Regulation 19 provides for the notification of serious incidents at any registered children's homes to a variety of people, identifying the type of incident and the persons to whom notification must be provided.

Regulation 20 provides for the maintenance of a policy and procedure in relation to unauthorised absence from the home by children. Regulation 21 provides for the procedure in relation to absence from the voluntary or registered children's home of the person in charge. Regulation 22 provides for the accountability of those responsible for operating children's homes, if not the person in charge of the home, and contains provisions similar to those concerning absent owners of residential care homes or limited companies operating residential care homes, to ensure regular visiting and reporting as to the conduct of the home. This provides, in effect, a degree of self-regulation.

4.7.7 The 1991 Regulations and community homes

Although, for reasons already given, there are no regulations in relation to community homes, reg 22 does provide that the Secretary of State may give directions requiring local authorities and voluntary organisations to accommodate, in community homes, a child looked after by a local authority for whom no places are available, or to take action to ensure that the child is accommodated elsewhere.

4.7.8 The 1991 Regulations and voluntary homes

Regulation 24 provides the procedure for application for registration of voluntary homes and specifies, through Sch 4, the information that must be made available to the Secretary of State on submitting an application for registration of a voluntary home.

4.7.9 The 1991 Regulations and registered children's homes

Regulation 25 provides the procedure for application for registration of a children's home and identifies, through Sch 5, the information which is to be required from an applicant for registration. Regulation 26 provides for a discretion to limit the number of children to be accommodated in the home, as one of the conditions to be imposed. Regulation 27 requires the registered owner to notify, on annual review or any previous review, the local authority of changes that have occurred in the home, after the original registration.

Regulation 28 provides for inspection of registered children's homes (absent in relation to community homes and voluntary homes). Inspection must take place (inspections may take place as frequently as the authority thinks is appropriate):

(1)   before the application for registration is granted;
(2)   within one month after each anniversary of registration in relation to the review;
(3)   at least once more in each year.

Registration authorities may give notice of inspections to the person in charge except in the case of inspections carried out otherwise than on registration or review.

Regulation 29 provides for the procedure to be carried out by a registered owner should he wish the registration to be cancelled and, interestingly, provides a requirement to take action to provide alternative accommodation for children at the home. Regulation 30 requires at least one month's notice of a change in the person in charge in a registered children's home. This may cause difficulty in the event of termination of employment otherwise than by at least one month's notice. This point may need to be watched carefully.

Regulation 31 provides, by incorporating Sch 7, the particulars to be sent to the Secretary of State within 3 months of establishment of a voluntary home and annually. Regulations 32 to 34 require that local authorities visit children accommodated at registered children's homes as a separate obligation from the obligation and entitlement to inspect.

4.8   FOSTERING CHILDREN AND CHILD MINDING

4.8.1   Private arrangements for fostering

A child may be placed with foster parents by a local authority, voluntary organisation or privately. The Children Act 1989, Part X and regulations made thereunder govern the private placement of children with foster parents.

According to the Children Act 1989, a child is privately fostered if he or she is being looked after by someone other than a parent, relative or a person with parental responsibility, is not looked after by a local authority, and has been so looked after for more than 28 days.[17] There are a number of provisions exempting certain arrangements from being classed as private foster care.[18] Also, a person may not foster more than three children, although there can be exceptions.[19]

Local authorities are under a duty to promote and safeguard the welfare of privately fostered children in their area and to make sure that carers are given the necessary guidance.[20] A local authority must be notified not less than 6 and not more than 13 weeks before a child is received into private foster care

---

17   Children Act 1989, s 66(1).
18   Ibid, Sch 8.
19   Ibid, Sch 7.
20   Children (Private Arrangements for Fostering) Regulations 1991, SI 1991/2050.

by the private foster parent(s), the child's parent(s), any person with parental responsibility with knowledge of the proposed foster placement, and anybody else directly or indirectly involved with the placement. However, if a child is placed in an emergency, then the parties previously mentioned must notify the local authority of the placement within 48 hours. Such a notice must contain certain details and a local authority must also be notified when the child ceases to be in private foster care.

An officer of the local authority must visit children in private foster care every 6 weeks during the first year of a placement and every 3 months thereafter.[21] The officer also has the power to inspect premises where children are being or will be accommodated and any children there.[22] Requirements can be imposed on foster parents by a local authority, and written reasons for the requirements must be supplied.[23]

Certain persons are automatically disqualified from being private foster parents.[24] A person is also disqualified if he or she lives in a household with a disqualified person or where a disqualified person is employed. If a disqualified person wishes to foster a child then he or she must disclose the fact of disqualification to the local authority and the local authority may, if it considers it appropriate, consent to the proposed foster arrangement. It is an offence for a disqualified person to foster a child without local authority consent, although it is a defence if the person is disqualified by virtue of the disqualification of another person and did not know and had no reasonable grounds for believing that that other person was disqualified.[25]

A local authority can prohibit a person from privately fostering a child on the grounds set out in the 1989 Act. Such a prohibition can relate to an individual generally, the premises where such a child is or will be accommodated or, a specified child at a specified place. Such a prohibition must be cancelled by the local authority where it is no longer necessary and the local authority must give reasons in writing for the imposition of the prohibition.[26] It is possible for a prohibition to be imposed on a foster parent at the same time as a requirement. In such a situation, the prohibition will only become effective if the requirement is not complied with.

The 1989 Act sets out a large number of offences which can be committed in respect of private foster arrangements,[27] including failing to notify the local authority of private fostering. Private foster parents are given a right of appeal against local authority decisions in the Family Proceedings Court.[28] Such appeals must be made within 14 days of receiving notification from a local authority of its decision.

---

21 Children (Private Arrangements for Fostering) Regulations 1991, SI 1991/2050.
22 Children Act 1989, s 67(3).
23 Ibid, Sch 8, para 6.
24 SI 1991/2094, Children Act 1989, s 68.
25 Children Act 1989, s 70(1)(d).
26 Ibid, s 70.
27 Ibid, s 70.
28 Ibid, Sch 8, para 8.

4.8.2   Arrangements for fostering by local authorities and voluntary organisations

Local authorities have a duty on them to maintain and provide accommodation for children in their care.[29] One way to do this is to place children with foster parents.

Foster placements arranged through local authorities and voluntary organisations are governed by the Foster Placement (Children) Regulations 1991.[30] The local authority or voluntary organisation must approve any foster parent before placing a child with them. Each foster parent must have references from two people and the authority or organisation must interview both these people. Certain information must also be ascertained.[31] Approval for a foster parent can be restricted to a particular child or children, a specified age group or number of children and by any other circumstances.

A written agreement must be entered into with the foster parent and the authority or organisation. The suitability of the foster parent and household must be reviewed at least once per year. As with private foster placements, a person authorised by the local authority must visit children which that authority has placed at least every 6 weeks during the first year of the placement and every 3 months thereafter. Children placed by voluntary organisations must be visited by a local authority officer within 28 days of the placement and at least every 6 months thereafter. Obviously, visits should be made if certain circumstances arise. It is possible for a local authority to make arrangements for a voluntary organisation to discharge the authority's duties. In such a situation, the child must be visited by an officer of the authority as if he or she had been placed by that authority.

Authorities or organisations can terminate placements. A local authority must keep a register of approved foster parents in the area and must also compile case records in respect of each foster parent. There are different rules which apply to emergency placements.

4.8.3   Child minding and the provision of day care

The Children Act 1989[32] requires local authorities to keep a register of child-minders who use domestic premises and other persons who provide day care for children on non-domestic premises. In essence, child-minders look after children in their own homes and 'day care centres' or are providers of care in a discrete place designed for the purpose – perhaps better described as a 'nursery'. It is only necessary for a person to register if that person is looking after an unrelated child or children under the age of eight for more than two hours a day and child-minders are only required to register if they are receiving a reward for doing so. However, 'reward' is an expression which is much wider in meaning than remuneration or profit and embraces benefits of a non-

---

29   Children Act 1989, s 23.
30   SI 1991/910.
31   Children Act 1989, Sch 1.
32   Ibid, s 71.

financial nature. Most schools, hospitals and the like are excluded from the registration requirements, as are parents, foster parents and nannies.

There are detailed regulations and provisions relating to the making of applications for registration.[33] Details of the people who will be assisting or living on the premises must be provided and all applications must be accompanied by the appropriate fee. A local authority can refuse to register a person if it is satisfied that the person who will be looking after the child or children, or the applicant if the applicant is a child-minder, is not fit to do so or that any person living at or employed on the premises where the child or children will be looked after is not fit to be in proximity to them. Registration can also be refused if a local authority is satisfied that the premises where the children are likely to be looked after is not fit to be used for that purpose. The register must be kept open to the public and an applicant must receive a certificate when registered.

There are also provisions relating to disqualification from registration.[34] If a person is disqualified but wishes to be registered, he must disclose the fact of disqualification to the local authority which can then consent to the registration.

A local authority must impose on an applicant any reasonable requirements it considers appropriate in addition to requirements relating to matters set out by statute, which include the maximum number of children to be looked after, the maintenance and safety of the premises where they are to be looked after and the necessity to keep certain records.[35]

A local authority can cancel the registration of a child-minder or day care provider on a number of grounds.[36] The child-minder or day care provider must be given at least 14 days' notice in writing with reasons for the authority's intention to cancel their registration. A local authority also has the power to cancel, impose, remove, vary or refuse an application, or to remove or vary a requirement, and the same procedure as set out above must be followed. An applicant can object and if the local authority proceeds, the objector has a right of appeal to the court.[37]

However, in emergencies, a local authority can make an ex parte application to the court for an order to cancel a person's registration, or to vary or remove a requirement imposed, or to impose an additional requirement. The court will make the order if it is shown that the child is suffering, or is likely to suffer, significant harm. The order is effective immediately and the local authority must serve it on the registered person, along with the written statement of the authority's reasons which supported the application.

A local authority has the power to inspect premises where child-minding is taking place, or day care is being provided, at any reasonable time. This

33   Children Act 1989, Sch 9, para 1 and Child Minding and Day Care (Applications for Registration) Regulations 1991, SI 1991/1689.
34   Disqualification for Caring for Children Regulations 1991, SI 1991/2094; Children Act 1989, Sch 9.
35   Children Act 1989, s 72 and s 73.
36   Ibid, s 74.
37   Ibid, s 77.

contrasts with inspection of residential care and nursing homes where inspection may be at any time. Premises must be inspected at least once each year and there is a fee payable by the registered person for each annual inspection.[38]

A person child minding or providing day care in contravention of the Act will, unless certain circumstances prevail, be committing a criminal offence.[39]

4.9   REGISTERED HOMES TRIBUNALS

The provision for the establishment of the Registered Homes Tribunal is to be found in Pt III of the Registered Homes Act 1984 and the rules under which the Tribunal operates are the Registered Homes Tribunal Rules 1984.[40] The law relating to the constitution of panels constituting a legally qualified chairman and professionally qualified members are set out in ss 40 to 42 of the 1984 Act.

Section 43 of the 1984 Act makes statutory provision for the procedure at Registered Homes Tribunals; that is the source of the rule-making power of the Secretary of State, under which he has made rules, namely the Registered Homes Tribunal Rules 1984. It is interesting to note that the provisions of the Arbitration Act 1950 are specifically excluded by s 43(3), save to the extent that the rules are incorporated by the rules made by the Secretary of State under this section.

Accordingly, procedure at a Registered Homes Tribunal is governed by the rules made by the Secretary of State and not by rules as they apply to other courts, arbitrations or statutory tribunals. Common law principles of natural justice may, no doubt, be advanced, but general principles of procedural rules as they apply, for example, in High Court litigation do not apply to the Tribunal procedure.

Section 44 makes provision for the assignment of staff to the Registered Homes Tribunal and s 5 provides for the payment of members and the expenses of Tribunals by the Secretary of State.

4.9.1   Regulations

All appeals to a Registered Homes Tribunal lie against the decision of an authority. That decision, made under ss 15 or 33 of the 1984 Act (in relation to residential care and nursing homes and para 8 of Sch 6 to the 1989 Act, in relation to registered children's homes) concludes the registration authority's deliberation. Within 28 days, the aggrieved applicant or owner may appeal to the Registered Homes Tribunal. If he does so appeal, then the appeal is governed by the rules set out in the Registered Homes Tribunal Rules.

---

38   Children Act 1989, s 76.
39   Ibid, s 78.
40   SI 1984/1346.

The Rules are simple and logical. Rule 3 sets out certain procedural requirements in relation to the notice of appeal and requires the registration authority to send it to the Secretary of State. Rule 4 deals with the procedure for appointing the Tribunal when the notice of appeal is received. Rule 5 sets out the pre-hearing procedure in relation to the Tribunal. It is limited, intended to be simple and without some assistance from the parties and the Tribunal, largely unsatisfactory.

4.9.2 Time-limits

The hearing may not commence less than 42 days from the service of notice giving the time and place for the appeal. The registration authority must send a copy of its reasons for a magistrate's order, or reasons for its own decision, to the appellant not later than 30 days prior to the hearing. The appellant must serve grounds of appeal not later than 21 days before the hearing. Those are the limits of the pre-hearing procedural requirements.

Rule 6 deals with rights of audience. Rule 7 requires the Tribunal to sit in public. Rule 8 deals with the provisions relating to the adjournment of a hearing. Rule 9 deals with procedure at the hearing.

Rule 10 deals with matters relating to evidence. The general law of evidence applies. Note should be taken of r 10(2), which enables the Tribunal to receive in evidence documents or information which would not be admissible in a court of law. Rule 10(3) gives the chairman of the Tribunal (but not the parties) power to call for further information or reports.

Rule 11 deals with the decision and the manner in which the decision shall be communicated. Rule 12 deals with withdrawal of appeal. It is important to note here that the withdrawal of an appeal carries with it the inevitable loss of right to restore the appeal. Appeals should not be withdrawn lightly.

Rule 13 deals with hearing more than one appeal at the same time. Rule 14 concerns the right of the chairman of the Tribunal to extend time-limits. Rule 15 provides that the Tribunal may regulate its own procedure, thus conferring a degree of flexibility. The Schedule specifies the form for notice of hearing of a Registered Homes Tribunal appeal.

4.10 OFFENCES

Part IV of the 1984 Act specifies matters which are offences against the Registered Homes Act 1984. This Part is of great importance and has attained greater importance following the amendments to Pt III of the National Assistance Act 1948 by Pt III of the National Health Service and Community Care Act 1990 and particularly, the new s 26(1)(e) of the amended legislation:

> 'No arrangements may be made by virtue of this section with a person who has been convicted of an offence under any provision of:
>
> (a) the Registered Homes Act 1984 (or any enactment repealed by that Act); or
> (b) Regulations made under Section 16 or Section 26 of that Act (or under any corresponding provisions of any such enactment).'

As to relevant regulations made under ss 16, 26 and 27, it does not seem to the author that the omission of s 27 means that an offence against that section is necessarily saved from this Draconian measure (it is surely a 'corresponding' provision).

The sections list the offences:

(1)   section 46 – the offence of carrying on a care home business without being registered;

(2)   section 47 – the offence of failing to affix the certificate of registration and, whilst fixing a low level of fine, provides for a daily fine if the certificate is not affixed within such time as may be prescribed by the court;

(3)   section 48 – the offence of breach of conditions of registration (s 5(5) or s 29(4) of the 1984 Act);

(4)   section 49 – offences against the regulations made under the 1984 Act.

(5)   section 50 – the offence of representing premises to be a nursing home when they are not registered as such;

(6)   section 51 – the offence of obstructing registration authority officers in the course of inspection;

(7)   section 51(1) – the offence of obstructing officers in relation to the inspection of a residential care home, and s 51(2) provides for the offence of obstructing officers in relation to the inspection of a mental nursing home (offences concerning obstruction of officers in relation to the inspection of a registered nursing home are offences under the regulations made under s 27 of the 1984 Act).

Section 52 provides that, with appropriate evidence, directors and officers of limited companies who are prosecuted may themselves be prosecuted if it can be shown that they are directly responsible for the offence. Section 53 supplements the normal rules about who may bring criminal proceedings.

There are no changes in relation to residential care homes, but in relation to nursing homes, only the Secretary of State (ie the Health Authority) or a party aggrieved (whoever that may be) may bring a prosecution for carrying on a nursing home unregistered[41] or failing to display a certificate of registration.[42] An exception is that another party may bring a prosecution only if they have obtained the prior consent of the Attorney-General.

Local social services authorities may prosecute for breach of the provisions in relation to the obstruction of an inspection of mental nursing homes.

4.11 GENERAL MATTERS

Part V of the 1984 Act deals with various general matters, some of which are of significant interest:

---

41   Registered Homes Act 1984, s 23(1).
42   Ibid, s 23(6).

(1)   section 54 makes provision in relation to the service of notices under the Act to supplement the provisions that are made under the regulations;

(2)   section 55 provides some useful definition provisions (it is worth noting that the definition of mental disorder expressly incorporates conditions which might, by technical experts, be described as mental illness as well as mental handicap and that this reflects the definition in s 1 of the Mental Health Act 1983);

(3)   section 56 deals with the power to make regulations and the form in which regulations should be made;

(4)   section 57 deals with consequential amendments and transitional provisions;

(5)   section 58 deals, importantly, with the extent of the Act (the Act does not extend to Scotland or Northern Ireland and, in the absence of primary legislation, this cannot be extended to those areas; the Act does not extend to the Isles of Scilly unless the Secretary of State makes an order directing it so to apply; at the date of writing no such order has been made);

(6)   section 59 deals with the coming into force of the Act.

Chapter 5

APPLICATIONS FOR REGISTRATION

5.1 INTRODUCTION

This chapter examines the process whereby the applicant for registration secures a certificate of registration or notification of registration, as the case may be. The participants involved will be the prospective care home owner (or, in certain circumstances, the care home owner already registered) and the appropriate regulatory authority.

The application process will be discussed in relation to:

(1) residential care homes;
(2) nursing homes;
(3) registered children's homes.

The discussion involves:

(1) identifying the nature of the application, whether registration is a matter of right, subject to statutory restriction, or a matter within the discretion of the regulatory authority;
(2) where the authority is bound to grant registration, the grounds upon which registration may be refused;
(3) where the authority is not bound to grant registration, the matters which it may take into consideration;
(4) the material that an authority is entitled to receive in the course of an application;
(5) the material that an authority may reasonably require in order to enable it to decide whether or not it shall exercise any discretion as may exist.

5.2 THE APPLICANT

Whatever may be the position as to the authority's duty to register or discretion to register, no duty or obligation falls upon the authority until the applicant has made an application and, with that application, supplied at least such information as is required by statute or regulation. Without a properly completed application, it may be said that there is no application and the duty to register does not arise. Thus, the efficiency and speed of the process whereby an application will be considered are in the hands of the applicant.

Accordingly, two items are required:

(1) a formal application; and
(2) the information required to be provided by regulations controlling registration.

That required information is to be found.

(1)   in relation to applications for residential care homes, in Sch 1 to the Residential Care Homes Regulations 1984;[1]
(2)   in relation to nursing homes, in Sch 2 to the Nursing Homes and Mental Nursing Homes Regulations 1984;[2]
(3)   in relation to registered children's homes, in Sch 5 to the Children's Homes Regulations 1991.[3]

5.3   FEES TO BE PAID ON APPLICATION

In addition, the application should be accompanied by the prescribed fee. Registrations are not transferrable. Every application is an original application and a prescribed fee will be payable. The fee may vary as between situations where the application is for the first registration of a home or where the application is by an applicant for registration on transfer of ownership.

5.3.1   Residential care homes

The current fees are:

(1)   residential care home owner and controller: £840.00;
(2)   residential owner and controller (small home): £230.00;
(3)   residential care home manager not in control: £230.00.

In addition, every year, the person registered as being in control, ie the business owner, shall pay an annual fee computed by multiplying the maximum number of persons for which the home is registered to care by £41.00, or where the home is a small home, by £30.00.

5.3.2   Nursing homes

In relation to nursing homes, the current fees are:

(1)   on registration: £678.00;
(2)   on registration of change of ownership: £410.00.

In addition, the registered person shall pay an annual fee equal to the maximum number of patients for whom the home is registered to care multiplied by £22.00. Where the home does not provide overnight care for patients, the registration fee is £190.00.

In the first year of registration, the annual fee is payable within one month of first registration and, thereafter, the fee shall be paid not later than the day before the anniversary of a date one month after registration. Owners should note that the practice of registration authorities is to issue invoices in respect of registration fees on a regular basis – not always linked to the statutory days. This is a practice for which there is no statutory authority.

The regulations require payment of the annual fee and, accordingly, as a tenant should seek out a landlord to pay rent, then a registered care home

1   SI 1984/1345.
2   SI 1984/1584.
3   SI 1991/1506.

owner should seek out the authority and pay the fee, whether demanded or not.[4]

5.3.3   Children's homes

In relation to registered children's homes, the fee payable on application for registration, which shall accompany the application, is 'such reasonable fee as the authority may determine'. This gives a degree of licence to the authority to fix fees as it sees fit. As the fee must be reasonable, it must be set against reasonable criteria, such as measuring the cost of providing the service of registration and inspection of registered children's homes for the particular local authority, and dividing that figure by the number of prospective applications for registration and renewal of registration in each year.

There is no provision for annual registration fees. The reason is simple. All registered children's home registrations are reviewable annually on the basis that the registration shall only continue if the authority shall so decide – the test being that the authority must be satisfied that the home is conforming with the relevant requirements. Once again, a reasonable fee must be paid within 28 days from the date upon which notice is received.[5]

5.3.4   Imminent change in fees

It is proposed that all fees will be increased from 1 May 1998 to the following amounts (at the moment this is only a proposal for consultation, but one should anticipate that it will be effected):[5A]

PROPOSED FEE INCREASES

Residential care homes	Current fee (£)	Proposed new fee (£)
Initial registration fee	840	952
Change of ownership	840	952
Registration of Manager (where manager is not owner)	230	261
Annual fee per bed	41	46

4   Residential Care Homes Fee Regulations 1984, reg 3; Residential Care Homes Regulations 1984, reg 5; Nursing Homes Regulations 1984, reg 4(1) and Sch 1; Nursing Homes and Mental Nursing Homes Regulations 1984, reg 5 and Sch 3.
5   As a matter of practice, many registration authorities charge the same fees as for residential care homes.
5A   See Department of Health circular letter, 19 January 1998.

Small residential care homes	Current fee (£)	Proposed new fee (£)
Initial registration fee	230	261
Annual flat fee	30	34
Nursing homes	**Current fee (£)**	**Proposed new fee (£)**
Initial registration fee	678	952
Change of ownership	410	952
Annual fee per bed	22	46
Annual flat fee (nursing homes with no beds)	190	215

5.4 NATURE OF APPLICATIONS

The first issue for an applicant, for registration of a residential care, nursing or registered children's home, is to consider the nature of the application. The question will be:

'Is the application one which the Authority are bound to grant unless they are satisfied that there are reasons why the opportunity should be restricted, or is this an application within the sole control of the Local Authority?'

This is an important question and upon it may rest the decision to proceed with an application.

An application, the grant of which is within the discretionary control of the local authority, is an application the conduct of which cannot be influenced by the applicant. An application which the authority must grant, unless it can show reasons for refusal, is an application over which the applicant has more influence and in respect of which he may be able to predict the outcome and timing.

Whatever step the applicant takes, it must be remembered that the fee must be paid and minimum information supplied, as a condition precedent to making an application.

A surprising number of prospective applicants, critical of delay, are found not to have submitted a formal application. An application form is not required, but there must be a definite application accompanied by minimum information. No amount of discussions about possibilities of registration or potential requirements for registration amount to an application and applicants are disappointed and surprised to find that, where they have thought a procedure to have been started by discussion with an authority, in fact no process has been started because there has been no formal application, no information and, of course, no fee.

The fee is a once and for all payment and is not subject to any refund should the applicant seek to withdraw or should the application be refused. Furthermore, the fees for registration, being prescribed by regulations made by the Secretary of State, under statutory authority, there is no discretion as to increase, reduction or waiver save where the amount of the fee is not predetermined as with registered children's homes. An exception is that s 5(2)(a) of the 1984 Act provides specific discretion for registration authorities to waive registration fees (but not annual fees) in respect of small homes.

5.5 IS REGISTRATION MANDATORY OR DISCRETIONARY?

The problem, in each case, is solved by reading the statute and, where appropriate, any relevant regulations. Section 5(1) and (2) of the 1984 Act sets out the scheme:

'(1) An application for registration under this part of this Act shall be made to the Registration Authority and shall be accompanied by a registration fee of such amount as the Secretary of State may by regulations prescribe.

(2) Subject to Sections 9, 12 and 13 below, on receipt of an application for registration and of the registration fee, the Registration Authority shall register the Applicant in respect of the home named in the application and issue to him a Certificate of Registration.'

It will be seen immediately that registration is a matter of right, subject to the application of ss 9, 12 and 13.

Section 9 provides reasons which must be established if the authority is to have a discretion to refuse registration. Section 12 and s 13 provide for the procedure to be followed, either in granting registration in accordance with the authority's duty or refusing registration in accordance with such discretion as is granted.

Section 9, then, is the key and should be quoted in full:

'(1) The Registration Authority may refuse to register an Applicant for registration in respect of a residential care home if they are satisfied –
  (a) that he or any other person concerned or intended to be concerned in carrying on the home is not a fit person to be concerned in carrying on a residential care home;
  (b) that for reasons connected with their situation, construction, state of repair, accommodation, staffing or equipment, the premises used or intended to be used for the purposes of the home, or any other premises used or intended to be used in connection with it, are not fit to be used; or
  (c) that the way in which it is intended to carry on the home is such as not to provide services or facilities reasonably required.

(2) The Registration Authority may refuse to register an Applicant for registration in respect of a small home only if they are satisfied that he or any other person concerned or intended to be concerned in carrying on the home is not a fit person to be concerned in carrying on a residential care home, ie sub-paragraph (a) of sub-section 1 only is to apply to the small home.'

The authority is only permitted to refuse registration if one or more of reasons (a) to (c), or reason (a) in respect of small homes, is established.

The statute would seem to suggest that the process involves identifying one or more reasons within paras (a) to (c), or para (a) in relation to a small home, identifying the evidence that supports the reason, evaluating the evidence and then proceeding, if a permitted reason is found to exist, to exercise a discretion as to whether or not to refuse registration.

Doubt as to this proposition has been suggested in *Zaman v Lancashire County Council.*[6] The Tribunal took the somewhat narrow view that the word 'may' (which, in the author's view, clearly infers a discretionary permission to refuse as opposed to the usual course of mandatory registration) should be construed restrictively, upon the basis that Parliament could not have intended that, once the registration authority was satisfied on credible evidence that matters of unfitness arose, it should have a further discretion as to registration. There is, in the author's opinion, no logic to this argument.

No doubt, in many cases, the established unfitness will be such as to lead to the inescapable conclusion that the application should be rejected. However, had Parliament intended the result suggested by the Tribunal decision, it could quite easily have so provided by substituting for 'may' the words 'must' or 'shall'. There may be many circumstances where the authority establishes one or more matters which may be of a relatively insignificant nature, and which can be remedied in due course and which, on their own, indicate lack of fitness or a failure to provide services or facilities required. However, taking a broad view, considering undertakings to do work or works done, and character references, as well as the interests of residents or potential residents, it will be right to exercise a discretion to register, albeit subject to such limited conditions as may exist.

A failure to honour an undertaking on registration is likely to be the clear evidence of 'unfitness' in cancellation proceedings. Section 9 should also be read together with s 10 which provides for cancellation of registration, again on a discretionary basis. The first ground for cancellation of registration is the existence of grounds which will entitle the authority to refuse an application for registration. It seems barely credible that Parliament should have intended a discretion to exist in relation to cancellation of registration, but compulsion to exist in relation to refusal of registration under the same circumstances and using the same language, having a perfectly clear option to prescribe compulsion as with registration itself in s 5(2) of the 1984 Act.

It is suggested that, in considering an application for registration of a residential care home, the local authority as regulator operates a three-stage process:

(1)   identify that a proper application with full information has been supplied (this to be supplemented by such further information as the authority may reasonably require);

(2)   decide whether permitted reasons for refusal of registration arise;

---

6   Registered Homes Tribunal decision No 103.

(3)   then decide whether or not to exercise the clear discretion given by the statute.

The detailed reasons for refusal of registration will be considered after an examination of the nature of the application in relation to nursing homes and registered children's homes.

5.6   NURSING HOMES

The statutory basis for the grant of registration in respect of a nursing home is almost the same as that in respect of a residential care home, under Pt I of the 1984 Act.

Section 23(4) of the 1984 Act reads:

> 'Subject to section 25 below, the Secretary of State shall on receiving an application under sub-Section 3 above *[ie an application for registration of a nursing home]* register the applicant in respect of the home named in the application and shall issue to the applicant a certificate of registration.'[7]

Two points should be noted:

(1)   unlike Pt I, and possibly without any relevance, the obligation to grant registration is not made subject to the procedural review procedures which, in the case of nursing homes, appear in s 31 and s 32 of the 1984 Act, being the sections corresponding with s 12 and s 13 of the 1984 Act in respect of residential care homes;

(2)   an application for registration of a nursing home is treated in exactly the same way as an application for registration of a mental nursing home, save that in the case of registration of a mental nursing home, the application must state whether or not it is proposed to receive into the home patients who are liable to be detained under the provisions of the Mental Health Act 1983.

5.6.1   Secure patients

Interestingly, the applicant for the registration of a mental nursing home must decide, at the first stage, whether it is intended to care for secure patients and indicate that to the authority. It is not merely an option which is to be included in the application form.

For this, as well as other reasons, it is suggested that the owner of a registered mental nursing home cannot change category of patient to include patients liable to be detained under the Mental Health Act 1983 without preparing and launching a fresh application. The logic is that such a home for secure patients will be quite different in location, construction, staffing and operation. It seems unlikely that secure and voluntary patients would be mixed, for voluntary patients would then be required to participate in a secure regime.

---

7   Words in italics supplied by the author.

5.6.2   The obligation to register

Once again, in s 23(4), there is an obligation upon the Secretary of State (who has devolved powers to Health Authorities) that, upon receiving the application, he *shall* register and *shall* issue a certificate of registration. Thus, there is clear indication of a duty to register and the corollary of an entitlement to expect registration.

Registration may only be withheld upon matters contained within s 25. Accordingly, it is accepted law that in considering an application for registration, the registration authority, in determining the issue, may only take into account matters arising under s 25.

5.6.3   Conditions of registration

This is to be contrasted with the secondary function of the authority in imposing conditions of registration, whether mandatory or discretionary. The essential difference is that, in considering whether or not to impose conditions and if so, what conditions should be imposed, the authority can take into account any relevant material.[8]

Section 25(1) sets out the grounds which entitle the Secretary of State to refuse registration. The preamble follows the wording of s 9:

> 'The Secretary of State may refuse to register an applicant in respect of a nursing home or a mental nursing home if he is satisfied –.'

Once again, it will be seen that the permissive, as opposed to the directive, word 'may' is used in relation to the Secretary of State's position on the application. The position is suggested to be the same as that in relation to residential care homes and the author suggests that this is a discretion to be exercised by the Health Authority in the name of the Secretary of State, once the Health Authority is satisfied that one or more of the permissible reasons for declining registration are present.

The reasons are as follows:

(1)   lack of fitness on the part of the applicant or persons who are working or may work at the home;
(2)   lack of fitness in relation to the home itself, its staffing, or the way in which it is commissioned;
(3)   use or proposed use which is improper or undesirable;
(4)   that the home will not be in the charge of an appropriately qualified person, being a medical doctor or a qualified nurse;
(5)   that the appropriate number of nurses will not be on duty in the home from time to time.

Consideration needs to be given not only to the arguments as they stand in relation to the imposition of conditions of registration and/or impact upon decisions to cancel registration for breach of conditions, or lead to criminal

---

8   See *Isle of Wight County Council v Humphreys* [1992] COD 308.

prosecution, but also, in the context of consideration of an application for registration, as to whether or not prospective failure to meet such potential conditions disqualifies the applicant from the beginning. Quite clearly, such provisions may be disentitling requirements.

If an authority is concerned about the quality of the qualifications of the person in charge, or of the nursing establishment, it is clearly open to it either:

(1)   to grant registration, subject to conditions, retaining the right to prosecute for breach of condition, should a breach occur; or

(2)   to refuse to register at all.

Authorities will need to tread carefully, for if minded to refuse registration at the outset on the basis that such staffing conditions will not be met, the authority must:

(1)   ensure that the condition that it has in mind, when construed in accordance with the statute, is a proper and enforceable condition; and

(2)   be satisfied that there is clear evidence that such a condition will be broken.

In practice, it is difficult to see how evidence that would satisfy an authority that the staffing of a home was such as to indicate potential breach of proposed conditions of registration, would not also be evidence that the staffing proposed at the proposed home was such that the home was not fit to be so used, ie ground 2 may be used.

5.6.4   Problems with staffing levels

Early disagreements about staffing levels, where strongly held views may arise, may provide the authority with strong evidence of an expressed intention by the prospective owner to fail to comply with staffing conditions, or conditions as to the qualifications of a person in charge. In appropriate circumstances, enforced agreement to a staffing condition, against a background of disagreement about staffing levels, may in itself still provide the authority with sufficient doubt to justify refusing registration, rather than granting registration upon agreed conditions – there being at least a strong suspicion that the grudging acceptance will lead to less than complete compliance. Bearing in mind that the purpose of registration is to protect potentially frail and vulnerable patients in a home, refusal under those circumstances might well be justified.

Staffing is a tortuous and difficult issue in relation to an application. Home owners will not wish to engage or even identify prospective members of staff unless they are sure that the application for registration will be granted. Authorities will wish to know that staff of particular grades, qualification and experience are in place and will wish to know the identities of such persons, so that they can be as sure as possible that the particular nurses or nursing auxiliaries or other staff are appropriate. In relation to the information to be provided regarding an application for registration, the law provides authorities with the ammunition that they require. Full staffing establishments may be insisted upon by an authority before a registration certificate is issued. The suggestion that registration should be granted and then the owner, possibly with the authority's assistance, think about staffing, is wrong.

An example of how an applicant willing to provide proper staffing might still fail in his application would be where it is known to the authority that there is a shortage of appropriately skilled or qualified nursing or auxiliary staff in a particular location. The owner might be first class. The prospective home might be ideal, but if the authority's experience is such that, with the best will in the world, the home owner is unlikely to be able to attract suitable staff because supplies of such staff are not available, then that might entitle a refusal of registration.

Certainly, it would be argued that this view protects existing owners (as in the Isle of Wight with Mr Humphries) and discourages active competition. However, the authority's discretion to withhold registration if it is not satisfied that proper staffing establishments can be maintained surely entitles it to protect the frail and vulnerable clients and potential clients within such an area by avoiding over saturation of nursing home providers, leading to competition for staff and possibly to a position where a new applicant will only succeed by seducing staff from existing employers.

A good guiding principle to authorities in such circumstances is that it is better to prevent an applicant from being registered (if there are permitted grounds) than to take the soft option of registering and then having the more difficult task of cancelling registration when certain frail and vulnerable clients will have already become involved in care.

5.7   REGISTERED CHILDREN'S HOMES

The position with regard to registered children's homes is quite different and may be ascertained from sub-paras 4, 5, 6, 8 and 9 of para 1 of Sch 6 to the 1989 Act. It is proposed to take the paragraphs one by one with appropriate commentary. Such little established authority, as there is, about the registration or cancellation of registration of registered children's homes is contradictory.[9]

5.7.1   1989 Act, Sch 6, para 1(4)

This reads:

> 'If a Local Authority is satisfied that a children's home with respect to which an application has been made in accordance with this Schedule complies or, as the case may be, will comply –
>
> (a)   with such requirements as may be prescribed; and
> (b)   with such other requirements (if any) as appear to them to be appropriate.
>
> They shall grant the application either unconditionally or subject to conditions imposed under paragraph 2.'

---

9   See decisions of Registered Homes Tribunal *Hett v Gwynedd County Council* (No 214) and *Bryn Alyn Community Ltd v Clwyd County Council* (No 231).

It will thus be seen that there is a different regime. Whereas, for residential care homes and nursing homes, registration and the issue of a certificate are an obligation of the authority, only to be refused if permitted reasons exist, in relation to registered children's homes, the authority is only required to grant the application if it is satisfied that the children's home complies or will comply with such conditions as may be prescribed and such other matters as appear to it to be appropriate.

Accordingly, the registration authority is given a carte blanche. Not only must it be satisfied of matters that are prescribed, but it is also permitted to exercise its judgement without limit over any other matters that appear to it to be appropriate. The application for registration of registered children's homes is, therefore, a lottery.

The authority does have to identify detailed reasons for refusal, but that may be merely to express itself dissatisfied in relation to certain requirements. The authority's obligation seems to be to identify the requirement about which it has concerns and express itself as dissatisfied. The authority does not seem to have to argue a case to justify its reasons for dissatisfaction. It is clearly for the applicant, the prospective home owner, to satisfy the authority.

The author suggests that the requirements which concern the authority must be requirements which are germane to the application and which are reasonable for a reasonable authority to consider. Furthermore, it is clear that the authority must act reasonably in considering whether or not its concerns are satisfied. However, if those concerns are not reasonably satisfied, the authority, it is suggested, merely has to express the fact of dissatisfaction and cannot be limited in arguing its case, either in relation to the application or subsequent appeal.

5.7.2 1989 Act, Sch 6, para 1(5)

'Before deciding whether or not to grant an application, a Local Authority shall comply with any prescribed requirements.'

This provision merely sets out that the authority must follow the requirements of regulation before deciding the application, ie an application cannot be rejected out of hand because the authority decides that it will refuse the application on one particular point, for example the character of the applicant. An applicant must have his application considered fully in relation to the requirements.

5.7.3 1989 Act, Sch 6, para 1(6)

'Regulations made for the purpose of sub-para 5 may, in particular, make provisions to the inspection of the home in question.'

The regulations are contained in the Children's Homes Regulations 1991.[10] They do, in fact, provide for inspection of the home so that an authority will not be entitled, referring back to para 5, to reject an application on the basis of the character of the applicant without viewing the home.

---

10 SI 1991/1506.

5.7.4   1989 Act, Sch 6, para 1(8)

'If the Authority are not satisfied as mentioned in sub-paragraph 4, they shall refuse the application.'

It should be noted that there is an obligation to refuse and not a discretion to refuse. This, of course, contrasts sharply with the arguments in relation to s 9 and s 25 of the 1984 Act. Furthermore, the obligation to refuse arises out of a lack of satisfaction rather than being satisfied that grounds for unfitness exist.

Accordingly, in relation to a registered children's home, the authority are obliged to refuse to register if the applicant has not persuaded it that all is in order. This contrasts sharply with an obligation to register and a discretion to refuse only if the authority are satisfied that permitted reasons for refusal exist in the case of residential care and nursing homes.

5.7.5   1989 Act, Sch 6, para 1(9)

'For the purposes of this Act, an application which has not been granted or refused within the period of twelve months beginning with the date when it is served on the Authority, shall be deemed to have been refused by them and the Applicant shall be deemed to have been notified of their refusal at the end of that period.'

This is indeed a curious paragraph which has already given and will give rise to serious problems. It does, however, emphasise the author's submission about the burden of proof in relation to applications for registered children's homes.

If an application has not been determined within 12 months, then the application is deemed to be refused, opening the door to appeal. The only conclusion that one can draw is that the authority shall be assumed to have determined it was not satisfied that all reasonable requirements in relation to the proposed children's home had been fulfilled.

The applicant then has a right to appeal. As a part of the appeal process, the authority will have to give a statement of its reasons for the decision. However, in this case, it has made no decision. The decision to refuse has been assumed. The authority thus has no reasons, even if it is obliged to give reasons, which might, at the highest, be to indicate those matters upon which it was not satisfied. A correct and tenable position for an authority faced with such an appeal, where its refusal has been assumed in accordance with the provisions of Sch 6, is to indicate that, as a consequence of the rule of law, the authority is not satisfied that all reasonable requirements had been satisfied by the applicant, leaving the applicant before the Tribunal to make a complete case on all relevant issues.

The debate then moves to the Registered Homes Tribunal, whose jurisdiction is set out in para 8 of Sch 6 to the 1989 Act and is in like terms to the jurisdiction in relation to both residential care homes and nursing homes, under Pt III of the 1984 Act. The Tribunal will have to hear the application from the applicant as a re-hearing of the application to the authority.

There is, it is suggested, no compulsion whatsoever upon the authority to assist the applicant's case. Accordingly, inconvenient and time consuming as it may appear, the correct course is for the applicant to present his case and expect challenge and cross-examination from the Tribunal and, indeed, from the respondent authority without any limit upon subject matter. The grounds of appeal, therefore, will need to be fulsome, covering every aspect of the application. An appeal will not be limited to matters canvassed by the grounds of appeal and the authority or the Tribunal of its own motion may raise with the applicant any matters whatsoever which arise. The Tribunal will then be considering such requirements for registration as they consider to be appropriate. They will be exercising, upon an appeal by way of re-hearing, the jurisdiction originally granted to the authority. It follows that very experienced professional members of Tribunals may be required.

Whether or not this curious result was intended by Parliament, the author does not know.

5.7.6   Burden of proof in appeals concerning children's homes

It is the issue of the burden of proof that has caused difficulties in those appeals heard by Registered Homes Tribunals.[11] This issue is central to the conduct of any judicial or quasi-judicial proceedings. Such proceedings are concerned with determining disputes of fact and law by adversarial procedure. The principle is that any proposed activity which is to the disadvantage of a person should be justified by the proposer, ie he who asserts a claim against another must prove it. Such proceedings are to be contrasted with Public Enquiries, the rationale of which is to establish the truth about an issue without, as a part of that procedure, purporting to determine issues as they affect individuals. In such a process, identifying the issues to be proved and, by whom they must be proved, is crucial.

As all decisions are taken by the authority, it is convenient if the authority is placed in a position of having to prove facts to justify its decision. However, mere convenience does not settle the matter. Where jurisdiction is conferred by a statute, it will be the statute that indicates where the burden of proof lies, ie balancing the interests of owners who wish to conduct business and residents who are vulnerable and in need of the protection of the law.

In terms of residential care and nursing homes, the burden of proof clearly lies upon the authority and that is now accepted as the practice of the Tribunal. In *Hett's* case,[12] the Tribunal seems to have simply decided (perhaps by way of assumption) that the same position should apply to children's homes. In the *Bryn Alyn* case,[13] more powerful submissions were made and the Tribunal appears to have been persuaded, correctly in the author's view, that the burden of proof lies upon the appellant. If Parliament has decided that those who wish to register children's homes should face greater difficulties than those who apply to register residential care and nursing homes, it is not for the Tribunal to change the law.

It is accepted that the authority must give reasons for refusal but those reasons do not limit the Tribunal jurisdiction and may be in general terms, for

---

11   *Lyons v East Sussex County Council* (1988) 86 LGR 369, (1988) 152 JP 488, CA.
12   Registered Homes Tribunal decision No 214, *Paul Hett v Gwynedd County Council.*
13   Registered Homes Tribunal decision No 231, *Bryn Alyn Community Ltd v Clwyd County Council.*

example 'we were not satisfied that the appellant should be registered'. At most, identification of areas where there was a failure so to satisfy the authority might be indicated. If the appellant fails to satisfy the Tribunal that he should be registered, the authority need not call any evidence.

In *Bryn Alyn*, the Tribunal sought to distinguish the 'legal' and 'evidential' burden of proof so as to suggest that the burden could switch between the parties during the course of proceedings. This is to confuse a rule of law with practice. Evidence, once adduced, may be seen to have discharged the burden of proof, unless rebutted. This cannot dilute or dispel the rules as to the party upon whom the legal burden lies throughout the case: 'The legal burden is the burden of proof which remains constant throughout the trial; it is the burden of establishing the facts and contentions which will support a party's case . . .'.[14]

Accordingly, appellants have to prove their whole case for registration of children's homes to the extent that issues are not conceded by the authority. It may be that, whilst individual matters are satisfactory, the picture presented as a whole is not satisfactory, so as to justify registration.

Observations as to the evidential burden lying upon the authority, where they rely upon evidence of past performance to justify refusal,[15] should be approached with caution. In decision 321, the Tribunal was approaching the issue pragmatically, the authority voluntarily accepting the burden of proof with the appellant's consent and for technical reasons the case was really a cancellation case.

5.7.7 Annual review of registration of a children's home

Registration of residential care homes and nursing homes is permanent, subject to cancellation. Whether or not this is the result achieved in relation to registered children's homes, once again is the subject of debate.

The relevant provisions to consider are para 3 and 4 of Sch 6 to the 1989 Act. Whilst the whole needs to be read and will be the subject of comment, the operative provisions are para 3(2) and (3) and para 4(3).

It seems that the time for considering cancellation of registration of a registered children's home is on an annual review. The person carrying on a registered children's home may seek to cancel his registration at any time. If a school ceases to be a school within the meaning of the 1989 Act the registration may be cancelled at any time.

Registration may be cancelled at any time on the grounds that the person carrying on the home has been convicted of an offence under the regulatory procedure or if any other person has been convicted of an offence in relation to the home. Curiously, this is restricted to offences under Sch 6 to the 1989 Act or the regulations made thereunder. However, it is suggested that other serious criminal offences would themselves necessarily trigger offences under the appropriate parts of the 1989 Act. Authorities facing such situations should remember to encourage or institute prosecutions under the 1989 Act, as well as

---

14   *Halsbury's Laws of England* Fourth Edition Vol Evidence p 11, para 13 *et seq.*
15   Registered Homes Tribunal decision No 321, *Berry and Berry v Calderdale Metropolitan Borough Council.*

other criminal law offences, in order to be in a position to cancel registration otherwise than on annual review.

Sub-paragraph (2) of para 3 reads:

> 'the responsible authority for a registered children's home shall at the end of the period of 12 months beginning with the date of registration, and annually thereafter, review its registration for the purpose of determining whether the registration should continue in force or be cancelled under Paragraph 4(3).'

There is a positive duty upon the authority to review the registration with a view to a result, ie should the registration continue or should it be cancelled. There is a clear duty upon the authority and the authority can be forced to comply with this duty and be forced to comply with it properly. One applicant to enforce such an obligation might be the registered owner, although the consequences of review might not be acceptable to him. Another interested applicant might be central government or another relevant public authority, those representing children, or relatives of children accommodated in the home. Failure to comply with the duty to review the children's home registration annually could have serious effects on those accommodated in the home, particularly if standards are less than satisfactory.

Sub-paragraph (3) of para 3 reads:

> 'if on any such annual review the responsible authority is satisfied that the home is being carried on in accordance with the relevant requirements, they shall determine that subject to paragraph 4 the registration shall continue in force.'

The relevant requirements are those in Pt VIII of the 1989 Act and regulations in relation to registered children's homes, ie the Children's Homes Regulations 1991 (as may be amended). There is an unfettered discretion to impose conditions as the authority thinks fit.[16]

Relevant requirements include requirements under Pt VIII, which itself incorporates Sch 6,[17] suggesting that the reasonable requirements include any other requirements as appear to the registration authority to be appropriate under sub-para (4) of para 1 of Sch 6.

The authority is under a clear obligation to determine that the registration should continue. It cannot leave the matter hanging in the air. The word is 'shall' and not 'may'. Following the decision that requirements are met and the mandatory decision that registration could continue, the authority is obliged to notify the owner and to notify the owner of the reasonable fee payable.

Continued registration is subject to payment of the fee within 28 days from the date of notice. As it is a condition of continued registration that the fee should be paid, non-payment of the fee irreversibly triggers cancellation of the registration. There would appear to be no flexibility and registered children's homes owners should be very careful.

There will clearly be debate as to whether a fee is reasonable. The matter is in the hands of the authority. It will be an imprudent owner who risks loss of registration by challenging the fee by way of non-payment. If such a challenge

---

16   Children Act 1989, Sch 6, para 2(1).
17   See ibid, s 63(11).

were to arise, it is suggested that the challenge and reasons for the challenge should be outlined, the fee should be paid and the authority should be warned of an application for judicial review of its decision to determine an unreasonable fee. Demanding an unreasonable fee must surely be any unreasonable under the 'Wednesbury' principles. In practice, such cases will be rare but the greater risk will be losing registration irreversibly by missing the time-limit.

Sub-paragraph (3) of para 4 reads:

> 'if on any annual review under Paragraph 3 or at any other time it appears to the responsible authority that a registered home is being carried on otherwise than in accordance with the relevant requirements they may determine that the registration of the home should be cancelled.'

The Parliamentary draughtsman has here left an interesting dilemma. The decision to renew registration is a mandatory decision, following satisfaction with requirements. The decision to cancel registration is a discretionary requirement following evidence of conduct outside relevant requirements. Why should Parliament have provided a situation where, although there is compulsory review, compulsory renewal and notification, if there is perceived dissatisfaction with performance, the cancellation is merely discretionary.

There can be no real distinction between satisfaction under para 3(2) and an appearance that a home is not being conducted properly in accordance with para 4(3). As there is an obligation to continue registration if the authority is satisfied, surely there must be an equivalent obligation to cancel if the authority is not satisfied. In this area, perhaps the Tribunal's substitution of 'shall' for 'may' might be a more persuasive argument.[18]

5.8   THE REGISTRATION PROCESS

The registration process will be an important period, both for the registration authority and the applicant, ie the prospective home owner. The applicant should not overplay reliance upon his entitlement to registration. The registration authority should not be overawed by the entitlement to registration and should not shrink from carrying out its duties correctly in the process of ascertaining, first, whether or not grounds for refusal exist and then determining whether or not the discretion to refuse should be exercised.

The conduct of a home owner is one of the vital ingredients in establishing unfitness to operate. So, with an applicant for registration, his conduct during the registration process is a good pointer to how he will conduct himself as a registered owner.

An applicant who prepares his application swiftly and efficiently, supplying all relevant information, with explanations for omissions, and approaches the process in a professional and polite manner, is an applicant who is likely to be a good home owner. An applicant who muddles the application, fails to understand questions, dodges difficult areas, withholds information from the authority, delays, complains about the authority's delay

---

18   Registered Homes Tribunal decision No 103, *Zaman v Lancashire County Council.*

when the circumstances are within his control and generally presents an unprofessional image, is an applicant who will appear as one who is likely to be unsuitable for the rigours of operating a regulated care home business.

Authorities should not shrink from declining to register persons who present themselves in that way, as they should not shrink from seeking to cancel the registration of those who, despite producing technically efficient homes, conduct themselves in relation to the authority, their staff, clients or those with whom they have to do business in a way that is less than professional or less than satisfactory, given the intimate nature of the business of operating a registered care home.

The registration process is a golden opportunity for the authority to organise itself so as to judge objectively and fairly whether the applicant is suitable to operate a care home. If in doubt, the advice is to decline registration. The applicant will then have a right of appeal to the Registered Homes Tribunal. The authority should, however, ensure that it acts on the basis of reasoned judgement based upon evidence, and certainly not simple prejudice.

In the course of operating a registered care home, the registration authority will be entitled to expect frequent disclosure of information about the business of the care home, during the course of the inspection process. The authority must be able to rely upon the owner as a person of integrity, whose word can be trusted and accepted.

Any action which is seen to mislead the authority will be regarded seriously. Tribunals tend to regard misleading the authority in relation to applications for registration, whether the issue arises in connection with a refusal to register or a cancellation of registration after the dishonest conduct has been revealed, as very serious. Non-disclosure will be regarded more seriously in many cases than the gravity of that which has been concealed.

In *Alatan v Wandsworth Health Authority*,[19] one of the applicants, the husband, was found to have failed to disclose a criminal conviction which his wife had received. The offence, whilst appearing serious, itself does not seem to have impressed the Tribunal as being a crucial reason in up-holding a decision to refuse registration. What was overwhelming was the applicant's failure to disclose something which was not necessarily serious. The Tribunal took the view that the if the applicant failed to disclose such a matter, how could the authority trust him to disclose important matters during the course of the operation of a regulated care home.

5.9 PERMITTED REASONS OR GROUNDS FOR REFUSAL OF REGISTRATION

This section examines the permitted reasons for refusal of registration, other than staffing conditions in relation to nursing homes, which have already been discussed. In relation to refusal of registration of registered children's homes,

---

19 Registered Homes Tribunal decision No 159.

there is no discernible limit to the matters which may be considered germane for consideration in respect to such applications.

In most cases, the grounds to be established are negative in nature. The exception is the impropriety or undesirability of use of the home, which requires a positive view.

5.9.1   'Fit' or 'unfit' – or 'suitability'?

Issues relating to the grounds for refusal of registration are bedevilled by the word 'fit'. Is he a 'fit' person or not a 'fit' person? Are premises 'fit' or 'unfit'? Are staffing levels 'fit' or 'unfit'? When considering what is meant by 'fit', the first point to note is that neither an authority nor a Tribunal is ever required to decide who or what is fit. What is to be established is 'unfitness'.

Every case depends upon its individual circumstances and, therefore, attempts at exhaustive definitions are redundant. An attempt to define an unfit person is a waste of time. The question will always be whether that person or situation is unfit, to be judged against the particular facts of the particular case.

Second, authorities and Tribunals are only required to determine what is not fit and not what is fit. It is suggested that what is not fit is something that can only be recognised from an examination of particular facts, using the experience and expertise of the decision-maker.

A distinguished expert in the English language, when asked to define a tea pot, stated that he found the task difficult but that he knew a tea pot when he saw one. The Tribunal, when offering indications for criteria of fitness, recognised that it was probably easier to recognise the quality of fitness than to attempt to define it.[20] It is suggested that attempts to provide exhaustive definitions of fitness should be abandoned in favour of the 'tea pot' approach.

Time may be spent identifying qualities such as 'trust', 'integrity', 'uprightness', 'honour' and 'truthfulness', as the Tribunal has attempted.[21] The problem that seems to have arisen is the pejorative tone with which some attempt to interpret the concept of fitness. The *Concise Oxford Dictionary*, 1991 edition defines 'fit' as:

(1)   well adapted or suited;
(2)   qualified, competent worth;
(3)   in a suitable condition;
(4)   good enough;
(5)   in good health or athletic condition;
(6)   proper, becoming, right.

It is suggested that a simple approach is the correct conclusion. In essence, 'fit' equals 'suitable'. If 'fit' is synonymous with 'suitable', all that the regulator or Tribunal is asked to decide is whether the applicant or the premises or the staffing, whatever issue may be at stake, is suitable for the purpose in hand.

---

20   Registered Homes Tribunal decision No 76, *Eleanor Azzopardi v London Borough of Havering*.
21   Ibid.

Suitability, less pejorative than fitness, simplifies the task. The Tribunal approved this approach in *Oldfield v Stockport Health Commission.*[22]

Indeed, if some circumstances associated with an application for registration of a regulated care home suggest 'unsuitability', no one would argue against a refusal of registration. Similarly, tests of unreasonableness, impropriety and undesirability are, essentially, objective tests of suitability for the conduct of the regulated care home business.

It is to be assumed that those responsible for making decisions about registration, whether the officers or members of a public authority or members of the panel constituted for a Registered Homes Tribunal, have knowledge and experience relevant to considering issues about the regulation of care homes. Such persons can be relied upon to use their common sense and their experience to make sensible decisions about suitability (including unreasonableness, impropriety and undesirability).

It is, it is submitted, unsatisfactory, that lawyers or others should seek to limit words which are in themselves limitless. The categories of fitness or suitability or propriety should never be closed and will certainly change as society evolves and, develops its attitudes to regulated care. More sophisticated facilities, greater training for staff, greater opportunity for qualification for those who aspire to operate care home businesses will all mean that that which is suitable or fit today, may be unsuitable or unfit tomorrow.

Care home businesses must keep pace with the times. One often hears the cry from an owner whose registration is criticised: 'If I were fit in 1966 how can you say that I am not fit now?' The answer is depressingly simple. Nothing stands still and a home that does not develop or develops in a way that is inappropriate will cease to be fit. It will cease to be suitable for its task.

5.10 CRITERIA FOR REASONS TO REFUSE REGISTRATION OF RESIDENTIAL CARE AND NURSING HOMES

This book will not attempt an analysis or even a listing of various circumstances that have or have not been found to be fit or unfit, unreasonable, undesirable or even suitable. Readers are referred to the Registered Homes Tribunal decisions. There are helpful notes compiled by Richard Jones in the *Encyclopedia of Social Services and Child Care Law,*[23] but all of such are only anecdotal and do not address issues of principle. Each case must be looked at upon its own facts and any attempt at demarcation is to risk attempting to create rules in an area where goal posts move so very frequently.

5.10.1 Fit persons and persons concerned or employed

Section 9(1)A of the 1984 Act reads, in relation to residential care homes:

'That he or any other person concerned or intended to be concerned in carrying

---

22 Registered Homes Tribunal decision No 289.
23 Sweet & Maxwell, 1993.

on the home is not a fit person to be concerned in carrying on a residential care home.'

Section 25(1)(a) of the 1984 Act provides, in relation to nursing homes:

'that the applicant or any person employed or proposed to be employed by the applicant of the home, is not a fit person (whether by reason of age or otherwise) to carry on or be employed at a home of such a description as that named in the application.'

Little distinction exists between the two. Those, in addition to the applicant, to be considered are those concerned in residential care homes or nursing homes.

An appellant sought to argue that 'employed' should have a restricted meaning limited to circumstances amounting to employment as a matter of law. The Tribunal had little difficulty rejecting such an argument.[24] What was clearly intended by Parliament was that the decision-makers should be concerned to evaluate the character, experience and aptitude of those persons who are going to be principally involved in carrying on the home. Artificial distinctions created by rules of law dividing workers into categories separated largely by methods of payment and taxation can surely have no place in such a consideration.

The nursing home requirement introduces the idea of age as being a category for fitness, but then widens the category with the words 'or otherwise'. Arguments that 'otherwise' should be construed 'ejusdem generis' must surely fail. There can be no limit as to the categories of fitness. The consequence of arguing the categories of fitness are limited to those similar to age would be to leave a position whereby an authority or Tribunal were obliged to grant registration for someone unfit by reason of character, habit or behaviour simply because age and matters that might be considered similar to age are not against the applicant.

Clearly, age is an appropriate category for determination of fitness, but it helps re-emphasise the author's point that fitness is not necessarily synonymous with pejoratively negative criticism. An old person may be of excellent character and considerable experience, but their physical capacity may simply not be sufficient to meet the demanding tasks of operating what may be a significant business over a seven day a week, 24 hour a day schedule.

It is submitted that the additional words in relation to nursing homes add nothing to the general principles. The issue for those making a decision is to decide if the applicant or those associated with the applicant are unsuitable to carry on the business. Put in that way, whilst difficult to complete, the task is simple to formulate.

Although it has been suggested that issues of fitness of the person cannot relate to issues that overlap into issues relating to the premises or method of operation of the home, the author would suggest that that must be wrong.[25] It has been held that the decision of fitness of the person was the all important

---

24 Registered Homes Tribunal decision No 39, *Jutlandia Limited v Plymouth Health Authority.*
25 Registered Homes Tribunal decision No 191, *Taylor and Taylor v East Sussex County Council.*

and all embracing issue, thus releasing an authority that had failed to plead allegations of unfitness of premises and staffing from difficulties faced by having limited itself to the unfitness of the person.[26] The reasoning was that viewing the operation of care homes, or other care homes, controlled by the same owner is an excellent way of judging suitability or fitness of the owner to be registered, in respect of the premises in question in the particular appeal.

In *R v Humberside County Council, ex parte Bogdal*, Brooke J was persuaded that it could well be that the way in which a home was operated might influence decisions about fitness of the person concerned.[27] Indeed, it is surely inappropriate to determine any issue in relation to registration of a care home without addressing the question of fitness of the operator. Can an applicant who presents premises which are unfit be himself regarded as fit? Is an applicant, who suggests unfit staffing levels, a fit person to carry on a home? Is an applicant who proposes to carry on a care home so as to provide unreasonable facilities, or a nursing home in an improper or undesirable way, a fit person? The answer is surely no.

The lesson of *Crammer* is that authorities should not fall into a potential trap by failing to plead unfitness of premises, staffing or unreasonableness of operation. Authorities should always consider unfitness, ie suitability of the person, unless they are satisfied that the applicant and those associated with the applicant are fit and the issues in question do not relate to fitness of the person.

It is suggested that, on a true analysis, very few cases will be appropriate for refusal of registration where the applicant is perceived to be a fit or suitable person.

5.10.2   Fitness of premises and establishment

Section 9(1)(b) of the 1984 Act reads:

'that for reasons connected with their situation, construction, state of repair, accommodation, staffing or equipment, the premises used or intended to be used for the purposes of the home, or any other premises used or intended to be used in connection with it are not fit to be used.'

Section 25(1)(b) of the 1984 Act provides:

'that, for reasons connected with the situation, construction, state of repair, accommodation, staffing or equipment, the home is not, or any premises used in connection with the home are not fit to be used for such a home.'

Again, there is no material difference between the two provisions. Wide ranging issues covering the entire potential operation of a registered care home are covered. These will be the issues that are identified in the course of the registration process. During such process, it may be that issues which arise under one or more of the heads identified under the two paragraph b's may be remedied. However, it may be that a matter, such as the location or the construction of a particular home, is such that it cannot be remedied.

It may be that a home is located in a place, or is constructed in such a way as to be so unsuitable that it cannot be conceived as being appropriate for

---

26   Registered Homes Tribunal decision No 138, *Crammer v Harrogate Health Authority*.
27   [1992] COD 467.

registration. The authority may consider that the staff proposed for a home, by background, inclination and philosophy, are wholly unsuitable to conduct that type of home. Equipment may be inappropriate, although, in the absence of a refusal by the prospective owner to update it, it is likely that this defect may be overcome.

The attitude of the applicant at and during the course of registration, to criticism of these issues, may reveal reasons for the unfitness of the applicant which did not appear at first light from the application.

5.10.3   Re-registration

It will be remembered that each and every change of ownership involves a fresh application for registration by the transferee. Where difficulties arise in a transferee's application, both the transferor and the transferee are likely to be critical of the authority if the authority is unwilling to, as it were, re-register a home which has been in operation for some time. The authority should be sensitive, but not over-sensitive, to such criticism.

Re-registration is an opportunity for review. Proposals to cancel registration may run into difficulties particularly if criticisms regarding standards of care are not great when the authority comes to consider the interests of existing residents.

On re-registration, the authority will in effect, by registration, be re-endorsing facilities and standards in a particular home. It is one thing to defer to cancel registration, it is quite another to re-register. That said, it is suggested that a reasonably objective observer will expect that, if a home's operation is unchallenged as to standards in the hands of one owner, then it is reasonable that that owner and any prospective purchaser would expect the home to be re-registered without difficulty, provided the new applicant satisfies the criteria of fitness.

Over enthusiastic demand from an authority for change may amount to an unwelcome intrusion in the negotiating process between transferor and transferee. To avoid such criticism, authorities should be astute during the inspection process to ensure that they are drawing owners' attention to standards which are falling or standards which are being superseded by changes in facilities within the care business generally. This will lighten the load when difficulties over re-registration by a transferee emerge.

However, authorities will appreciate that they are charged with ensuring that proper standards for registered care homes apply. The fact that poor standards may have been permitted, perhaps for a long period of time, is no reason why such poor standards or bad behaviour should continue to be tolerated. Re-registration presents an opportunity for re-consideration and if an authority is satisfied that there are serious issues concerning standards it should not be shy to stand up and require change, on pain of refusing re-registration.

5.10.4   Unreasonable, impropriety and undesirability

Section 9(1)(c) of the 1984 Act provides:

> 'the way in which it is intended to carry on the home is such as not to provide service or facilities reasonably required.'

Section 25(1)(c) of the 1984 Act provides:

> 'that the home is or any premises used in connection with the home are used or proposed to be used for purposes which are in any way improper or undesirable in the case of such a home.'

Here, the thinking diverges and, it is suggested, one has two quite different situations. In relation to residential care homes, the mischief clearly aimed at is a method of carrying on the home that fails to provide services or facilities reasonably required.

Section 9(1)(c) may well be seen as subsumed in s 9(1)(a) and (b) and particularly s 9(1)(b). It is indeed difficult to see how a home that was judged fit by reference to its premises and establishment and fit in respect of the character of its proposed operator could be unfit on the basis that the use of that establishment by a fit operator was found to be unreasonable to achieve the desired aim. Such an operator, seeking to deliver care unreasonably or being seen to deliver care unreasonably, cannot surely be accepted as 'fit', even if 'fit' on other grounds.

In relation to nursing homes, a different test arises. This is one of impropriety and undesirability. The distinction here is clear. The applicant and the establishment may be first class, but the use or proposed use may be seen as improper or undesirable.

It is impossible to attempt to guess at or catalogue circumstances that might arise. Perhaps first class premises that were used to provide nursing or out-patient surgery, procured on a private basis by dubious sales practice, might meet such a criteria. Perhaps a home, whilst established in a first class manner, operated in accordance with curious and potentially damaging philosophies and theories, might be seen as improper or undesirable. The operation of a home in such a way that clients were encouraged to provide for or pay fees at such levels or in such ways as to deprive themselves of substantial assets, or evidence that experience in a particular home showed an unacceptably high level of gifts either before or at death, to the owners or staff, might amount to such evidence. The categories cannot be limited.

Clearly, a different mischief is envisaged by the statutory draughtsman for nursing homes than for residential care homes. If such concerns arise in relation to residential care homes, then an authority wishing to prevent operation would have to rely on s 9(1)(a) unfitness of the applicant or persons concerned, as opposed to having the fall-back provision of s 9(1)(c), for nursing homes.

It should be noted that, in relation to small homes, the sole criteria for an authority in refusing registration is the s 9(1)(a) reason of unfitness of the person.

For the reasons argued previously, it is suggested that this distinction is illusory. As unfitness of the person is or should be the overriding criteria for refusing registration and if it will be judged, as it surely must be, by reference to evidence of conduct in the operation of such homes, then the restriction is merely a restriction to a category which itself embraces the excluded categories.

It is submitted that it is not possible to argue that category (b) and (c) criteria in the case of a residential care home are excluded from category (a) criteria simply because of this restriction in relation to the small homes, introduced by the Registered Homes Amendment Act 1991 some 7 years after the 1984 Act had been passed.

5.11   THE REGULATORY REQUIREMENTS

The regulations in question are:

(1)   Residential Care Homes Regulations 1984;[28]
(2)   Nursing Homes and Mental Nursing Homes Regulations 1984;[29]
(3)   Children's Homes Regulations 1991.[30]

The issue is to determine from the regulations information required to be submitted as part of an application for registration. The information which is required or may be sought by an authority is not limited to that provided in the regulations.

In relation to residential care homes, the basic requirements are set out in the regulations. Regulation 2 of the Residential Care Homes Regulations 1984 introduces the information, which is to be found in Sch 1. In regard to nursing homes, reg 4(2) of the Nursing Homes and Mental Nursing Homes Regulations 1984 introduces the requirements to be found in Sch 2. The Children's Homes Regulations 1991, reg 25 introduces Sch 5, which outlines particulars to accompany applications for registration of such homes.

A study of the regulatory requirements will show that, such is the detailed information required, it is inevitable that the prospective home will have been constructed, equipped and staffed before any application is able to proceed. Staff must be in place, construction completed and equipment in place before an authority may be required to consider any application. Many will consider that it is unreasonable and impractical for an applicant to invest in equipment and hire staff unless it is known that registration will follow. Financiers may be reluctant to extend credit unless registration is ensured. Staff may be unwilling to commit to employment unless a job is guaranteed.

However, registration is a licence to commence business forthwith. The Secretary of State has clearly decided in favour of preventing the commitment of registration until all is in place. The alternative would be to risk approval of businesses which, by their own admission, were not ready. Applicants must appreciate that this is the law. Fairness to potential owners is not an issue. Protection of the vulnerable is the issue of paramount importance.

It is not intended to review the regulations, in so far as they provide requirements to be part of an application for registration, item by item. Readers are referred to the regulations in detail.

---

28   SI 1984/1345.
29   SI 1984/1578.
30   SI 1991/1506.

5.12   THE INFORMATION REQUIRED TO ACCOMPANY A PROPER APPLICATION

Before an authority is required to register a registered care home, it must be satisfied that the home is ready to operate in all respects. The issue of the certificate of registration, or notification that registration has been granted in the case of a children's home, is a licence to trade. Registration does not pre-date the provision of appropriate and adequate facilities.

It is now suggested that an application for registration may itself not properly be delivered until the vast majority of items required for the home to operate shall have been delivered or precise information be available.

Many authorities, acting pragmatically, process applications before homes have been constructed, repaired, refurbished, staffed or commissioned. That is an excellent practice which should not be discouraged. However, those taking a purely legal view will argue that the authority is concerned to process applications properly made. Regulations made by the Secretary of State specify when applications are fit for consideration.

Considerable public resources, in terms of time and money, will be devoted to such applications, which may not even be proper applications as they are incomplete. Authorities who are concerned about particular applications may find it helpful to insist on precise supply of all the information which has to be supplied by applicants for registration in order to determine that the application is in order.

5.12.1   Staff

Under all the regulations, applicants are required to identify specifically categories of management, care and nursing staff who will be employed in the particular homes. Prudent applicants will not wish to employ, engage or even offer employment or engagement to staff until they know that registration has or will, with certainty, be granted (there may be no certainty about registration until the certificate or notification is actually issued).

It will be difficult, if not impossible, in most cases to identify staff as required by the regulations. It seems in order for an authority to decline further to process an application until all important staff positions have been identified and candidates, who have accepted appointment, have been identified. The authority will not be able to determine the application until this information is supplied, for the authority will wish to consider, in respect of all such staff who are to be concerned or employed in the particular home, whether each and every one of such staff is fit to hold such a position.

From the applicant's point of view, it is not until all such information has been supplied (whether upon the official form published by the authority or otherwise) that the applicant can be sure that he has lodged an application properly. It is not until this information is to hand that an applicant will be able to make any serious complaint about delay in the processing of the application.

In the case of serious delay, if an applicant were minded to seek a prerogative order of mandamus to compel an authority to make a decision in relation to a registration application, such application would not succeed unless the applicant were able to show serious delay following the submission of a properly completed application with all information required by statute.

There are other issues than staff, but staff is the most obvious. It is indeed an onerous obligation upon an applicant to have to identify all relevant staff at the start of the application process rather than immediately before registration.

5.12.2   Criminal convictions

It has always been regarded as good practice that the registration authority should enquire of applicants for registration as to details of any criminal convictions. This is one of the circumstances to which the Rehabilitation of Offenders Act 1974 does not apply, by virtue of the Rehabilitation of Offenders Act 1974 (Exceptions) Order 1975.[31] Following the Registered Homes Amendment Act 1991, the information required to be supplied in relation to an application for registration for residential care homes and nursing homes was extended specifically to include details of convictions and spent convictions, and the applicant is told that he is not entitled to shelter behind the protection of the Rehabilitation of Offenders Act 1974.

Amendments to the Children's Homes Regulations in October 1997 extend the requirements for disclosure of criminal convictions to registered children's home (applications and operations). Procedure, now included within the regulations, in relation to residential care and nursing homes, was outlined in Department of Health Circular No LAC(91)(4) and was, in any event, already regarded as a matter of standard and good practice by all registration authorities in relation to applications for registration.

The reason behind the formalisation of the requirements was the inclusion of so-called small homes within the registration requirements, with effect from 1 April 1993. Concern about those with criminal convictions operating small homes was one of the moving causes behind bringing small homes into the ambit of regulation. It was said that operators with criminal convictions were operating small homes, which did not then require to be registered. As with so much of the legislation bringing small homes into regulation, it appears to have proceeded upon a misunderstanding. Simply requiring small homes to be registered would have meant that authorities would have pursued the usual police checks and enquiries as to criminal convictions. The regulations do now authorise authorities to carry out police checks without the consent of the applicant. Prudent authorities would previously have asked for consent to a police check. Anyone who refused would surely be seen as 'unfit'. There was no need for specific regulations to underline what was already practice, but with the information now included within the information required to be supplied, it can be said that the onus is now switched to applicants to supply the information rather than upon authorities to request it. That said, a request for information about criminal convictions, together with warnings as to the non-applicability of the Rehabilitation of Offenders Act 1974, formed a standard part of registration

---

31   SI 1975/1023.

applications and a standard section in the most commonly used application forms.

The existence of criminal convictions can be said to be the single most common cause for refusal of an application for registration. One would not expect a person who has a criminal conviction to be regarded as suitable to carry on a care home except in exceptional circumstances.

It is only in rare cases that Tribunals have allowed appeals by those with criminal convictions against a refusal for registration. It is difficult to discern any general principle, save that each case must be looked at on its own merits. It certainly cannot be said to be the law that any criminal conviction of any type operates as an automatic disqualification from registration for the operation of a regulated care home. However, it can be said that the presence of such a conviction will place considerable obstacles in the applicant's path.

Any attempt to conceal, withhold or delay disclosure of the conviction will almost certainly lead to a refusal of an application.[32] It may also be said that, if the nature of the offence, no matter how trivial, impacts directly on the operation of the care home business, then it is unlikely that such an application will be successful. Convictions for fraud, or offences of violence clearly fall into these categories. Nevertheless, those whose convictions lie in the past and who have displayed exemplary evidence of rehabilitation over a considerable period of time may reasonably expect such convictions, whilst noted and always within the authority's knowledge, to be disregarded and not unnecessarily to hinder an application which has merit. Those cases where a Tribunal has excused non-disclosure or 'understood' non-disclosure by reference to poorly drafted information requests are in a minority and should not be regarded as persuasive, whoever forgets a criminal conviction?

It is thought that evidence of the commission of offences under the Registered Homes Act whether or not the subject of conviction, ie offences committed and identified in a notice but not repeated, would prove an immense obstacle to registration. If an applicant has in the past so transgressed as to break the rules of registration, it will, in the author's submission, be virtually impossible for him, with any credibility, to argue that he remains other than an unfit person to carry on a regulated care home.

In one Tribunal case, an applicant had been convicted, in the past, of operating a residential care home with numbers of residents in excess of the maximum provided by her certificate. Although there was no evidence of abuse, maltreatment or lack of care, the Tribunal found that it was appropriate to cancel her registration upon the ground that she was not fit to remain registered. Failing to observe the cardinal condition of registration (ie the maximum numbers within the home) was thought to be the strongest possible indication of unfitness to carry on such a home.[33]

5.12.3 Categories of client

Information required to be supplied with an application for registration includes information as to the types or categories of residents or patients to be

---

32 Registered Homes Tribunal decision No 159, *Alatan v Wandsworth Health Authority*.
33 Registered Homes Tribunal decision No 118, *Piper v Birmingham City Council*.

accommodated. Such provisions, in relation to registered children's homes, are limited to identifying particulars of the children in residence on the date of the application. Such a requirement was clearly introduced taking into account the novel nature of the registration and that all applications, at the beginning, would be for registrations of homes which had previously been operating on an unregistered basis. A new home starting from scratch will obviously have no children in residence. If it has, then the owners will have committed an offence and, almost inevitably, be found unfit to be registered (unless currently only accommodating three children, or less).

In relation to residential care homes, para 3(g) of Sch 1 to the 1984 Regulations provides that the numbers, sex and categories of residents should be identified by reference to a category letter. Regulation 9 of the Nursing Homes and Mental Nursing Homes Regulations requires that the type of home be identified. Regulation 10 requires that not only the number of patients for whom the home is proposed to be used be identified, but that there be a distinction between different categories and age ranges.

The author suggests that the requirement to supply information as to type and categorisation of the patient, as a matter of course, during the pre-registration process, is not to be confused with the imposition of conditions of registration at the time when registration is granted. The requirement to supply information is so that the authority shall be fully informed in making a decision and, in particular, making a decision as to whether or not a discretionary condition as to category of residents should be imposed.

Failure to impose a condition of registration, following disclosure of the categories of residents proposed to be accommodated, cannot be taken as an imposition of condition by implication. However, as with other cases of misleading behaviour, fraud or concealment, introducing patients into a home who are different from the categories indicated in the application may clearly change the basis upon which the application was granted and registration issued and may lead to a justified proposal to cancel registration, upon the basis that circumstances have changed; that the home owner or applicant are no longer fit; that the premises as staffed or commissioned are no longer fit; or that the applicant is not fit because of the way in which he appears to have misled, or failed to inform the authority.

5.12.4   Other information

A study of the provisions of the appropriate schedules of the relevant regulations will reveal a wealth of detailed information, some obvious and some slightly obscure, required as part of a registration application. The information required by the regulations does not limit the information which the authority may seek, but is merely an indication of the minimum information required to make a reasonable decision. The authority, in coming to a decision, will be expected both by the applicant and by others, but in particular the general public, to ask such questions as may be appropriate as to elicit the information necessary to make a sensible decision.

There can be no categorised limit to the extent or detail of information that may be required by an authority before it can make a decision upon an application for registration. Requests for irrelevant information may lead to an allegation that the authority has broken its statutory duty in relation to process of the application for registration, which may lead to litigation or a complaint to an Ombudsman, being the Local Government or Health Services Commissioner.

5.12.5   Obscure or irrelevant requests for information

It is important that the main issues are extracted so as both to be understood and distilled into such form upon which the authority can make a proper decision. However, the authority should not be over concerned that applicants be troubled with seemingly irrelevant material, but rather that over sensitivity to the applicant's convenience may cause the authority to register without having discovered or considered a relevant issue.

5.12.6   Other issues to be taken into account by the authority

There can be no limit on the material that an authority may consider appropriate to examine, in relation to an application for registration. The approach must be if in doubt ask for information. Many authorities take the view that, whilst their powers may be limited, there is no reason why they should not probe extensively and request information. When resistance is encountered, then the reasons for resistance will be analysed.

In one case that went to the Local Ombudsman, authorities were criticised for requesting medical reports on directors of a company who would not be concerned in the day-to-day management of a company. Officious concern for long spent criminal convictions perhaps might be an example of irrelevant material, but the authority is attempting to establish the information, first, to assist it in performing its duty of registration and, second, to enable it to take a proper view of any material that may be relevant to that duty or, if appropriate, in exercising a discretion to refuse registration.

There follows a list of issues which, in the author's experience, may arise and may be of importance.

Police checks
Whilst it is clearly established by practice and by the various regulations that applicants should be requested and should give information as to their criminal convictions, that in itself may not be sufficient. Applicants should, it is suggested, be required to consent to a check by the police. Applicants who have been frank and full in their disclosure will have nothing to fear, and those who have not would at least be given a final opportunity to consider their position before inevitable exposure of non-disclosure.

Aspirations of the applicant
One of the most important questions to ask of an applicant is: 'why do you want to become registered to operate a care home?'.

Motives in applying for a care home registration may be all important. The answer will be illuminating and, whilst it may not be determinative of the issue, applicants who express interest and concern for care of vulnerable groups will emerge; but if those applicants show a lack of knowledge or experience or aptitude for coping with the problems required in caring for or supporting those in need, so that their aspirations do not meet the reality of their ability, their applications may be in difficulty.

Similarly, whilst not closing the door immediately, if applicants indicate that their interest in the business of operating a regulated care home is related to making a profit as a primary consideration, this may serve as a warning for a registration authority.

Applicant's experience

Many of the matters upon which the applicant is required to supply information will touch upon his experience in life. Authorities should be astute to explore and investigate the full extent of an applicant's experience, particularly where applicants are individual applicants or applicants operating in partnership. The situation may be less important for the directors of limited companies who will not themselves have day-to-day control of the management of the particular business.

Financial resources

Financial resources create sticky problems. Applicants, naturally, are concerned that their financial position is a matter of confidentiality. This should not necessarily impact upon the registration authority's decision. Registration authorities are rightly concerned to ensure that applicants have sufficient resources and those resources should include sufficient working capital to service what is very often substantial capital borrowing, to acquire or build businesses and to pay the operational costs of the business. Both the applicant and the authority will be in some difficulty if the applicant has insufficient resources to provide for the needs of the patients.

It has been said that it is better to refuse registration than for an authority to find itself in the position of having to cancel registration as a result of the applicant-turned-owner's inability to deliver services.

The author's view is that a middle course must be steered through these positions. It is inappropriate for an authority to expect to receive the most detailed financial information, but sufficient working capital must be available to satisfy the authority that the applicant is able to deliver a service.

An authority does not require to know the identity of lenders. However, many lenders will wish to be introduced to the authority. An authority does require, in the author's submission, to know the extent of monies being borrowed to fund the acquisitions or development and to show that sufficient income remains after providing for repayment of capital and interest to meet the proper and reasonable costs of providing a service. If an applicant indicates that the needs of the business will be met from resources derived from sources outside the income generated by the business, it is not unreasonable to seek broad information as to the identity of those sources and guarantees that the sources will remain available to the applicant.

Applicant's business capabilities

The operation of a regulated care home is a business. In the past, it may have been seen as a vocation and the relatively easy availability of public grants to support clients has suggested that applicants needed to concentrate less on standard business acumen skills. With the change in 'Community Care' implemented from 1 April 1993, if those distinctions were ever valid, then their justification will be seen to be diminishing.

Applicants should be questioned about their policy in relation to marketing, their understanding of the needs of client groups for care and the anticipated requirements of the growing business.

5.13 ROLE OF THE APPLICANT

Applicants will appreciate that they are entitled to registration subject to the authority's discretion to refuse, or in the case of children's homes, that they have the problem of persuading an authority with an unfettered discretion that their plans are suitable to be incorporated into a registered children's home. The role of the applicant should be seen as one of attempting to assist the authority to discharge its duty with maximum speed and minimum inconvenience.

The applicant should not approach registration on a confrontational basis. The more confrontation, the more likely are applicants to raise doubts as to their character and thus doubts as to their fitness to carry on a home. Relationships with the authority are vital. Registered owners often find themselves the subject of proposed cancellation as a result of inability or unwillingness properly to co-operate with the regulatory authority in the regulatory process.

Sensible applicants will prepare their application having taken advice about the law, the regulations and the practice. They will complete an application form, incorporating all the information required by the regulations, and such further information as the applicants consider to be helpful to the authority in assisting the authority in making a decision; which is then the more likely to be favourable to the applicants and much more likely to be made with the speed that the applicants will consider appropriate.

Applicants should remember that their conduct in the course of an application will be one of the yardsticks by which the authority judges personality, character and business ability. That in itself, rather than detailed responses to requests for information, may have a significant effect upon the authority's judgement on issues such as fitness.

Applicants should be sufficiently experienced to know where the application will meet difficulties. Applicants should be aware of national practice and of the authority's locally established view of practice, even where that may differ from the applicant's view or from established national views.

Sensible applicants will meet such issues head on and address the concerns within the application, rather than hoping that the authority will overlook any difficulties.

5.14 ROLE OF THE AUTHORITY

The authority is the appointee either of Parliament or of central government to process the application for registration on a local basis. It is not an adviser to the applicant in relation to the application, and should avoid appearing to give guidance and support to an application.

Some applications may take months or years. Principles of policy and practice may change. An authority exposes itself to risk if it indicates that it will grant registration in respect of certain facilities only for the applicant to find expectation dashed because policies or practices which have been sustained have changed.

An authority which encourages an applicant to refurbish, develop or construct a home to a certain standard only to refuse to register it later because of changes in practice may be exposed to an action for damages based upon the tort of negligent misstatement. Such an action would face difficulties. Authorities will not usually be exposed to liability in tort if the registration process is conducted in accordance with legal limits, but if the officer embarks on a course outside the limited role of regulator and creates a special relationship upon which the applicant relies, cost and expense wrongly incurred as a result of such reliance may found a claim for damages for which the authority is vicariously liable.[34] Such a situation often arises where applicants or architects or other professional advisers of applicants seek an authority's approval for particular plans and specifications.

No home is fit for registration until it is built, furnished, commissioned and staffed. Any indication of approval should be made quite clearly on the basis that plans are considered appropriate for registration in accordance with current law and practice and the current policy of the particular authority, but all plans are subject to review when prospective homes are inspected prior to registration, having been constructed and commissioned.

Some authorities have developed a stamp for plans in terms similar to the following:

> 'Approved in principle, but subject to reconsideration and final approval on final inspection for registration after the buildings and facilities shown in these plans and/or specifications have been constructed, furnished and commissioned.'

In the registration process, the regulator or authority's position is to wait, question and review. The authority is not an initiator of action. It is for the applicant to get its material in order and to bring the application to the authority in a form which is sufficiently full to enable the authority to make a decision.

It is not for the authority to tell the applicant where there are gaps in information. Naturally, the authority will wish to be helpful, but an authority should not be required to spend considerable time endeavouring to educate each applicant into how an application should be presented. Failure to present an application in an appropriate form may be indicative of lack of fitness or suitability to be registered.

An authority is only required to make a registration decision once all information is available and once the unit is ready to operate. If authorities are pressed to make decisions earlier, inevitably some information will be unavailable, or buildings or facilities will be incomplete. Injudicious pressure from applicants for early determination of registration applications can only lead to disappointment when the applications are rejected. Once rejected, the

---

34 *Hedley Byrne & Co v Heller & Partners* [1964] AC 465; *Welton v North Cornwall County Council* [1997] 1 WLR 570 (CA).

applicant's opportunities are for appeal to the Registered Homes Tribunal or if that time is lost, for reapplication.

5.15 RESTRICTIONS ON RE-APPLICATION

In relation to residential care homes and nursing homes, there are no restrictions on the time or frequency of re-application for registration following failed applications. Applicants should, however, be aware that most lawyers practising in the field consider that the process of registration is one of on-going review through the registration process, past the decision of the authority and up to the decision of the Tribunal. Accordingly, it is the author's view that, if an application for registration failed before the authority because facilities were not yet in place or seemed to be inadequate, an appeal would probably be allowed if those criticisms had been corrected in the period between authority decision and Tribunal hearing.

The position is not the same in relation to registered children's homes. Paragraph 9 of Pt I of Sch 6 to the 1989 Act makes it clear that, from the effective date of determination of the decision for refusal of registration or cancellation of registration of a registered children's home, the applicant or owner is not entitled to make a further application or application for re-registration until the expiry of 6 months commencing with the effective date.

With regard to cancellation, it is clear that the restriction is in respect of registration of the home in question. In relation to refusal of registration, the restriction is on a further application. Future Tribunals and courts may have to determine whether or not that restriction is on all applications in relation to registered children's homes or applications in relation to the particular home. Logic does not seem to suggest that an applicant refused registration of a registered children's home would have an equitable cause for complaint if he was banned for 6 months from making further applications in relation to other homes or prospective homes.

5.16 VARIATION OF REGISTRATION CONDITIONS

By variation of registration is meant variations of the conditions attaching to registration, from time to time. There will always be at least one condition of registration, ie the mandatory condition as to the maximum number of persons to be accommodated or kept within the home.

The 1984 Act makes provision for applications for variations of condition of registration in respect of residential care homes or nursing homes. However, there is no provision for an appeal against the rejection of such an application. The procedural provisions of Sch 6 to the 1989 Act are drafted in virtually identical terms to the provisions of ss 12 to 15 and ss 31 to 34 of the 1984 Act.

Whilst the matter has not arisen in practice, there is no reason to suppose that it will be argued successfully that there is any opportunity for an applicant to appeal against a refusal to vary conditions of registration in respect of a registered children's home. Perhaps this might be argued more strongly as, within a registration of a registered children's home, the authority has the power to impose such conditions as they think appropriate without limit, as opposed to the more restricted field in relation to residential care homes and nursing homes.

The authority does, in all cases, have power to initiate variation of condition of registration. It does not have to entertain an application for variation of conditions of registration. This was determined in the leading case of *Coombes v Hertfordshire County Council*.[35] Mr Coombes wished to extend his residential care home. He had constructed an extension and extra rooms were available. He applied to Hertfordshire County Council to vary conditions of registration. Increases in size of residential care homes did not commend themselves to Hertfordshire County Council, who declined to entertain his application. Mr Coombes appealed to the Tribunal. The authority argued successfully that there was no procedure for an applicant to challenge a refusal to vary conditions of registration and, accordingly, there was no jurisdiction for the Tribunal to hear the appeal.

5.16.1   Procedure for increase in number of persons accommodated

The owner makes an application to re-register the home. Out of an abundance of caution, the owner may make the application in a different name, ie adding partners, seeking to change operation to a limited company, joining in a spouse, or by some other method. In the author's view, a care home owner is entitled to make an application for re-registration of the home as a whole. The process will be one of re-registration and the new applicant will have to pay a full registration fee and annual fee thereafter. Most owners regard such charges as a relatively small sacrifice compared with what is at stake in having capital assets capable of business operation but which cannot be exploited due to lack of a registration certificate.

Once the application is a full application for re-registration, then not only must the authority consider the application, but, it is submitted, this is no different from any other application for registration. Not only must it be considered, but it must also be granted, unless permitted reasons within s 5 or s 25 are sustained. The open field for conditions of registration in relation to registered children's homes would suggest that only a very confident businessman would seek to increase registered numbers at a children's home without the concurrence of the regulatory authority.

Owners may reasonably expect that if they are operating homes in good standing with the authority, it is reasonable to suppose that there will be no sustainable objections to their operating larger homes. Such may not necessarily follow. The authority may consider that the owner is competent to manage a home of the current size, but that if size is increased, competence will be an issue. Furthermore, it may be that the authority is tolerating inadequate accommodation within the existing care home. Extension may

---

35   Registered Homes Tribunal decision No 115, *Coombes and Coombes v Hertfordshire County Council* (1991) 89 LGR 774.

provide the opportunity for the authority to phase out inadequately sized accommodation or shared accommodation. A home with four double rooms, operating in an area where the authority favours only single rooms, should approach such an extension with caution. It may well be that there are very good reasons why the shared accommodation is inadequate. Construction of an extension of four more single rooms may not necessarily advantage the owner, unless the shared accommodation is so criticised that the authority is likely to seek to reduce the number of persons who may be accommodated. It is a disaster, in terms of capital expenditure, to build an extension only to find that the number of persons who may be accommodated does not increase. Such a situation occurs frequently in practice.

Whilst it is right to say that an authority will be hard pressed to justify refusing registration for the numbers proposed by an applicant simply on grounds of policy, if the actual physical attributes of the accommodation, particularly shared accommodation, can be shown, on sustainable grounds, to be inadequate, then the authority is not only likely to restrict numbers on registration but has reasonable prospects of sustaining that position on appeal. In determining the issue as to conditions to be imposed as opposed to the fact of registration itself, the authority is not limited in the legitimate issues which it may take into account – including its own policies.[36]

Decisions to extend should never be made without considering the context of the authority's likely response to applications for variation of registration. A hostile authority will at best delay and at worst frustrate the purpose of the application, which may have been funded from borrowed capital. That funding, if not serviced by increased income, is likely to place the care home operation in jeopardy.

5.17 DISTINCTION BETWEEN APPLICATION AND CANCELLATION OR VARIATION

The procedure for application is remarkably similar to procedures for variation and cancellation at the instigation of the authority. The only significant difference is that cancellation or variation can only be instigated by the authority. Application can only, obviously, be instigated by an applicant, ie the prospective owner.

However, after the initiation of the particular process each follows the same course and, in the context of the different procedures for residential care homes and nursing homes as opposed to registered children's homes, the same procedures, with the same burdens of proof, apply.

5.18 THE DECISION PROCESS

The procedure for a decision by the authority follows a common form whether the issue is an application for registration, a proposal to vary conditions of

---

36   See *Isle of Wight County Council v Humphreys* [1992] COD 308.

registration, or a proposal to cancel registration (in the latter case, save where the cancellation is taken via the emergency route for residential care home and nursing homes). The procedure is identical and follows identical statutory wording in Pt I of the 1984 Act, Pt II of the 1984 Act and Sch 6 to the 1989 Act.

In relation to registered children's homes, there is no power to seek urgent cancellation of registration; references to such power are omitted from the procedural sections.

The procedures are to be found:

(1)   residential care homes – ss 12 to 15 of the 1984 Act;
(2)   nursing homes – ss 31 to 33 of the 1984 Act;
(3)   registered children's homes – in paras 5 to 7 of Sch 6 to the 1989 Act.

Any authority proposing to take such action needs to study the procedure in detail. It is simple, but it is very easy for mistakes to be made. There is no substitute for following the provisions of the Act line by line.

The common procedure follows this form:

(1)   notice of proposal;
(2)   an opportunity for and the receipt of representations from the owner;
(3)   a decision by the authority.

5.18.1   Notice of proposal

In relation to the proposed refusal of an application for registration, the notice must be in writing and it must:

(1)   either indicate that the application is granted as requested, or is granted subject only to agreed conditions; (in these cases no further formality to the notice is required for obvious reasons) or
(2)   give notice that the authority proposes to refuse the application; or
(3)   give notice of proposal to grant the application subject to conditions which are not agreed.

In the two latter cases, the notice must give the reasons for the proposal. Most importantly, the notice must (see ss 13, 32 of the 1984 Act and para 6 of Sch 6 to the 1989 Act) give notice that the disappointed applicant or owner has the right to make representations to the authority about the issue, orally or in writing, and that he should indicate whether or not he proposes to make such representations within 14 days.

5.18.2   The need to give reasons

Much debate is centred upon the need to give reasons. The author is of the opinion, not shared by all, that an authority proposing a course of action should be in a position to give its reasons and the evidence which sustains those reasons at the time when the notice of proposal is issued.

Submissions to Tribunals that authorities are bound by the evidence supporting reasons presented with the initial proposal for refusal of registration, or indeed cancellation, have met with no success. Tribunals favour the view that, whilst the registered care home remains in operation, the subject is constantly developing and authorities have the opportunity to supplement, expand and develop reasons and even to rely upon matters that have come to light after the service of the initial proposal.

However, it makes sense that, where reasons are known, these should be identified in the fullest and most particularised detail at the first opportunity for formal communication with the applicant. The reasons should be supported by the evidence upon which the authority relies. It will not be possible to keep such evidence secret forever. Production of further evidence will, in accordance with the rules of natural justice, delay the opportunity to make the decision.

Further, the authority will then be ready for the subsequent procedures. The applicant will know the position. The Tribunal and, indeed, members of the authority, before the Tribunal, will see the issues from an early stage and have greater confidence in the approach of the authority's officers.

Where information is to hand and evidence has been gathered, there can be no justification whatsoever for not making it available. This is a matter of principle in accordance with the rules of natural justice, or simply a matter of common sense. Many Tribunal hearings and disputes have collapsed because authorities have provided minimal reasons at the outset, only fleshing these out with detail and serving supporting evidence days before a substantial Tribunal hearing.

Very often, appellants to those Tribunal hearings decide to withdraw their appeals when they see the strength of the evidence. Surely, it is likely that they might have withdrawn earlier had they known the full extent of the case. They would certainly have received advice from their lawyers and been in a better position to judge their own actions, even if they chose to rely upon the entitlement to trade up until the last minute.

Full details of reasons make it easier for the applicant to prepare sensible and full representations. The purpose of the procedure is to enable the authority to come to a decision, having understood the case put upon its own behalf by its own officers and having received representations which may well meet that case. The procedure is not a procedure whereby the authority is being asked to rubber stamp the decision of officers. Nor should it be seen as such either by officers or members of the authority. The authority is the decision-maker and, as such, should be fully informed.

Some take the view, wrongly, that reasons can be identified by simple recitation of sections of s 9 and s 25 of the 1984 Act. Grounds for refusal of registration are identified in s 9 and s 25. Sections 12 (5), 31(5) and 5(5) of the 1984 Act and Sch 6 to the 1989 Act all provide that the authority shall give reasons for a proposal. It is submitted that the permitted grounds are simple limitations upon the type of reasons that may be given. To require reasons to be stated, as a matter of right for the applicant, is not simply to require general grounds or headings for reasons. The applicant, and indeed the authority making a decision, will require to know the substance of the reasons in order to be able to make a real and fair decision.

To state without giving reasons that applicants should not be registered because they are not fit persons to be registered is wholly insufficient to enable any reasonable authority to make a decision or any reasonable applicant to make sensible representations.

5.18.3   Representations

The opportunity to make representations is often misunderstood. A notice of proposal is not valid without indicating the opportunity for representations. All that is required, within 14 days, is a simple indication as to whether or not the applicant wishes to make representations. If that indication is not given, the authority may proceed to make a decision. If the indication is given, then the authority may not make the decision until:

(1)   either the representations have been received; or
(2)   a reasonable time has passed for such representations to be made and such representations have not been made.

What is reasonable will cause difficulties. It is suggested that the test of 'reasonableness' will depend on the subject matter at issue.

Where an application for registration has been refused, the only person disadvantaged by delay is the applicant. Applications should not remain outstanding forever, but within very generous limits, almost any amount of time can be allowed. For applicants are not in a position to conduct business or take their case further until the representations are made.

In cases of variation of condition and cancellation of registration, different considerations will apply and much will depend upon the subject matter of complaint. In relation to applications for registration, authorities are encouraged, it is submitted, to control the process by encouraging efficiency and speed. The authority should, following an indication that representations are to be made, press for a timetable. The authority should seek to set dates at which committees or persons appointed to hear representations will be convened, or dates by which written representations are to be received.

The authority must always be sure to be reasonable, and in setting a timetable, it will have opportunity to extend the timetable on request, supported by good reason. The authority should not fall into the trap of allowing matters to drift, particularly in cases where care homes are in operation.

5.18.4   Should representations be made orally or in writing?

This is entirely a matter for the applicant. The representations are an opportunity for applicants to put their case. Different cases will present different situations. In relation to applications for registration, the issues may be more those of principle than of fact. Such may more conveniently be contained within a written representation rather than expounded in oral submissions.

Oral representations are received by committees of the local authority in relation to residential care homes and registered children's homes, or persons appointed by the Health Authority, in relation to nursing homes. In practice, most authorities appoint a panel of non-executive and executive members of the authority, who have not been concerned with the issues, to review the decision of those who have been concerned in the application.

Oral representations are not an opportunity to give evidence, to challenge officers or to cross-examine or be cross-examined. They will only be chosen where applicants or their advisers believe that presentation orally may advance the case.

5.18.5   Is there a procedure for representations?

There is no procedure. Many authorities fall into the trap of treating the receipt of representations as an opportunity for the hearing of a mini-tribunal. There is no statutory basis for this. Some think that it is providing an opportunity for the applicant to have a full and correct hearing of their representations. This is to misunderstand the statutory provisions.

Proper conduct of a Tribunal hearing requires proper procedures and takes considerable time. Authorities will never have sufficient time to have a mini-tribunal conducted. Many authorities will conduct such representations otherwise than in accordance with the established rules for courts or Tribunals. There are rules limiting the evidence to be produced at Tribunals, but confrontations at representational hearings can become conversational and anecdotal.

Owners will wish to approach such a situation with caution. Everything that is said will be written down or recorded. Explanations given (which can only truly be checked if given in writing) will be presented at the Tribunal not only by applicants but by the authority. Inconsistencies will be exploited. If evidence is given or there is cross-examination, inconsistencies or differences between performances will be examined in detail.

Whilst the authority must not rubber stamp the proposal, applicants need to understand that, in reality, the authority is likely to adopt the proposal of its officers unless there is a dramatic change of circumstances, new facts arise or the authority is persuaded as to the lack of competence of its officers. Such would be a grave matter.

If the matter is proceeding to be heard as one of representation to the authority, then owners should assume that it is more likely than not that the proposal will be upheld. Some argue that the procedural step of 'representations' is illusory, as non-expert representatives are set to review the 'decisions' of the authority's experienced professionals.

Authorities should not seek to establish mini-tribunals. The expense can be quite large and it might be difficult for the authority to justify incurring such expenses without statutory authority.

5.19   THE DECISION

Once the representations have been received, the authority needs to make a decision. The authority must consider the issues that arise on the proposal and which are answered by the representations. That decision will be issued and notified even if it is a decision to grant registration upon conditions agreed or imposed.

If the decision is to grant registration on agreed terms, then it will take immediate effect. If the decision is other than to grant on agreed conditions, ie to refuse, or to grant subject to conditions which are the subject of contention, then the decision will not take effect until:

(1)   the twenty-ninth day after the decision of the authority; or
(2)   immediately after the abandonment or determination of the appeal.

The appeal is determined by the issue of a decision in writing by the Tribunal. It is not likely that such a decision will be issued earlier than 6 months from the date of the authority's decision. It is more likely to be 6 months and, perhaps, a year. Applicants who are exercised about proposed conditions of registration which they may not like should bear these time-limits in mind since the home may not be operated until the conditions have been accepted or the appeal abandoned.

The notice of the decision must give details of the right of appeal conferred by ss 15 and s 34 of the 1984 Act and para 8 of Sch 6 to the 1989 Act. All that is required of such notice is that it should identify the right of appeal and indicate that it shall be notified within 28 days from the date of the decision. The procedure is simply to notify a request for appeal to the authority. The authority must then notify the Secretariat of the Registered Homes Tribunal.[37] Thereafter, the Secretariat of the Tribunal takes over the procedure.

There is no formality regarding notice of appeal. One Circular, issued by the Department of Health in the late 1980s, suggested that appellants should be told to give reasons, in short terms, for deciding to appeal. There is no justification for that. Authorities should not follow it and appellants should ignore it. Before the Tribunal, the burden of proof and the burden to establish reasons falls upon the authority (save in children's home cases upon an appeal against a refusal to register). There is no reason why appellants should be forced to identify reasons, or establish the reasonableness of their case. An appeal is a matter of right.

5.19.1   Decision to grant registration subject to conditions

Where the decision is to grant registration subject to conditions which are not agreed, an anomaly exists. Many prospective appellants would be prepared to observe the conditions pending appeal. The position will often arise because this is an area where conflicts will be on matters of principle rather than issues of fact. The procedure does not permit for registration to be granted with the conditions binding pending a decision of appeal. An applicant must decide:

(1)   to accept the conditions, in which case they are binding and not subject to further appeal; or
(2)   to fight the appeal and take the consequence of delay.

It is doubtful that a grant of registration upon an undertaking to observe conditions of registration pending appeal is valid.

The result of such an agreement is not easy to determine. If the Tribunal accept jurisdiction, then it may be argued that registration has been effected without conditions in force and that the authority is required to serve notice to

---

37   Address: Area 217, Wellington House, 133–135 Waterloo Road, London SE1 8UG; telephone
       number: (0171) 972–4035; fax number: (0171) 972–4525.

propose to vary conditions or impose additional conditions. However, it is arguable that the registration is a nullity, for without the condition, the authority would not, in any event, have granted registration.

Such difficult issues obstruct the common sense approach of operating a care home, subject to the disputed condition, pending registration. The difficulty can be seen in this way:

(1) there is no power to accept conditions conditionally;
(2) accordingly, if conditions are accepted, the issues are complete and there is no jurisdiction for the Tribunal;
(3) if the conditional acceptance of conditions is invalid as a matter of law, then the consent does not take effect and the registration has not been correctly effected, as the decision of the authority cannot take effect;
(4) accordingly, the operation of the care home is unlawful and unregistered. Section 18 of the 1984 Act, in relation to residential care homes, may provide a defence where such a situation has been encouraged by the authority or its officers. No such defence exists for nursing homes, so that owners who give conditional consent run the risk of an argument from the authority that jurisdiction has been ousted, or that if jurisdiction is validly assumed, then operation of the care home pending tribunal is unlawful. It is suggested that amendments to the legislation to allow conditional acceptance of conditions pending appeal would be sensible.

Some suggest it appropriate to accept the conditions and then, by agreement, to lodge a 'paper' application for re-registration which enables the issue to be argued. Such can only work by agreement. Difficulties remain even then. The Tribunal will view a home operating as suggested by the Authority. Will they readily sanction a reduction in facilities? How will the Tribunal view an applicant accepting conditions on the one hand and challenging those same conditions on another? In any event, if the home operates in compliance with the conditions, it may be difficult to show that a lower standard is adequate.

5.19.2 Registration made with invalid conditions

The effect of a registration purporting to be made with invalid conditions, raises an interesting debate, which will depend for its results on the facts of each particular case as to whether the illegality of the conditions vitiates the whole decision or permits the decision to stand with the offending conditions being excised.

The argument proceeds in this way:

(1) an authority is only entitled to make a decision within its powers;
(2) a decision 'ultra vires' is void, ie of no effect;
(3) if an authority makes a decision subject to invalid conditions – is it the whole decision or simply the conditions which are invalid;
(4) to decide this, the court will look to see if the authority would have made the decision at all if it had known that the conditions were invalid;
(5) only if satisfied that the decision would have been made irrespective of the offending conditions, may the decision stand, ie are the conditions

an integral part of the decision or may they be seen as ancillary to the decision?

Courts have been reluctant to leave decisions on licences to stand where invalid conditions are imposed.[38] If authorities concerned with applications for registration of residential care or nursing homes (this can never apply to children's homes) grant registration subject to invalid conditions, similar issues will arise.

If the conclusion is that registration would not have been granted without the offending condition, then, it is submitted, the registration will be a nullity. However, where conditions purport to govern operational matters, ancillary to the fact of registration itself, the court may be prepared to excise the offending condition. A crucial factor will be whether or not the issue of concern covered by the condition would have been a matter upon which the authority could have refused registration. Concerns that would not have justified refusal of registration, but are protected by an unlawful condition, should surely not lead to a finding of nullity of registration.

For authorities, the watchword remains, if in doubt refuse to register and express doubts within the ambit of reasons for refusal permitted by s 9 and s 25 of the 1984 Act. Great caution is needed on the part of owners, the lawfulness of whose actions is dependant upon valid registration, and for authorities who will not wish to act outside or beyond their powers, such powers being the only justification for action or decisions of any nature.

---

38   *R v Leicester Licensing Justices, ex parte Bisson* [1968] 1 WLR 729; *R v North Hertfordshire District Council, ex parte Cobbold* [1985] 3 All ER 486; *R v Inner London Crown Court, ex parte Sitki (Akmen Ali)* [1994] COD 342.

Chapter 6

CARRYING ON A CARE HOME

6.1 INTRODUCTION

This chapter reviews the day-to-day operations of the care home and the legal effect of issues that may arise in the course of such operation, viewed from the standpoint of the owner, the person in charge, the authority as regulator and the authority as purchaser.

6.2 THE ROLE OF THE OWNER

The owner is recognised to be a fit person to carry on a home which itself, as presented at registration, is considered to be fit in all material respects. It is the role of the owner to operate the business of the regulated care home.

The owner is responsible to the clients for the proper delivery of care, and to the regulatory authority for the operation of the care home to a proper standard, in accordance with established practice and the proper expectations of the regulatory scheme. The owner is not, under any circumstances, entitled to pass the blame for errors, faults or omissions to others, including the person in charge and thereby escape the consequences of default. Insofar as the owner does not have professional qualifications or individual skills to perform particular tasks required, then it is the owner's responsibility to ensure that such skills are delivered by persons with appropriate qualifications and experience and that such tasks are performed. Excuses of shortage of labour or lack of understanding should never be tolerated.

It would be foolish for an owner to seek to operate a regulated care home business without understanding, in depth, the requirements of that business. Authorities should identify such inadequacy in the pre-registration process and decline to register any person who shows a lack of aptitude or understanding. There should never be a case of an owner learning on the job. In a registered care home business, an owner is taking on responsibility for some of the most frail and vulnerable members of society. It is right that high standards should be expected.

6.3 THE ROLE OF THE PERSON IN CHARGE

The person in charge is distinguished from the owner and is sometimes described as the 'manager', or in nursing homes, 'matron', or in some circumstances, 'head of care'. The notion of a person in charge has a statutory basis only in relation to the registration of nursing homes, where the expression 'in charge' appears in s 25(1)(f) of the 1984 Act, in relation to permitted refusal (or indeed cancellation) of registration if the home were not 'in the charge' of a registered medical practitioner or an appropriately qualified nurse.

The role of the person in charge, or manager, has already been examined. It does cause concern in practice and, therefore, it is proposed to examine it further in the context of the day-to-day operation of the home.

6.3.1   What is meant by 'in charge'?

A number of meanings may be given to this expression. It may refer to a person in charge of the conduct of the home at any particular time. The expression 'in charge' may be used loosely to refer to the person who has effective control of the home at a moment in time, perhaps when an inspection takes place. In that context, the person in charge is the person responsible for what happens on a minute by minute basis. Such a person may be the ultimate manager or matron, or indeed the owner, or may be a senior and appropriately skilled member of staff leading the shift, for the time being ('heading the shift' is not the proper meaning of the term 'person in charge' either for the purposes of s 25(1)(f) of the 1984 Act or generally).

'Person in charge' may mean simply the person who runs the business. That may be the owner or, in the case where the owner is an absentee owner, a manager to whom full powers of control of the business have been delegated. It may in this context, in effect, be a deputy manager or matron where the owner takes overall responsibility, visiting regularly but not taking day-to-day responsibility. The owner will take important decisions, but day-to-day control of the delivery for care will be in the hands of a qualified or experienced person who takes charge of the home and responsibility to the owner for day-to-day matters.

The author's understanding of the position of 'person in charge', as distinct from the owner of a business, is that the person in charge is the person who undertakes professional responsibility for the delivery of care to the patients, residents or clients within the establishment, as opposed to the person who takes responsibility for the business and administrative responsibility. Of course, the position of owner and manager, or person in charge, may be held by the same person. Indeed, the position of manager and person in charge may be held by the same person.

However, whatever classification occurs, it must be the case that the home is in business to deliver care. Many owners will wish to be engaged in the business of care but will not themselves have the aptitude, skill or experience to deliver or control the delivery of care. They will thus need to appoint a person to take control of care and, in a nursing home, will require the care to be under the control of a medical doctor or a nurse. Where a nurse is in charge, that nurse must be a registered nurse holding what is regarded as a first level qualification, ie a nurse registered in Pts I, III, V, VI and VII of the Nurses Midwives and Health Visitors Parts of the Register Order 1993.[1]

It is an integral part of the operation of any care home that proper care be delivered. Someone (even if the leader of a group of experienced care

---

1   SI 1993/588.

professionals) must take ultimate responsibility for delivery of care. Quite obviously, every care home requires such a person who has appropriate skill and experience to meet the needs of those in care within the home.

6.4 THE ROLE OF THE PERSON IN CHARGE OF CARE

6.4.1 Responsibilities to the owner

Such an individual is responsible for the delivery of adequate care to the owner, ie their employer, where the roles are split. It will be an essential term of the job description in the contract of employment of someone who is taking on responsibility for care that they are responsible and accountable for failings in the delivery of care. The person in charge often receives an additional payment for taking on the responsibility of being 'in charge'. Other staff, even senior professional staff, are usually paid by the hour. The person in charge must recognise that he does not have regular hours of work. They are expected to work the hours that are necessary to ensure the delivery of care and, if absent through sickness or on holiday, it is their prime responsibility to the owner to ensure that the continuation of care is delivered. The owner is ultimately responsible, but under a properly drawn-up contract with the person in charge, the owner may look to that person to deliver such a service. If the person in charge fails to do so, the owner may be accountable to clients and to the regulatory authority. It will be no excuse for the owners to blame the person in charge. The owner must ensure that the person in charge understands their responsibilities and that the consequence of failure may be a loss of appointment and professional reputation.

Failure by staff (however senior) to report for duty is the responsibility of the person in charge and they will be accountable to ensure that appropriate steps are taken to meet the shortfall (even if, in extreme cases, they have to attend themselves). A competent person in charge must work as a direct care professional. He should split duties between various shifts and should expect to work anti-social hours, ie weekends and nights. The person in charge should himself, as should the owner, make irregular and unannounced visits at anti-social hours when not expected, so that they know that the scheme of care which they have devised works when they are not there. Attendance at only recognised hours is a recipe for disaster.

An owner who cannot sustain a relationship with the person in charge may be categorised as unfit to continue in operation. A person in charge who fails in his duties may face dismissal and may find it difficult, in the absence of suitable references, to find an alternative appointment as a person in charge, or possibly in any senior position in the nursing or residential social care professions.

6.4.2 Responsibilities to the clients

The person in charge is also responsible to the clients not by reason of direct contract, but by reason of his professional duty to ensure that a proper and adequate standard of care is delivered. These issues may not have been tested in the courts, as owners are the most likely defendants for 'breach of duty to care' litigation. Persons in charge are not likely to be seen as appropriate defendants, usually due to lack of substantial means. 'Persons in charge' should, perhaps, consider having legal liability insurance, in these days of increasing risk of involvement in litigation. Persons in charge should check that their employers hold sufficient indemnity insurance against legal liability, to cover such claims, and that insurers will not seek an indemnity from senior employees, whose alleged default may have caused the claim to arise. Insurance should be on a 'non recourse' basis with a waiver of rights of subrogation.

6.4.3   Regulation of conduct of nurses in charge

The conduct of nurses is regulated by the United Kingdom Central Council of Nurses and Midwifery, which will regard the nurse in charge, or indeed any registered nurse engaged, as responsible for patient care. Where there is a failure to care appropriately or a failure to deliver a service, particularly by a nurse who has undertaken the responsibility of being in charge, the UKCC will take a serious view.

The consequences of breaches of professional standards by nurses were revised in April 1993. Previously, the consequences of breach of duty were either removal from the register or that no action be taken. It was almost inevitable that, following a finding of professional misconduct, some action was required to be taken and, as the only course was removal from the register, many nurses found themselves so removed in circumstances that were surprising to their colleagues.

In 1993 the remedies for misconduct were extended to include the delivery of a reprimand and a suspension from registration. This gives the disciplinary tribunal a greater flexibility to 'make the punishment fit the crime'.

Nurses who undertake the responsibility of 'taking charge' of the delivery of nursing care in a private nursing home should be in no doubt that their professional body will regard them as wholly accountable for the proper delivery of nursing care to patients.

6.4.4   The position in residential care and children's homes

As yet, those responsible for the delivery of social and personal care in residential care homes and registered children's homes are not controlled by statutory regulation in same way as nurses, and thus are not accountable to any professional body. It is likely that professional bodies will be formed and that there will be statutory regulation by the end of the 1990s.

6.4.5   Responsibilities to the regulatory authority

Where there is an appointed person in charge, as opposed to an owner, the regulatory authority will regard the person in charge as the person with whom they will have contact in relation to issues concerning the delivery of care in individual cases. This is not to say that the owner is removed from or is able to abdicate responsibility.

Some authorities fall into the trap of considering that, with the appointment of a so-called manager or person in charge, they can exclude the owner from dialogue. The person in charge, manager, or head of care is the delegate of the owner. The owner should be involved in serious discussions about issues of concern. It is not for the authority and/or the person in charge to instruct the owner as to what the owner is required to do. Both the person in charge and the authority must remember that the person in charge works for the owner and, subject to being required to operate in accordance with good professional practice, are subject to the direction of the owner, in reasonable terms, as to how their duties are to be discharged.

The person in charge does not have a responsibility to the regulatory authority which by-passes the owner. Nevertheless, if regulatory action is contemplated and issues include those of failing to deliver proper care, the person in charge will be concerned. It will be their conduct which is criticised and, if such charges are sustained, they will be accountable both professionally and to the owner.

6.4.6 Notice of absence

So important is the role of the person in charge, that both regulation of residential care and nursing homes requires the person registered (person in control, in the case of residential care homes – probably synonymous with person registered) to give notice to the regulatory authority of the absence of the person in charge/manager, if that absence is to be a period of 4 weeks or more.

Clearly, it is sensible to ensure that contracts of employment with persons in charge and/or managers provide that no more than 3 to $3\frac{1}{2}$ weeks' holiday may be taken at one time.

The notice must be given not less than one month before the beginning of the absence, or one week in the case of an emergency, and detail the length of the absence and the arrangements for running the home in the absence of the person in charge. In the case of residential care homes, the reason for the absence is required. The person registered or in control is required to inform the regulatory authority when the person in charge returns.

Failure to give the notice constitutes a criminal offence. Prosecutions may not be launched, however, until after notices identifying the offence and requiring its remedy have been served and the offence continues after the time for remedy has expired.[2] In such a case, given that the authority will only discover the breach by identifying the absence, it is difficult to see how a prosecution could be successfully pursued. The particular default (as opposed to failure in ongoing standards) cannot, in fact, be repeated. However, failure to have a proper person in charge may give rise to questions about the fitness of the owner or perhaps the home.

Owners are warned that termination of employment of the person in charge amounts to absence which, accordingly, requires notification. This

---

2   Residential Care Home Regulations 1984, reg 20; Nursing Homes and Mental Nursing Homes Regulations 1984, reg 19.

provision does not merely relate to occasions of holiday or long-term sickness.

6.5   THE ROLE OF THE AUTHORITY

The role of the authority may be regarded as being in two distinct forms:

(1)   regulatory;
(2)   purchasing.

6.5.1   Regulatory role of the authority

The authority is responsible for the registration and the cancellation of registration. Otherwise, the role of the authority is to monitor the operation of the home. An authority should not seek to become involved in the day-to-day operation of the home.

The inspectors appointed by a regulatory authority will, in most cases, be experienced providers of care. They will be either social workers with experience of residential care, or qualified nurses. In the course of inspection, they may discover such shortcomings on the part of those operating the home that they need to intervene, in accordance with their own professional standards of duty, to protect the vulnerable residents or patients. Inspectors should be slow to take that course. They should examine options and should not intervene unless they are satisfied, after consultation with senior colleagues, that there is no alternative. It is suggested that, if inspectors feel compelled to intervene in care or management in order to protect the clients, then it should follow that the gravity of the situation is such that action will be taken to seek to cancel the registration.

It is not part of the function of the authority regularly to intervene to manage or supervise care for clients in a regulated care home. The authority will observe, note and possibly take action in relation to major decisions of the home. It is not the authority's role to take those decisions on behalf of the registered owner.

It is not the function of the authority to appoint senior staff, nor is it the function of the authority to veto the appointment of senior staff, or to seek to interview senior staff so as to advise the owner on a short list for appointment. If such steps are considered to be necessary, it is an indication that the owner is not capable and thus not fit, ie not suitable to be registered.

The authority is not an official adviser to the owner. In the course of inspection, particularly where the owner's representative and the inspectors share common professional standards, there is bound to be interchange and discussion about topics of mutual interest. However, the authority should stop short of giving formal advice in specific situations. The authority will, of course, organise training sessions for owners, persons in charge and staff. This constitutes guidance as to general standards of care. What is beyond the proper remit of the authority is to give specific advice or instruction. It is the owner who runs the business, supported in appropriate cases by the person in charge. Failure to make the right decisions is an indication of unfitness.

The officers of an authority should not advise the owner, for, in giving advice, they may assume a duty of care either towards the owner or, more likely, increase any duty of care that the authority may owe towards the vulnerable clients within the home.

6.5.2 The role of the authority as purchaser

Local authorities with social services power have, since 1948, been potential purchasers of residential care and child care services. Health Authorities and their predecessors have been potential purchasers of health care for a similar period. Local authorities are now also potential purchasers of health care, following the implementation, on 1 April 1993 of Pt III of the National Health Service and Community Care Act 1990. Further, frequency of local or Health Authority purchase of community care services from private sector care homes has increased and will continue to increase, so that such purchasers and, in particular, the local authority responsible for social services, will become the dominant purchasers of residential community care services.[3]

The role of the local Health Authority as a purchaser is to be distinguished completely from that as regulator. In purchasing residential care, the authority will be performing a duty to a client in making appropriate arrangements to fulfil the care needs of that client. The statutory duty is to a particular client rather than to the generality of clients. The authority acts to ensure the fulfilment of the contract as opposed to adherence to the regulatory requirement. Thus, as a purchaser the authority is concerned to fit the particular care home to the particular client. As a regulator, the authority is concerned that the care home provides a proper standard of care for the generality of clients who may be attracted by the service offered by that particular care home.

Quite clearly, it would be unethical for the authority to use information and experience gained as a regulator to influence its position as a purchaser. Where the purchasing and regulatory authority are different, then it will be easier to create separation. Where the authority is the same, the officers are urged to create so-called 'Chinese walls' so as to preserve the distinction.

The system which has been established will start to falter if regulators are seen to use their special position in relation to registered care homes to influence the market and commercial viability, particularly where they have a role as dominant purchaser. The developing policy of open reporting of inspection and demands for information by regulators from purchasers within the public market are putting pressures upon this vital distinction.

Any protection for a care home owner lies in the confidential nature of the relationship between regulator and regulated. Information obtained by the regulator is obtained in confidence. The regulator is not entitled to impart that confidential information other than to those within the contemplation of the parties, ie those directly concerned with regulation, as opposed to other aspects of operation of a care home. Clearly, once information about a care home is in the public domain, for example, there has been a decision to cancel

3   See *Wollon v North Cornwall County Council* [1997] 1 WLR 570 (CA).

registration, then there can be no restriction on dissemination of the information. Where the information remains as between regulator and care home owner, it is confidential and capable of protection by the legal remedies and claims for compensation that support a right of confidentiality.

An authority which supplies confidential information about the conduct of a care home, discovered during the inspection process, and imparts that information to another authority, or to officers of its own authority who are responsible for purchasing, is likely to face a serious and substantial action for damages. The consequence might be the loss of the business. Authorities should hesitate before embracing policies of exchange and publication of information of this nature.

6.6   RELATIONSHIPS

6.6.1   Between the owner and the person in charge

This relationship will, inevitably, be circumscribed by contract, whether that contract be a contract of employment or a contract for the provision of services. Both parties must take care over the preparation and negotiation of such an agreement. The owner must be sure that the selection of the person in charge is suitable both in the sense that he is competent to supervise care services and that he will relate constructively with the owner.

The necessity to have a person in charge indicates that the owner is either unable by reason of lack of skill and competence, or through other commitments, to deliver the care services personally. The owner will thus expect a full service, unlimited in time or extent, from the person in charge. The owner should ensure that the job description or service specification in the contract is fully and completely drawn so that the person in charge is truly in charge, responsible and accountable to the owner.

The person in charge should understand the responsibility of the role which is being undertaken. If there is any doubt as to his ability or willingness to undertake the enormous responsibility of taking charge of a business owned or controlled by others, he should withdraw. Great responsibility and great accountability will be required. Errors may lead not just to termination of the relationship with the owner but to lack of credibility with the regulatory authority and, in many cases, loss of professional reputation. The person in charge should understand that, even if the job description or service specification is not fully drawn, the concept of being in charge is one of ultimate responsibility. It cannot be shirked.

6.6.2   Interference or obstruction by the owner

Having appointed such a person in charge, the owner must permit that person to discharge their functions fully and must not interfere with the role of the person in charge. Any such interference would undermine the professional position of the owner's appointed senior officer. It may cause the regulatory authority to be concerned about the fitness of the establishment, from the staffing point of view, upon the grounds that the person in charge is being restricted in delivering care in the way which he would wish and, in consequence, the owner may risk the resignation of the person in charge. Frequent unexplained resignations can lead to the conclusion that the owner, who is unable to delegate, is an unfit person to operate a care home.

By appointing a person in charge, the owner abdicates responsibility for day-to-day care. Therefore, the owner must accept that if the person in charge requires services or facilities for staff, those services or facilities must be provided. An owner who declines or obstructs the person in charge in procuring appropriate equipment, facilities or staff will be seen to be obstructing the delivery of proper care and, almost inevitably, be labelled unfit, thereby placing the registration in immediate jeopardy. In an extreme case, such conduct could lead to urgent action to cancel registration.

The person in charge is thus in an invidious position. He is professionally responsible for the delivery of care, but is not in direct control of resources and may not be in direct control of decisions about the purchase of supplies, equipment or staff. The conflict between the duty to obey instructions from the employer and the duty to deliver proper standards of care is a constant dilemma in many regulated care homes.

Each problem is a question of degree. However, the person in charge will remain, in the eyes of the regulatory authority, responsible for the proper delivery of care. He will not be able to avoid responsibility on the basis of a defence of superior orders from the owner or lack of facilities, staff or equipment, which are to be provided by the owner. In those extreme circumstances, the person in charge must resign to protect his professional position, albeit reserving their remedies. Such conduct by an owner could well amount to constructive dismissal from employment or repudiation of a contract for services. An owner who appointed a person to take charge of care and persistently refused to make available the appropriate facilities, equipment and staff would have acted so as to repudiate the contract of employment or contract for services and resignation would be lawful. Compensation would follow as to consequence of constructive dismissal from employment or repudiatory fundamental breach of a contract for services.

6.6.3 Between the owner and the authority

After registration, the relationship between owner and authority is limited. The authority are responsible for inspection, ie the monitoring of the registered care home on a regulatory basis. The relationship of the authority with the owner will be one of an enforced visitor entitled to observe the conduct of the registered care home and to inspect its records, meet and discuss issues with staff and interview clients. Whether the relationship is cordial, indifferent or strained, the relationship is a difficult one.

The relationship between owner and authority is not one of partnership. The authority and the owner may be partners in the supply of care services in other roles, but the authority as regulator is not a joint venturer with the owner. Where the authority acts as purchaser, the relationship between owner and authority is as between service purchaser and service provider. The relationship will be governed by contract, not a contract of partnership, but a contract to provide services. The provider will wish to ensure that the quality of service required is met and the purchaser will wish to ensure that that quality is maintained so that the authority's clients, for whom care is arranged with the owner, are satisfied, and are satisfied with the performance of the authority, in so providing care for them pursuant to the authority's statutory duty.

6.6.4   Between the authority and the person in charge

This relationship is only indirect. The person in charge will be in contact with the authority, as a senior employee or service provider of the owner. In that capacity, the person in charge is standing in the shoes of the owner, and that relationship is thus similar to the relationship between the owner and authority.

There is no separate contractual relationship between the person in charge and the authority. The person in charge will owe duties to the owner and is not entitled to breach those duties (eg loyalty and confidentiality) because of some perceived supervening responsibility to the authority. If the person in charge feels, as a result of the authority's activities or otherwise, that their professional position is compromised by the conduct of the owner then their remedy lies in termination of their contract for services or employment.

The authority will regard the person in charge as the embodiment of the owner on professional care issues and will expect to speak with the person in charge, as if the owner, on such professional issues. The authority will expect the person in charge to be suitably experienced, qualified and skilled not only to deliver care but to manage care, plan care and answer the authority's questions about the delivery of care as between the owner and the client. This is the fundamental relationship which lies at the root of the operation of each and every registered care home.

6.6.5   Between the owner and the client

The owner has agreed with the client, or a sponsor on behalf of the client (for example, public authority, relative or charity), to look after the client, who is not able to look after himself. The owner is thus responsible to deliver the care required and that responsibility cannot be shirked.

The relationship between owner and client is normally governed by contract. Where the contract is made between the owner and the sponsor for the client, the client may be a party to the contract but even if not, the contract is made for the benefit of the client and the client can seek performance of those obligations, on the part of the owner, made specifically for his benefit either directly or by complaining to the sponsor.

Increasingly sophisticated and complex agreements for care and the provision of services are negotiated. In essence, the fundamental term of any contract for care is that the owner will ensure the provision for the client of such care as the client may need, whatever that care may be. Under no circumstances is an owner entitled to withhold necessary care, irrespective of contract terms, where that care is needed. That is not to be confused with the supply or non-supply of optional extras.

If the owner is unwilling to expand care services to meet needs, or if the owner is unable, because of increase in client needs, to meet those needs, then the owner must ensure, and must ensure that the contract so provides, that the client is discharged to another provider, who is both able and willing to provide such care.

6.6.6 Safe custody of clients' property

One issue which gives frequent difficulty is where the owner takes safe custody of money or valuables on behalf of the client. No specific provision for such is made in relation to nursing homes or registered children's homes. In relation to residential care homes, para 17 of Sch 2, introduced by reg 6 of the Residential Care Homes Regulations 1984, provides that the owner shall keep:

> 'a record of all money or other valuables deposited by a resident for safekeeping or received on the resident's behalf specifying the date on which such money or valuables were deposited or received and the date upon which any sum or other valuables was returned to a resident or used at the request of the resident or on his behalf and the purpose for which it is used.'

It is suggested that this provision should be adopted in relation to each and every type of regulated care home. It is a common sense principle that, where the property of another is held, that property should be properly recorded and movements in that property (ie return to the client or given back to the owner) should be recorded. This applies equally to valuables and to money.

Furthermore, although there is no requirement to keep such valuables or money separately, or in a separate account in the case of money, it is suggested that where monies are held or valuables kept on behalf of a number of clients, those items should be kept in individual lockers, safes or accounts so that they do not become mixed either with the owner's monies or valuables or monies or valuables belonging to other clients. There is no rule that requires payment of interest on monies held, although common sense and fairness suggest that if money is placed in safe keeping, it should earn interest if held for significant periods of time.

Owners who mix valuables and monies of clients with that of other clients and with their own monies court disaster and will have only themselves to blame if others, for example regulatory authorities, relatives of clients or, indeed, the police, take an adverse view of such conduct. It is very simple to avoid such difficulties and all owners are advised to be meticulous about book-keeping.

6.6.7 Appropriation of clients' money

Clients' money should never be appropriated to the owner on the basis that extra charges have been or will be incurred, thus giving the owner a general proprietary right over the clients' money. This may seem obvious, but all too frequently, in the operation of care homes, owners make that simple mistake. In an extreme case, owners may have some difficulty in proving that they have acted honestly. Appropriation of such monies in such a way, seen to be permanent deprivation, only lacks the element of dishonesty before being converted into the serious offence of theft.

A conviction for theft is very serious. Among its consequences will inevitably be cancellation of registration. A person who steals from clients cannot be said to be a fit person to operate a care home.

6.6.8   Application of social welfare benefits

The operation of the social welfare benefits system produces complex problems. Clients, who are unable or unwilling to understand or take control of their own affairs, will receive substantial monies. That money will all be payable to the account of the client. A client who is unable to look after his own affairs will, in certain circumstances, appoint another to handle benefit claims upon his behalf. That other, sometimes known as an appointee, may be the home owner. Thus, home owners will be receiving money that belongs to the client, which they will expect to appropriate to meet fees.

It may be that the benefits received are insufficient to meet fees. It may very well be, although this should not be assumed, that there is an implied authority to appropriate, from monies received, that which is due to the owner. Such should never be assumed and there is no substitute for explanation at the beginning of the relationship. However, some monies may be in excess of the requirements. It is easy for an owner to take all the benefit monies due to a client and appropriate them to the owner's account. Combinations of retirement pension, attendance allowance, mobility allowance, disability living allowance, income support, including the residential boarder supplement and the personal expense allowance incorporated in income support, all raise complicated issues.

Most elderly clients will receive significant social security benefits and pensions. Such monies always belong to the client. Insofar as they are in excess of the client's obligations to the owner, they should not be appropriated to the owner.

6.6.9   'Pocket money'

The personal expenses allowances, sometimes known as 'pocket money', show the classic example of difficulty. 'Pocket money' is paid to the client as part of the client's social security benefit. It is not appropriated for personal spending. If fees agreed exceed welfare benefits and require a contribution of all or part of the 'pocket money', then provided the client understands, there is no reason why the money should not be so appropriated by the owner. However, an arrangement should be set out in the contract at the outset of the relationship. If clients believe that they have been accommodated at so called 'public benefit' rates, they and their relatives may well believe that the 'pocket money' will be available to them. If it is to be available to them, it will have to be received, credited to their account and appropriately recorded.

If the client's care is sponsored by another, particularly a local authority, then the contract of care will be fully paid by payment of the agreed sum pursuant to that agreement. There will be no provision for seeking a supplement from the client. Accordingly, in such circumstances, any benefits payable to the client and not retained by the sponsor are the client's money and may only be used with the consent of and to the advantage of the client. It is wrong to suggest that such monies will be collected and appropriated on a regular basis on the understanding that various general extras will also be provided on a regular basis. Extras should be treated as a matter of choice and should be debited individually, just as the 'pocket money' or other surplus benefits should be credited individually.

Owners who fail to follow this course diligently will face enormous difficulties. Clients may accumulate substantial balances of public welfare benefits for which they have no apparent need, but those surpluses belong to the clients and not to the home owners.

6.7 LIABILITIES OF PARTICIPANTS

This section examines the potential liabilities of participants in the operation of a care home both to one another and to third parties. The liabilities may be grouped as follows:

(1) of the owner to the regulatory authority;
(2) of the owner to the purchasing authority;
(3) of the owner to the client;
(4) of the client to the owner;
(5) of the authority to the owner;
(6) of the authority to the client.

6.7.1 Liabilities of the owner to the regulatory authority

Save for the obligation to pay the registration fee and annual fees, the owner owes no financial responsibility to the regulatory authority. The owner does, however, owe the all-important duty to operate the registered care home to a proper standard in accordance with such conditions of registration as may exist and up to a level of acceptable professional practice. The consequences of failure to perform that duty are:

(1) the cancellation of the registration and loss of livelihood;
(2) prosecution for breach of those statutory obligations which amount to offences prosecutable by the authority.

6.7.2 Liabilities of the owner to the purchasing authority

These will be the liabilities which the owner has undertaken pursuant to the contract with the purchasing authority. Such a contract will define financial responsibility of the authority with the owner subject to all remedies available as a matter of law for breach of contract.

The owner should be aware, when negotiating with the authority, that they are negotiating a contract which will be enforceable to the letter. Such contracts were rare prior to 1 April 1993, but are now the standard vehicle for establishing obligations of care. The terms of the contract are important and if those terms are inappropriate, the owner should seek to negotiate. Once contractual obligations are established, both parties are bound, subject to renegotiation, whether or not they are content with the result.

The reality of the market place is that the authority, as a dominant purchaser, is likely to be able to impose its own will in relation to contractual terms upon the basis that it can choose, or not, to deal with the owner.

Various attempts were made, in the early days of community care, to see whether or not the authority's position as a dominant purchaser could be limited by rules of public law. Two cases have come before the courts – the *Newcastle* case[4] and the *Cleveland* case.[5]

In the *Newcastle* case, Auld J held that, in dealing with care home owners for the negotiation of community care contracts, local authorities were entitled to insist upon such contractual terms as they thought appropriate and were available in the market. Insisting on terms that were tough was a fact of commercial negotiation and not a matter that was subject to judicial review. Registration did not carry with it a right to expect 'public authority trade' if facilities and services, although 'adequate' for registration, did not meet those that the authority expected for its clients.

In the *Cleveland* case, Potts J appeared to take a different view. Whilst following much of that which was said by Auld J, Potts J was persuaded that the particular actions of the particular authority went beyond what was reasonable and, therefore, those actions were capable of judicial review. Following a period of discussion with local care home owners, the authority had issued forms of contract, stated the contracts were not negotiable and, with less than 2 months to go before the commencement of community care service provision, indicated that the contracts were required to be signed within less than 2 weeks by anyone who wished to have a contract to provide services for the whole of following year. The contractual provisions were such that a large number of the care home owners were not able to meet the standards of service and facility identified in the contract and, thus, if they chose to sign, would immediately place themselves in serious breach of contract. The authority declined to phase in these arrangements or to provide a period within which higher service standards could be met, even when invited to do so by the judge.

There seems to have been no evidence that the owners would have been able to meet the increased requirements from operating revenues, within the relatively short periods suggested by the judge, for example installation of lifts, call systems, etc. If it is right (per Auld J) that authorities are entitled to set the terms of contracts, as they see fit, in order to ensure a proper service (and this was accepted by Potts J), how can it be right that an authority should accept an inferior service for a period and thereafter, if there is no improvement, terminate the agreement? Authorities clearly can and should only purchase proper standards of care. Surely it cannot be right that authorities are required to purchase inadequate care from inadequate facilities upon a temporary basis, simply because they have, understandably, upset the court by their conduct.

Such an approach overlooks the fundamental interests of the clients in care. Potts J's decision should, perhaps, be regarded with caution. In considering an authority's approach to terms of contract, it is submitted, with respect, that Auld J's approach was the more sound.

The *Cleveland* decision may be a more useful authority for judicial review of an authority's decisions where:

---

4   *R v Newcastle City Council, ex parte Dixon* (1993) 17 BMLR 82.

5   *R v Cleveland County Council, ex parte Cleveland Care Homes Association* [1994] COD 221.

(1)   it fails to respond to genuine expectations for real consultation;
(2)   it seeks to impose contract terms which cannot be met by a significant
       number of registered providers – thus restricting client choice. How can
       it be rational to register establishments as fit for use and then state that
       those establishments provide inadequate facilities?

6.7.3   Owner's liabilities to the client

The relationship between the owner and the client is similar to the relationship
between the owner and the purchasing authority. The relationship is based
upon contract. The owner's liabilities to the client will stem from the
contractual obligations which have been undertaken. However, the owner
should not seek to avoid fundamental obligations by negotiating tight or
meaningless contracts.

The contract may be directly with the client, or, may be with a sponsor,
relative, charity, or purchasing authority. Unless the client is actually a party to
the contract, the client may have difficulties in enforcing contractual
obligations, but will not have contractual responsibilities. Save where services
are purchased by a local authority, the owner should seek a commitment from
both the sponsor and the client to avoid confusion, should a dispute arise. In
the case of local authority community care contracts, parts of the payment
obligation may be taken by the client discharging their contribution
responsibilities direct to the home owner,[6] or by an independent third party
sponsor. In the former case, the local authority's responsibility is only
extinguished to the extent that the client actually discharges the contribution
obligation. Some local authorities seek to avoid that responsibility, in effect
seeking to divide the payment obligation into one or more parts. Such attempt
may be unlawful and unenforceable.

The agreed 'fee for care' is all that the home owner is entitled to receive,
from anyone. Accordingly, where an authority has agreed to purchase a care
package, the owner may not charge any additional sum for the delivery of that
care. Personal expense allowance (paid to a client as a part of social security
benefit) may not be claimed to cover a shortfall in fees. There is no such
shortfall. Any additional payment may only be legitimately charged for
additional service or extra goods supplied.

Whether or not the same could come within the principles of the Unfair
Contracts Terms Act 1977, it is clear that the basis of a contract to provide care
for a client who cannot look after himself is that the owner will provide such
care as is required from time to time or, if unable or unwilling so to do, will
ensure that that care is supplied or that the client is discharged from the
contract. In so far as the contract does not express this fully and accurately, it
is suggested that such a term will always be implied.

Failure to meet that standard is not just a matter of breach of regulation
but also of contract enforceable by reference to the usual contractual
remedies. Indeed, it will be implied into any contract for care for a client, that
the owner will ensure that the home in which care is supplied will remain
registered with the appropriate regulatory authority.

---

6   National Assistance Act 1948, s 22 and s 26, as amended.

Such disputes will be rare, but it seems to the author that, if a client is required to vacate at unreasonably short notice, either because of failure of care standards or loss of registration in respect of premises, and the new care home charges higher fees, then for whatever period might be considered to be a reasonable period of notice, such additional fees may be recoverable by the client from the first owner as damages for breach of contract.

6.7.4 Liabilities of the client to the owner

These liabilities are the reverse of the owner to the client. They may be based upon contract or, where the client is not a contracting party, upon general principles of law.

The principal liability is to pay the fee for the care service rendered. This issue needs to be addressed by owners during contractual negotiation. If the client fails to pay the fee, a difficult issue as to legal contract and moral responsibility arises. The natural remedy for a hotel keeper who is not paid is to require the guest to vacate. Thus, with care homes, the natural remedy for the owner who is not paid is also to require the client to vacate. Clients may not be able to understand the consequences of their actions. Non-payment may not be the fault of the client. To evict clients who are frail and unable to care for themselves, may well be seen as not the action of someone who wishes to be regarded as a fit person to carry on a regulated care home. Therefore, a balance must be struck. Clearly, reasonable notice must be given, unless an emergency arises. Such an emergency might be where the conduct or condition of the client deteriorates to such an extent as to make the client a danger to himself, others, or so as to be in such need as cannot properly be met by the owner within the particular establishment. It is suggested that an emergency would never arise as a matter of non-payment of fees.

It is suggested that, in such circumstances, there would be an implied duty on the owner to take reasonable steps to assist the client in resolving financial difficulties, procuring payment from other sources, for example sponsors, or realising assets to met the liability. One would expect an owner to research such difficulties in advance. Owners, who find themselves unpaid, would not receive sympathy if they proceeded to evict a client whose capital assets were sufficient to meet the liability, but, were not immediately available, for example awaiting realisation or sale.

An eviction might be successful, but the owner's character might suffer long-lasting damage, both in commercial terms as regards other potential clients or purchasers, and in the eyes of the regulator – would a fit person behave in this way? Owners should, therefore, approach such situations with caution. Clients whilst responsible, may not be in a position to understand the consequences of their liabilities.

6.7.5 Liabilities of the authority to the owner

This may be divided into two sections:

(1) liability as a purchasing authority;
(2) liability as a regulatory authority.

6.7.6 Liabilities as a purchasing authority

This liability is the reverse of that of the owner to the purchasing authority. The liability of the purchasing authority is clearly circumscribed by contract. The relationship of the parties is not bedevilled by the difficulties of lack of capacity on the part of the client. The purchasing authority's liability will be to pay on time and in accordance with the provisions of the contract, provided that the owner has supplied care to the appropriate standard.

Owners may wish to attempt to negotiate that the obligation to pay and the provision of services to specified standards should not be linked. This will, undoubtedly, be resisted by purchasing authorities. However, the authority should appreciate that a regular, steady flow of funds is the only method whereby the owner can guarantee to deliver the service which the client requires and which the authority has procured for the client, pursuant to the authority's statutory duties. Officious interference with cash flow, in the absence of grave concerns about care, can only make matters worse. A responsible authority would never seek to disrupt cash flow for trivial reasons.

Owners, meanwhile, should be astute in negotiations to try to protect themselves against what some might see as opportunistic local authorities assisting their own cash difficulties by seeking to delay or postpone payment beyond the agreed schedule, on excuses which may be less than genuine.

6.7.7 Liabilities of the authority as regulator

This issue has raised much debate over recent years, as to whether the authority owes a duty to the owner in respect of the manner in which regulation is conducted. It can now be said with some confidence that authorities are not liable for their actions in the conduct of regulation or other public duties unless:

(1) they have acted maliciously so as to use their powers for an inappropriate purpose so that the tort of malicious prosecution or abuse of power is established;

(2) an officer of the authority has created a duty of care (usually professional) for which the authority is vicariously responsible. It may be that, in the conduct of their duties, officers so exceed their authority so as to assume the responsibility of an adviser in a special relationship with an individual and that the authority becomes vicariously responsible for the duties that have been so assumed;[7]

Authorities do not owe a duty of care to individuals in the way in which they perform the obligations of regulation nor will the courts find a privately enforceable statutory duty as to the manner or form of performance of their statutory duty of regulation.

---

7   *X (Minors) v Bedfordshire County Council* [1995] 2 AC 633 (HL); *Harrison v Cornwall County Council* (1992) 156 LG Rev 703; *Hedley Byrne & Co v Heller & Partners* [1964] AC 465; *Martine v South East Kent Health Authority* (1993) *The Times*, 8 March (CA).

The rule is established as one of public policy. Those entrusted with public duties to protect vulnerable members of society should not have to look over their shoulders in the conduct of their duties.[8]

6.7.8 Malicious prosecution/malicious abuse of power

The authority acts as an enforcer and prosecutor and thus will clearly be seen in the position of a policeman. The tort of malicious prosecution will apply to the regulatory authority as it does to others in a position of public enforcement.

The essential requirements for a claimant to establish the tort are:

(1) there shall have been a prosecution or similar exercise of executive power;
(2) that prosecution shall have failed;
(3) there shall have been no reasonable grounds for bringing the prosecution or taking the action;
(4) the prosecution or action shall have been pursued for an improper or inappropriate motive (malice).

To state the principles is to show the difficulties which a prospective plaintiff may face. Errors of judgement in the course of routine regulation can never seriously be said to give grounds for such an action.

It is not proposed to dwell on this subject, for it will be seen immediately that the circumstances in which such a remedy could apply will be rare. The remedy could only apply where the authority prosecutes and fails, or where the authority obtains an order urgently cancelling registration and that order is not upheld on appeal. Furthermore, the appeal should not just be allowed, but it would have to be clear that there was no justification for the authority in making the application to the magistrate.

Failure of prosecution or loss of an appeal against a decision of a magistrate urgently to cancel registration would never be sufficient to found the tort. The authority must be proved to have acted unreasonably and for improper motives. The circumstances in which such a case could be advanced will be rare and should be readily identifiable should circumstances arise.

6.7.9 Breach of statutory duty

Actions for breach of statutory duty have been developed alongside the development of actions for negligence. It is necessary to establish:

(1) that the regulatory authority owes a duty; and
(2) that that duty is owed to the owner who makes complaint; and
(3) that the duty has been broken; and
(4) that ascertainable damage computed in accordance with the law has flowed from the breach of duty;
(5) further, and most important, it must be shown that the duty is one which Parliament intended to be accompanied by a private right to claim damages should a breach be established. Each and every case will have to

---

8 *Martine v South East Kent Health Authority* (1993) *The Times*, 8 March (CA).

be reviewed to see if it passes this final test even if all other tests are satisfied. Many regulatory duties are clearly not duties in respect of which Parliament would have intended a private right of damages to arise.

It is worth noting the caution expressed in the Court of Appeal in *Lyons v East Sussex County Council*,[9] in another context, to the effect that the 1984 Act exists to protect frail and vulnerable members of society, and not to protect home owners. It exists to regulate and restrain home owners in the interests of residents. Therefore, it is suggested that it will be only in unusual cases that the court is likely to find that the breach of a duty to an owner was actually intended to carry with it a private right of damages for that owner. In the final analysis, each case will be determined by the interpretation that is made of the provision in question.

6.7.10 Duty of care

In the absence of breach of statutory duty upon which an action may be maintained, and in the absence of malicious prosecution or abuse of power, the authority does not owe the home owner a duty of care as regards the manner in which it conducts the regulatory procedure or any parts of it.

The view of the Court of Appeal in *Lyons v East Sussex County Council* is relevant here. Given that the purpose of regulation is to protect the clients and not the owners, it would perhaps be surprising if a duty of care was owed. None the less, the actions of regulatory authorities can have devastating effects upon home owners; businesses may be lost and lives may be ruined.

Perhaps the harshest example is the cancellation of registration without warning and/or notice under the urgent cancellation procedure outlined in s 11 and s 30 of the 1984 Act. The issue came before the Court of Appeal in the case of *Martine v South East Kent Health Authority*,[10] upon an interlocutory point. In that case, the Health Authority had applied successfully for an order cancelling Mrs Martine's registration, as a matter of urgency. Mrs Martine's appeal to the Registered Homes Tribunal was allowed. Indeed, the Health Authority offered no justification for its action and suggested that it was content that the appeal be allowed. Nevertheless, the Court of Appeal held that there was no duty of care upon officers of the Health Authority when making an application to a magistrate. Clearly, there was material which entitled the magistrate to make the order. It was the presentation of the application and the investigation that lead to the application that gave rise to complaint.

The strength of this decision is beyond doubt, but may be slightly weakened following the decision by the House of Lords in *Spring v Guardian Assurance*.[11] The House of Lords, overruling the Court of Appeal, found that there was a duty of care on an employer supplying a reference for an employee, to that employee and to the party requesting and receiving the reference. The Court of Appeal had held that the employee was not entitled to invent a new cause of action relying upon an alleged duty of care, so as to avoid the

9 (1988) 86 LGR 369, (1988) 152 JP 488 (CA).
10 (1993) *The Times*, 8 March (CA).
11 [1995] 2 AC 296 (HL), overruling [1993] 2 All ER 273 (CA).

difficulties created by having to establish the tort of defamation. The House of Lords overruled that view and ruled that the duty of care existed. In *Martine*, the Court of Appeal held, in addition to the public policy issue on duty of care, that it was not open to Mrs Martine (following *Spring*) to invent a cause of action based on duty of care, in order to avoid the difficulties created by having to establish the tort of malicious prosecution. In view of *Spring*, this part of the Court of Appeal's judgment in *Martine* must now surely be regarded as suspect and likely to be overruled on similar grounds by the House of Lords.

In argument, the Court of Appeal, in *Martine*, took the *Spring* case as the primary point. In the judgment, the public policy issue features as the principal *ratio decidendi*. The author suggests that the overruling of *Spring* cannot be taken to overrule *Martine* on both points. The Court of Appeal's decision that no duty of care exists, as a matter of public policy, must be regarded as good law at least until that issue is reviewed in the House of Lords, or possibly by the Court of Appeal under its inherent powers.[12] Furthermore, the decisions of the House of Lords in *X (Minors) v Bedfordshire County Council*[13] give a clear statement that no duty of care lies in the performance of a public duty even where such a duty is exercised for the benefit of the claimant and has failed that claimant in a way which is said to amount to a breach of a duty of care.

The best view at the present time is that regulatory authorities hold no duty of care to care home owners in relation to the way in which regulation is conducted.

6.7.11   Liabilities of the authority to the client

Authorities, enjoined as they are to regard the interests of the frail and vulnerable within society, may be liable to such individual clients for breach of a duty of care should they fail to carry out their regulatory duties in a proper, effective and competent way. Such liability might arise in two ways:

(1)   a breach of a statutory duty;
(2)   liability for breach of a duty of care.

Breach of statutory duty

The essential ingredients of the tort of breach of statutory duty have been outlined above when considering the liability of an authority to an owner. The claimant will need to identify an express statutory duty to the individual which has been broken and which has given rise to damage, and go further to show that that duty was intended to be accompanied by a private right to claim damages in the event of breach.

Such express rights are rare, but it is suggested that it would be simpler to argue that private rights in damages do arise, given that the purpose of the regulatory scheme under the 1984 and 1989 Acts is to protect frail and vulnerable members of society.

---

12   See the argument in *Young v Bristol Aeroplane Co Ltd* [1944] 1 KB 718.
13   [1995] 2 FLR 276.

Duty of care

To find that there was a duty of care would indeed extend the potential liability of local authorities and Health Authorities and would be said by those who favour closing such doors as being a classic example of opening the floodgates to wide-ranging and speculative claims.

In reply, it might be said that there is little point in having a system of regulation to protect the frail and vulnerable if those who are frail and vulnerable are not entitled to seek compensation when they are damaged because the regulator has not acted in accordance with normal standards (perhaps the standard of the ordinary reasonably competent regulator dealing with a particular circumstance).

Resources are scarce. Without a duty of care that gives rise to a claim for compensation, some local authorities will, perhaps, ration resources so as to meet those areas where greater risk of liability arises.

The matter has come before the courts recently in the cases of *M (a Minor) v Newham LBC; X (Minors) v Bedfordshire County Council and Others.*[14] These cases involved claims by or on behalf of children and parents of children alleging breach of statutory duty and breach of duties of care by local authorities, and officers for whom local authorities and Health Authorities were responsible, in the implementation of the protection of children pursuant to the requirements of the 1989 Act.

The majority of the Court of Appeal (Bingham MR dissenting) dismissed the claims and held that there was no cause of action against the authorities. The majority found that, in the appropriate provisions of the 1989 Act, Parliament had not intended to give to children and their parents a private right in damages supporting breach of statutory duties. Furthermore, the majority held that a duty of care was not owed by such authorities and their servants and agents to children whose protection was the prime concern under the principles of the Act. Public policy, restriction of potential claims against public authorities and the opening the floodgates to potential claimants were cited as grounds for what is essentially a policy decision.

The House of Lords upheld the decision of the Court of Appeal. Even where public duties are owed for the protection of a vulnerable group, those duties are, as a matter of policy, owed to the wider public and not to the individuals concerned in particular cases, so as to create a potential private right to claim damages. It is different if an individual officer owes a particular duty of care for which the authority is vicariously liable.

6.8   CARE HOME MANAGEMENT

This section will consider three specific items:

(1)   complaints about the care service;
(2)   record-keeping;
(3)   employment of staff.

6.8.1   Handling complaints

The handling of complaints is a necessary skill in the operation of a care home business. Complaints are inevitable. Some will be justified and some will not. Both local authority and home owners (including the person in charge) are likely to be involved on a regular basis in complaint issues. A satisfactory complaints procedure is a part of good quality assurance in relation to service.

Complaints may arise internally. They may also arise externally where the complaint is made not to the home owner or person in charge, but publicly, perhaps through litigation, or direct to the authority.

6.8.2   Internal complaints

Within every group of persons accommodated in an establishment for communal living there will arise complaints about the standard of various aspects of the service supplied. The inevitability of such complaints must be recognised and the owner (together with the person in charge, if one is appointed) must, as a matter of good care practice, establish an open and available complaints procedure. Clients, staff and friends and relatives of clients must know that there is a complaints procedure, and must know that it works, so as to have confidence in it. A proper complaints procedure is thus a part of good care practice within a registered care home.

None of the relevant regulations appear to give direct authority for the requirement for a complaints procedure in a nursing home, but there is such a provision in the Residential Care Homes Regulations 1984, reg 17. However, it would be surprising if anyone would suggest that a well-run home could function appropriately without an effective procedure for handling complaints.

Such procedure should be explained as a part of the pre-admission or pre-contractual procedure. Clients and their relatives should know exactly what is to be done if a complaint arises. It is much better that the procedures are understood before there is a complaint, rather than angry requests being made for details of a complaints procedure in an emotionally charged atmosphere.

Details of the complaints procedure should appear in the home's promotional material and operational brochures. The home should have a complaints procedure policy. Details of the complaints procedure should be available openly in those parts of the home which are visited frequently by the public, and should be available in every client's personal accommodation. The safest course is to make sure that, in every possible place, there is seen the means to initiate the complaints procedure. Such an open invitation to refer complaints may very often be seen as a safeguard against inappropriate complaints.

The 1984 Regulations[15] require that it should be a part of any complaints procedure that clients and their relatives should be told the name and address of the local authority responsible for regulation (guidance and good practice

---

15   Regulation 17.

suggest that this should also include the telephone and fax numbers of the authority) and indicate that if dissatisfied or, even as a first course, they may take such a complaint to the authority. Clients should also appreciate, and this will no doubt be reinforced by the authority, that complaints to the authority are likely to be met, in the first instance, by the question as to why the matter has not been pursued internally. There may be a good reason, but external complaints procedures are normally only appropriate if internal procedures have been exhausted.

Complainants often say that they have been fearful that the making of a complaint will rebound against them or against their friends or relatives in care. Owners should take pains to ensure that this view is dispelled and should work actively to encourage complaints so as to bring into the open concerns that may otherwise develop into serious issues. It is suggested that any evidence of attempt by staff to dissuade clients or their relatives from using the complaints procedure should be regarded as a serious disciplinary offence.

Not only should the complaints procedure be open and available, but so also should be the results of that procedure. Complainants, their supporters and others will be satisfied if they can see that an investigation is taking place, has been conducted fairly and has produced a result which answers the allegation.

Proper conduct of complaints procedures is a matter which a local authority will study carefully in the investigation of a regulated care home. The existence of a complaints procedure is therefore important, as is the existence of a procedure that works and is seen to work quickly and fairly.

6.8.3   External complaints

If a complaint gives rise to a cause of action at law, then the courts are the appropriate forum to pursue the issue. If the complaint does not give rise to a cause of action, or if litigation is not an appropriate remedy, then the aggrieved party will have to consider other options.

One clear option is to complain, where the complaint relates to a regulated business, to the regulator of that business. Authorities should, therefore, establish procedures to encourage complaints to the authority about the conduct of registered homes. Such procedures should always suggest that complaints should be made, in the first place, to the registered care home owner or person in charge. Complaints should only be referred to the authority if no satisfactory conclusion is reached.

Complaints are an important indication for authorities as to the breakdown of services within a registered care home. Although some owners argue to the contrary, an authority must investigate each and every complaint that is made. The investigation may be short. There will be cases where the simplest examination will show that the complaint is unsustainable.

The purpose of the authority in receiving and investigating the complaint is the better to carry out its functions as the regulator of a registered care home. The authority will not be able to provide a remedy for the complaint, save to recommend other causes of action to the complainant or to arrange reconciliation between the care home owner and the client, where relations have broken down.

The authority will gain a valuable insight into the operation of the registered care home, when the authority is not physically present. Such evidence will be invaluable and form an important part of the picture of operation of the care home as seen through the eyes of the regulator.

How an authority investigates a complaint depends entirely on the nature of the complaint and the gravity of the issues raised. There is no requirement for the authority immediately, or at all, to notify the owner that a complaint has been made, or the nature of that complaint. If the complaint is sustained and the authority feels it appropriate to take regulatory action, then it will have to reveal sufficient of the complaint to justify the allegations of breach of regulatory standards as are made in the course of such subsequent action.

To reveal the nature and source of the complaint at an early stage of the investigation might be to frustrate the investigation itself. To reveal the source of the complaint may put the complainant at risk. Anonymous complaints or complaints from those who require the authority to preserve their anonymity are, therefore, frequent. Difficult issues of principle arise.

An authority should always regard anonymous complaints with great caution. Similarly, save in exceptional cases, the fact that complainants wish their identity to be kept secret and are not prepared to be named to support the complaint does suggest that the veracity of the complaint may be questioned. Those who tell the truth about serious issues are seldom concerned about being associated with the evidence. There are, of course, exceptions.

Where information is supplied in confidence, the authority should respect that confidence. That is no reason not to investigate the complaint. It may be that, as a result of the complaint, the authority investigates and itself finds evidence which will justify regulatory action.

The authority must understand that any regulatory action may be challenged, with the consequent requirement for objective justification in courts or Tribunals. In those cases, the evidence which justified the action must be available for challenge. Necessarily, evidence which the informant will not support and will not appear to adduce, is evidence which will be valueless in terms of regulatory action. It may not be valueless, however, in putting the authority upon the trail of serious issues.

Tribunals will not insist upon technical rules of evidence in relation to issues concerning the operation of a care home. Authorities should not do so either. However, this does not mean that sensible rules of practice as to credibility of evidence should be discarded so that authorities and their officers proceed upon the basis of supposition, circumstantial inference and rumour. Too often, the officers of authorities, persuaded by the genuine nature of complaints, assume truth prior to investigation and continue to assume truth even in the absence of corroborative material or, sometimes, in the face of contradictory material.

If the subject matter of the complaint, when investigated, produces corroborative evidence and the matter is so grave as to justify further regulatory action, the authority should put the issues to the owner or person in charge, or other relevant staff, as a matter of good practice. If the material discovered gives rise to a suspicion that a criminal offence, whether under the Registered Homes Act 1984 or otherwise, may have arisen, then serious consideration should be given to the provisions of the Police and Criminal Evidence Act 1984. If the authority wishes to rely in evidence upon anything that may be said once reasonable suspicion of a criminal offence has arisen, the standard caution or words to the effect of the caution should be administered. Slavish adherence to the formula:

> 'You are not obliged to say anything, but anything you do say will be taken down and may be given in evidence and if at a subsequent stage you seek to rely in your defence upon any material which might reasonably have been disclosed now that matter may be drawn to the attention of the court hearing any proceedings which may subsequently have been instituted.'

is not necessary, but the message must be conveyed that interviewees need not respond but if they do respond, they are warned that what they say may be taken into account and used and that they should give explanations reasonably available rather than spring them by surprise on the prosecution at a later date when it will be more difficult for prosecutors to check the facts.

As soon as inspecting officers reasonably believe that an offence may have been committed they should caution the suspect (if they wish to rely on material subsequently admitted).

Although the statutory codes on investigation of offences under the Police and Criminal Evidence Act 1984 apply to care home inspectors as 'police officers',[16] such are of limited effect as inspections of registered homes are occasions upon which the consent of the property owner is not required for searches that come within the definition of 'inspection', as such 'inspections' are authorised by statute and not dependent on owner-approval or individual sanction, for example a search warrant authorised by a Justice of the Peace.

Those inspecting, with the owner's permission, must advise the owner if they discover material which causes them to suspect that an offence has been committed. They may only continue with the inspection if permitted by law or if they have the owner's consent.[17] Authorities will only be authorised to search if they comply strictly with all the conditions precedent to inspections: see Chapter 8.

There is no obligation upon the authority to share with owners the detailed results of investigations or even the fact that investigations are taking place. However, authorities should bear in mind that, if they wish to rely upon the results of investigations immediately or at a later date, then they will be criticised if they have not taken action at an appropriate time to canvass the results of the investigation with those directly concerned, ie the owner and senior staff.

In the investigation of complaints, authorities should be astute to appreciate that certain types of complaint are motivated by self-interest and, sometimes, are made by those obsessed by emotions such as fear or guilt. On occasion, a desire for revenge may be discerned. The evidence of dismissed staff should always be treated with caution, particularly when their complaints are made contemporaneously with dismissal. Complaints by relatives should also be approached with caution. A number of emotions may affect relatives in

---

16   Police and Criminal Evidence Act 1984.
17   Ibid, Code B.

relation to family members being in care and those emotions may prevent a truly objective reaction to events about which they have heard or which they have observed. Also, junior members of staff may not fully appreciate the reasons why senior professionals operate in a particular way.

Authorities should not be dismissive of complaints, but nor should they be too swift to accept complaints as justified.

6.9 RECORD-KEEPING

6.9.1 General

An efficient business run appropriately will keep well-ordered records and the business of a registered care home is no exception. Records are required to be kept as a matter of law and as a matter of good practice. In some cases, records that are required as a matter of practice, although not as a matter of law, may become so important that their absence would reflect upon the fitness of the owner to continue to be registered.

The regulations do not require owners to keep records of the numbers and identities of staff employed from day to day, or to keep records of individual care plans in respect of clients. However, to find a care home that failed to keep such records would be surprising. Absence of such records suggests unfitness to operate the care home.

The 1984 and 1989 Acts, and particularly the regulations made under those statutes, require certain records to be kept.

6.9.2 Statutory record-keeping

It is not intended to comment here in detail upon each and every record required to be kept. The sources will be identified with certain examples.

6.9.3 Residential care homes

The obligation to keep certain records is introduced by reg 6 of the Residential Care Homes Regulations 1984. The powers of the inspector to call for inspection of records at a residential care home is limited to the statutory records.[18] The records are set out in Sch 2 to the 1984 Regulations but the owner of a small home is exempted from keeping many of them.

Upon studying the exceptions, one may wonder whether the exemptions have advanced the owners of a small home very far, or whether, indeed, they would not wish to keep those records. The keeping of records is as much for the protection of the owner as for the convenience of the authority or for the protection of clients.

Authorities will wish to inspect such records on all full inspections and most other inspections. The records are to be kept at the home. Keeping them elsewhere is not acceptable.

---

18   Registered Homes Act 1984, s 17(3).

6.9.4 Nursing homes

Records to be maintained at nursing homes are less extensive than those required at residential care homes. Nursing homes are controlled by registered medical doctors and registered nurses. The requirements of professional practice of such doctors and nurses include requirements to keep proper records. No doubt, the limited statutory requirement took into account the extra requirements of proper professional practice on such doctors and nurses.

An authority inspecting a nursing home is entitled to inspect any records and is not limited to the statutorily required records.[19] The records required to be kept by statute are identified in reg 7 of the 1984 Nursing Regulations, which introduces Sch 4, identifying particular information to be recorded in the case records of patients in nursing homes. The records required to be kept pursuant to these regulations do not need to be kept at the home (in contrast with the position in residential care homes), save for the case record dealing with the daily statement of the patient's health and condition or any investigations made, surgical operations carried out and treatment given. A distinction is drawn between working papers which professionals within the nursing home may require for on-going treatment and other records. Note that this description does not include a modern 'care plan'; it is submitted by the author that 'care planning' is now such standard practice that failure to maintain such plans would be evidence of 'unfitness'. However, whether such a plan would be a clinical record remains an interesting question.[20]

6.9.5 Registered children's homes

The statutory requirement for the keeping of certain records is introduced by Part II of Sch 6 to the 1989 Act and, in particular, para 10(1)(f).

6.9.6 The Children's Home Regulations 1991

Paragraphs 15 and 17 of these regulations provide for the keeping of records. The person responsible for keeping the records at a registered children's home is the responsible authority, ie the person responsible for the operation of the home. Records are divided as between confidential records which that person shall arrange to be kept and to be kept securely and treated as confidential, and other records which that person is obliged to keep.

Schedule 2 to the regulations sets out the information which the owner must arrange to keep confidentially and Sch 3 sets out other records which the owner is merely obliged to keep.

6.9.7 Voluntary records

The need to keep records does not stop with the limits of the statutory requirement to that effect. It is suggested that complete and detailed records should be kept by every regulated care home owner in respect of every aspect

---

19 Nursing Homes and Mental Nursing Homes Regulations 1984, reg 10.
20 See reg 10(3) of the Nursing Homes and Mental Nursing Homes Regulations 1984.

of the business, particularly as that aspect impacts upon the care supplied to clients who are not able to care for themselves.

Record-keeping is a burden but it is essential for the following reasons:

(1) without records, proper care cannot be supplied;
(2) without records, what has occurred in relation to care or other issues cannot effectively be discerned;
(3) records are kept so as to simplify investigations which may occur in the future and to protect the home owner from being unable to defend claims through lack of information.

6.9.8 How long should records be kept?

Records should be kept as long as may reasonably be thought necessary. Minimum periods are prescribed. In relation to statutory records at residential care homes, records must be kept for a minimum of 3 years from the date of the last entry of the record.[21] In relation to nursing homes, the only limits on keeping records are that records in relation to medical or nursing intervention and statements of health and condition should be kept for one year from the date of the last entry.

Records under the Mental Health (Hospital Guardianship and Consent to Treatment) Regulations 1983[22] are required to be kept for not less than 5 years from the date that the patient left the home.

In relation to registered children's homes, records are required to be kept, where the records are of a confidential nature, for 75 years, unless the child dies before attaining the age of 18, in which case the records must be kept for 15 years from date of death. Other records, other than records of menus, must be kept for at least 15 years.

Save in relation to registered children's homes, given the purpose for which records are kept, the time-limits prescribed by the Residential Care Homes Regulations 1984 and the Nursing Homes and Mental Nursing Homes Regulations 1984 are inadequate. The periods suggested in the Children Homes Regulations 1991 in respect of all records other than confidential records, ie a retention period of 15 years, seems a minimum safe period. Records will be a vital source of evidence and information if claims are brought against owners alleging lack of care. Legal liability insurers may well decline cover if records are not maintained and preserved.

Claims for damages for personal injury may be brought within 3 years from the date when the incident giving rise to damage occurred. Other claims at law may, generally, be brought within a period of 6 years from the date when the incident arose. The periods during which claims may be brought may be extended if it can be shown that the claimant did not have sufficient knowledge and understanding of the potential claim until 3 or 6 years from the date when such knowledge first arose. In the case of confused or mentally ill clients, the limitation on bringing legal proceedings is never closed. In the case of damage to children, the limitation periods do not begin to run until the

---

21 Residential Care Homes Regulations 1984, reg 6(4).
22 SI 1983/893.

child has attained full age, ie 18 years. It would, therefore, be foolish to discard records too early.[23]

In respect of such legal liability, most owners will be insured. Owners will probably find that insurers have their own requirements about the keeping and retention of records and failure to keep or preserve such records for appropriate periods of time may enable insurers to disclaim liability under the relevant policy. Owners should read insurance policies with care. If in doubt, insurers should be consulted. If in any doubt, a record should be retained rather than discarded.

6.9.9 Nature of records

To be meaningful, records must be complete and legible. A home owner should establish policies about the method and regularity of keeping records. Modern practice suggests different styles of record-keeping. Proper record-keeping is a professional responsibility of qualified care workers, particularly nurses and registered medical practitioners.

6.9.10 Alteration of records

If an error has occurred in the records, the error should be recorded in a rider or note so that subsequent readers can see the original note and the correction. Original records should not be altered under any circumstances. At best, such gives rise to suspicion of falsification; at worst, it is found to be falsification itself. Falsification of records points inevitably to unfitness to carry on a regulated care home where the maintenance of records is an essential obligation.

6.10 STAFF

The operation of a registered care home is a labour intensive business. Second only to the core business of delivering satisfactory care is the proper and effective management of staff. Without efficient, properly skilled and well-managed staff, a regulated care home cannot operate. Where staff are not properly managed, it may be suggested that the home is unfit to remain registered.

The staff to be managed will not only be substantial in numbers but varied in skills and functions. The owner must be able to increase and reduce staff establishments as patient requirements reduce and increase. In relation to those staff engaged in the direct provision of care, whilst the owner may rely to an extent upon agency staff supplied on a temporary basis, the regulatory authority will expect to see permanent staff, who are able to assimilate and develop care for individual clients on a personal basis.

Detailed examination of employment law is beyond the scope of this book. However, certain issues will be addressed for the sake of completeness:

(1)   contracts of employment and particulars of employment;

---

23   References to Limitation Acts.

(2)   disciplinary action;
(3)   trade unions;
(4)   transfer of employment and TUPE.

6.10.1   Contracts of employment and particulars of employment

The law does not require employers to enter into formal written contracts of employment with employees. Nevertheless, it is good practice for such contracts to be negotiated. The law does require that every employee should, within (not later than two months) after the commencement of employment, receive a statement of particulars of the terms of employment, including the following material[24] (changes in terms of employment must be notified within four weeks):

The basic particulars
   (1)   the name of the employer and employee;
   (2)   the date when the employment began;
   (3)   the date upon which the period of continuous employment began, if different from the date in (2) above.

The terms of employment
   (4)   the rates of pay (or method of calculating pay);
   (5)   the frequency of payment;
   (6)   the hours of work;
   (7)   holiday entitlement;
   (8)   any terms relating to incapacity due to sickness or injury and any provision for sick pay;
   (9)   any terms and conditions relating to pensions and pension schemes;
  (10)   the length of notice which the employee is obliged to give, and is entitled to receive, to terminate the contract of employment;
  (11)   the title of the job which the employee is employed to do;
  (12)   details of whether or not there are any disciplinary rules and grievance procedures and if there are any, details of where those rules and procedures are set out (if not in the statement);
  (13)   as an alternative to the job title, a brief description of the work for which the employee is employed;
  (14)   if the employment is not intended to be permanent, details of the period for which it is expected to continue, or if it is for a fixed term, the date on which it is to end;
  (15)   either the place of work, or, where the employee is to work at various places, an indication of that and the address of the employer;
  (16)   details of any collective agreements which directly affect the terms and conditions of the employment;
  (17)   if the employee is required to work outside the UK for more than one month, particulars of:

---

24   Employment Rights Act 1996, s 1(2).

(a) the period for which the employee is to work outside the UK;

(b) the currency in which remuneration is to be paid during that period;

(c) details of any remuneration paid or *ex gratia* benefits provided by reason of the employee being required to work outside the UK; and

(d) any terms and conditions relating to the employee's return to the UK.

Good employment relations and practice suggest not only that particulars of employment should be given but that a full contract should be made. Both employer and employee should understand their position in relation to the vital aspects of the relationship of employment.

The required particulars of employment may be included in a contract of employment. The particulars may be contained in more than one document but items (1) to (7), (11) and (15) *must* be in the same document.

Even a small regulated care home is likely to have a substantial staff. Care must be delivered 24 hours a day, 7 days of the week, every week of the year, every year. To meet the requirements, significant numbers of employees are required. It is impossible to manage such numbers of employees without the basis of employment being written down. This is as much in the interests of the employer as the employee.

It is beyond the remit of regulatory authorities to be concerned about individual terms and conditions of employment, save to the extent that those conditions may impact upon the willingness or ability of staff to deliver care. Lack of ability to provide the service of care will impact upon the owner whose obligation it is to provide the care and satisfy the regulatory authority that care is provided.

Unhappy staff will function poorly. Staff who are required or encouraged to work excessive hours will not function as well as staff who work moderate hours with reasonable overtime allowances. Staff will expect and require holidays. Performance will suffer where staff are required, encouraged or permitted to work without holidays. Holidays are not an alternative to payment, but an important recreational break, ensuring that employees are the more easily able to fulfil their required tasks.

Exclusion of holidays is not the same as the exclusion of holiday pay. Rates of pay may be enhanced so as to ensure that the period of absence has been covered. If such a policy is adopted, it must be plainly stated in the particulars of employment.

Authorities should avoid being prescriptive about terms and conditions of employment or seeking to translate into private sector regulated care homes the sort of conditions which are negotiated in the public service. However, it is legitimate for authorities to consider terms of employment of staff in the context of whether those terms and conditions are conducive to delivery of adequate care services. The authority will also consider whether the numbers of staff employed are sufficient to deliver services. By numbers is meant sufficient numbers working reasonable hours to deliver an adequate service. The hours can be supplied by smaller numbers of care workers, but those hours will be less effective. Authorities and owners should be aware that the moment at which the highest level of skill is required is not predictable, may arise suddenly and may well arise at an anti-social hour. Night-times and weekends are times at which vigilance and skill are required to be of the highest.

6.10.2   Disciplinary action

Disciplinary action is an unpleasant but inevitable part of operating any business which requires a substantial labour force. The owner must not shrink from the responsibility to administer constructive discipline. Such may be required in the interests of patient care.

A reasonably substantial work force always benefits from the introduction of a code of discipline. Staff at all levels require to know where they stand. An essential element of effective disciplinary action is that it is seen to be fair. A hallmark of fairness is that a code of discipline is established and that the code is followed.

The code should indicate breaches of employment, and the results, or the range of results, that will follow. Offences which are liable to serious disciplinary action, ie a final warning before dismissal or summary dismissal, should be identified. Appropriate review and so-called 'grievance procedures' should be established. In smaller homes where the management is in the hands of the owner, it may be impossible to establish a grievance procedure with any real meaning. The owner or person in charge will make the decision and will be unlikely to change that decision on review. Employees should appreciate this.

Where the person in charge is separate from the owner, it may well be appropriate for an employee to have a right to have a grievance, in relation to discipline imposed by the person in charge, reviewed by the owner. Dismissal of employees can lead to time-consuming and expensive disputes.

6.10.3   Dismissal

Dismissal may occur where an employer terminates an employee's contract of employment with or without notice. It may also occur where the employee terminates the contract of employment on the basis that his continued employment is no longer possible, because the circumstances of his treatment are such as to make it impossible for him to continue. The prospect of such an allegation (known as 'constructive dismissal') becomes more likely the greater the seniority of the staff concerned. Employees should be slow to make allegations of constructive dismissal. Employers will allege that no dismissal has occurred and that the employee has resigned. Courts and Tribunals are slow to accept that the treatment of an employee was such as to justify such an allegation. Sometimes, this is seen as an excuse for resignation, in the hope that resignation may lead to compensation (which, frequently, does not follow). The consequences of losing a complaint based upon an allegation of constructive dismissal, following voluntary termination of employment by an employee, are dire for the employee. The employee is deemed to have resigned without remedy.

If there is a dismissal, then the employee is entitled to two types of remedy:

(1) a remedy at common law for damages for breach of the contract of employment;
(2) a remedy for compensation for unfair dismissal under the Employment Protection legislation.

6.10.4 Dismissal at common law

At common law, an employer is entitled to dismiss an employee without reason. The employee's entitlement is to the period of notice provided by contract or a minimum period imposed by statute if the contract is silent or seeks to provide for notice less than that minimum, or a reasonable period of notice established by custom and practice within a particular area of activity.

An employee's rights will be to seek damages, which will be broadly equivalent to the period of notice which the employee was entitled to receive, less any payments already made. An employee will be expected to minimise his losses by seeking alternative employment and taking any reasonable offers of employment that are available.

6.10.5 Unfair dismissal

The remedy of unfair dismissal arose from recognition that common law rights were insufficient to compensate employees who had lost their livelihood. Where it is established that an employee has been dismissed, it is for the employer to establish the reason. That reason must be permissible. If the reasons are not permissible, then the fact of dismissal is deemed to be unfair.

The permissible reasons for dismissal are:

(1) incapacity to work denoting inability as opposed to incompetence or misconduct;
(2) redundancy;
(3) misconduct;
(4) some other substantial reason.

Not only must the reason for dismissal be a permitted reason, but the sanction of dismissal must be appropriate to the behaviour of the employee.

Neither incapacity to work nor redundancy are necessarily pejorative of the employee's conduct. An employer is not expected to continue to employ an employee who is not able to do the work. Nor is an employer expected to continue to employ an employee for whom he no longer has work.

Redundancy is never simple and special rules will be employed to ensure that redundancy is not used as an excuse for unfair victimisation of employees or selection of undesirable employees for redundancy, as opposed to those who should, generally, first be selected for dismissal where work shrinks. A basic principle is the last to be employed should be the first to be dismissed.

An employer is not expected to continue to employ an employee who misbehaves. However, misbehaviour must be such as to justify dismissal and not lesser disciplinary action.

Recognising that there will be many and various circumstances which may justify a dismissal, it is also provided that other substantial reasons may be advanced. Even if dismissal is for a permissible reason and dismissal is a sanction appropriate to the circumstances, the manner of dismissal must be conducted fairly. Whether a dismissal is fair in the circumstances will be judged upon the view of the reasonable employer in the position of the employer taking the decision at the time when the decision was taken.

The manner of dismissal may not stand if not conducted with care and proper advice. Instant dismissals can rarely be justified. Allegations of incapacity to work cannot arise overnight. Steps should be taken to see if alternative employment is available. Time should be taken to see if the incapacity can be overcome. Investigations should be conducted to see if training will assist. Candidates for redundancy must be selected with care, and proper notice of redundancy must be given. Redundancy can never arise by way of summary dismissal.

Misconduct can arise immediately, but a sensible employer will reflect before making a decision. It will rarely, if ever, be appropriate to dismiss instantly in the context of employment within a regulated care home. The more proper course of action is to suspend the employee pending investigation. The suspended employee (who will be under instruction from the employer whilst suspended with or without pay) should return at an appointed time to be faced with the results of the investigation. Actions should not be taken at that time, but a further appointment made at which the employee will be ready to give their side of the story and probably be supported by a representative, perhaps a solicitor or friend.

Such a procedure may not affect the result but it should be followed to show not only that the employer has considered matters seriously, but also that the employer has been seen to act in a way that enables the employee's side of the case to be heard, thus demonstrating fairness.

Authorities will expect to see owners of regulated care homes conduct their employment practices in a proper way. An owner who is seen to act in a high handed and unfair way may be thought to act similarly in relation to business and care decisions. Such a person may be thought to be unfit to be a registered care home owner.

However, there are circumstances when an employee cannot be retained within a care business irrespective of the consequences. An owner will be faced with a family type business where staff are working closely together and providing a service to care for those who cannot care for themselves. Disaffection and incompetence or poor conduct, which creates lack of confidence, on the part of the owner, in the employee, cannot be tolerated. Such conduct undermines the constructive spirit that is required in a well managed staff, in order to deliver proper care.

The cases will be rare, but there will be cases where, even though it appears to the prudent employer that he may be acting unfairly, it is more important in the interests of the clients in care that members of staff should be dismissed than that their employment should be preserved. The more senior the staff, the more likely this is to occur. It is unlikely that the relationship between an owner and person in charge would survive an allegation of serious misconduct even if, on strict standards of industrial practice, dismissal was not justified. A regulated care home cannot risk having a disaffected person in charge.

Owners may well think it appropriate, and their decision may be respected by regulatory authorities as well as other members of staff, to remove disaffected senior staff, rather than risk continuing difficulties in the operation of the home. In those circumstances, owners will have to accept that the price of protecting the business may be substantial compensation for unfair dismissal.

Complaints for unfair dismissal cannot be brought until the employee has been employed continuously for 2 years. The time is reckoned from the commencement of employment until the date when proper notice for termination of employment would take effect (the effective date of termination of employment). Similar restrictions apply to applications for payments of redundancy payments following dismissal by reason of genuine redundancy.

There is a limit on the maximum compensation payable in respect of unfair dismissal. The award is divided into a basic award (intended to protect against the loss of redundancy rights) and a compensatory award. The basic award is computed by multiplying the number of years of continuous employment by a multiplier which will be fractions calculated by reference to the employee's net wages. The multiplier will be: 3/2 for employees over 41 years of age, 1 for employees over 22 but under 41 years of age and 1/2 for employees under 22 years of age.

A maximum net wage, for the purpose of calculation of compensation, is set and is currently £210 per week. The maximum basic award is £6,300 and the maximum compensatory award is currently fixed at £11,300.[25]

Employers should remember that there are important exceptions to the imposition of these limits. The limits are increased rapidly and dramatically if an employee is dismissed for an impermissible reason, for example, trade union activity. Dismissal for trade union activity, which is an impermissible reason, and a failure to re-instate leads rapidly to an increase in the maximum award to £27,500. Where dismissal is found to be on grounds of sex discrimination, there is no limit to the amount of the award that can be made.

Employers should remember that allegations of sex discrimination may not only be made by women, but also by men. This is important to remember in a sector of business where a large proportion of the employees are women.

Remedies of re-engagement and re-instatement can be sought in relation to unfair dismissal. Re-engagement is hardly ever relevant in relation to the operation of regulated care homes, as re-engagement implies engagement in a different capacity from that in which employed. Substantially different employments in different locations or with different responsibilities are not a reality in regulated care homes.

Re-instatement is a possibility, but it is unlikely, save in case of impermissible dismissal for trade union activities or possibly dismissal as a result of sex discrimination, that a Tribunal would award re-instatement in a situation where the employment is essentially intimate and involves the provision of personal services. Re-instatement is rarely awarded where it would produce an unworkable relationship between employer and employee and

---

25 Employment Rights Act 1996, s 124(1).

particularly where that would adversely affect the service provided by the employer's business to others, in this case the care of those who are not able to care for themselves.

6.10.6   Trade unions

Trade unions seldom impact on the day-to-day operation of care homes. There is no obligation to recognise a trade union. If a trade union has entered into a recognition agreement with the owners of a regulated care home, then the owners must conduct themselves in accordance with the recognition agreement and only negotiate with the recognised trade union.

In reality, trade unions can be influential and, even if not recognised, where a significant number of employees within the regulated care home are members of the union, the reality is that the owner will have to listen to the union and deal with the union representing the employees.

The authority will only be concerned in relation to dealings with trade unions, as with other employment practices, insofar as those impact on an owner's ability to deliver care to clients in need in accordance with proper standards and to follow the requirements for operation of a regulated care home.

Taking steps which cause confrontation or disrupt the willingness of staff to perform their contracts of employment without good cause may be a reason which gives rise to concern as to the continued fitness of the regulated care home owner.

6.10.7   Professional bodies and trade associations

Whilst it is not for regulatory authorities to give specific advice to owners as to particular problems arising in care home operation, there are a number of well-established and respectable trade associations. The four principal associations are:

The Registered Nursing Home Association
Calthorpe House, Hagley Road, Edgbaston, Birmingham B16 8Q7
Telephone: (0121) 454–2511
Fax: (0121) 454–0932

The British Federation of Care Home Proprietors
852 Milton Road, Thurmaston, Leicester LE5 8BN
Telephone: (01533) 640–095
Fax: (01533) 640–141

The National Care Homes Association
5 Bloomsbury Place, London WC1A 2QA
Telephone: (0171) 436–1871
Fax: (0171) 436–1193

Independent Healthcare Association
22 Little Russell Street, London WC1A 2HT
Telephone: (0171) 420–0537
Fax: (0171) 242–2681

In addition, there are a number of local associations of care home owners, growing in number and efficiency since the introduction of community care contracting and the necessity for good working relations with local authorities, both as purchasers and regulators.

Such associations, whether they be national or local, welcome the opportunity to advise both in relation to applications for registration and the conduct of regulated care home business.

It is often thought that local authorities are sufficiently well resourced and informed as not to need support and assistance from others. In the author's experience this is not so. Increasingly, groups of registration officers from local authorities and Health Authorities gather on a regional and national basis. Inspecting officers are represented by:

National Association of Inspection and Registration Officers (NAIRO)
Heather Wing, Chief Executive, 28 Broom Lane, Rotherham S60 35L
Telephone and Fax: (01709) 366–237

Society of Nursing Inspection and Registration Officers (SONIRO)
Royal College of Nursing, 20 Cavendish Square, London W1M 04B
Telephone: (0171) 409–3333
Fax: (0171) 495–6104

In addition, Health Authorities have their own professional association:

NHS Confederation
(formerly the National Association of Health Authorities and Trusts (NAHAT))
26 Chapter Street, London SW1P 4ND
Telephone: (0171) 233–7388
Fax: (0171) 233–7390

This organisation has a specific division dealing with the regulation of nursing homes from the local authority point of view.

Day-to-day problems that may confront authorities or owners in the operation of care homes will always benefit from being referred to such national or local associations, who will have a wider experience and will usually offer encouragement and solutions.

6.10.8 Transfer of Employment and the Transfer of Undertakings (Protection of Employment) Regulations 1981[26] (TUPE)

These regulations protect the employment status of employees when the ownership of a business changes hands. Employees will be entitled to have continuity of employment from the date when first they began to work in the business and protection of the terms and conditions of their employment.

Employees thus do not need to be concerned where ownership of a regulated care home changes hands. The new owner will not be able to negotiate without their consent in relation to terms and conditions of employment and will certainly not be able to impose changed terms and conditions of employment.

The new employer, for his part, must appreciate that he will be bound by the terms and conditions of employment which already exist. If prudent and

---

26 SI 1981/1794.

well advised, he will investigate those terms and conditions carefully, particularly any working practices that may not be recorded in documents, before proceeding to purchase.

The provisions apply equally where a private employer takes over the operation of care homes previously operated in the public sector and brought into the private sector, where they will be regulated. The terms and conditions allowed to public sector employees will be transferred under TUPE to the private sector employer with the transfer of the business and the transfer, in consequence, of the employment.

Refusal to accept transfer of employees amounts to unfair dismissal on the part of the new employer. Insisting, unlawfully, on disadvantageous changes in terms of employment may constitute constructive dismissal and that will be unfair dismissal. However, the employees may simply insist on performance by the transferee employer of all the transferred terms. This may be more expensive for the employer.

Attempts to avoid the regulations by dismissal prior to business transfer will fail. If the business is transferred, the employee will be entitled:

(1)   to any 'redundancy' payment made by the old employer; and
(2)   to insist that the new employer honours all the 'old' terms and conditions of employment.[27]

An employer who flouted the interests of employees in breach of the legal requirements under TUPE might clearly be seen to be a person unfit to be registered to carry on a regulated care home. As with other instances, isolated circumstances might not necessarily lead to such a conclusion, but a conglomeration of such allegations will come together to present an inescapable conclusion of unfitness.

Even where no trade union is recognised, an employer must remain aware of the substantial sanctions for dismissal that may be held to be related to trade union activity. If members of trade unions are actively pressing for trade union recognition, or pressing their claims through trade union representatives, and in that context or shortly thereafter they are dismissed, there is likely to be an allegation that the dismissal was related to trade union activities. The owner/ employer should be aware of this risk and be particularly careful to avoid punishing awards of damages or facing reinstatement, which is not only a loss of face but which, in those circumstances, might be quite ruinous to the continuation of the business.

6.11   CRIMINAL RECORDS

It has long been regarded as good practice that employers of prospective staff to care for vulnerable clients in residential care should question applicants as to their previous criminal record.

The restrictions on dictation for the disclosure of criminal offences contained within the Rehabilitation of Offenders Act 1974 do not apply to such

27   *Wilson v St Helens Borough Council* (1997) *The Times,* 18 July.

questions in relation to employment within residential care or nursing homes or registered children's homes.[28]

It is now required that before employing or engaging a person who is to have substantial and unsupervised access to children on a sustained or regular basis an operator must take steps to obtain information about that prospective employee's criminal record.[29] The Government has set up a scheme whereby the police will co-operate with this requirement provided that requests for information are made through a nominated officer at the local authority.[30]

There clearly may be room for significant discussion in relation to what amounts to 'substantial and unsupervised access' and whether or not such is upon 'a sustained or regular basis'. Owners should, as a matter of practice, check all staff unless it is quite clear that such staff will have nothing to do with direct care of children or have no contact whatsoever with children. A wise course would be to check all staff.

---

28   See generally Rehabilitation of Offenders Act 1974 (Exceptions) Order 1975.
29   The Children (Protection from Offenders) (Miscellaneous Amendments) Regulations 1997. Inserting new para 5(3) of the Children's Homes Regulations 1991, SI 1991/1506.
30   LAC (97) 18. Police checks on staff working in registered private children's homes and small unregistrable children's homes.

Chapter 7

PURCHASE AND SALE OF CARE HOMES

7.1 INTRODUCTION

Since a registered care home is a valuable business asset, its sale and purchase should not be viewed as a simple property transaction. Whilst the underlying principal asset supporting a care home business is an estate in real property, whether it be freehold or leasehold, that real property estate will be of diminished or possibly little value unless accompanied by the other important elements which need to be transferred to a purchaser in order that that purchaser may both inherit and exploit the business which he has purchased.

7.2 PRELIMINARY MATTERS

Solicitors and other advisers acting in relation to such a purchase need to take particular care. In addition to the estate in land, transfer of the following will also be required:

(1) the goodwill of the business;
(2) title to fixtures, fittings and loose furniture;
(3) the full benefit and advantage of existing contracts with patients or residents, or with those who sponsor such patients or residents; and local authorities purchasing community care services; and
(4) contracts of employment with the staff, including key staff and in particular, the principal nursing officer or residential care home manager (although such contracts will automatically transfer with the business purchasers will wish to be sure that staff remain and do not leave on transfer leaving the business unmanageable).

These elements are to be found in a wide variety of business transfers. However, with transfers of care home businesses, there is the all-important addition that the purchaser must acquire property, real and personal, and physical conduct of the business, so that he is in a position to conduct that business lawfully by holding an appropriate registration certificate. Without such certificate, any purchaser would trade unlawfully from the moment at which he completes the purchase, which may well lead to prosecution for unlawful conduct of a care home business. The purchaser has no right to expect any period of grace within which to complete registration formalities.

It is essential that any purchaser does not complete such a purchase and does not enter into any contract which commits him to complete such a purchase until he has received a certificate of registration. In most cases, the certificate of registration will itself not be sufficient. The conditions which limit the registration must be in terms at least identical to those which were applicable to the business prior to transfer, or in terms which the purchaser finds satisfactory. An agreement to purchase, subject to the issue of a certificate of registration, will not suffice. Vital issues which concern the conditions as to numbers of persons to be accommodated, categories of persons to be accommodated and in the case of nursing homes, the levels of nurses who must be employed as a condition of registration, will have a direct impact on the financial viability of the home. It is beyond the scope of this book to deal in detail with general aspects arising on the conveyancing of real property or upon the transfer of a business, but before turning to issues directly relating to registration, some aspects in relation to general transfer issues are worthy of special attention.

7.3   PROPERTY CONSIDERATIONS

7.3.1   Restrictive covenants

Nursing homes and residential care homes are very often conversions of substantial property formerly occupied as a single mansion house residence, or possibly a conversion from a hotel, guest house or block of residential apartments. Much conversion work has been done to properties originally built in the latter part of the nineteenth century and the early part of the twentieth century. Where such properties were developed on substantial estates, it was common practice for the business user to be severely restricted, so as to promote the interests of the estate as a whole. Frequently, only certain professional uses, for example a solicitor's office or a doctor's surgery, were permitted.

Despite the external appearance of the property continuing to resemble a substantial private dwelling house, most residential care and nursing home use will contravene such standard restrictive covenants, and the issue will need to be addressed carefully. In the author's experience, a number of care homes have been conducted in breach of such covenants because the issue has been overlooked in previous conveyancing.

7.3.2   Planning consent

Planning consent for the operation of the particular nursing or residential care home needs to be evaluated carefully. Substantial development by way of building works will usually have required planning consent and if no evidence of such consent is forthcoming, careful attention should be paid before accepting representations from a vendor or a vendor's advisers that planning permission was immaterial (almost certainly never right) or not required, by reference to some statutory exemption. Although the Town and Country Planning (Use Classes) Order 1987[1] provides for change of use (as regards use as nursing home, residential care home and school) without the need for particular planning consent, care should also be given to examine existing

---

1   SI 1987/764 as amended.

planning consents, if any. Many planning authorities are concerned about over-development, in particular areas, of residential care homes and nursing homes for the elderly, as this may have an adverse effect on property values or cause particular areas to become linked with this type of resident. In order to mitigate against the flexibility of the order, planning authorities very often seek to limit the beneficial effect of planning consent by either imposing conditions to such consent which inhibit full flexibility of movement for different use, or seek to enter into planning agreements under s 106 of the Town and Country Planning Act 1990, the effect of which is to severely restrict the ability of the property owner to change use or expand development. All such matters need to be investigated very carefully.

An increase in patient numbers may require planning consent even if there is no visible external development or such development is permitted under the general development order. Greater intensity of operation may be 'material' development. Registration for increased numbers does not imply planning consent.

A particular feature of nursing and residential care home development is that such homes tend to develop by slow expansion over a period of years. Small extensions or new day rooms, or extra recreational or therapeutic facilities may be added, as time goes by. Unfortunately, this often occurs without approval from the local planning authority or appropriate consents under Building Regulations being obtained. These matters need to be carefully checked. Most planning authorities regard an increase in the number of persons for whom the home may provide accommodation as being a material change in use which requires additional planning consent. In the course of operating a home, where such increased facilities may arise as a result of internal rearrangements, many owners have overlooked the need, if there is indeed such a need, to seek such consent from the local planning authority. A purchaser should obviously not purchase, nor should a mortgager lend, unless satisfied that there is full and effective planning permission to enable the purchaser to conduct the business which he has agreed to purchase.

Vendors are often extremely surprised to learn that securing consent to an increase in registered numbers by the appropriate registration authority was not sufficient in itself to satisfy all the regulatory requirements. Some might suggest that this is, in any event, a minor technicality, but it cannot safely be regarded as such. Increases in numbers affect not merely the internal operation of a registered care home, but also impact on its locality and the amenities within that locality. Increases in numbers will mean, almost certainly, increases in staff and certainly increases in movement, in the sense that there will be a greater number of visitors for the increased number of residents.

It cannot safely be assumed that a planning authority will automatically rectify an omission on the part of a vendor. It cannot even safely be assumed that the matter will be dealt with at the level of Senior Planning Officers. It may be referred to the authority itself for a decision. Residents within a locality may perceive the potential impact as being greater than that which will occur. Regrettably, there still remain certain prejudices about interaction in the community with particularly vulnerable groups in care. In some cases, groups who are in care may differ so fundamentally that some concerns may have serious local repercussions. The change of use of a small residential care home from care for frail elderly ladies to the provision of care for young adults suffering from learning difficulties combined with challenging behaviour will effect a very significant change and owners should take careful steps to ensure that all planning requirements have been fully satisfied.

7.4   TRANSFER OF BUSINESS – CONSIDERATIONS

7.4.1   Goodwill

The goodwill of a business comprises reputation and the bond forged with customers together with the circumstances, whether of habit or otherwise, which tend to make that bond permanent. An examination of the types of goodwill shows a distinction between goodwill that can be seen to be personally attributable to the owner and goodwill that flows from the property and the location in which the business is situated, for example a retail shop in a prime trading site. Whilst there is an element of personal goodwill attaching to the reputation of particular owners, it is suggested that, in general, the goodwill attaching to residential care homes and nursing homes is attached to the situation and property location, rather than personal goodwill. It is unlikely that existing residents will wish to leave a care home merely because there is a change of owner. Equally, it is likely there will be a limited number of care and nursing homes within a particular area and the needs of that area will indicate a reasonably steady flow of clients. However, a word of caution is needed, given the changes in funding of community care provision implemented on 1 April 1993.

Prior to 1 April 1993, social welfare benefit funding was directed towards individuals who were given the opportunity to purchase care facilities of their choice. The emphasis has now changed to an increase in funds available for social welfare for purchasing local authorities, who will be the first resort for those prospectively in need of care and who, as local authorities, will purchase care for an individual rather than funding the individual to purchase care for themselves. It therefore seems likely that greater value in the future may be attached to so-called personal goodwill, to the extent that a particular owner, through excellence in care practice, has achieved a particular relationship with a local authority. Although it is not likely that an authority, which has consented to the transfer of community care contracts to a purchaser, would seek swiftly to remove patients satisfactorily accommodated, the risk of damage to goodwill if the in-coming purchaser is unable to continue the satisfactory service to the standard and in the method expected by officers of that particular local authority, is greater than when the number of purchasers are spread out among individual members of the community, rather than small numbers of large and effective purchasers.

A crucial line of enquiry for a prospective purchaser is to establish that the notional goodwill associated with the business is in reality goodwill and not something that might be described as 'mediocre will' or 'bad will'. Accordingly, the relationship of the care home owner with the relevant local authorities, both as regulators and purchasers, must be investigated. Detailed enquiries should be made about the relationship with the local registration authority. A purchaser should seek copies of all recent correspondence with the registration authority and should be prepared to ask searching questions about matters which appear to be less than satisfactory. At the very least, all inspection reports prepared within the last three years should be copied and delivered to the purchaser. If there are difficulties disclosed in the relationship with the registration authority, the purchaser will wish to meet with the registration authority to ascertain the authority's attitude and whether or not its criticism is directed to the home as such and/or the particular owner.

7.4.2 Contracts

A purchaser will also wish to examine copies of the contracts with individual residents and patients accommodated within the home and, particularly, to examine contracts with purchasing local authorities, whether community care purchasers, ie social services authorities, or National Health Service purchasers. The purchaser will, as he will be purchasing the benefit and advantage of such agreements, wish to have disclosure of correspondence with such purchasing authorities as to the conduct of community care contracts. The purchaser will wish to evaluate the real extent of goodwill and the extent to which that goodwill will carry over to a new business owner rather than evaporate once established loyalties no longer apply to the relationship between the purchasing authority and the particular business.

When assessing the value of goodwill, the purchaser should be aware not to accept blindly business transfer valuations prepared by so-called experts in the field. The value of goodwill will be established in relation to the true adjusted net profit of the business and the purchaser must, together with appropriate professional accountants, examine carefully the balance sheets and profit and loss accounts of the business. If no balance sheets are available, then the purchaser should, as a matter of good practice, insist on the preparation of balance sheets or instruct his own accountants to construct balance sheets from available information.

7.4.3 Funding

Different levels of borrowing and personal drawings will have a significant effect on cashflow and profitability. Certain purchasers will be able to fulfil major professional roles within the business and others will need to purchase such services by engaging or employing those who can supply such skills. All such matters need to be taken into account in adjusting a profit and loss account to show what is the likely profit for a purchaser of a particular business.

However, some figures will be constant and the most important of those is the cost of staff, in terms of salaries and wages, to the business. This figure may be expected to be somewhere between 45% and 60% of the turnover. Percentages at the higher end of this range or in excess of that range would suggest over-staffing and the possibility of increasing profit by rationalisation. Percentages at the lower end of or below the range indicated would suggest under-staffing and possible difficulties with the authority, which may result in significantly increased staffing levels being required of or suggested to a prospective purchaser. A purchaser should take care to analyse wage and salary bills and to investigate actual staffing levels on a week-by-week basis so as to calculate the cost of staff.

Occupancy levels are a crucial factor in evaluating a care home business. Unlike many hotel businesses, residential care and nursing homes will expect to operate to near capacity. A prudent purchaser should ask for details of occupancy levels in respect of the proposed home over a period of at least six months prior to enquiry. Sudden variations and, in particular, sudden drops in occupancy levels should be explained. A purchaser should also attempt to correlate variations in staffing levels with variations in occupancy levels.

It is also necessary to evaluate the source of referrals to the business. Following 1 April 1993, many homes will still have a combination of patients who pay their fees privately, patients whose fees continue to be paid by the Department of Social Security (their rights to social welfare benefit established prior to 1 April 1993 being maintained by so-called 'preserved rights'), residents and patients wholly supported by local authority community care contracts or by Health Authority private bed contracts and, in some cases, private patients who fund their fees by continuing to draw upon those remaining social welfare benefits which are payable for care, supplemented by their own resources.

There can be no doubt that, for most care home businesses, the future lies in establishing and maintaining good contractual relations with the community care purchasers, ie County Councils, Metropolitan Borough Councils and London Boroughs, being social services authorities and unitary authorities. A purchaser will wish to ensure that such relations have been secured for the home and that the continued turnover and profitability of the home is not secured precariously on those whose rights to funding are based upon sources of benefits which have been discontinued.

All these elements will need to be drawn together to form a view about the potential value of the goodwill of a business and a simple reference to an apparent expert would be insufficient in itself and may be dangerous. This would be even more so if that expert, in the post-1993 climate, is relying on prior trading history, for prior trading history, where income has been derived from discontinued benefits, may be dangerously misleading.

7.5   FIXTURES, FITTINGS AND FURNITURE

7.5.1   Leasing agreements

A purchaser should be aware that, historically, care home owners have made extensive use of medium-term leasing facilities for a wide variety of equipment, furniture and fittings within nursing homes. Extensive enquiries need to be made about the existence of such leasing arrangements. In virtually all such cases, the lessors will need to be consulted and will need to approve any transfer of the burden of the leasing obligations to the purchaser. However, the purchaser will wish to consider if it is desirable to take on the burden of such leasing obligations, rather than to require the vendor to pay off the leasing agreements. The value of the business, as specified by expert valuers, will normally be upon the basis that proper title can be made to all business assets. If, for example, nurse call systems, lifts or even carpets are not actually the property of the vendor, the value of the business is significantly diminished.

Any purchaser who does decide to take on the leasing obligations should ensure that the leases do not continue for a period beyond the useful life of particular equipment: contracts on, for example, carpets for periods of up to 7 years – a period clearly beyond the anticipated life, even of the heaviest duty carpet, in a nursing home environment.

7.5.2 Warranties

The purchaser will seek a warranty that the assets transferred include all those necessary to continue the business. It will be difficult for a purchaser to check the detailed inventory supplied by the vendor and it is not unknown for significant items to be excluded from the inventory by the vendor, who removes them at completion much to the surprise of the purchaser. It is always a wise course to allow for time to check the inventory room by room.

7.5.3 Secured/mortgaged goods

The question of loose furniture items being mortgaged creates its own difficulties, both for the lender, who may wish to take such security and for the purchaser, who may wish to ensure such property is free from mortgage, either to principal lenders or to hire purchase finance companies. Of course, the matter will be subject to detailed investigation by the purchaser's advisers, but they should also seek clear confirmation from any mortgagee or lender redeeming security at completion, that that lender has no further claim or entitlement to any fixtures, fittings, furniture or items at the home.

7.6 THE BENEFIT OF CONTRACTS FOR CARE OF RESIDENTS

A contract for care is a personal contract. Therefore, unless it is renewed with the purchaser of the business, it is probably discharged by transfer of the business by the original care home owner. In practice, patients and residents are likely to be more concerned that a new owner may seek to remove them from occupation or to change the material terms and conditions of their accommodation and care contracts.

In practice, with ordinary private patients and residents as clients, the matter may usually simply be addressed by the vendor notifying the patient of the transfer of ownership, coupled with identification of the new business owner. A novation agreement may be inferred from that documentation and subsequent billing and payment by the new owner and the existing patient.

7.7 COMMUNITY CARE

More care would need to be taken when community care contracts had been established between the business owner and the local authority or Health

Authority. Such contracts are likely to be long, as compared with individual contracts, and may contain surprising terms and conditions. Purchasers should study all such contracts to ensure that they understand and are prepared to deliver the level of care which may have been specified in the contract.

By far the most important matter, however, is that almost all community care contracts are expressed to be personal to the particular care home owner and to require the prior written consent of the authority before they are transferred. This gives the authority considerable power in relation to the proposed transfer of ownership of a registered care home. In order to be sure that the existing goodwill of the business has been secured, the purchaser's advisers must ensure that the necessary formalities in relation to the transfer of those contracts have been completed at or before completion of the main transaction. It may be that mere written approval to transfer is required or it may be that a full document authorising the transfer needs to be drawn up and signed on behalf of the appropriate authority.

The vendors may regard this with concern and potential vendors should take particular care, in negotiating community care contracts, to ensure that their ability to transfer the business is not restricted by omitting an unqualified power of veto over a buyer for a purchasing local authority. There are limits to which an authority, as a regulator, may intervene to prevent the transfer of ownership by declining or seeking to change conditions of registration. If the same authority, as a purchaser, has an absolute power to decline consent to transfer the benefit of care contracts, then that authority, in effect, will have total control over the marketability of the business concerned. Those valuing such businesses or seeking to lend money against the security of such businesses must ensure that any valuation and, consequently, any loan takes into account the marketability of the contracts underlying the business.

Another hidden trap awaits the unwary in relation to local authority community care contracts in nursing homes. Local authorities may only enter such contracts provided they contract within their powers and in accordance with the restrictions imposed on their contracting powers by enabling legislation. The legal authority for the purchase of such care is s 26 of the National Assistance Act 1948, as amended by the National Health Service and Community Care Act 1990.

Where arrangements are made for the purchase of care in residential accommodation where nursing care is provided, then the premises in which such accommodation is provided must either be registered under Pt II of the Registered Homes Act 1984 or be exempt from such registration. No such arrangements may be made by a local authority for the accommodation of any person in such a nursing home without the consent of the Health Authority. This requirement is being very substantially overlooked. If that is so, then arrangements made with nursing home owners for the provision of nursing care which has not been specifically approved by the Health Authority will be ultra vires the local authority. Issues may arise as to payments made under such contracts, but purchasers will be concerned to learn that such approval has been granted, so as to ensure that the benefit of the contract which they are purchasing is a valid and enforceable contract. Section 26(1)(d) of the National Assistance Act 1948 provides some relief for admissions to nursing home made as a matter of urgency, but re-enforces the need for Health Authority consent by indicating that such arrangements may only be temporary, so as to require Health Authority approval confirming the placement to be obtained as soon as possible.

7.8　THE BENEFIT OF CONTRACTS OF EMPLOYMENT

The employees in a registered care home will form a vital part of the assets of the home. The purchaser may be concerned, in the event of over staffing, to be able to trim the staff at the earliest possible time and a vendor will be concerned to ensure that all staff are transferred.

A purchaser may be seriously concerned to ensure that the loyalty of certain key staff, for example the person in charge of a nursing home or the recognised or registered manager in relation to a residential care home, remain loyal to the business and will give their loyalty to the new owner.

A detailed examination of the provisions of the Transfer of Undertakings (Protection of Employment) Regulations 1981 ('TUPE')[2] is beyond the scope of this work. However, a number of points are worthy of comment.

(1)　The transfer of the business of a care home is a transfer of an undertaking for the purpose of the Regulations.

(2)　In consequence, irrespective of contractual provisions, the full benefit, advantage and burden of the contracts of employment will transfer with the transfer of the business from the vendor to the purchaser. This will include all benefits or conditions of employment, irrespective of acceptability. Therefore, the purchaser must make the most careful enquiries and obtain full disclosure of the obligations which he is undertaking. A vendor must be equally careful to ensure that all matters, no matter how seemingly trivial, which arise in relation to the contracts of employment are disclosed. Non-disclosure, to the dissatisfaction of a purchaser, may lead to a claim for breach of contract if the purchaser finds himself saddled with unanticipated liabilities.

(3)　If, for any reason, any employees are not transferred to the purchaser, then such non-transfer will be regarded as unfair dismissal, leaving a potential liability in respect of such dismissal upon either the vendor or purchaser (but usually the purchaser), depending upon when the dismissal is deemed to take effect. Dismissal prior to transfer will almost certainly fix the vendor with substantial liabilities to pay compensation and dismissal by the purchaser, at or closely after the transfer date, is likely to face the purchaser with similar compensation liabilities.

If, for any reason, the vendor or purchaser does not wish particular employees to transfer, or individual employees have expressed a wish not to transfer (perhaps their employment may be relevant to other aspects of the vendor's

---

2　SI 1981/1794.

businesses), then great care must be taken to address the issues arising under TUPE, before exchange of contracts.

7.9 VALUATIONS

Great care should be taken in placing reliance on professional valuations in relation to nursing and residential care home businesses. In this specialist business, more than any other, particular firms of valuers have acquired a reputation for special expertise. The author suspects that this has arisen because of the unusual nature of the business, which leads to each business operating at or near capacity, so that it is possible to assume that similar businesses in similar areas carry readily reckoned valuations; which can circumvent the normal exercise of analysing business accounts and trading performance. This is so because, given capacity trading, the potential for gross profit is present in each and every business and net profit will be determined merely by reference to individual tastes and expenditure in operation.

Such practices have resulted in less experienced valuers suggesting that nursing homes in particular areas have a value per bed. This is a dangerous assumption. If there were ever any justification for this proposition, it dates back to the time when not only each and every individual could claim a right to cash limited social security benefit, but when there was no such cash limit on such benefit, prior to April 1985, and each area effectively fixed a going rate for publicly funded residential and nursing care. That was then the rate payable to all applicants to the local office of the Department of Social Security.

A never ending stream of potential customers, who were able to secure funds from a public source, simply by proof of insufficiency of capital and income to meet certain low limits, provided a golden opportunity for an almost risk free business. Those days are long gone and the final move away from social welfare benefit funding of individuals in care home placements to public authority contracting on behalf of those whom it assesses to be in need, means that it is vital that valuation, however useful as a rule of thumb, is cross-checked both against business performance and business potential, taking into account, inter alia, the factors which have been outlined in this chapter.

However, purchasers should note the following. Lenders, as a matter of policy, cannot possibly undertake such an examination on their own account. Lenders will be looking to ensure that the business proposition is sufficient to secure the repayment of the monies being advanced and, the lower the proportion of monies advanced to the purchase price, the less concerned will the lender be to ensure that the purchase price is realistic.

Purchasers may find specialist valuations useful in order to secure the support of traditional lenders, but this should not in any way be regarded as a substitute for careful analysis of the important business indicators, both past and future, before determining whether the valuation suggested represents true value or something less than true value.

The element of change in business means that underlying business cannot truly be valued against past performance unless it is matched by performance in the new community care environment. This cannot be overstated. There is no doubt that residential care and nursing home business provides an opportunity for outstanding cashflow (certainly to the extent that the business is based on social welfare benefits and private individuals' own resources). Such cashflow may not be so regular in the short term with community care based contracts payment being made against invoices issued to a local authority, but, nevertheless, local authorities will recognise that non-payment will place their sponsored patients and residents in jeopardy. Cashflow will still be good compared with many comparative businesses, particularly as occupancy levels, being near to capacity, should ensure that most well run businesses are operating to their potential – a potential not as affected by seasonal variations as are businesses such as hotels and guest houses.

7.10 HOW SHOULD THE VENDOR PREPARE FOR SALE?

Too often, the vendor first directs his attention to the instruction of a business transfer agent. This might be the normal course in respect of other business transfer agreements, but in the case of registered care homes, should only come after the vendor has considered the implications for the registered care home business.

No transaction will be in a position to complete, other than in the case of a purchaser who shows a total disregard for the security of the business, unless a new certificate of registration in respect of the home is issued to the purchaser. Clearly, any purchaser will have to overcome the hurdle of satisfying the registration authority that he, as a purchaser, is not an unfit person to be concerned in the operation of the care home business. In addition, the purchaser will also have to satisfy the registration authority that the premises, location, situation, staffing and method of operation of the care home business will continue to be satisfactory. At this stage, the registration authority will reconsider whether or not to refuse the purchaser registration, re-evaluating all the material that it considered in relation to the vendor's application. It may be that matters over which the authority was satisfied in respect of the current owner's application may give cause for concern with a less experienced or less well-funded prospective owner.

Untold damage can be done to prospective sales if purchasers make early and ill-prepared applications, or even approaches, to a registration authority. Registration authority officers may talk frankly and openly with the purchaser, who appears to have a genuine interest, and speak of matters of such concern that the purchaser may be dissuaded from continuing his interest. Whether or not the prospective vendor has any recourse against the authority in respect of anything that has been said, is a difficult question. In practice, the vendor will suspect that this has happened but may not even get any direct evidence of the conversation, let alone its substance. A dissuaded purchaser will just disappear.

7.10.1 Particulars of sale

It is also important to ensure that the particulars of sale, prepared by a business transfer agency, do not misrepresent the position in regard to the registration. If particulars suggest a particular basis of business, which then turns out to be different, purchasers will expect reductions from the asking price which might not have been expected if the particulars had been drafted accurately.

7.11   REGISTRATION AUTHORITIES

Registration authorities expect (although they are not entitled as of right) to be kept informed as to developments in the operation or potential disposal of a care home business. Early approach by the vendor to the registration authority may secure the registration authority as an ally, who will endeavour to provide constructive information so as to support the transfer. The registration authority's interest in relation to a home, which it regards as in good standing, is that the transfer should proceed smoothly in the interests of the vulnerable residents and patients.

The crucial issue for the vendor is to clarify with the authority both that it will not seek to place unnecessary objections in the path of the transfer, and also ascertain any matters which the authority considers will need to be addressed before it will issue a new registration certificate.

In the author's experience, early approaches to registration authorities yield dividends. Authorities are pleased to be involved and to be made aware of the process, and thus be able to deal more easily with enquiries from prospective purchasers or valuers appointed by those purchasers or their prospective lenders. Establishing the matters which may be of concern to an authority and require change will aid the vendor in negotiations, for the vendor will then be able to approach the purchaser, with a view to identifying these areas of difficulty. These may be confirmed in conversation with the registration authority, so that the vendor will be seen to be dealing in an open and accurate way.

It may be that there will be genuine disagreement between the authority and the prospective vendor as to matters which need to be addressed. The purchaser's reaction to the vendor in relation to those disagreements will be much more sympathetic if the purchaser has been told of the difficulty prior to discussion with the authority. A prospective purchaser who makes enquiries of the authority, having been told that there are no difficulties, and discovers a list of problems, if not dissuaded, is likely to become a difficult and demanding purchaser in relation to other details in the transaction. Such a prospective purchaser is more likely to seek to reduce prices.

Clearly, the issues which will be central to the mind of any prospective purchaser, in addition to the process of registration, will be the numbers for which the home will be registered to care, the categories of patient or resident for whom the home is registered to care (if any restrictions be imposed) and, in relation to nursing homes, the extent of any proposed nursing establishment conditions which the authority may seek to impose.

An authority may well use the opportunity of a transfer of ownership to seek to secure changes which it would not seek against an existing owner. This is understandable. Changes in condition or even the cancellation of registration are difficult to enforce (in terms of expense of time and finance), where the authority would have to battle against an existing home which can continue in operation until the authority's case has been established. Every application for registration on transfer of ownership is, in effect, a new application. The authority knows that the prospective vendor's desire for sale cannot be consummated until the prospective purchaser has obtained a new certificate. The authority is thus in a stronger position to advance its case, in the knowledge that a transaction may be delayed or even frustrated by delay in effecting re-registration.

All parties must appreciate that re-registration on transfer of ownership is not a matter of right. The vendor has no right to expect the authority to register any third party and the purchaser only has the same right to expect registration as any other applicant for registration. The matter is subject to reconsideration and hence the need to prepare grounds for the application for re-registration on transfer of ownership is one of paramount importance in approaching the negotiations for sale.

It may be that a registration authority has accepted a situation that it regards as less than satisfactory, but not so unsatisfactory as to justify changing registration conditions or cancellation of registration, pending a possible change of ownership. In those circumstances, the vendor will know perfectly well that any purchaser will face changed ground rules. If a vendor fails to disclose such a situation, then he will have only himself to blame if the purchaser takes an adverse view or tries to negotiate a price reduction.

7.11.1 How should the authority react?

In the vast majority of cases, a registration authority will wish to assist a smooth transfer of ownership. The concern of the authority is the continued care of the frail and vulnerable residents and patients who are accommodated in the registered care home business. Any disruption to a seamless service of care may be to the disadvantage of such clients. If the sale fails and the home is repossessed by a lender or closes for some other reason, the registration authority, in its role as purchaser of community care or health care, may find itself having to re-accommodate or assist in the re-accommodation of the residents who have been cared for in the home.

Nonetheless, the registration authority will recognise that each application for registration is to be considered upon its own merits. Registration may not have been considered fully for a number of years and accepted standards of practice and service may have changed. The fact of re-registration operates as a statement on behalf of the registering authority that the applicant, the home and its services, facilities and staffing are all considered re-fit for registration, as is the manner in which the applicant proposes to conduct the home. An authority which registers a home out of convenience, whilst holding misgivings about particular aspects of the care service or the facilities, accommodation or location, must expect both criticism and complaint. More importantly, if it seeks to regulate the new owner in respect of matters known and material at the date of change of ownership, the authority will be met with the forceful argument that, if matters of concern were already known to the authority, they should have been brought to the attention of the purchaser at the time of re-registration. The purchaser will have a compelling argument that, if he had known that he would be required to change services and facilities at the time of change of ownership, he would then have had the opportunity to review the price which he was prepared to pay for the business.

It may be difficult for a home owner to seek to establish that the registration authority holds a duty of care in relation to information given during the course of the application for re-registration. However, in certain circumstances and particularly if the authority takes it upon itself, through its officers, to offer guidance and comfort about registration, it is not inconceivable that such a claim could be founded if an authority seeks at, or shortly after, re-registration to suggest that facilities and services which have been acquired are inadequate or unfit for the purposes of the particular home.

Upon receipt of an application from a prospective vendor advising the authority of a proposed sale, it is suggested that the authority should co-operate with that approach and should seek to agree with the proposed vendor what the authority will require of a prospective applicant (in addition to being satisfied that the applicant is not unfit to be registered) and arrange with the prospective vendor that such matters will receive attention prior to the application, or will be the subject of agreement between the prospective vendor and the registration authority in their dealings with any prospective applicant for registration.

It is often argued that if a particular home is considered fit to operate in the hands of the existing owner then, subject to the establishment of fitness in any prospective applicant, it should be considered fit in the hands of such prospective new owner. Whilst there is force for such argument, it is not overwhelming.

Chapter 8

INSPECTION OF CARE HOMES

8.1 WHAT IS INSPECTION?

Inspection of registered care homes is the cornerstone of the regulatory process, without which no other action may be judged or taken effectively. Inspection is a power to enter into premises and view those premises, the activities carried on and documents retained there, with a view to reporting back to the regulatory authority on the current state and condition of the care home.

An inspector may suggest and recommend. An inspector may never instruct. It is no part of the inspection process for the inspector to threaten enforcement action which is, in any event, beyond the power of the individual inspector. The inspector should regard himself as a guest, although a guest whose entry cannot be denied.

The powers of the inspector either to be present or to request to see information or activities are circumscribed by legal authority. If the inspector over-steps the legal authority, he will be in the position of a trespasser to the home owner's property. A more difficult issue is the extent to which an inspector, who receives information in the course of inspection, must regard that information, insofar as it relates to the care home business, the owner or the residents or patients, as confidential. This topic has gained in importance with the current trend for open reporting of inspection, designed originally to calm public disquiet about the conduct of local authority operated residential care homes and NHS hospitals.

The inspector, as a visitor, may have an implied licence to attend at the premises and to proceed insofar as he or she is invited, in the same way as any other visitor, including the police or central or local government officials. Once that implied licence is revoked, the continued presence or insistence upon continued presence constitutes a trespass and that continued presence can only be justified if allowed by the statutory requirements. A visitor may only proceed with an inspection to the extent that the property owner consents. An inspector to whom access may not be denied, may so proceed without consent. This is important where the inspector is investigating a suspected statutory criminal offence, and Code B of the Police and Criminal Evidence Act 1994 applies. The ability to proceed against refusal of access once the suspected offence has been notified is invaluable.

8.2   STATUTORY AUTHORITY FOR INSPECTION

8.2.1   Residential care homes

Inspection is dealt with by s 17 of the Registered Homes Act 1984. No power is given to make regulations as to the inspection of residential care homes, save for s 17(4) of the 1984 Act, which enables the Secretary of State to make regulations as to the occasions and intervals at which inspections may take place. The Residential Care Homes Regulations 1984[1] provide, in reg 18, that inspection shall take place not less than twice in each year. There is no limit upon the number of inspections.

It will also be argued, with some force, that a registration authority is, by implication, obliged to inspect sufficiently so as to satisfy itself that the home is conducted in accordance with statute and regulations, and that the authority must devote sufficient resources to ensure that such inspections are carried out sufficiently frequently and to such effect as to protect the residents. No claim for damages at law will lie for breach of such a duty, but such a failure will attract criticism and may result in a successful complaint of maladministration against the authority to the Health Services Commissioner.

8.2.2   1984 Act, s 17(1)

> 'Any person authorised in that behalf by the Secretary of State may at all times enter and inspect any premises which are used or which that person has reasonable cause to believe to be used for the purpose of a residential care home.'

This sub-section provides authority for inspectors appointed not by the registration authority but by the Secretary of State. Such inspections will be rare, but it is clear that if the Secretary of State, for any reason, perhaps dissatisfaction with the conduct of the registration and inspection service provided by the registration authority, wishes to inspect, the Secretary can authorise inspections.

'Premises' clearly extends to premises used as a small home, for the definition of residential care home in s 1 of the Act is now widened so as to embrace a small home. A small home is still a residential care home, but one which has to face different requirements of regulation.[2]

Clearly, premises known to be used as a residential care home will be registered premises and the fact of registration provides the authority for inspection of such premises. If premises are not registered, then it would be difficult for an inspector to argue that the premises were so used unless and until he had conducted the very inspection for which authority was required. Hence the entitlement to inspect is extended to premises which the inspector 'has reasonable cause to believe to be used' as a residential care home. This is not a 'carte blanche' to inspect any premises. The inspector must have reasonable cause to believe, ie there must be some information, albeit not necessarily information which can be sustained by the highest standards of

---

1   SI 1984/1345.
2   Contrast ss 1, 2, 4, 4(1)(a) and (b) of the 1984 Act.

evidence, that the activity defined in s 1(1) of the 1984 Act is being carried on from premises which are not registered. Furthermore, that cause must be reasonable, so that if the inspector is to justify enforced entry, he must show not only that he has received information which leads him to believe that an offence may be committed, but also that he has objectively tested that evidence and come to the conclusion that it is reasonable for him to proceed.

As inspectors may well be criticised and be the subject of legal action alleging trespass to land, if they force entry to premises where their entry turns out to be unjustified. They should also be prepared to produce objectively verifiable evidence of the information which led them to take the step of entry and inspection.

The power is a power 'to enter and inspect'. Therefore, this is not a power which is dependent upon the continued consent of the care home owner before it can be enforced. The inspector who is prevented from exercising these powers may force entry and inspection. Only reasonable force may be used. What will be 'reasonable' is a matter of judgement in a particular case. Often, inspectors will seek the support of police officers both to emphasise the powers of inspection and to ensure that breaches of the peace do not occur. Section 17(6) provides that it is an offence to obstruct any person authorised in exercising their power of inspection and the offence is complete at the moment of obstruction. Obstruction followed by an acceptance of the position still provides material sufficient to sustain a conviction. The offence is prosecutable without notice and the penalty is set out in s 51(1) as a fine following summary conviction.

8.2.3   1984 Act, s 17(2)

This provides identical powers for persons authorised by the registration authority. The distinction between subss (1) and (2) is that those authorised by the Secretary of State may inspect premises anywhere and those authorised by the registration authority may only inspect premises within the area of the authority.

Both sub-sections refer to entry 'at all times'. This is clear authority for the proposition that inspectors may enter at any time of the day or night and without regard to the reasonableness of the hour or the effect upon those within the premises inspected. It is wrong to suggest that inspectors, under Pt I of the 1984 Act, have to make their visits at reasonable times. This is different from powers of inspection of premises accommodating children under s 80 of the 1989 Act and powers of inspectors of child-minders and 'under eight' Day Care Centres, under s 76 of the 1989 Act.

8.2.4   1984 Act, s 17(3)

This gives power (but, in effect, limits power) in relation to the inspection of records. The power of entry is coupled with the power to inspect the premises. Sub-section (3) gives power to inspect records to be kept in accordance with regulations made under Pt I of the 1984 Act. Therefore, the power does not extend to inspect records which are not obvious in inspection of the premises and which are not required to be kept. An example would be that there is no obligation on a registered owner, under Pt I of the 1984 Act, to keep staff duty rosters. Therefore, inspecting officers cannot demand such records. Inspecting officers, being astute to stay within their powers, should make sure that when they ask for documents or records which are not immediately available, that those are records which the owner is required to keep as a matter of statutory law and not those which are kept as a matter of business practice.

It will be seen that there is a significant difference in the powers in relation to the inspection of registered nursing homes.

8.2.5   1984 Act, s 17(5)

This places some limitation on the power of 'entry and inspection' by requiring that the person who proposes to exercise the power, ie the person who is demanding entry, must, if required, produce a duly authenticated document showing his authority to exercise that power. Inspectors and registration authorities should be careful to ensure that inspectors are properly armed with such authority. It is no defence to say that the owners know the identity of the inspector. The document must be clearly authenticated by the authority upon whose behalf the inspector is acting. The document must show the authority for the inspection, not merely that the inspector is employed by the authority, and must identify the inspector. Quite clearly, it is necessary that the inspector be not only named, but that he has a properly authenticated photograph. If the document which purports to be the inspector's authority is insufficient, then those within the home will be entitled to resist the entry and inspection, which may defeat the whole purpose of the authority's policy in relation to a particular home. An inspector forcing entry after being required to supply such a document and having been told that such a document is ineffective, will be going beyond his powers and will be acting as a trespasser.

It is, in the author's view, no defence at all for the authority to say that the registered owner and staff knew the identity of the inspector. The requirement to produce the authenticated document is a condition precedent to the power of entry and inspection, should the document be required. All inspectors should have such a document at all times.

It is important that *anyone* exercising power of inspection be actually authorised so to act by an appropriately empowered officer of the authority, even if acting 'ad hoc' and even if that person has other powers of entry. Failure to take the simple step of ensuring proper authority and authenticated evidence of such authority may cause difficulties if there is a subsequent challenge.

The power of entry and inspection does not include the power to make copies of documents or to take items away from the care home. However, common sense dictates that an inspector should make notes (which may include his own handwritten copy of documents) so as to be able to report and give credible evidence about the visit. It is suggested that inspectors may be assisted by cameras and should consider the use of recording equipment. Many owners will permit use of photocopying equipment, but an inspector might consider taking a portable photocopier. Inability to make copies would frustrate the purpose of inspection which is to report and recreate the observations made by the inspector.

The power of inspection does not include a power to demand that the care home owner prepare and send documents to the authority on a regular or any basis. It will be seen that there is a different position in relation to registered nursing homes.

8.2.6 Duty to inspect

There is clearly wide-ranging power to inspect. There is a duty to inspect only residential homes other than 'small homes' twice per year.[3] This is often used to justify non-inspection of 'small homes'. However, inspection visits are required to inspect *all* residential care homes by para 3 of the Inspection Unit Directions 1994.[4] The exemption from registration duties seems to apply only to the minimum required number of inspections.

8.3 REGISTERED NURSING HOMES

The statutory authority is to be found in s 27(d) of the 1984 Act:

> 'The Secretary of State may make regulations with respect to entry into and the inspection of premises used or reasonably believed to be used as a nursing home.'

Details are not included, but it will be seen immediately that, in common with residential care homes, the regulations authorise entry and inspection to premises used or reasonably believed to be used as a nursing home.

8.3.1 Nursing Homes and Mental Nursing Home Regulations 1984[5]

The relevant regulations are regs 10 and 11 of the 1984 Regulations. Regulation 11 provides for frequency of inspection and provides that inspection shall take place at such intervals as the Secretary of State may decide, but not less than twice in each year. Here again, inspections are required twice per year, but an emphasis that the Secretary of State (ie Health Authority) can inspect as frequently as may be thought appropriate.

8.3.2 1984 Regulations, reg 10

Regulation 10 is the all-important regulation to assist inspection.

> 'Any person authorised, on producing (if asked to do so) a duly authenticated document showing that he is so authorised may enter and inspect any premises which are used or which he reasonably believes to be used as a nursing home and in the course of such inspection may require the production of records.'

The provisions follow those of s 17 of the 1984 Act in relation to residential care homes. In addition, the inspector may require the production of records

---

3 Residential Care Homes Regulations 1984 (SI 1984/1345), reg 18.
4 Annexed to LAC (94) 16 issued by the Department of Health.
5 SI 1984/1584.

– not the records required to be kept in accordance with the Act, as under s 17, but 'the production of records'.

Cross-reference to reg 15 shows that anyone who, without reasonable cause, refuses to allow an inspector to inspect a home or a record at a home, under reg 10(1), shall be guilty of an offence. That offence is prosecutable without warning.

8.3.3 'Records'

It is submitted that, with no limitation to the records required to be kept by the 1984 Regulations, 'records' is wide enough to embrace any records kept at the nursing home, including records maintained by owners for their own purposes.

Sub-paragraphs (3) and (4) of reg 10 restrict the entitlements of inspectors. Although those sub-paragraphs are specifically made a condition precedent to sub-para (2), it is suggested that they equally apply to the request for records under sub-para (1). Clinical records may not be inspected other than by a medical practitioner and no one is required to disclose information contrary to the provisions of the Human Fertilisation and Embryology Act 1990. That Act is beyond the scope of this work, but in essence, persons granted licences or given directions thereunder are restricted from allowing others to view the information.

The issue as to what is a 'clinical record', may give rise to serious problems. The restriction is not merely on requesting inspection but upon actually inspecting. A non-medical practitioner who inspects records which may be described as clinical records has gone beyond the intrusive inspection power. No decided cases on this issue are known to the author and, in practice, nursing home inspectors inspect all records within nursing homes.

'Clinical records' may be defined as being records created as a result of interaction between patient and medical practitioner, as opposed to nurse. At the other end of the scale, 'Clinical Record' may be interpreted as a record which relates to individual patient care, as opposed to records as to the general operation of a health care unit.

If the latter interpretation, or anything like it, were to be adopted, then the practical scheme of inspection of nursing homes, as understood in the UK at the present time, would face grave difficulties. The very records which nursing home inspectors may wish to inspect in order to satisfy themselves as to standards of care will be the nursing records and, indeed, the daily records of patients' condition maintained under reg 7 of, and Sch 4 Part 1 to, the 1984 Nursing Homes Regulations. Those records are records about individual patient care. Inspection of nursing homes could not be conducted properly without access to such records.

It is unusual for nursing home inspection teams to include a medical practitioner. However, in cases of difficulty, registration authorities can ensure that a medical practitioner attends on the inspection so as to avoid technical arguments.

Health Authorities, it is suggested, would be well advised to take the robust approach that, as the restriction on inspection is limited to medical practitioners, clinical records should be construed in this context as being limited to records relating to interaction with other medical practitioners. This both makes sense of the regulations and makes them workable in the modern context.

Home owners, who may be advised to take an alternative course, should bear in mind that if their contention for a wider construction fails, then they will have failed to provide information within reg 10(2) or permit the inspection of records within reg 10(1) and that will have constituted an offence under reg 15(1) or (2) of the 1984 Regulations. By that time, it will be too late and the offence will have led to a conviction, for the argument can only be settled in the magistrates' court, and the consequences of conviction will follow.

It is suggested that it will be a bold owner who would stand on a point of principle, to withhold information, when the consequences of being wrong would be so grave, ie a conviction under the 1984 Act (under s 26(1)(e) of the National Assistance Act 1948, such a conviction would act as an automatic bar to community care contracts). Withholding access to such information wrongly could ruin a nursing home business.

8.3.4   1984 Regulations, reg 10(2)

This entitles the person authorised by the Health Authority to require the person registered to furnish 'such information in relation to the nursing home as may be reasonably required for the purposes of inspection'.

'Such information in relation to the nursing home' must surely be interpreted to cover any material relating to the operation of the nursing home and can clearly be distinguished from the production of records identified in reg 10(1).

The limits are that the requirement must be reasonable and that the requirement must be made in relation to a particular inspection process. It is submitted that almost any information that relates to the nursing home, as opposed to matters not relevant to the nursing home (eg the owner's personal affairs), must be such as is reasonable for the owner to produce if required and that all that the inspecting officer has to show in making the requirement (whether at, before or after inspection – the purposes of inspection are not limited to the inspection itself) is that the information is required in relation to preparation for the conduct of or the evaluation of inspection.

Given the criminal sanction, Health Authorities might well consider it appropriate to make wider use of requests for such information and, indeed, to ease their own work by making such requests in advance of the actual inspection.

8.4   MENTAL NURSING HOMES

Section 35 of the 1984 Act provides detailed provisions giving statutory authority for the inspection of mental nursing homes and specific rights to interview patients in such homes. The mental incapacity of patients in such homes requires extra statutory control, particularly where such patients may be less well supported or intellectually equipped to make and maintain complaints or criticisms of their surroundings, than those in general nursing homes.

8.4.1   1984 Act, s 35(1)

'Subject to the provisions of this section, any person authorised in that behalf by the Secretary of State may at any time, after producing, if asked to do so, some duly authenticated document showing that he is so authorised, enter and inspect any premises which are used, or which that person has reasonable cause to believe to be used, for the purpose of a mental nursing home and may inspect any records kept in pursuant of Section 27(b) above.'

The scheme of inspection rights will thus be seen to be repeated in relation to mental nursing homes. 'The Secretary of State' will include those to whom the powers of the Secretary of State have been delegated pursuant to the National Health Service Act 1977, ie the Health Authorities. The person authorised must thus have the authority of either the Secretary of State, or the Health Authority, and must have a duly authenticated document to prove that authority. As previously argued, this document needs to specify the purpose of the authority, ie the inspection of a mental nursing home (and authorities should be aware to specify that the authority is to inspect mental nursing homes and not rely on a general permission to inspect general nursing homes), clearly identify the person authorised and, it is suggested, identify them not merely by reference to name, but by reference to a photograph.

The power is one 'to enter and inspect', so it is important that there is no doubt about the authority of the inspector, whose authority is all that removes him from the position of an unlawful trespasser. What is to be inspected are premises used or premises which the inspector has reasonable cause to believe to be used as a mental nursing home. This will be established either by the fact of registration or, if the inspector believes, on objectively credible evidence that one or more persons suffering from a mental disorder[6] are accommodated and receiving care. Inspectors need not have a reasonable suspicion that someone is actually suffering from a mental disorder. The appearance of suffering from a mental disorder is sufficient.

Such an inspector may also inspect records kept in pursuance of s 27(B), ie records kept not as a result of general practice, but as a result of the requirements made under the 1984 Nursing Homes Regulations. The powers of inspectors of mental nursing homes appear to be limited to statutory required records, whereas the power of inspectors of general nursing homes is wider.[7]

Section 26 authorised the making of regulations relating to the inspection of both nursing homes and mental nursing homes and subs (3), after dealing with some transitional matters, authorises the Secretary of State to include in such regulations, regulations relating to the timing and occasions for visits to mental nursing homes. This is to be found in reg 11 of the 1984 Nursing

6   1984 Act, s 22.
7   Nursing Homes and Mental Nursing Homes Regulations 1984, reg 10(1).

Homes Regulations, merely specifying that inspection should take place not less than twice in each year.

Specific reference in s 35(3) of the 1984 Act to the power to make regulations under s 26 in this way would seem to suggest that the general regulation power derived from s 26 in relation to general nursing homes is not (as embodied in reg 10 of the 1984 Nursing Homes Regulations) applicable to mental nursing homes. Inspectors should tread extremely carefully before deeming it appropriate to demand production of records other than those records for which they can find express regulatory authority in the 1984 Regulations.

8.4.2   1984 Act, s 35(2)

An important additional power is given to an inspector appointed on behalf of the Secretary of State or the Health Authority. Sub-section (2) provides that such an inspector may visit and interview a patient residing in a home, who is or appears to be suffering from a mental disorder, for the purpose of investigating any complaint as to his treatment made by or on his behalf, or if the inspector has reasonable cause to believe that the patient is not receiving proper care. Where the inspector is a medical practitioner, he may examine the patient and may require the production of of medical records relating to the patient's treatment in the home.

This wide and extensive power, which is a power not only to intrude into premises operated as a mental nursing home, and to ask questions and inspect records in relation to the operation of the business of that home, but also to interview patients without obtaining the consent of the home owner, also appears to give the inspector power to interview and, if a medical doctor, to examine the patient against the patient's will.

As with general nursing homes, there will be a wide variety of mental nursing homes; and some registered mental nursing homes, not being those who have specifically given notice that they intend to take in 'secure' patients, have no more right to restrain or restrict patients than other organisations or businesses operating within the community.

It is suggested that the right answer is to be found by examining the word 'interview'. The concept of an interview involves an exchange of information prompted by questions and answers voluntarily given. Interviews are never compulsory (save where there may be a contractual obligation for the provision of information) and, under the Police and Criminal Evidence Act 1984, information obtained at police interviews is inadmissible at trial unless the formalities of a 'caution' have been followed. Those formalities are designed to ensure that there is full knowledge of the consequences of answering questions at interview before it can be regarded as safe to rely upon answers which may tend to incriminate.

Therefore, it is submitted that if a patient, as opposed to an owner, does not wish to attend or proceed or continue with an interview, then the inspector cannot insist, against those wishes. Inspectors conducting such an interview will need to be astute to ensure that the patient consents to the interview and continues to consent to the interview, but mental nursing home owners must beware before they intervene, for there are strict sanctions for obstructing the inspection of a nursing home and the penalties are even stricter in relation to obstruction of the inspection or refusal to permit visiting and interviewing of persons at mental nursing homes.

8.4.3   1984 Act, s 35(5)

This sub-section outlines those areas where a criminal offence is committed:

(1)   *refusal to allow the inspection of the premises*
      It should be noted that refusal in itself amounts to an offence. There is no apparent defence based upon a reasonable cause for refusal;
(2)   *refusal without a reasonable cause to allow visiting, interviewing or examination of a patient*
      Here note that the owner may establish a defence by reference to 'reasonable cause'. Any such cause would need to be both substantial in itself and reasonable in the circumstances;
(3)   *refusal to produce for inspection documents or records which may be required;*
(4)   *other obstruction of the inspection.*

The defence of 'reasonable cause' only applies to refusal in relation to visiting, interviewing or examining the patient. Clear evidence that the patient refused to agree to the interview, or the continuation of the interview, might be just such a cause as might be deemed reasonable in the circumstances. However, those relying upon such a defence should be aware that the right to seek interview is a cornerstone of the protection of the vulnerable mentally ill and courts and tribunals are likely to expect clear evidence that there was a genuine disinclination on the part of the patient, not encouraged by the owner, before finding that such a situation existed.

The 1984 Act, s 35(6) gives some assistance with definition of 'obstruction' or refusal to allow interview 'without reasonable cause'.

A person who insists on being present when requested to withdraw by an inspector authorised to interview and examine a person in private is guilty of an offence. Once again, there is no limitation which provides for a defence of 'reasonable cause' to a refusal to withdraw. Thus an inspector has the power (for the protection for the patient) in the conduct of the inspection, interview and examination, that even if it might be seen as a reasonable excuse to attend and object to the interview (either in principle or without the owner or staff being present), to require a withdrawal. Refusal to withdraw thereafter constitutes an offence without a defence. The penalty for conviction in respect of such an offence is not only a substantial fine but the possibility of a maximum term of 3 months' imprisonment, as an alternative to or in addition to such a fine. This is the only provision of the 1984 Act which specifies as a penalty for the commission of an offence a period of imprisonment. The offence is only to be tried summarily by magistrates and there is no right to trial by jury.

8.5   MENTAL HEALTH ACT 1983

NHS Trusts, Regional Health Authorities and Health Authorities who maintain patients in registered mental nursing homes may discharge patients from such mental nursing homes (ie secure detention) pursuant to s 23 of the

Mental Health Act 1983. Additional powers to visit and examine patients are provided by s 24 of the 1983 Act, in order to assist those whose duty it is to consider whether or not to discharge a patient from such secure detention. The powers are:

(1)   to visit the patient;
(2)   to interview and, if a medical practitioner, examine the patient;
(3)   to require production of records relating to the patient's treatment and to inspect such records.

Once again, the right is one that cannot be resisted and, accordingly, visiting medical practitioners must be careful to remain within the limits of their authority. Given that the patient is in compulsory care and, in effect, detained, it will be seen as an open question as to the extent that a patient may resist interview. However, as has already been suggested, a non-consensual interview may be seen as a contradiction in terms.

Section 129 of the Mental Health Act 1983 provides an offence for anyone obstructing such a visit or interview, in similar terms and with similar penalties to s 35 of the 1984 Act.

Section 115 of the Mental Health Act 1983 provides that an approved social worker employed by the local social services authority has a power of entry and inspection to a mental nursing home if it is believed that a mentally disordered patient is not under proper care. The power extends to any premises other than a hospital. What is a 'hospital' for the purpose of this section is not entirely clear. Certainly, NHS hospitals and local authority accommodation come within the exclusion. The power does extend to unregistered premises and is an important protection for the mentally ill who are the subject of 'care in the community'. The power may be exercised only at 'reasonable times'.

By s 120 of the Mental Health Act 1983, the Secretary of State and persons authorised by him or her have power to visit and interview private patients detained under the Mental Health Act 1983 in registered mental nursing homes. The Secretary of State has directed that these functions be exercised by the Mental Health Act Commission.

By Annex C to Health Circular 21 of 1984, the Secretary of State directed each Health Authority to secure that any premises which are not registered as nursing homes or mental nursing homes in their district and which it has reason to believe should be so registered, be inspected.

Where a mental nursing home (or a residential care home or nursing home) is used to accommodate children, the Secretary of State may cause that home to be inspected, from time to time, pursuant to s 80 of the Children Act 1989. It is inspection by the Secretary of State and is clearly intended to be an inspection, in effect, to monitor the regulatory inspectors. In relation to registered nursing homes or registered mental nursing homes, the power does appear to be slightly superfluous as the Secretary of State has ample such power either through the Health Authority, or by the officers of his or her own department, under s 35 of the 1984 Act or, in relation to general nursing homes, regs 10 and 11 of the Nursing Homes and Mental Nursing Homes Regulations 1984, made under s 27 of the 1984 Act.

8.6   COMMUNITY HOMES, VOLUNTARY HOMES AND CHILDREN'S HOMES

The statutory authorities are the 1989 Act and the 1991 Regulations.[8]

8.6.1   Community homes

In respect of community homes, which are units not operated otherwise than by local authority or voluntary organisations, no specific powers of inspection are provided or, indeed, required.

8.6.2   Voluntary homes and children's homes

The statutory powers of inspection in relation to voluntary homes and children's homes are to be found in s 62(6) to (9) of the Children Act 1989, in relation to voluntary homes, and applied to children's homes by s 64(4) of that Act. The purpose of these sections is to introduce the power of entry and inspection for local authorities and their officers.

The supervisory power of entry and inspection is reserved to the Secretary of State by s 80 of the Children Act 1989, wherein are reserved to the Secretary of State general duties and powers in relation to children. The power of the local authority is to be exercised by a person authorised by the authority, who, once again, shall produce a duly authenticated document showing that authority, if asked to do so.

So far, the position mirrors that of the power of inspection for nursing homes and residential care homes. However, the power of inspection may only be exercised for the purpose of enabling the authority to discharge its duties under this section. In relation to voluntary homes, it will be remembered that the homes are not registered by the local authority but by the Secretary of State, whereas with children's homes, these are registered by the local authority itself. The purpose of entry is the wide purpose of 'safeguarding and promoting the welfare of the children in accommodation'.[9]

The powers are different in important respects:

(1)   to enter and inspect premises, but only 'at any reasonable time';
(2)   to inspect the children;
(3)   to inspect records of a kind required to be kept by the regulations, set out in para 7 of Pt II of Sch 5 to the Act. The power to inspect includes the power to direct the home owner to furnish the records to the inspector, which clearly avoids the argument that an inspector is only entitled to see that which is obvious.

8.6.3   Information held on computer

Section 62(8) of the 1989 Act provides an additional power which reflects advances in information technology over the years. If records are maintained upon computer, the inspector may require access to the computer, the right to

---

8   SI 1991/1506.
9   Children Act 1989, s 62(1)(b).

inspect the operation of the computer and associated material and material which has been used in connection with the computer, and may require the computer owner or operator to assist in using the equipment.

If, however, an inspector receives and misuses copyright information he and his employer will be liable for substantial damages.[10]

Use of these wide-ranging powers to demand access to computer software may very well give to the inspector (particularly an inspector who is computer literate) sufficient information to understand the nature of the computer operation and sufficient source material to replicate computer programs. Lest inspectors feel that the statutory power to require assistance effectively authorises them to make use of computer software, it is suggested that they should receive very clear advice as to the limitation of their powers. Information so obtained is obtained in confidence and the recipient clearly holds that information in confidence for those whose property it may be. The power to use the material, which would otherwise be a breach of confidence, is restricted to the purposes for which the information has been obtained, ie the regulation of the registered voluntary and children's homes and matters arising directly out of the regulatory process or the inspection. Any use of the material beyond those limited objectives would be regarded as a misuse and the offending authority and its officers would face actions for breach of copyright, for which the remedies include an injunction and damages, and a liability to pay the substantial legal costs that may be associated with such an action. Registration authorities would be well advised to remind their officers of this potential hazard.

8.6.4 Criminal offences

A criminal offence is created for those who obstruct officers in the exercise of their powers of inspection of voluntary and children's homes, but it is prosecutable only summarily and is punishable by a moderate fine. Section 62(9) of the 1989 Act creates an offence only where the obstruction is carried out intentionally. This can be contrasted with the absolute offence created in relation to residential care homes (s 17 of the 1984 Act), mental nursing homes (s 35(5) and (6) of the 1984 Act) and nursing homes (regs 10(1) and 15(2) of the Nursing Homes and Mental Nursing Homes Regulations 1984).

8.6.5 Occasions for inspection

Part II of Schs 5 and 6 to the 1989 Act specify the material which may be comprised in regulations to be made by the Secretary of State as to the operation of and the keeping of records in relation to voluntary homes and registered children's homes. The inspectors will need to rely upon the statutory authority for the power of entry, but the inspections provided for in the regulations are mandatory. The following occasions are prescribed for inspection:

(1) the registration authority must inspect before deciding whether or not to grant the application (interestingly, even if the authority is minded not to

---

10 Copyright Designs and Patents Act 1988, s 16(3).

grant the application for reasons relating to the application or the applicant), there must still be an inspection;

(2)   within one month prior to the anniversary of the registration. Since registration must be reviewed every year, there must be an inspection in the last month prior to the review date;

(3)   upon at least one other occasion during the year.

The authority is entitled to warn the person in charge of the home of its intention to conduct the required annual inspection, but is forbidden to give warning of any spot inspections. It is important that registration authorities appreciate this. It is considered to be good practice to arrange routine inspections of residential care and nursing homes by appointment with the owners and their managers or nurses in charge. In relation to children's homes, that is only permissible in relation to the single annual review inspection. Otherwise, inspections must be made without warning.

Authorities are obliged to take into account the reports of the inspection of the home when reviewing the registration of the home on an annual basis. Adverse inspection reports will lead inevitably to the cancellation of the registration, for no reasonable authority could overlook a seriously adverse report unless there were overwhelming reasons, for example satisfactory explanations for failure, change of staff or change of procedures. The adverse inspection report of a registered children's home will thus be a very damaging document for the owner.

8.6.6   Functions of the Secretary of State

Part II of the Children Act 1989 provides for the Secretary of State's supervisory functions and responsibilities in relation to the care of children. Section 80 provides, at length and in detail, a comprehensive power of entry and inspection for inspectors appointed by the Secretary of State in relation to accommodation where children are living away from their parents and clearly includes children's homes, residential care homes, and nursing homes or mental nursing homes required to be registered under the 1984 Act and used to accommodate children.

The inspector must be authorised by the Secretary of State and that inspector may not be an officer of a local authority unless that particular authority has consented.

The Secretary of State may require information or inspection of records which relate to any matters relevant to the accommodation of children (the specific areas are outlined in s 80 (4) of the 1989 Act). The people from whom information may be required are set out in s 80(5) and are, in essence, the persons responsible for owning or managing the accommodation provided for children.

Inspectors may inspect the children and may examine, in such a way as they think fit, the state and management of the home and the treatment of the children. Full powers to require access to and co-operation in the operation of computers are provided for such inspectors, in similar terms as those provided for local authority inspectors of registered voluntary homes and registered children's homes.

The inspectors are given the power to enter the premises at any reasonable time, as are their local authority counterparts. It will be remembered that this does not apply to residential care and nursing homes and thus does not apply to inspectors of such homes which accommodate children. The inspector must produce the duly authenticated document showing authority to inspect and inspectors must be astute to remember upon whose behalf they are inspecting, particularly if they are local authority officers. An inspection made on behalf of the Secretary of State, but only with authority on behalf of the local authority, might place inspectors in difficulty if challenged as to their authority.

Obstruction of such an inspector is an offence, punishable by fine on summary conviction, but once again the offence will only be made out if the obstruction is shown to be intentional. This is similar to the provisions for offences in connection with obstruction of inspection of registered voluntary and registered children's homes, but in sharp distinction with the provision for the offences in relation to residential care and nursing homes.

8.7   GENERAL PRACTICE

Having examined in detail the statutory authority for the power of entry for the purpose of inspection of various types of registered care home, the remainder of this chapter will examine practice and procedure in relation to such inspections. The purpose of these practical notes is to assist owners, staff and registration authorities in the preparation for and evaluation of such inspections and, beyond their statutory requirements and context, to consider the purpose of the inspection and how the inspection may be used for the better enforcement of the regulatory requirements.

8.7.1   Timing of inspections

There is no restriction upon the number of times in any year that an authority may inspect. Put simply, the authority must inspect as often as it considers necessary in order that it may properly discharge its duty to the public to be satisfied that a proper and sufficient standard of facilities, service and care is being delivered in the particular care home. There are, however, statutory requirements for an authority to inspect on a minimum number of occasions in each year.

8.7.2   Resistance by home owners

Authorities and their advisers will often be faced with the allegation that, by frequent and often critical inspections, the authority are in some way intimidating the owners of the home, the staff, or possibly even the patients. The style of the inspection must at all times be sensitive to patients and staff and be conducted on a basis of courtesy towards the owners. Authorities do not usually inspect frequently unless they have genuine cause for concern about the care of the patients, residents or children within the particular unit. Fulfilling their public duty to inspect regulated care home businesses properly can never be described as harassment and the common law knows no such tort as 'harassment' by a local authority.

A new tort of harassment was introduced by the Protection Against Harassment Act 1997. Lawful authority is a defence to such an action. It is hard to think that registration officers acting under the 1984 or 1989 Act would not have the benefit of such a defence.

On many occasions, it may be sensible to arrange to give notice of the intended inspection, but there is no requirement to do so and, often, notice of the proposed inspection may go a long way towards defeating its object.

The officers of the authority are entitled to inspect as often as they think fit, and should not be intimidated by owners who may seek to impede the inspection of premises, records or the interviewing of clients. Reference to the statutory and regulatory provisions will remind officers of their considerable powers of inspection and of their powers to enforce those rights by prosecution – on many occasions without the need to give notice. In relation to inspection of records and interviewing patients in mental nursing homes, there is also the prospect that a convicted owner, who has obstructed the inspectors, may, in addition to other difficulties, face a period of imprisonment.

A home owner who obstructs the inspection process may also expect to be characterised as an unfit person to continue to be registered. Home owners should take legal advice and should only seek to restrict the inspection process under that advice and if they are sure that they can genuinely assert that officers are exceeding the very wide powers granted to them by the legislation.

An analysis of those cases that have come before the Registered Homes Tribunals, where allegations have been made either of so-called 'harassment' or of inappropriate or improper conduct on the part of officers, will reveal that Tribunals recognise the delicate position of inspectors, the difficult task that they have to perform, and are disposed to support those officers. Officers of inspecting authorities should derive encouragement from that and home owners should be on their guard against inappropriate complaints.

8.7.3   Inspection at reasonable times

It is often suggested that registration officers should only inspect at reasonable times of the day or night. This is quite incorrect in relation to residential care homes and nursing homes within England and Wales. It will be observed that inspection of children's homes is limited to reasonable times. That is against the background of the very much greater restrictions on obtaining a registration of a children's home or the greater frequency with which the fact of registration is reviewed. Registration authorities are entitled to inspect by day or by night whenever they see fit and the owner is not entitled to exclude them provided, of course, that they are able to produce the appropriately authenticated authority for their presence.

Out of hours inspections made without warning are very often the best way in which to ascertain the manner in which a care home business is conducted. The very best registered home owners conduct their own out-of-hours inspections to ensure that their staff perform when they, the owners, are away.

The restriction on inspecting children's homes to 'reasonable times' is not restricted artificially to times which might be considered to be objectively reasonable in ordinary circumstances. The reasonableness of the time of inspection will surely be judged by reference to the purpose of the inspection and the matters which have caused the inspection to be planned and implemented. If allegations are made that children are locked in rooms at night, then clearly it cannot be suggested that it is unreasonable to inspect the home during the night hours. However, where an authority is expressly required to act in a way which is characterised as 'reasonable', senior officers of the authority should always consider whether or not their proposed conduct will meet a standard that may be considered reasonable and not assume that all actions will automatically be considered so. It may be sensible to test the matter with an independent officer of the authority, whose views would be extremely helpful.

8.7.4 Who may inspect?

The simple answer to this question is that anyone properly authorised and supported by an authenticated authority may inspect on behalf of the registration authority.

Questions are often raised as to whether persons without professional experience or practical knowledge may inspect. The answer remains clear. Anyone who is authorised may inspect. Thus, the authority may, in principle, authorise authority members, councillors, trade union officials, competitors or others who may not be to the liking of the registered owner to carry out the inspection. They may not be excluded from the home on any ground whatsoever. Obstructing an inspector who is unwelcome by identity, as much as by the fact of his presence as an inspector, is just as much an offence as obstructing one who is known to be the regular authority inspector.

Many authorities are now following the course of engaging lay assessors, particularly in residential care homes, where they suspect that lay assessors may be able to bring common sense to disputes about technical standards in what is essentially required to be a homely environment. The principal role of the lay assessor may be to report independantly on the conduct of the inspection and its outcomes.

In difficult cases, authorities may wish to appoint a different or independent inspector or possibly an inspector from the private health and social welfare sector, or even an inspector employed by another authority, in order to check the reports they are getting from their regular inspectors. A registered home in trouble will necessarily face a number of inspections which will inevitably be critical of that home. Relationships between the individual inspector and the home owner and senior staff will be difficult. The authority should be sensitive to the proposition that such inspectors may become fixed in their view as a result of their own perceptions, formed over the course of the period of inspection, and be astute to engage independent inspectors before regulatory action is contemplated.

In relation to mental nursing homes, the Secretary of State reserves the right to conduct inspections upon his own behalf throughout the country, but that rights of inspection for local authorities or nominated social workers, in respect of mental health care premises, are restricted to the officers of the authority in whose geographical area those premises are situated.

8.8   TYPES OF INSPECTION

Three types of inspection can be identified:

(1)   a routine inspection;
(2)   an unannounced inspection;
(3)   an inspection stimulated by a particular complaint or cause for concern.

8.8.1   Routine inspections

The authority is required to carry out, in most cases, not less than two inspections in the course of the year. At least one of those will normally be characterised as a routine inspection. At this inspection, the authority will be checking, in addition to standards of care, facilities and service, the general documentary record-keeping and establishment of the premises.

It is obviously sensible and conducive to the efficient completion of the inspection that home owners and nurses in charge, or managers, have notice of such an inspection so that they can be present when the authority visits. It is suggested that the practice of sending pre-inspection questionnaires, although criticised by some, is a very useful practice for assisting home owners and authorities in concentrating their minds on the information that has to be gleaned and checked, thus shortening the inspection process. If inspectors know the number of patients in residence and their conditions and needs, together with the number of staff engaged and similar matters before they arrive to inspect, then the course of the action will be quicker and easier.

It may well be that an authority will wish to do more than one routine inspection during the course of the year, but those inspections should be distinguished sharply from inspections that are designed to discover facts as to the conduct of the home, as opposed to checking that all is running smoothly.

8.8.2   Unannounced inspections

The right to visit, enter and inspect at any time of the day or night is a right which should be used with planning and care, as a means of discovering exactly what is happening, under the most favourable circumstances, ie without the owners or staff knowing that the visit is likely to take place.

In relation to registered children's homes, it will be remembered that at least one inspection during the course of each year is to be conducted without notice to the owners. The author would suggest that this should be practised for all registered care homes, irrespective of whether or not they are considered to be homes in good standing and, therefore, not the subject of criticism. Homes that appear to be running smoothly need to be subjected to the full rigours of the inspection process, just as those homes perceived to be 'of concern'.

Similarly, inspections which are unannounced should, on occasion, be conducted at anti-social hours, even where the home is not perceived to be a home with difficulties. Anti-social hours inspections may reveal things which would never be uncovered by inspections in normal working hours and certainly never uncovered by routine inspections.

8.8.3   Inspection caused by specific complaint or concern

Local authorities receive a number of complaints from a wide variety of sources about the conduct of registered homes. Some will come from people with an obviously biased view, ie dissatisfied relatives of residents or disaffected staff. Others will come from well-meaning members of the public. In all such cases the authority must react sensibly to the complaint and owners and senior staff must appreciate that such complaints require to be investigated, if only so that they may be dismissed. Uninvestigated complaints lead to a lack of satisfaction, which benefits neither home, nor residents, nor patients, nor the authority.

Of course, authorities should take steps at least to satisfy themselves that the complainant has some genuine basis for the information that is relayed. However, if the complaint cannot be dismissed as wholly fanciful upon the basis of an initial interview with the complainant (who may well wish to remain anonymous), authorities will need to investigate those complaints.

Some forethought is required as to the conduct of such an inspection. If an inspection relates to things that happen at a particular time of the day or night there is little point in inspecting at a different time, but it may also be sensible to inspect at a variety of times to compare what is found. Authorities will need to consider whether they need to engage specialist inspectors, for example pharmacists or medical officers, to accompany the inspection team as a result of the particular type of complaint which is under investigation.

Whilst it will often be sensible to share the facts of the complaint with the home owner at some stage during inspection, it will only rarely be sensible to tell the home owner of the complaint before some form of inspection has been conducted to assist the authority in forming a judgement about the complaint. Certainly, authorities will not wish to announce to owners that a particular type of complaint has been made in a way that would enable the owner to conceal material that would be of assistance in an investigation.

Owners and authorities must appreciate that the authority owes a public duty to inspect and regulate registered care homes and that public duty will only be discharged so as to gain the respect and confidence of the public if the public feel that information that they reveal is processed sensitively and effectively.

8.9   PREPARATION FOR INSPECTION

Whichever type of inspection may be contemplated, that inspection is an important part of the creation of a case history for the particular registered home.

In the case of a routine inspection, the authority's officers will need to review exactly what it is that they require to inspect and cross-check matters of concern on previous inspections so they are sure to follow up previous suggestions or requirements, in order to ensure that these have been taken seriously and remedied effectively. If this is not done and there are gaps in the chain of fault identification, then the authority will be subject to forceful criticism and the suggestion either that the views of its officers vacillate or that standards which may very well not have been maintained or corrected have, in fact, improved so as to be seen to fluctuate, rather than to have been consistently bad.

The authority's evidence will be almost entirely based upon the records of inspections. The inspection itself and the records which are taken afterwards can only be properly prepared if the inspection itself is the subject of normal and meticulous pre-inspection work.

It should be rare for inspectors to go alone and the inspectors who do go should go with a plan designed to discover the information which they require efficiently and effectively. Inspectors preparing for such inspections should consider carefully if they wish to be assisted by specialist inspectors or by technical equipment. Endless arguments can occur about absence of materials, or cleanliness, or similar issues. Those matters can be settled quickly and effectively by the use of a camera. The inspectors should, however, remember that they need to acquire information in a form which can be proved at a later date. A photograph must be able to be identified by the photographer, who must be able to give evidence as to the time and place the photograph was taken. The most effective way of doing this is to use a polaroid camera. The instant photograph can not only be shown to the owner or staff present, but also be marked for identification purposes immediately. If this is not possible, then the film must be developed at the earliest possible moment and the rolls of film carefully marked so that they can be proved to be photographs taken at a particular time and place.

Issues may well arise as to the conduct of owners or staff during the course of an inspection. It seems to the author that there can be no objection to officers carrying with them portable tape recorders upon which they may record the way in which they are received. Similarly, these recordings will need to be identified and proved as to the time and place of recording. They can, however, be invaluable, as can photographs, to show what was seen or heard. Such evidence may then be distinguished from the way in which the same persons behave at a registration authority meeting or before a statutory Tribunal.

8.10   CONDUCT OF INSPECTION

Having prepared for the inspection, the inspectors should attend and follow through the plan that they have formulated. It may be that other material comes to light. It may be that there is time to consider such material or that that material may be of such importance as to overshadow the pre-planned purpose of the inspection. Unless either of these circumstances appertain, the advice to inspectors should be to follow through the pre-planned formula and, if necessary, to return on another occasion further to inspect any new material which was discovered and may not have been germane to the particular purpose of inspection. Registration authorities and Registered Homes Tribunals will welcome evidence about the conduct of inspections that is presented in an orderly manner rather than appearing to be haphazard, save in a grave emergency.

The inspectors should always be aware of the extent and the limitation of their powers, during the course of inspection. Inspectors should remain courteous and should remember that they are inspectors and reporters. It is not the function of the inspector to give instructions to the owner, on the spot. It is not the function of the inspector to cause concern for owners, staff, patients or residents. The function of the inspector is to collect evidence and deliver that evidence to their senior officers at the authority in order that those officers may form a view as to the conduct of the particular home and whether any, and if so, what, further action is required.

There is no reason why owners should not accompany inspectors on their visit or delegate members of staff to accompany and assist them. Inspectors are not entitled to restrict such accompaniment, but owners must understand that neither they nor their staff should impede the course of the inspection. It is not for the owner, or his staff, to select what it is that the inspectors view or inspect during the course of the inspection.

Inspectors must observe carefully and to ensure that they record, in an effective manner, what they have seen, heard or witnessed so as to be able to report, and, if necessary, give evidence on the subject at a later date. Inspectors must be very careful to remain objective observers.

Inspectors should remember, as should owners, the extent of the inspectors' right to demand inspection of records – not at a later stage but at the time of the inspection – and to require, in the case of nursing homes, information in relation to the operation of the nursing home to be furnished for the purpose of inspection, ie before, during or possibly after inspection. A distinction is drawn between information which is to be furnished for the purposes of inspection and information requested generally. The former is a compulsory requirement and the latter is a voluntary one, which should not be ignored, as it may be in the interests of responsible owners and effective authorities to build up a bank of information in order to assist future inspections.

8.11 POST-INSPECTION DEBRIEFING AND RECORD-KEEPING BY INSPECTORS

The purpose of the inspection, from the point of view of the inspector, has been to gather evidence which will either form a part of the record or will be used as the basis for evidence about what was discovered during the course of the inspection, or both. It may be that regulatory action is anticipated at the time of the inspection but even if it is not, each and every inspection is a vital occasion upon which to observe the operation of the registered home.

As soon as possible after the conclusion of the inspection, inspectors should revisit their notes. Ideally, this should be within hours and certainly on the same day. Inspectors will be challenged by owners' advocates, on cross-examination, about the contemporaneous nature of notes and the contemporaneous nature of a review of those notes and the translation of those notes into reports, statements or formal Proofs of Evidence.

When the notes have been revisited and reviewed, the visiting inspectors should work together to check accuracy, compare differing recollections and identify areas that may have been witnessed by one rather than another of the inspecting team. The inspectors will then have to decide what further action, if any, is required.

Whilst it is appreciated that there are limited resources for inspectors, it is suggested that, after all inspections, inspectors should be debriefed by senior officers, who should review the notes, consider the recollections of the inspectors and reconsider with the inspectors whether further action is required and if so, what further action is required.

It is suggested that it will be a rare inspection from which no further action is required. It is important for the authority to place upon record any matters found during the course of an inspection, whether positive or negative, and particularly any criticisms or misgivings. It is vital for the authority that these records be kept internally, but if matters of criticism are not reported to owners and managers, then there is bound to be the legitimate complaint, at a later stage, that the criticisms were not communicated to the owners. Owners are not obliged to agree inspection reports. It may be useful for inspectors to invite owners to agree, but owners should always be aware of the criticisms that are made.

Following the post-inspection debriefing sessions, an inspection report should be produced. It is suggested that the contents of the inspection report should be shared with the owner and/or manager of the registered home. At the very least, a letter should be written to the owner and/or manager (and it is important that both are aware, for both have separate responsibilities and may not know of shortcomings on the part of the other), identifying those areas which the authority considers to be 'of concern'. The owner will then have the opportunity to respond. Many owners do not respond. An owner who fails to respond to complaints will be very poorly placed to initiate criticism of the officers' conduct, or their conclusions, at a later stage.

It will be at the stage of post-inspection debriefing that inspectors and their senior managers will decide whether or not further regulatory action is to be taken. The inspectors should have in mind that it is not for them to decide whether or not action should be taken, but for the registration authority on the recommendation of senior officers, based upon the inspectors' reports and probably supplemented by experienced legal advice.

Whatever steps the authority decides to take, it is vital that detailed records of the inspectors' discoveries, views and decisions are kept so that there is a constantly developing history of the registered home concerned.

8.12   POST-INSPECTION DEBRIEFING AND RECORD-KEEPING BY OWNERS

From an owner's point of view, the departure of the inspectors is certainly not the end of the inspection visit. A prudent owner will have arranged for senior staff to have observed the course of the inspection and those senior staff should make immediate reports on the course of the inspection, possibly within an inspection record book. There may have been disagreements during the course of the inspection and senior staff should note disagreements and report to their employers. If there have been agreements about failings in services or facilities, then owners and managers should make immediate efforts to correct those errors, so that they are corrected even before any critical inspection reports and letters arrive.

Owners will not be able successfully to challenge the veracity of critical comments in inspection reports unless they themselves have a contemporary record of what is said to have occurred. Good practice within any registered home requires detailed recording by owners and their staff of what occurs during inspection visits, and, similarly, there should be 'debriefing' sessions between owners and staff to review what has occurred during the course of an inspection. Owners must be in a position to respond to criticism and to respond quickly, promptly and efficiently. The level of that response will speak heavily as to the owner's commitment and professional ability.

Whatever else may or may not occur, letters from registration authorities must not go unanswered. Looked at from the point of view of the owner, it is a grave, and possibly fatal, error to ignore correspondence from the registration authority. At the very least, this shows an attitude which is careless or possibly even contemptuous of the authority. At the worst, it may be taken as acceptance of criticism which will, very often, be impossible to counter at a later date.

Owners should be aware that registration authority inspectors have every right to make allegations or, in appropriate cases, prosecute in relation to inspection. Allegations by owners of harassment and intimidation by inspectors, therefore, may well be seen as whinging, rather than complaining in a way which may found a sensible legal cause of action. Allegations that cannot be sustained should be avoided. They reflect badly on the person making the allegation and may even enhance the case of those against whom the allegation is made.

8.13 HOW OWNERS MAY PREPARE FOR INSPECTION

Inspection is an on-going process and whilst consideration should be given to their reaction to inspections that have taken place, owners should not overlook the on-going nature of inspection and the fact that prudent authorities will be creating a history of the home's operation from their inspection reports. Owners should regard inspection visits as an opportunity to enhance their reputation in the eyes of the registration authority.

An owner who knows of an announced inspection should make sure that his house is in order. He should ensure that records are up to date, easy to find and easy to understand. Inspection is a difficult task which may strain the normal courtesies. If the inspection may be made easier by the owner appearing to be efficient and able to answer questions and produce documents as and when required, the atmosphere will be less charged and the inspection will go more smoothly – leaving a better feeling with the inspectors and, almost certainly, a more positive result than would otherwise be achieved.

8.14   PRE-INSPECTION QUESTIONNAIRE

Many authorities are now following the course of sending a pre-inspection questionnaire. In the author's view, this is to be applauded. The information as to the operation of the home may, if the home is a nursing home, be quite properly required within the terms of the appropriate statutory regulations. Whether or not that is the case, it is surely common sense that time is saved and the opportunity for misunderstanding avoided by routine material being prepared by the owner in advance and submitted to the authority. Typical information would relate to the numbers of patients and conditions of patients. Naturally, the owner will have concerns about patient confidentiality, but the owner should remember that where the authority is merely asking in advance, in relation to a proposed inspection, for information to which it is entitled when the inspection takes place, all that is being requested is advance knowledge. Clearly, the authority, in receiving information which has been held by the owner in confidence, also holds that information in confidence and may only use it for the legitimate purpose of regulation of the registered care home.

8.15   'OPEN-REPORTING' OF INSPECTION OF CARE HOMES

The campaign for openness in government is gathering pace and, in relation to the regulation of registered care homes, has caused attention to be focused upon the inspection and inspection reporting procedures.

Central government is pressing local authorities and Health Authorities to publish material which they discover in the course of inspection visits. Authorities should approach the matter with great caution. The fact that the central government suggests that there should be openness in the reporting of inspections of registered care homes does not mean that authorities can so report with impunity.

The difficulties may have arisen because attention was first concentrated on open reporting of inspection of homes operated by or on behalf of social services departments, local authorities or Health Authorities. Clearly, subject to individual patient confidence and subject generally to the law of defamation as it affects individuals, authorities are in a position to report to the public upon the inspection of homes operated by them or on their behalf. The position is by no means the same in relation to the reporting to the public of inspection of privately operated registered care homes.

Clearly, the reporter must have regard to the rights of third parties. First, the patients or residents at the particular home and their individual circumstances will clearly be matters confidential to them and should be excluded from any reports. Second, anyone publishing material about the inspection of any care home will have regard to the law of defamation, for any persons named, especially by implication, may very well be able to bring an action for damages. However, within the ambit of sensitive and appropriate reporting through the appropriate media by local authorities, the standard defences of privilege and, possibly for media publication, fair comment on a matter of public interest, will no doubt suffice to ward off attacks against any such publication which cannot be shown to be malicious.

The difficulty for authorities in reporting to the public upon their inspection of private care homes is that authorities, by their inspectors, are entering and inspecting as a matter of statutory right. During the course of such inspections, they will discover matters which they would not be entitled to view save as a result of their statutory powers. They are thus, in the author's view, in the position of those who have received information in confidence. Where information is imparted in confidence, the owner of the information does not expect that information to be used other than for the limited purposes for which it is imparted.

In the case of information obtained upon the inspection of a registered care home, the inspector is not receiving much of the information as a voluntary disclosure. Some home owners would wish to tell the inspector as little as possible. The information that is being obtained is being obtained because the inspector is authorised to demand it. The information is received in order to enable the inspector to do a proper job in reporting to his employing authority about the conduct of a particular registered care home, so that that authority may make an informed judgement as to any action that may be taken and may make that informed judgement in the public interest of ensuring that registered care homes operate to a particular standard. The information is not imparted with a view to it being generally disseminated either for the purpose of assisting the public or other public authorities, as potential customers, in making choices about a particular care home.

Any publication which brings the material into the pubic domain does not absolve another publisher from obligations of confidence. Those who republish in breach of confidence may find themselves responsible although they may have a right to claim an indemnity from the original publisher.

Information, good or adverse, which is published in breach of confidence, may bring upon the publisher a substantial action for damages. As the local authority or Health Authority will be the publisher of the information and responsible for any damage which occurs, they should view such matters with great caution. It is they and not central government who will face the legal action if they publish material in a way which goes beyond the implied licence granted to them when information is supplied to an inspector.

By LAC (94) 16, the Government directed local authorities, so as to be binding upon them under s 7 of the Local Authority Social Services Act 1970, that they should publish inspection reports both in relation to residential care homes operated by the authorities themselves, and by private operators but regulated by their applicable local authority.

Such directions were not replicated in respect of nursing homes, but in January 1998 the NHS Executive issued guidance forewarning the issue of directions that all inspection reports of nursing homes should be published.[11] It is anticipated that these directions will be published in March 1998 and become binding from May 1998. Directions are expected to include a standard

---

11   Department of Health circular letter, 19 January 1998.

form of inspection report. Both the direction issued in respect of local authorities in 1994 and the anticipated direction in respect of nursing homes in 1998 will require authorities to publish reports but cannot override third party legal rights which may or may not exist and may or may not be infringed by the publication. However, these directions should give good grounds for a claim to an indemnity for the authorities from central government should any such claims be made or sustained.

Chapter 9

REGULATORY ACTION

9.1 WHO TAKES THE ACTION?

Regulatory action is always taken by a regulatory authority. There is no opportunity for the regulated care home owner to initiate regulation procedure. This may be considered by some to be a serious omission. There is no route whereby a regulated care home owner can test in advance whether or not particular standards or facilities meet the regulatory standard.

In relation to residential care homes and registered children's homes, the power and duty to take regulatory action is conferred upon the local authority responsible for social services. With regard to registered nursing homes, the power is conferred by Parliament upon the Secretary of State for Health. Parliament has empowered the Secretary of State for Health to delegate such functions to Health Authorities.[1]

Health Authorities should have in mind the source of their delegated authority. They act in the name of the Secretary of State. They may be required to produce that authority, particularly when taking extreme powers of a regulatory nature. As the Health Authority acts in the name of the Secretary of State, the Secretary of State could take action of his own motion. This is highly unlikely. It is suggested that if circumstances arose whereby a particular home was attracting such adverse attention, and the Secretary of State was minded to take action over the head of the Health Authority, the Secretary of State would issue a direction to the Health Authority to take action rather than take action in his own name.

However, the power to act unilaterally, as with power of inspection and certain powers in relation to mental health functions, does remain an option for the Secretary of State.

9.2 WHO ON BEHALF OF THE REGULATORY AUTHORITY TAKES ACTION?

This is an important issue. Regulatory authorities are substantial authorities. The powers vested in them by Parliament or delegated to them by the Secretary of State are detailed and extensive. Those powers will need to be apportioned and delegated within the authority.

Whereas a Health Authority, meeting either in public or private,[2] may make individual decisions, it is quite impossible for a County Council, London

---

1 See National Health Service Act 1977, s 13 and s 14; National Health Service (Functions of Health Authorities and Administration Arrangements) Regulations 1996, SI 1996/708.

2 Usually, nursing home regulation business is reserved to the private part of the agenda of Health Authority meetings.

borough, or Metropolitan borough to reserve such detailed issues to decisions of the authority at such a meeting. Further, the authorities and their officers need to be sure that the authority has appropriately delegated functions and, taking into account the principle that sub-delegation is not permitted, the authorities need to ensure that there is sufficient statutory authority for delegation of particular functions.

Section 101(1) of the Local Government Act 1972 permits local authorities to delegate decision making to certain specialist committees. Clearly, the regulation of registered care homes will be delegated to the social services committee. As in all areas of sub-delegation, the existence of the power to delegate is one thing and the fact of delegation or renewal of delegation, where required, is another. Officers and advisers to authorities should take pains to ensure that delegated authorities are in place and that further delegation, through what are sometimes known as 'standing orders', is kept up to date.

Such power of sub-delegation does exist for a Health Authority, in practice. The important decisions of the Health Authority are taken by the authority. It is unusual to find generic decision making delegated to committees of Health Authorities (or indeed officers). Such is usually the norm with local authorities. This may very well reflect volume of business. However, a Health Authority may determine, by properly constituted standing orders, that a committee of the authority may act as the authority in urgent cases. In appropriate cases, the authority may delegate a particular decision or a particuliar type of decision to a committee of the authority.[3]

It is necessary to distinguish between decisions that are final decisions of the authority, ie actual decisions to implement regulatory action, as distinct from decisions to take various steps along the route to the decision to take regulatory action.

The decisions of the local authority which one would expect to be made by the authority or a committee to which power has been delegated are those made pursuant to s 15 (residential care homes), s 33 (nursing homes – in this case by the authority only) and para 7 of Sch 6 to the Children Act 1989 (registered children's homes). Other decisions, for example a decision to serve a notice of proposal or the decision to serve notice pursuant to reg 20 of the Residential Care Homes Regulations 1984; or s 15 of the Nursing Homes and Mental Nursing Homes Regulations 1984 to warn of imminent prosecution, are administrative decisions which may be taken by officers or groups of officers or sub-committees of members to whom relevant standing orders have delegated such power.

It is, however, necessary to ensure that standing orders which delegate the power to take action are seen to have been approved and ratified by the authority, which has the statutory power, or a committee of that authority to which statutory power has been delegated.

---

3   National Health Service Act 1977, ss 13, 14 and 16; National Health Service (Functions of Health Authorities and Administration Arrangements) Regulations 1996, SI 1996/708.

9.3 DECISION TO PROSECUTE

Prosecution itself is not a formal decision, grave as it is, in view of the provisions of s 26(1)(e) of the National Assistance Act 1948. A decision to prosecute is not a decision to take effective action. The effective action, in the author's submission, is the conviction for the offence and that decision is taken by the appropriate court and not by the prosecuting authority. Similar considerations apply to a decision for urgent cancellation of registration under s 11 and s 30 of the Registered Homes Act 1984.

However, as the discretion to prosecute is a public authority decision, if taken capriciously or for improper purpose or, as a course wholly disproportionate to the cause of complaint, it may be the subject of proceedings for judicial review. Any such action, it is submitted, must be taken *very* promptly, and certainly well within the maximum 3 months allowed. If 'warning' is given, action should be taken before the expiry of the remedial period.

9.4 WHERE URGENT ACTION WILL BE REQUIRED

An application for urgent cancellation of the registration of a residential care home or a nursing home (no such power exists for a registered children's home) will need to be taken in the name of the authority. The decision, however, is not the decision of the authority. As with prosecution, the decision to cancel the registration will be the decision of the magistrate. The regulatory authority will simply be the body that makes application. The requirement for the intervention of the magistrate is part of a system of checks and balances which prevents abuse. Accordingly, a decision to make an application to the magistrate is a decision which is appropriate to be delegated to a sub-committee of the appropriate authority or to individual senior executive officers or, possibly, the Chairman of an authority.

Nevertheless, appropriate standing orders must be in place to show who has the authority and such orders must have the legal authority gained from their approval by the authority itself. Officers of authorities who act otherwise than in accordance with the standing orders or beyond the powers delegated to them by standing orders will be acting not only beyond their own powers, but not on behalf of the authority. Their action will be invalid and, whilst they are likely to be entitled to an immediate indemnity, the authority will be vicariously liable for their actions, and they may face personal liability. In extreme cases of abuse of power, the authority may not provide an indemnity and may, indeed, seek an indemnity for any losses that the authority suffers, being vicariously liable for unlawful action. Such contractual and employment indemnities may not stand up to that, if the underlying action is beyond the authority's powers as opposed to a power exercised inappropriately. It may be unlawful for authorities to indemnify officers for liability incurred in actions beyond the authority's powers.[4]

---

4 *Burgoine v Waltham Forest London Borough Council* (1996) *The Times*, 7 November (ChD).

Officers should check the existence and the satisfactory nature of the content of standing orders so as to ensure that they will be able to discharge their functions as and when required. This is particularly important in relation to the urgent applications to cancel. If such issues are urgent, they will require immediate attention. In the author's experience, they are usually effected within 48 hours of matters of concern being discovered. Any longer period suggests that urgency does not exist. Without standing orders, it may be practically impossible to use such powers.

Owners should not be shy to challenge authorities to produce the authority for the actions of individual officers or committees. Owners should not, however, expect to find authorities acting improperly. None the less, some authorities, surprisingly, pay insufficient attention to establishing an effective chain of command, so as to control the operation of powers to take regulatory action. Authorities may head off such challenges by ensuring that they provide, upon request, a full chain of authority to their action.

9.5   AGAINST WHOM IS REGULATORY ACTION TAKEN?

In almost every single case, the regulatory action is taken against the owner, ie the person registered. In those rare cases where a manager will be properly registered, the action may be taken against the manager as a registered person. It will be recollected that, where a manager is registered, he is registered because he is deemed to be carrying on the business and thus is, in effect, an owner.

Prosecutions of those who are carrying on regulated care homes without being registered, or holding out premises as registered nursing homes with an intent to deceive, will be conducted against persons who are inevitably unregistered. They will, however, be the persons proven to be carrying on the particular home, ie the equivalent of a registered person. It is the fact of non-registration that leads to the prosecution.

There are exceptions relating to prosecutions for the obstruction of inspection. It is highly likely that the persons present at an inspection will not include the person registered. Inspections will occur without warning and at anti-social hours. There needs to be an effective sanction for obstruction of inspection. Accordingly, any person who obstructs is likely to be charged with an offence.[5]

9.6   TYPES OF REGULATORY ACTION

There are three categories of regulatory action:

(1)   action to vary conditions of registration or impose new conditions of registration;

---

5   See Registered Homes Act 1984, s 17(6) (residential care homes); 1984 Act, s 35 (5), (6) (mental nursing homes); Nursing Homes and Mental Nursing Homes Regulations 1984, SI 1984/1578, reg 15(1)(c), (2) (nursing homes). There is no entitlement to a warning of prosecution under reg 15(2).

(2)   action to cancel registration;

(3)   action to prosecute registered persons for offences committed in the operation of the regulated care home.

In all cases, the registration authority acts as a regulator. Whilst the action may impact seriously upon the relationship between the owner and the authority as a purchaser, that relationship is affected by the consequences of the regulatory action and is not a factor in the action itself. Decisions to take regulatory action should not be governed by considerations of the authority's position as purchaser. Regulatory action should not be used to influence the authority's behaviour as a purchaser. Attempts to regulate by use or abuse of dominant purchasing powers or inappropriate mixing of powers of purchase and regulation might be seen as an abuse of power.

9.6.1   Variation of condition or imposition of new conditions

There is no power for owners to seek to enforce (by way of appeal) applications to vary conditions of registration or seek the imposition of new conditions of registration unless the authority accedes to their application. This prevents an owner from increasing the number of persons who may be accommodated in the regulated care home other than at the discretion of the regulatory authority.

Action to vary conditions of registration may be rare, save in the case of registered children's homes, given the limitation on valid conditions for which provision is made in the 1984 Act.[6] Variation of condition or imposition of additional conditions is to be conducted through the normal registration process, ie notice of proposal, representations, decision and appeal before the Registered Homes Tribunal or, in urgent cases, by application to the magistrates in relation to residential care home or nursing home registration, under s 11 or s 30 of the 1984 Act.

Section 5(4) of the 1984 Act provides that the regulatory authority may vary conditions of registration or impose additional conditions:

'The registration authority may from time to time:

(a)   vary any condition for the time being in force in respect of the home by virtue of this part of this Act;
or

(b)   impose an additional condition, either on the application of a person registered in respect of it or without such application.'

The procedure is identified in s 12(4). The authority shall give notice of the proposal to vary or impose an additional condition, and reasons for the proposal shall be given.

In relation to nursing homes, s 29 of the 1984 Act provides that the Secretary of State may make regulations as to the variation of conditions in force or the imposition of additional conditions. Such regulations have been

---

6   See Roch J in *Warwickshire Country Council v McSweeney* (unreported) 8 December 1988 and Chapter 5 generally.

made and are contained in reg 6 of the 1984 Nursing Homes Regulations, which provides:

'(1) the Secretary of State may vary any condition for the time being in force in respect of home by giving notice in writing to that effect to the person registered;

(2) a notice given under Paragraph 1 shall specify a date which shall be reasonable in the circumstances on which the variation specified in the notice shall have effect;

(3) where it is a condition that the number of persons kept at any one time in the home shall not exceed a specified number (the original maximum) and the Secretary of State varies that condition by specifying a lower number, he shall specify that the original maximum shall continue to apply so long as all the patients in the home are patients who were resident there at the date on which notice of the variation was given under Paragraph 1.'

This regulatory provision is in conflict with s 31(3) of the 1984 Act which provides:

'except where he makes an application under Section 30 above, the Secretary of State shall give any person registered in respect of the nursing home or mental nursing home notice of a proposal –

(a) to cancel the registration;

(b) to vary any condition for the time being in force in respect of the home by virtue of this act; or

(c) to impose any additional condition.'

Section 31(3) provides for the 'proposal', right to 'representation', decision, and appeal procedure.

Regulation 6 of the Residential Care Homes Regulations 1984 suggests that an authority can impose new conditions or changes in conditions without the right for the owner to respond. However, the statute must surely take precedence.

The drafting of the 1984 Regulations pre-dates the introduction of the ordinary procedure for variation of condition or cancellation of registration. Accordingly, the position can be reconciled on the basis that the draughtsman has not taken the changes into account when up-dating the regulatory procedure, so as to provide remedies of appeal for the regulated nursing home owner.

Nowhere is this more important than in relation to so-called 'staffing notices' issued under s 25(3) of the 1984 Act. Such are described as and are clearly conditions of registration. Many authorities fall into the error of believing that such staffing notices can be imposed by the simple service of the notice. They could, indeed, be so imposed, under a regime providing for the imposition of staffing conditions supported by powers of reg 6 of the 1984 Regulations. However, surely, that would not work, given the introduction of the rights to appeal of the regulated nursing home owner by s 31 et seq of the 1984 Act.

An interesting problem remains with the interpretation of regulation 6(3). No such provision is to be found in relation to residential care homes or registered children's homes. The provision that reductions in numbers of persons who may be accommodated shall not take effect until the numbers of patients have reduced to that number seems, on its face, to be a sensible provision to protect frail and vulnerable patients from eviction.

The question is whether this provision can really be deemed to continue to have effect, given the new procedures introduced by the 1984 Act. If it is necessary to reduce numbers of persons accommodated because it is perceived that, at current levels, there is a serious risk to the life, health or well being of clients, how can it possibly be right that the magistrate, having been persuaded to make such an order, which s 30 states to have immediate effect, reg 6 defers the operation of the order until the regulated owner has seen fit to reduce numbers to those required?

That must be wrong. The author submits that the statute must override the anomaly. Parliament could not have intended that, if a grave situation arose in which there was a required reduction in numbers, that reduction in numbers should depend, despite the intervention of the law, upon the whim of the regulated owner. Furthermore, given the appeal procedure, can reg 6(3) of the 1984 Regulations really have any continued effect?

The proposal takes effect either upon its agreement or upon the expiry of 28 days from the date of the decision of the regulatory authority, or if the owner exercises a right of appeal, when such appeal is determined or abandoned. If the regulated owner agrees to the reduction, surely the reduction should take immediate effect. If the regulated owner does not appeal against a decision of the authority, why should the decision further be deferred? If, after the hearing of all issues on an appeal, the Tribunal decides that the variation or additional conditions should take effect, then why should it not take effect at that time rather than be deferred at the whim of the regulated owner.

Once again, the author submits that the statute, which states when the decision takes effect, overrides the postponing effect of reg 6 of the Nursing Homes and Mental Nursing Homes Regulations 1984. Any other conclusion would be illogical, would defeat the purpose of Parliament and would not work in the interests of frail and vulnerable members of society accommodated in regulated care homes.

It should be noted that, in relation to nursing homes, the statutory power for the Secretary of State to make regulations about variation of condition does not provide that such variation shall be made at the application of the registered owner. It is suggested that nothing turns upon this (given the effect of s 5(4)), but even if the owner makes application for variation, the regulatory authority has a complete discretion as to whether or not to entertain such application. Clearly, the regulatory authority has a discretion in relation to nursing homes in similar terms, even though not expressed in the 1984 Act. A complete discretion as to whether or not to entertain the application for variation does not help the owner.[7]

It remains an open question (given the lack of appeal procedure for an owner's application variation) whether an unreasonable refusal to grant variation of condition or even to entertain such an application, might be the subject of a successful application for judicial review.

---

7   See Registered Homes Tribunal decision No 115, *Coombes v Hertfordshire County Council.*

9.6.2   Registered children's homes

The provisions in relation to variation of condition or imposition of new conditions of registration for registered children's homes are to be found in Sch 6 to the 1989 Act, introduced by s 63(11) of the 1989 Act. It will be recollected that para 2(1) of Sch 6 provides that the local authority, in relation to the registration of a registered children's home, may impose such conditions as it sees fit. Paragraph 2(2) provides:

'a local authority may from time to time –

(a)   vary any condition for the time being in force with respect to a home by virtue of this paragraph; or
(b)   impose an additional condition, either on the application of the person carrying on the home or without such an application.'

The provision mirrors s 5(4) of the 1984 Act in respect of residential care homes. It is submitted that the principles of complete discretion as to whether to entertain applications from the registered owner, as made law in *Coombes v Hertfordshire County Council*,[8] apply equally to registered children's homes as to residential care homes.

The local authority has a complete discretion to vary conditions of registration or impose new conditions of any nature and at any time as it sees fit. The procedure is in identical terms to s 12(4) and s 31(3) of the 1984 Act. The provisions are set out in para 5(4) of Sch 6. In relation to variation of conditions, reference is made to conditions being in force by virtue of Pt VIII. This must mean Pt VIII of the 1989 Act, which is simply the Part dealing with registered children's homes.

Paragraph 5(5) of Sch 6 provides that the local authority must give reasons for its proposal. There is no urgent procedure for variation or imposition of new conditions in relation to registered children's homes.

9.6.3   Cancellation of registration

Cancellation of registration is the ultimate sanction of the regulatory authority. In relation to residential care homes and registered nursing homes, registration may be cancelled either by the administrative method of proposal, representation, decision and appeal, or by the urgent method of application to a magistrate. Registration of a registered children's home can only be effected by the so-called ordinary procedure.

9.6.4   Cancellation of registration of residential care homes

The authority for the power to cancel is s 10 of the 1984 Act, which reads:

'the registration authority may cancel the registration of the person in respect of a residential care home –

(a)   on any ground which will entitle them to refuse an application for his registration in respect of it;

---

8   Registered Homes Tribunal decision No 115 (1991) 89 LGR 774.

(b) on the ground that the annual fee in respect of the home has not been paid or paid before the due date;

(bb) in the case of a small home on the ground that the annual return has not been duly made in accordance with the regulations made under Section 8(a) above; or

(c) on the ground –

  (i)   that he has been convicted of an offence under this part of the Act or any regulations made under it in respect of that or any other residential care home;

  (ii)   that any other person has been convicted of such an offence in respect of that home; or

  (iii) that any condition for the time being in force in respect of the home by virtue of this part of this Act has not been complied with.'

Power to cancel is a discretionary power. It will always be an exercise of the discretion, both as to whether or not cancellation is sought and as to which procedure is adopted.

Sub-paragraph (a)

The grounds which entitle the regulatory authority to refuse registration are the three grounds set out in s 9 of the 1984 Act. In short, if the authority takes the view that circumstances have changed so that, if at the date of consideration of cancellation, they would not have granted registration, then they are entitled to redress the situation by cancelling that which has been granted.

In effect, there is an on-going review of the conduct of the owner, and of the regulated care home, to ensure that it maintains a standard which entitles the owner to retain registration.

Sub-paragraph (b)

The author is not aware of any cases where cancellation has been effected solely upon the ground of the annual fee not being paid. It is suggested, with respect, that non-payment of the annual fee, of itself, is unlikely to be sustained as a ground for cancellation, provided that the fee has been paid at or before the time of the decision of the authority or the Tribunal. The provision is intended to prevent owners simply refusing to pay fees. This must be contrasted with the annual fee payable if the registration of a registered children's home is renewed. There, non-payment appears to operate as automatic and irrevocable cancellation.

Sub-paragraph (bb)

The procedure for the preparation of an annual return for a small home was introduced by way of concession to those who suggested that small homes should not be subjected to the full rigours of registration.

Such a provision requires teeth. Cancellation is the only effective sanction that can be imposed for non-compliance with an administrative task. Once again, it is suggested that compliance, albeit late, is likely to avoid the rigours of cancellation.

Sub-paragraph (c)

This sub-paragraph identifies a number of issues which may arise out of misconduct within the home, but the author would suggest that each and every one of them would amount to material which would entitle an authority to refuse registration in respect of the home.

A person who has been convicted of an offence in relation to a regulated care home is surely not a fit person to be registered in respect of that home.[9] It is interesting to note that the right of cancellation applies to conviction for offences in respect of the home in question, or other homes.

Convictions of others (given the offences under the 1984 Act or the 1984 Regulations) can only really relate to staff who obstruct inspection. Serious obstruction of inspection either arises because the staff are acting in aberration or because they are acting upon instructions of the owner, for example the owner who states that his home will not be disturbed during the night, irrespective of the wishes of the authority.

It is submitted that, in practice, any apparent risk to the registered owner will be considerably diluted. It will be obvious if staff have acted without the instruction of their employer. The employer's attitude to staff thereafter will demonstrate clearly his position. An owner who instructs staff to obstruct the regulatory authority surely cannot be said to be a fit person to have conduct of a regulated care home.

Even though convictions of others in relation to other residential care homes is not incorporated within s 10(c)(ii) it is suggested that appropriate evidence of instructions to obstruct inspection in other homes surely makes an owner at risk of being considered unfit in respect of any regulated care home.

Section 26(1)(e) of the National Assistance Act 1948, as amended by the National Health Service and Community Care Act 1990, makes it unlawful for a local authority to contract with a regulated care home owner for community care services where that owner has committed an offence under the 1984 Act or the 1984 Regulations. The effect of convictions, being to exclude the provider from a significant source of business referral, is likely to have considerable economic impact on the underlying business of the regulated care home. That is likely to affect other issues which go to fitness under s 9(c) and (b) of the 1984 Act.

The procedure for cancellation of registration requires the established route of urgent application, pursuant to s 11 of the 1984 Act, or ordinary procedure, pursuant to s 12 of the 1984 Act.

9.6.5   Cancellation of registration of nursing homes

The power for cancellation of the registration of a registered nursing home is contained in s 28 of the 1984 Act:

> 'the Secretary of State may at any time cancel the registration of a person in respect of a nursing home or mental nursing home –
>
> (a)   on any ground which would entitle him to refuse an application for the registration of that person in respect of the home;
> (b)   on the ground that the person has been convicted of an offence against the provisions of this part of the Act relating to nursing homes or mental nursing

---

9   See Registered Homes Tribunal decision No 118, *Piper v Birmingham City Council.*

homes or on the grounds that any other person has been convicted of such an offence in respect of that home;

(c) on the ground that any condition for the time being in force in respect of the home by virtue of this part of this Act has not been complied with;

(d) on the ground that that person has been convicted of an offence against regulations made under section 26 or 27 above;

(e) on the ground that the annual fee in respect of the home has not been paid on or before the due date.'

Considerable similarity with the reasons for cancellation of the registration of a residential care home will be observed. Once again, there is a discretion to initiate the cancellation procedure.

Sub-paragraph (a)

Detailed analysis of the permitted reasons for refusal of an application for registration of a registered nursing home are set out in Chapter 5.

The regulatory authority monitors in order to ensure that a home remains up to standard. A registered nursing home must remain fit for registration on an application for re-registration at any time.

It is upon this basis that some argue that it is difficult for an authority to justify seeking to refuse registration or impose different conditions of registration for a transferee on change of ownership, where the authority has made no criticism or proposal to vary conditions or cancel registration. There is some force in that argument. Authorities who have misgivings or concerns should consider carefully whether or not to criticise if not to commence regulatory action. In that way the authority will avoid criticism from potential purchasers and greater criticism from vendors.

Sub-paragraph (b)

Once again, it will be seen that the grounds extend to any offences committed generally, in relation to nursing homes or mental nursing homes, by the person registered, or offences committed by others in relation to other nursing homes or mental nursing homes.

The principal offence for which others might be responsible would be obstruction of the inspection, including the extended inspection, interview and examination rights of patients in relation to mental nursing homes. Evidence of instructions to obstruct inspections in nursing homes would surely amount to evidence of unfitness upon the part of the owner.

Undoubtedly, authorities and Tribunals will look at the conduct of registered owners in relation to any nursing homes which they operate. Unfitness in one home is not necessarily unfitness in all homes, but it does raise a presumption that the owner needs to rebut. That presumption would be that if an authority found owners to be unfit in particular circumstances those owners must surely have a burden upon them to show why, having been found unfit in relation to that home by a particular authority or Tribunal, they are not so unfit in relation to any other home or all homes which they are operating.

Sub-paragraph (c)

Similarly, breach of condition of registration is a sensible reason for consideration of cancellation of registration. Interestingly, the breach does not have to be proven by successful prosecution to conviction, but merely established as a fact by the authority and sustained before the Tribunal.

Sub-paragraph (d)

Conviction of offences contrary to the 1984 Regulations is equated to conviction of offences contrary to Pt II of the 1984 Act. The need for this provision is simply that offences are established under Pt II of the 1984 Act and other offences are only established offences by the Regulations.

The power to stigmatise such conduct as offence is comprised within ss 26(e) and 27(g) of the 1984 Act, which permit the Secretary of State to provide that breach of the regulations shall be an offence. Substantial numbers of breaches of the regulations are designated offences pursuant to reg 15 of the Nursing Homes and Mental Nursing Homes Regulations 1984.

Sub-paragraph (e)

Non-payment of the annual fee is again included as a discretionary reason for cancellation of registration. As before, a sanction is required against the owner who declines to pay fees as a matter of principle. Once again, it is suggested that non-payment which has been remedied, save in exceptional circumstances, would avoid the consequence of cancellation by the authority or even by the Tribunal.

In considering cancellation of registration, the regulatory authority and the Tribunal will take into account the interests of the persons accommodated in the regulated care home.[10] Accordingly, it is submitted that relatively trivial breaches of regulation, for example non-payment of the annual fee, which are remedied, are unlikely to provide sustainable grounds for cancellation of registration. If all else is well with in a registered nursing home or residential care home, but the owner has forgotten or perhaps deliberately delayed payment of a fee, it cannot be right to take away the home environment of frail and vulnerable people. Authorities must bear in mind always that the purpose of regulation is to protect frail and vulnerable members of society requiring care and residential accommodation – not to punish registered home owners for the sake of it.

9.6.6   Cancellation of registration of registered children's homes

Provisions for cancellation of the registration of registered children's homes are contained in para 4 of Sch 6 to the 1989 Act.

The procedure for implementing cancellation is set out in para 5(4) and (5) and follows the ordinary procedure provisions in relation to residential care homes and registered nursing homes. There is no provision for urgent cancellation of registration of a registered children's home.

Registered children's homes are subject to regular review, ie annually. An authority is obliged to review the registration and, if it decides to continue the registration, to notify the owner.

---

10   See *Avon County Council v Lang* [1990] COD 365.

Non-payment of the annual fee within 28 days of notification of continuation of registration breaches the condition upon which renewal is granted. This would appear to be a provision of which time is of the essence and the registration will be lost automatically if payment is not made. If the effect of non-payment is that registration lapses, then not only can the owner not remedy the situation, but there is no appeal. Indeed, a registration authority might well be acting beyond its powers in waiving the breach. A further application for registration, albeit one which is granted swiftly, will, in the author's view, be required if the regulatory scheme is to be followed correctly. Such application will not be permitted for six months.

Paragraph 4 reads as follows:

'(1) The person carrying on a registered children's home may at any time make an application, in such manner and including such particulars as may be prescribed for the cancellation by the responsible authority of the registration of the home.

(2) If the authority are satisfied, in the case of a school registered by virtue of Section 63(6), that it is no longer a school to which that provision applies, the authority shall give to the person carrying on the home notice that the registration of the home has been cancelled as from the date of the notice.

(3) If on any annual review under Paragraph 3, or at any other time, it appears to the responsible authority that a registered home has been carried on otherwise than in accordance with the relevant requirements, they may determine that the registration of the home shall be cancelled.

(4) Any responsible authority may at any time determine that the registration of the home shall be cancelled on the ground –
   (a) that the person carrying on the home has been convicted of an offence under this part or any regulations made under Paragraph 10;
   (b) that any other person has been convicted of such an offence in relation to the home.'

Sub-paragraph (1)

Unusually, in terms of regulated care homes, a provision is made entitling the owner to apply for cancellation of the registration. No provisions are made indicating whether or not the authority is bound or has a discretion to grant such application. The assumption must be that the authority has a discretion to grant the application. Clearly, an authority might well wish not to accede to voluntary cancellation if it itself contemplates compulsory cancellation.

The Department of Health maintains a register of cancelled registrations and authorities who go to the time, trouble and expense to ensure cancellation of the registration of the former registered owner are often very concerned to ensure that the cancellation and the grounds for it are recorded, published and circulated. An erring owner, in respect of a registered children's home, would no doubt wish it to appear that the cancellation had arisen out of his own application rather than by compulsion.

Further, the cancellation of registration of a registered children's home will leave children accommodated in the home at risk. An authority may very well not wish to accede to cancellation other than in accordance with its own timetable. It will need to ensure that there are proper arrangements for the re-accommodation of children. The owner clearly remains responsible to the regulatory authority, to the children and to those who may purchase places or sponsor children at the registered children's home whilst the registration remains in force.

The Children's Homes Regulations 1991 do not prescribe any form of application or particulars to be supplied in relation to an application for cancellation by an owner. Perhaps this is not surprising as such an application is unlikely to require more than the fact of application coupled, possibly, with some detailed reasons.

Sub-paragraph (2)

This relates to notification of cancellation of the registration as children's homes of certain schools. Although sub-para 2 suggests that cancellation of registration takes effect immediately and that would be the natural consequence of the school having ceased to be a school registrable as a children's home, it is quite clear that the provisions for appeal and the so-called ordinary procedure for cancellation set out in paras 5, 6, 7 and 8 of Sch 6 to the 1989 Act apply equally.

A school might wish to be registered. Its source of some fees and/or some pupils might be dependent upon registration. Local authority support might be dependent upon registration. There may be a very real issue as to whether the school has ceased to be registerable and that issue may need to be determined as a matter of law by the Tribunal and ultimately by the courts.

Sub-paragraph (3)

This is the sub-paragraph that deals with cancellation of registration should it appear, upon an annual review, that the registered children's home is not being carried on in accordance with the relevant requirements.

It is curious that an authority is obliged to give notice that it is satisfied with the conduct of a registered children's home, so as to trigger renewal of registration, but appears to have a discretion as to whether or not to serve notice of cancellation, if not satisfied with the way in which the home is being conducted. The reality is surely that, if the authority exercises its discretion not to serve notice of cancellation, this must surely trigger an obligation to serve notice of renewal.

The wording of sub-para (3) is odd, for it does not speak in terms of serving notice in respect of cancellation. The words are:

'may determine that the registration of the home be cancelled'.

It may be arguable that, under these circumstances, the paras 5–8 procedure is not invoked. The effect of that would be that the authority has a discretion to cancel without appeal. The author suggests that such a conclusion cannot be right. In a scheme of regulation that provides universally for a similar procedure of cancellation of registration, it is manifestly unlikely that Parliament decided to confer upon authorities the power to cancel registration without appeal simply by omitting reference to a notice in one sub-paragraph of the Schedule. The wording is repeated in sub-para (4) and the author suggests that the only sensible interpretation is that the determination to cancel must be followed by the service of a notice of proposal pursuant to para 5.

It will be noted that the trigger for giving notice of renewal of registration or determination to cancel registration is merely that the authority is not satisfied that the home is being conducted in accordance with the relevant requirements. The authority is not obliged to fit its reasoning within the limits of permitted reasons. The relevant requirements include any matters which the authority may consider to be appropriate.[11]

Sub-paragraph (4)

The authority is given a specific discretion to cancel registration if the person carrying on the home has been convicted of an offence under Pt VIII of the 1984 Act, incorporating Sch 6, or any regulations made under Sch 6, para 10 of the 1989 Act. It is clear, as with the similar provisions for the owners of residential care and nursing homes, that such convictions would relate to the operation of any registered children's home and not just the one being considered for cancellation by the authority.

In contrast, the right to cancel registration as a result of the convictions of other persons relates to registered children's homes offences only in relation to the home being considered for cancellation.

The offences which may be committed in respect of registered children's homes are less extensive than those in relation to residential care homes. In short, they provide for:

(1)   an offence of carrying on a children's home without registration;
(2)   an offence of breach of condition.

Neither of these offences can be committed by anyone other than the person carrying on the home, whether registered or not.

Sub-paragraph (a) also deals with offences for breach of the regulations made pursuant to the power created in Sch 6 to the 1989 Act. Curiously, none of the regulations introduced by the Children's Home Regulations 1991 carry with them the stigma of offence or are capable of prosecution. However, the Children (Secure Accommodation) Regulations 1991[12] do provide that it is an offence for anyone to use accommodation registered as a children's home for the purpose of restricting the liberty of children, without reasonable excuse. It is suggested that this is the only offence, albeit a very serious offence, which can be committed by anyone other than the registered owner, so as to trigger cancellation within Sch 6, para 1(4)(b) to the 1989 Act.

9.7   PROSECUTION

Both the 1984 and the 1989 Acts provide that certain conduct in contravention of the provisions of both the statute and the regulations shall amount to an offence. This is, perhaps, best described as a statutory, rather than a criminal, offence. Nevertheless, the consequence of committing such an offence may be criminal prosecution.

---

11   See the 1989 Act, Sch 6, para 1(4)(b).
12   SI 1991/1505.

9.7.1 Notice of prosecution

Certain offences committed in respect of residential care or registered nursing homes may not be prosecuted without prior warning. Regulation 20 of the Residential Care Homes Regulations 1984 and reg 15 of the Nursing Homes and Mental Nursing Homes Regulations 1984 provide for the service of a notice upon a person registered who is considered to have committed an offence. In relation to residential care homes, no offence is committed prior to failure to comply with the notice, but, in relation to nursing homes, if the offence has been committed, it still stands as an offence, but no penalty may be imposed through the criminal courts unless and until there is a repetition of the offence following the service of the notice.

The service of a warning notice is not found in the regulations relating to registered children's homes. Perhaps this can be explained by reference to the relatively small number of offences that may be committed and the relative gravity of those offences. Warning notices are not required in respect of residential care and registered nursing homes where the offence committed is operating while unregistered (one would hardly expect a notice under those circumstances) and in respect of breach of condition. Breach of condition of registration of a registered children's home is an offence unless the owner has a reasonable excuse.[13] There is unfettered power to impose imaginative powers in respect of children's homes. That wide-ranging power combined with the sanction of prosecution fortify the authority's power for creative regulation of such homes.

9.7.2 Breach of conditions

The practitioner considering a prosecution, whether as a prosecutor determining whether to proceed or as a defendant contemplating whether or not the offence will be made out, will need to look carefully at the terms of the conditions of registration.

In relation to residential care and registered nursing homes, this will be a relatively simple task. The types of conditions are prescribed by the statute[14] and relate essentially to numbers and categories of clients, together with qualifications for the nurse in charge and the number of nurses to be on duty with regard to registered nursing homes. In relation to registered children's homes, conditions may be far more wide reaching.

There is no point in imposing a condition (unless it be to suggest a guideline to the registered owner, which would hardly be an appropriate regulatory practice) unless the sanction of statutory prosecution is contemplated. If the condition in respect of breach of which a prosecution is brought cannot be clearly understood, then the prosecution is bound to fail. Ambiguous conditions, or conditions which cannot be capable of any proper understanding, may not even be conditions of registration, so it will be almost impossible to found a prosecution.

---

13 Children Act 1989, Sch 6, para 2(3).
14 See *McSweeney v Warwickshire County Council* (unreported) 8 December 1988, Roch J.

When drafting a condition, care should be taken to advise regulatory authorities that the shorter and more succinct the condition the better. Lengthy, ambiguous conditions should be avoided. If the condition of registration is incapable of construction, so as to form the subject of proper prosecution, it may be argued that it is an invalid condition. An argument may then centre as to whether that condition can be excised from the registration or whether the whole registration fails, with the consequence that the owner is operating unregistered. Such an owner would have a statutory defence, under s 18 of the 1984 Act, in respect of a residential care home, but no such defence in respect of a registered nursing home. On a first occasion, the situation would probably amount to a reasonable excuse for the offence, under the terms of the 1989 Act.

The author would suggest that it is in the interests of both parties to ensure that a condition should be drafted in the clearest possible terms.

9.8 THE OFFENCES

Here, we will consider in brief order the groups of offences that can apply in respect of the conduct of each genus of regulated care home.

9.8.1 Residential care homes

(1) Carrying on a residential care home while unregistered (s 2 of the 1984 Act);
(2) committing a breach of conditions of registration (s 5(5) of the 1984 Act);
(3) committing offences created by regulations made under the 1984 Act, pursuant to s 16 of the 1984 Act (s 16(2) of the 1984 Act and reg 20(2) of the Residential Care Homes Regulations 1984);
(4) obstructing the inspection of a residential care home (s 17(6) of the 1984 Act).

9.8.2 Nursing homes

(1) Carrying on a nursing home or mental nursing home while unregistered (s 23(1) of the 1984 Act);
(2) breaching a condition of registration of a nursing home or mental nursing home (s 29(4) of the 1984 Act);
(3) holding out a nursing home or mental nursing home to be such, whilst not registered, with intent to deceive any person (s 24 of the 1984 Act). The ingredients of this novel offence are that:
  (i) it may be committed by any person;
  (ii) it must have been committed with intent to deceive any person; and
  (iii) by applying a name to premises in England or Wales or so describing or holding out premises as to indicate or reasonably be understood to indicate that the premises are a nursing home or maternity home or mental nursing home.
'A *person*'. Clearly, the statute envisages that anyone may commit this

offence. It may be the person who is actually committing the offending act. It may be a person conducting a registered home which is not registered as a nursing home, but is held out as such, for example a residential care home that advertises itself as providing nursing care, or providing nursing staff. The offence could also be committed by somebody unconnected with the operation of an establishment who holds out to others that the establishment is a nursing home, even if those responsible for the conduct of the establishment are innocent or ignorant of the circumstances.

'*With intent to deceive any person*'. Holding out to no particular purpose, possibly by way of gossip or rumour, does not create an offence. The intention must be to deceive but the person deceived may be anyone. The persons likely to be deceived are:

(i)   persons resident in the establishment;
(ii) persons who are encouraged to become residents of the establishment;
(iii) sponsors of persons who are or may become resident in the establishment, for example relatives, charities or sponsoring local authorities;
(iv) the Department of Social Security or a local authority, who may be encouraged to pay benefit for persons resident in an establishment or make arrangements for accommodation of persons within the establishment without checking the registration. Although this seems unlikely, circumstances may arise where units of accommodation associated with registered residential care, nursing or children's homes are used for what amounts to the purposes of a nursing home and held out as such without being so registered.
(v)   Persons who may purchase the establishment. An owner of an unregistered establishment would commit an offence if he persuaded a gullible and unwary purchaser to purchase it as a nursing home whilst it was not so registered.

'*Describes or holds out*'. The simplest case will amount to actually using the style 'nursing home', 'maternity home' or 'mental nursing home' in relation to the premises. However, it is argued strongly that suggesting that the premises provide the services of nursing care, or other services which require registration as a nursing home, is as much holding out premises as a nursing home as attributing a particular name, type or style. Accordingly, individuals have been successfully prosecuted where they have issued advertisements for homes (usually residential care homes) indicating that those homes are:

(i)   under the control of a qualified nurse;
(ii) providing 24-hour nursing care;
(iii) providing full nursing cover.

Any use of the word 'nurse' or 'nursing' in connection with the operation of an establishment which is not registered as a nursing home in a commercial context, must be a situation which places the issuer of such words at risk of prosecution. Certainly, there is a proviso that the words must be published or used with intent to deceive, but a plea of ignorance of the 1984 Act or ignorance of the likely effect of the words is not likely, in the author's submission, to make any progress.

It is a principle of the criminal law that a person is to be taken as intending the natural consequences of their action. If conduct of a person in relation to an establishment unregistered as a nursing home is such that ordinary people would expect others to infer from that conduct that the premises were a nursing home, then such a person must expect to be convicted. At the very least, during the course of the trial, the burden of proof will shift from the prosecution onto the defence to adduce evidence that no deceit was intended but only where the prosecution have raised a *prima facie* case of 'deception'.

'Indicate or reasonably be understood'. These words are carefully and cleverly drafted to sweep up arguments as to the construction of particular advertisements, publications, sign boards or hoardings. The author suggests that, with these words, no amount of quick footwork on the part of prospective defendants will avoid the consequences of their actions.

(4) Offences as a result of the contravention of the provisions of regulations made pursuant to the 1984 Act and, in particular, s 26 and s 27 (s 26(e), s 27(g)) and para 15(1), (2) and (3) of the Nursing Homes and Mental Nursing Homes Regulations 1984.

9.8.3   Registered children's homes

(1) Carrying on a children's home while unregistered (s 63(10) of the 1989 Act);
(2) breaching a condition of registration (para 2(3) of Sch 6 to the 1989 Act);
(3) breach of regulations made pursuant to Pt VIII of the 1989 Act (paras 10(3) and (4) of Sch 6 to the 1989 Act).

As previously indicated, it appears that no offence was created by the Children's Homes Regulations 1991, but an offence has been created in respect of restricting the freedom of children within a registered children's home or indeed a voluntary home, by reg 19 of the Children (Secure Accommodation) Regulations 1991. The provision reads as follows:

'(1) The use of accommodation for the purpose of restricting the liberty of children in voluntary homes and registered children's homes is prohibited.
(2) The contravention of, or failure to comply with the provisions of Paragraph 1, without reasonable excuse, shall be an offence against these regulations.'

No decided case is known to the author. Clearly, a debate might arise as to whether or not the offence is committed if the particular accommodation was used on a single occasion, rather than being set aside for regular use for the purpose of restriction. It is suggested that, given the subject matter and the social concern that would arise from restricting liberty of children without lawful authority, a finding that children have been restricted as to their liberty in a registered children's home would be sufficient to prove the offence.

Interestingly, a defence will be provided if a reasonable excuse can be shown.

9.8.4 'Reasonable excuse'

Out of all the provisions for the regulation of care homes, only the provisions in respect of registered children's homes provide that an offence shall be committed only if it is committed without a reasonable excuse. Such a provision contains two elements. There must be an excuse and that excuse must be reasonable.

In common with normal criminal law principles, the author would suggest that, as the offence, in each case, is created by the commission of certain acts without reasonable excuse, it is for the prosecution to prove beyond all reasonable doubt that the offence has been committed without reasonable excuse. That burden will lie upon the prosecution whatever steps the defence may make. However, if no excuse is proffered by the defence, the prosecution's task may be made easier.

Aside from the provisions of the Children (Secure Accommodation) Regulations 1991, children are protected, as are adults, by the law concerning the crime and tort of false imprisonment.

9.9 REGULATORY PROCEDURE

Consideration of the regulatory procedure will be divided into three sections:

(1) the 'ordinary' procedure for regulation;
(2) the urgent procedure for regulation in relation to residential care homes and registered nursing homes;
(3) prosecution in respect of the operation of registered care homes or the conduct of care homes which are not registered, including consideration of the effect and meaning of the service of notices pursuant to regs 20 and 15(3) of the 1984 Residential Care Homes Regulations and the 1984 Nursing Homes Regulations, respectively.

9.9.1 Ordinary procedure for regulation

The system first introduced with the 1984 Act has been repeated in the 1989 Act. The 'ordinary' procedure for regulation is appropriate in ordinary circumstances. If the regulatory authority feels that conditions need to be changed or that additional conditions need to be added, or, regrettably, that the registration needs to be cancelled, it will follow this course. The process is simple:

(1) a notice proposing what is intended;
(2) an opportunity, identified in the notice as a pre-condition to the validity of the notice, for the owner to make representations about the proposal;

(3) thereafter, a decision, not a rubber stamped decision, but a decision taking account of the proposal and its reasons and the representations which have been received;

(4) thereafter, for aggrieved owners, the further safeguard of an appeal to the Registered Homes Tribunal.

Much depends on the ability, integrity and impartiality of the Tribunal. Any regulatory action is bound to have been preceeded by correspondence and discourse between the owner and the officers of the regulatory authority. The issues will have been highlighted. Where the ordinary procedure is employed, it will be rarely, if ever, that the ingredients of concern come as a surprise to the regulated care home owner.

The authority acts by its officers. The authority must trust its officers or else their position becomes untenable and the authority's reputation must diminish. The officers responsible for the preparation and service of a regulatory notice will be senior. Care home owners should appreciate that it is unlikely that any representations that they make will persuade the officers that their action was misjudged. There will have been great consideration and debate before the preparation and service of the regulatory notice. Accordingly, it should come as no surprise to regulated care home owners and their advisers that, although an authority must consider fully both the reasons for the proposal and the owner's representations, it will be a rare occasion that a proposal to take regulatory action is not adopted by the authority.

The period between the decision of the authority, receipt of appeal and the hearing of the appeal is short. This is rightly so. Serious issues are at stake. A home owner's reputation, which has been impugned by a regulatory decision, should be redeemed quickly. If the decision is correct, it is wrong that it should have its effect delayed by the vagaries of litigation.

The period between notice of proposal and decision of the authority is a vital opportunity for both parties to the regulatory dispute to get their case into order. The preparation of the case will form the foundation of a subsequent appeal, which may well be inevitable. The right of appeal being absolute, and there being no possibility of an order for costs in the Tribunal, authorities should assume that every adverse decision will be the subject of an appeal. Nor should owners expect the miracle of success by submission of representations, which should be regarded as but a step leading to appearance before the Tribunal.

9.9.2 Cancellation of registration

It will be seen immediately that the emphasis here is different from a pending application for first registration. Whilst the application for registration is pending, the only person adversely affected is the applicant. With regard to a proposal to cancel or vary conditions of registration (almost always in a way adverse to the commercial interests of the owner), the home will be operating under a sword of Damocles. The clients in care may have an uncertain future. If poor care practices are alleged, then it is likely that those care practices will continue throughout the course of the procedure. Time here is of the essence.

A decision to cancel registration is a public decision. Delay will not help the owner. His reputation will have been damaged by public knowledge that his registration is in jeopardy. It is inevitable that purchasers of care will not be keen to undertake new contracts. Existing purchasers may seek to remove clients.

The very purpose of regulation, ie the protection of the frail and vulnerable, is effectively suspended while these matters are considered. It may be that the emergence of a serious risk could lead to further urgent action. However, it must be a matter of concern if there is any risk, albeit not serious, to the life, health or well being of clients. In the absence of any such risk, it may be a matter of debate as to why the action has been taken by the regulatory authority in the first place.

The Registered Homes Tribunal has consistently taken the view that adjournments of hearings are to be avoided at all costs. Adjournments are often the first thought of litigation lawyers. Many are surprised that applications for a first adjournment, so commonly accepted in other arenas, are met with a robust denial before the Tribunal. The Tribunal has adopted the principle that 'justice delayed is justice denied'.

9.9.3   The notice

The notice must:

(1)   be in writing;
(2)   indicate the action proposed;
(3)   inform the owner of his right to make representations and that such right must be exercised by a simple indication as to whether or not representations will be made, such indication to be given within 14 days;
(4)   give reasons for the proposal.

The reasoning that applies to giving full reasons, backed by available evidence, in relation to a refusal of registration must apply equally to a proposal adversely to change the conditions of registration or, indeed, to cancel registration. These matters should not arise casually. It is suggested that any authority conducting itself properly will not embark upon adverse regulatory action unless it has formed a firm view based on serious evidence. Regulatory action is expensive in terms of money and time. No properly advised authority, conducting its duties reasonably, could possibly enter upon such a course without due consideration.

It therefore follows that the authority must have detailed evidence to support the proposal. The sooner served the more powerful will be its effect. The procedure is designed, with fairness in mind, to tell an owner what is said against him and why an action is proposed. There can be no possible justification for not informing owners in the fullest possible way of the evidence against them.[15]

It may well be that the authority does not wish to disclose the identity of informants, or certain information that will reveal its sources. Such

---

15   See Registered Homes Tribunal decision No 323, *Woodfield Lodge Ltd v Hertfordshire County Council.*

information can, of course, be withheld. The authority should, however, bear in mind that it will never be able to rely upon material which is not disclosed to the owner. Withholding of important material is one possible ground upon which a Tribunal might be persuaded to grant an adjournment. There is no reasonable prospect that vital evidence will not have to be disclosed if the authority is to rely upon it. The authority should only omit to disclose such evidence if it can sustain its case before the Tribunal without adducing such evidence.

There is no restriction on adding, to reasons adduced by way of evidence before the Tribunal, material arising or discovered subsequent to the notice of proposal, or even material that was known or available on the date of proposal but omitted. However, occasions when this is allowed are rare. Administrative inconvenience and expense are poor reasons. However, there may be special circumstances:

(1)   the authority may be relying upon evidence from staff who need to remain employed, possibly for the safety of residents;

(2)   the authority may wish not to disclose sensitive sources of information until nearer to the hearing of the Tribunal. Such occasions will be rare and will probably only relate to circumstances where the safety of witnesses or that of frail and vulnerable clients is at stake.

An advantage of early disclosure is that it will indicate to the owner the strength of the authority's position. Insufficient notices may encourage owners and their advisers to anticipate success on appeal. On the other hand, full disclosure of the case, which sadly often happens only days before an expensive Tribunal hearing, often reveals to owners, and particularly their advisers, the futility of pursuing an appeal.

Those owners who have insurance to protect themselves against the enormous expenses of conducting regulatory disputes before the Tribunal will, in the current insurance market, inevitably have, as a term of such insurances, a clause which avoids the liability of the insurer unless the insurer has had legal advice that there are reasonable prospects of the owner succeeding in the appeal. The greater the information supplied in advance (and most such insurance policies only cover costs incurred after the authority's decision and in connection with the Tribunal hearing), the more likely it is that the owner's legal advisers or independent legal advisers will advise the insurers of the strength of the authority's position. Withdrawal of support for legal costs will, in all probability, diminish or eliminate the capacity to appeal effectively.

If the authority is presented with insufficient reasons by its officers, with detailed and persuasive representations from the owner, independent and non-executive members of the authority may be persuaded to side against the authority's officers in cases which are not justified. Full disclosure of the reasons will help to persuade the members of the authority of the correctness of the course taken by senior officers. Members of the authority may not be skilled and experienced in matters of regulation of care homes and detailed proposals may help to inform them about the issues that they have to consider.

Notices of appeal must be lodged within 28 days of the decision. Tribunal hearings may be fixed as early as 6 weeks from the date of notice from the Tribunal. An authority that is well prepared will be in a strong position to urge for an early hearing and to resist the plaintiff's pleas for adjournments.

There is no justification whatsoever for an authority to take the short cut of simply reciting, word for word, the permissible grounds for cancellation of registration from the 1984 Act, to support the proposal. Persuasive representations by the owner may be more successful, and lazy preparation will result in emergencies later in the day, when there will be less time to prepare and formulate a sensible campaign.

9.9.4   Representations

What may be seen as a misplaced desire to become involved in the creation of legal style hearings has often lead authorities to create quasi tribunal situations at the representational stage. This is an error. All that is required by statute is that the authority considers representations made by the owner. Representations present the opportunity to the owner, who has received a notice adversely affecting his registration, to put his side of the case. The owner is entitled to make those representations to the authority.

If the authority has served full and complete reasons for the notice of proposal, then the representations may be prepared the more swiftly and complaints for delay and further information more easily diverted.

It is a matter for the owner how he prepares the representations. They may be oral or in writing. Once the owner has indicated that he wishes to make representations, the authority is prevented from proceeding until either:

(1)   the representations have been received; or
(2)   a reasonable time for delivery of representations has elapsed without those representations being delivered.[16]

The opportunity to make representations is subject to the pre-condition that notice of such intention should be given within 14 days. There is no reason to suggest that this deadline is flexible. If the deadline expires without such a notice being given, the authority may proceed without further ado. Whilst it will probably look at any submissions or representations received before an actual decision is made, there is absolutely no obligation on an authority to give a further opportunity for representations or even to accept representations made out of time.

Representations, it is suggested, are a private stage of the procedure. Whilst the matter is awaiting decision by the authority, the fact that regulatory action is being taken and representations are being received should remain confidential and should not be disclosed to anyone other than those directly concerned, particularly purchasers of care, including purchasing divisions of the regulatory authority.

Owners should appreciate that representations, once made, are, in effect, set in stone. Changes of mind, variations of evidence or a tactical about face will become ever more obvious if the prior course had been set in stone in the form of representations made to the authority. An owner, if in doubt, should

---

16   1984 Act, s 13 and s 32; 1989 Act, Sch 6, para 6.

withhold submissions. Advocates for the authority will be able to make much capital out of changes in position. Changes in position cause concern as to the reliance which can be placed on parties and witnesses. Concerns as to the reliability of witnesses are the beginning of defeat in any litigation.

The authority should remain in control of the representational process. The opportunity for control will be improved, the greater the information attached to the notice of proposal. Owners should be encouraged to state at an early stage whether they wish to make representations in writing or orally. If representations are to be made orally, then special arrangements will have to be made.

In relation to residential care homes and registered children's homes, representations will be heard by a committee or sub-committee of the local authority. In relation to nursing homes, the representation will be heard by a person appointed by the Health Authority (usually a panel of persons). Those persons, who will be independent, have to be assembled, for which time must be set aside.

It is not unreasonable for the owner to be asked how he wishes to proceed. There is no provision for him to answer, but a failure to co-operate will be noted. In the absence of co-operation, it is suggested that the authority should fix a date by which written representations should be received or at which oral representations will be heard. There is no absolute rule that it must be fixed for the convenience of the owner. There is certainly no rule that it should be fixed for the convenience of a particular lawyer. Authorities should not be seduced into extending the period in which representations are to be received.

The nature of the allegations (largely determined by their immediate impact on the health and safety of clients) will dictate what may be a reasonable period. Requests for extensions, on reasonable grounds, should usually be granted, save in exceptional circumstances. However, the closer to the date the extension is sought, the more an authority should consider whether to deny it. The authority should remember that it is only taking action because it perceives the interests of frail and vulnerable clients to be in some risk. If that is so, then delay increases the risk – upon the assumption that the authority is right.

Determining what is a reasonable time will always be difficult. Any decision of an authority made without having allowed a reasonable time for representations, will be subject to judicial review. Assuming that very short periods are not involved, the High Court is unlikely to be impressed by such applications for review. There have been cases in which attempts have been made to postpone the hearing of Tribunals by taking proceedings for judicial review to impugn the conduct of the process of representation. Such applications have been spectacularly unsuccessful. It is unlikely that the High Court will interfere in the administration of the process whereby an authority makes a regulatory decision.[17]

Care must be taken not to introduce material before the authority, in considering whether or not to adopt a proposal, that has not been served upon the owner, or in respect of which the owner has not had a reasonable time to

---

17   *R v Leicestershire County Council, ex parte Thompson* (unreported) CO/ 109/ 91.

consider his position. If there is a full set of reasons appended to a notice of proposal, the problem is less likely to arise. In principle, there should be little need for an authority to respond to anything that is stated in representations by an owner. Rebuttal or denial of what is said by the authority does not need to be answered. Repetitious paperwork is redundant and annoys those considering decisions.

As the representations will be made in response to the reasons for the proposal, it should be unlikely that much new material arises. If it does, the authority should not be slow to expand its reasons and offer a further reasonable time for a response. However, those advising authorities should think very carefully before they allow the representational process to be expanded and extended in this way. They will need to consider carefully if a response is really needed or if this is merely indulgence in rebuttal for its own sake.

It may very well be that the proposal will still stand even if certain elements appear to have been successfully challenged or even abandoned. The underlying purpose is to take the regulatory action forward and not to score at every occasion on every point. A person registered as the owner of a regulated care home who appears to be unfit on a number of counts will still be unfit if one or more of those counts is withdrawn or successfully answered.

It should be rare, if ever, that registration officers of the authority, who may have conduct of the case, are present when the representations of the owner are received. The authority committee, or indeed the authority itself, may require the advice of its legal advisers. That is quite different from having officers responsible for formulating the proposal present to expand or even clarify terms of the proposal. Extra information supplied at this stage will suggest unfairness and may encourage more successful applications for judicial review of the decision to progress regulatory action.

If officers are available and it is thought necessary that they should participate, at the very most they should be asked to clarify issues which arise out of the proposal and the representations and, under no circumstances, should they be permitted to add additional information. Such a course could be fatal to the legality of the subsequent decision, with the consequent loss of time and increased risk by delay to those clients in care; ie those who the authority is endeavouring to protect by regulatory action.

If representations are presented orally, it may well be that owners will be asked to clarify what they or their representative says. If matters remain of concern to the authority or its committee thereafter, then the committee can adjourn to seek further clarification of the reasons for the proposal, while having to afford an opportunity to the owner to comment on any clarification received. The authority should be careful not to follow that course unless the need for clarification will make a difference to the decision that it would make.

9.9.5   The decision

In all cases, the decision is the decision of the authority. It must be made by the authority or by a committee, division or sub-committee of the authority to which power has been validly delegated.

It is unlikely that Health Authorities, by standing orders, will have effectively and lawfully delegated power to make the decision. The authority may, and usually does, make the decision as a matter of routine having heard the reports and recommendations of an independent sub-committee set up under appropriate 'standing orders' to consider the issue. An authority will certainly not have time to consider such detailed issues at a full authority meeting. Authorities very often only meet four times a year, given their restricted roles, following the creation of a new internal market in the National Health Service. Such infrequent meetings may be considered sufficient to justify the authority making, by further standing orders, provisions whereby groups of members of the authority may constitute a quorum for considering regulatory issues in relation to nursing homes.

Authorities can be convened at short notice, but this is inconvenient. Clearly, standing orders can provide for emergency action to be taken on the basis of a decision of less than the whole of the authority. Provided the standing orders have been approved by the whole of the authority, there is no reason why a facility for more frequent decisions should not be made. This must be consistent with the policy of the legislation in protecting the frail and vulnerable and, indeed, protects owners in the sense that it ensures swifter process of applications for registration and, to an extent, swifter opportunities to clear names and reputations which have been sullied by the prospect of adverse regulatory action.

The decision is simply a decision to adopt or reject the proposal. The authority does not have an opportunity to make any other decision. If a different decision is required, the procedure will have to be revisited. The decision to adopt (or indeed reject) the proposal shall be notified in writing to the owner.

There is no need for the notice to include any reasons for the decision and, in the author's submission, it should not. If there is an appeal, there will be reference back to the reasons for notice of proposal, but the conduct of the Tribunal hearing will rely upon further reasons promulgated on behalf of the authority, in accordance with Registered Homes Tribunal Rules 1984.[18]

The notice does require a written explanation as to the right of appeal. It simply needs to state that there is a right of appeal which may be exercised within 28 days after[19] service of the decision upon the owner.

It is important to note that decisions of the authority do not take immediate effect. The time-limit for appeal is important. It is not extendable. Upon the fact of appeal depends the time when the decision takes effect. In the case of a cancellation, the date when the decision takes effect is the date when conduct of the regulated care home by the owner ceases to be lawful. This is very important.

If there is an appeal, the decision takes effect only when the appeal has been determined or if the appeal is abandoned. An appeal can be abandoned by notice in writing withdrawing the appeal. The appeal is otherwise determined when the notice of the Tribunal is published and that notice is

---

18 SI 1984/1346. See r 5(2), (3).
19 1984 Act, s 15 and s 33; 1989 Act, Sch 6, para 7.

required to be published in writing. If no appeal is brought, the decision takes effect on the expiration of 28 days from service on the owner of the notice of decision.

There is a need for time to elapse, in the interests of frail and vulnerable clients, between a decision to cancel registration and the cessation of operation of the home. However, it is somewhat odd that, following the extended suspension of a decision, pending decision of the Tribunal upon the appeal, there is 'sudden death', in that the decision takes immediate effect as soon as the decision of the Tribunal is published. In other words, the owner is operating unlawfully at the very moment the Tribunal decision arrives through the post.

9.9.6   Emergency regulatory action

Emergency regulatory action in relation to regulated care homes is provided under the 1984 Act in relation to residential care homes and nursing homes. The source of the law in this field is s 11 of the 1984 Act, in relation to residential care homes and s 30 of the 1984 Act in relation to nursing homes. The urgent procedure was first introduced in the 1984 Act.[20] The provisions are identical and are as follows:

'If:

(a)   the Secretary of State/*Registration Authority* applies to a justice of the peace for an order –
    (i)   cancelling the registration of a person in respect of a nursing home or mental nursing home/*residential care home*;
    (ii)   varying any condition for the time being in force in respect of the home by virtue of this part of this Act; or
    (iii)   imposing an additional condition; and
(b)   It appears to the justice of the peace that there will be a serious risk to the life, health or well being of the patients in the home unless the order is made;

He may make the order and the cancellation, variation or imposition shall have effect from the date on which the order is made.

(c)   An application under sub-section (i) above may be made ex parte and shall be supported by a written statement of the Secretary of State's/*Registration Authority's* reasons for making the application.
(d)   An order under sub-section (i) above shall be writing.
(e)   Where such an order is made, the Secretary of State/*Registration Authority* shall serve on any person registered in respect of the home, as soon as practicable after the making of the order –
    (i)   notice of the making of the order and its terms; and
    (ii)   a copy of the statement of the Secretary of State's reasons which supported his application for the order.'[21]

At a stroke, without warning or notice, the registration of the regulated care home owner is terminated. The effect is immediate. The remedy is appeal to

---

20   First contained in the schedules to the Health and Social Services Administration Act 1983. This was never brought into force, being superseded by the Registered Homes Act 1984.
21   Section 30 of the 1984 Act; differences for residential care homes (s 11 of the 1984 Act) indicated by italics supplied by the author.

the Registered Homes Tribunal, with consequent delay. The home cannot operate lawfully, and the patients must be dispersed. Whatever the result on appeal, the effective result is termination of the regulated care home business, and the ruin of the owner.

In the author's experience, most exercises of this power have resulted in such disruption to residents and patients that at least one has died within a week or two following the event. The order is truly draconian. It has, however, been sanctioned by Parliament and is a part of the law.

In *Lyons v East Sussex County Council*,[22] Lord Donaldson, the Master of the Rolls, upholding the decision of Farquarson J, as he then was, held that the burden of proof in justifying the magistrates' order was upon the authority and, furthermore, that the authority could rely on newly acquired or amended material to support the decision on appeal. The Court of Appeal expressed the view that such orders would not be made without careful consideration by magistrates. The Court of Appeal, in *Martine v South East Kent Health Authority*,[23] expressed the view that, by the introduction of the magistrate, Parliament was ensuring checks and balances in the exercise of regulatory power.

The inevitable result is that any application made under s 11 or s 30 of the 1984 Act will be accompanied by sufficient material to make the success of any application a mere formality. An application would not be formulated or put forward without evidence that suggested a serious risk to clients' life, health or well being. In *Martine's* case, the Court of Appeal further held, that the applicant regulatory authority owes no duty of care to the regulated care home owner in preparation for or conduct of an application for an urgent cancellation order. The inevitability of the magistrates' decision and the inherent unfairness of the position were reported[24] by the Tribunal.

The remedies available to owners are those unattractive remedies, namely torts akin to malicious prosecution, ie malicious abuse of power. That involves proving not only that action was misconceived, but that taking the action itself was unreasonable and that the authority were improperly motivated. Clearly, if officers fabricated evidence, then such actions are likely to succeed. However, in the absence of such extremely unusual circumstances, the prospects of success for the unfortunate owner who finds his business stopped by such an order should be regarded as non-existent.

Sub-section (1)

The order can only be made if the regulatory authority apply to a magistrate. The 1984 Act is silent as to whether the magistrate should be a magistrate holding a commission for the area in which the home is situated. The general view of lawyers practising in this field and magistrates' courts clerks, is that only magistrates holding a commission for the area in which the home is situated would be competent to make the order. In extreme circumstances, there would not seem to be a reason precluding another magistrate from acting. However, it is suggested that such circumstances should be extreme.

---

22 (1988) 86 LGR 369; (1988) 152 JP 488.
23 (1993) *The Times*, 8 March.
24 Registered Homes Tribunal decision No 323, *Woodfield Lodge Ltd v Hertfordshire County Council.*

The application for the order can be in support of any regulatory action other than prosecution. The order takes effect from the date when it is made, ie the order takes effect even before it is served. This should be contrasted with the 'ordinary procedure' where it takes effect 28 days after service of the notice.

The Court of Appeal, in the *Lyons* case, held that the criteria for a satisfactory order under s 11 or s 13 were quite different to the criteria for ordinary regulatory action. The magistrate is not concerned to considered whether or not the regulated care home owner is fit, whether the premises are fit, whether the staffing establishment is fit or whether the business is being conducted in a way so as to provide facilities reasonably required or, in the case of the nursing home, in an improper or undesirable way. The sole criteria for the magistrate or the Tribunal appeal is the issue:

> 'will there be a serious risk to the life, health or well being of the patients/residents in the home unless the order is made?'

That must appear to the magistrate to be the consequence if he does not make the order. The evidence must show future risk, but evidence of what has been recently discovered will inevitably be taken as evidence that unsatisfactory circumstances will continue unless the order is made. The order being made takes away lawful permission for the regulated care home owner to operate. The serious risk will therefore be avoided, in effect, by closure of the home. The risk may arise from a temporary change or may be as a result of a build up of dangerous and unsatisfactory practice. Risks will always arise suddenly, and in the author's experience, such orders are not refused.

Sub-section (2)

This deals with procedure. The application may be made ex parte. Many, including the author, have argued over the years that an application should not be made ex parte unless truly grave and dangerous circumstances are identified. An authority, exercising its power properly, would not take such steps unless a truly grave situation had emerged. The authority must be satisfied, as must the magistrate, that a serious risk for the future exists. However, Parliament has provided that warning need not be given and, indeed, the author would suggest that if it is appropriate to give warning, it is unlikely that it is appropriate to take the action.

In *Woodfield Lodge* the Tribunal expressed a strong view that only in extreme cases should an application be made without notice to the owner.[25] Such a view has not yet been endorsed by the High Court. *Woodfield Lodge* was an unusual case and should be approached with caution. The owner had succeeded on the 'urgent' appeal upon the basis that the authority had disclosed no case to answer. On the ordinary appeal, after two years, the authority abandoned its case with two days to go. The Tribunal was surprised. However, power exists to protect the vulnerable in danger. That should not be

---

25 Registered Homes Tribunal decision No 323, *Woodfield Lodge Ltd v Hertfordshire County Council.*

diluted by reference to a hasty case. An authority should not be reluctant to act if satisfied of serious risk, but should not act unless objectively satisfied of need.

In the author's experience, all such applications are made ex parte. All that is required is a written statement of the Secretary of State's or local authority's reasons. Looking forward to the almost inevitable appeal, authorities and their advisers will wish to prepare the statement carefully, dwelling on such history as is available and identifying, probably with photographic evidence, the concerns that arise. The statement of reasons will form the unalterable statement of the authority's reasons when the matter is challenged before the Tribunal. The urgency is not so great that details cannot be particularised. The force of the application and success in sustaining it on appeal will be improved by attention to detail at the application stage.

As a matter of procedure, the authority needs a form of application and form of order. A statement of reasons and any other supporting statements, affidavits or exhibits should be annexed to the application. Sufficient copies should be available for the magistrates' court to retain the original and for the authority to have a copy sealed by the court for its retention and one for service upon each owner.

Service must be made as soon as practicable. Interestingly, the authority are not required to give a regulated care home owner information about the rights of appeal. Service of such an order is an emotive issue. In the author's submission, a prudent authority will write a letter to the owner explaining the nature of the order, explaining the owner's new unregulated position each explaining the rights of appeal.

9.9.7 Consequences of cancellation

Cancelling registration does not entitle an authority, without the owner's co-operation, to close a regulated care home. Tales of fleets of ambulances, wailing through the streets of northern cities at anti-social hours, cause excitement and anxiety. This should be avoided. The order was obtained for the interests of the frail and vulnerable clients. Their move to other accommodation for care should be effected as quickly and as painlessly and in as low a profile as possible.

The order, having been served, the authority has no right or power in relation to the premises in addition to the power of inspection. There will be a right to enter and inspect premises reasonably believed to be conducted as a regulated care home.

If clients have a low dependency, it may well be that their presence in the home will continue for a short period of time, albeit unlawfully. If they are supported by s 26 of the National Assistance Act 1948, both local authorities and Health Authorities have duties as to the social welfare and health care needs of those within their jurisdiction. Clients abandoned will be clients for whom those authorities continue to have a responsibility. Authorities must be careful not to condone continued 'unlawful' operations. If they do, their case on 'seriousness' may be undermined.

However, authorities must appreciate that adults not subject to a custodial prison sentence or a secure detention order pursuant to the Mental Health Act

1983 cannot be compelled to vacate premises. They commit no offence by remaining in place. The continued provision of nursing care in nursing homes or accommodation with board and personal care in residential care homes constitutes an offence by the owner. In extreme circumstances, it may be appropriate to consider seeking to have clients who are unwilling to move detained under the provisions of the Mental Health Act 1983 on the basis that they are suffering from mental disorders so as to be a danger to themselves or others.

Section 47 of the National Assistance Act 1948 provides for a local authority to make application to detain in secure accommodation persons who are certified to be:

(1)   suffering from grave chronic disease or, being aged, infirm or physically incapacitated, are living in unsanitary conditions; and
(2)   are unable to care for themselves and are not receiving from other persons proper care and attention.

At first sight, this section might appear to be useful for authorities forced to take further action following urgent regulatory procedures to cancel care home registration. The difficulty seems to be in establishing unsanitary conditions. Many reasons may have given rise to the order cancelling urgently a care home registration. It will not necessarily be the case, indeed it may be rare, that the premises may be shown to be unsanitary.

There will be a public duty to the clients, both from the local authority, under Pt III of the National Assistance Act 1948, to provide accommodation and from the Health Authority, under its general duty to provide for the health care needs of persons resident within its jurisdiction free of charge. The Health Authority may be involved even where the residential establishment was a residential care home and not a nursing home. Professionally, nurses are obliged to take steps for those whose needs come to their attention. Embarrassments may arise. If, as a result of a the cancellation, clients are abandoned, Health Authority nurses may feel obliged professionally to provide appropriate care, perhaps in the existing establishment. If that occurs, then it cannot be said that the clients concerned are not receiving proper care and attention.

Careful consideration of the risks of lack of co-operation from clients and alternative accommodation need to be considered in advance by any authority having to take this action. Obtaining the magistrate's order is relatively easy. Dealing with the consequences that flow, in an area not well covered by legal provision, may prove much more difficult. The authorities should remember that they may well have to bear the cost of supporting care in the interim (and the interim may not be short) and may ultimately have to bear the cost of alternative accommodation. Health Authorities should have in mind that nursing patients so dispossessed may become the responsibility of their sister local authority. Clearly, close co-operation is required if misunderstandings are to be avoided.

In the author's submission, such action should only be taken when circumstances are truly grave, ie in the words of the Act, 'there will be a serious risk to health, life or well being unless the order is made'.

9.9.8 Judicial review of the decision to cancel

The magistrates' decision is subject to judicial review. Such an order may be obtained quickly to suspend the order of the magistrates pending either a full hearing of the judicial review or the Registered Homes Tribunal appeal. Such an application may be a device to keep the home in business. It may be no more than a stalling tactic. It may ultimately fail, but it does show that the magistrates' order is not absolutely final. Such applications are now a more frequent event. In *R v Ealing, Hammersmith and Hounslow Health Authority*,[26] where such orders were made on an interim basis. However, the harsh words with which Laws J rejected the application on a full hearing are likely to cause subsequent judges to take a less accommodating view. The judge suggested that the courts should only intervene where such orders were clearly perverse. The court should not allow itself to be manipulated to stall orders for the protection of the frail and vulnerable. However, a number of judges have been persuaded to intervene in such circumstances. This is a poor reflection on the integrity of public authorities who make such applications and a reflection of the inadequacy of the statutory appeal.

Grounds for making such applications might include:

(1) reasons given cannot sustain assertion of 'serious risk';
(2) the authority does not make full disclosure of material facts which might have influenced the magistrates;
(3) the authority has been less than full and frank;
(4) delay between discovery of circumstances and action is so long as to negate the proposition of serious risk;
(5) the allegations are well known and subject to dispute rather than arising as a sudden emergency;
(6) the magistrate has been misled as to his discretion and the law by the material placed before him.

Those advising owners in these dire circumstances must give thorough and urgent attention to the possibility of judicial review to protect their clients' businesses. Any delay may be fatal.

9.9.9 May procedures for cancellation of registration be merged?

In *Lyons v East Sussex County Council*,[27] the Court of Appeal were invited to give some general consideration to the procedure for urgent cancellation of registration of nursing homes. The Court declined the invitation, but there was some discussion and comment upon the desirability for the urgent procedure and ordinary procedure to be merged. The Court of Appeal, with its usual foresight, expressed the view that it would be unfortunate if appellants were to succeed on an appeal against an urgent cancellation and remain in business

---

26 (1996) 30 BMLR 92.
27 (1988) 86 LGR 369, (1988) 152 JP 488, CA.

where the facts clearly indicated to the specialist tribunal that they or their premises or matters associated therewith were unfit to remain registered to care for the frail and vulnerable. It was suggested that decisions by both the urgent and the ordinary route could be made and the appeals joined in order to expedite one decision in relation to all aspects of the particular home. The Court expressed the view that it did not matter which procedure started first.

This has caused some surprise and some difficulty. Clearly, if a decision has been made by the authority following the ordinary route, there is no problem about an urgent decision to cancel registration pending appeal, being superimposed upon the decision of the appropriate registration authority. However, a different situation arises where the urgent order made by the magistrate comes first. How can there then follow the ordinary procedure to cancel registration, which has already been cancelled by the magistrates' court? The ruling of the Court of Appeal, if it may be so characterised, can easily be said to be *obiter dictum* and thus only of persuasive authority. However, it should not be lightly disregarded.

How then can it be possible for the registration authority to decide to cancel the registration which has already been cancelled? If the registration has been cancelled, then clearly the second decision can be of no effect. There may only be capacity for a double decision if the effect of the first order is merely suspending as opposed to cancelling the registration.

An examination of the statutory authorities suggests that this is possible. Using the authorities from Pt I:

(1)   section 11(1) of the 1984 Act provides, after providing for power for urgent cancellation, '.... and the cancellation .... shall have effect from the date on which the order is made.';

(2)   this is to be contrasted with s 14(3) of the 1984 Act, which provides, in relation to an authority decision, that the decision shall not take effect until the later of the determination or abandonment of appeal or a period of 28 days from notification of the decision;

(3)   it will be observed that, in both cases, the statute speaks in terms of the order or decision taking effect;

(4)   the jurisdiction of the Tribunal is outlined in s 15(4) and (5); in the case of both a decision of the authority and the order of the magistrates, the Tribunal merely have a jurisdiction to confirm the decision or direct that it shall not or shall cease to have effect;

(5)   there is an absence of provision for reinstatement of registration;

Accordingly, it would seem that the original decision or order to cancel registration operates as an executory act awaiting confirmation by a subsequent event. In the case of a decision of the authority, that act is completed by the appeal result, which either puts aside the original decision or confirms it; in the case of the magistrates' court order, the subsequent decision confirms the effect of the order or causes that order to cease to have effect.

It may be that the true effect of the magistrates' court order is to suspend rather than cancel the registration, leaving an underlying registration in place, which may probably be the subject of a decision of the authority. By this course, that which was debated in the Court of Appeal, seems to be sustainable and authorities should not be dissuaded from taking steps to confirm, by ordinary procedure, cancellations which have been the subject of a formal magistrates' order under the twinned urgent procedure.

An example of the position where an 'urgent' cancellation is set aside on appeal, with no complimentary procedure, may be seen in *Gya v Worthing District Health Authority*.[28]

9.9.10 Prosecution

Prosecution is always an option for statutory offences provided by Parliament. The prosecutor will be the regulatory authority. Prosecutions will be time-consuming and expensive. Given that conviction for an offence under the 1984 Act, or regulations made thereunder, operates as an inflexible and irreversible ban upon any local authority arranging a residential community care contract with the convicted owner, conviction, or even the prospect of prosecution, is serious.

Curiously, convictions under the Children Act 1989 in respect of registered children's homes do not carry with them a similar ban.

The author would suggest that, in these circumstances, it will rarely be appropriate to launch a prosecution unless the regulatory authority is also contemplating regulatory action to cancel registration. To prosecute, secure a conviction and ensure that the owner cannot obtain clients from the dominant purchaser of community care services is, in effect, to take steps to close the business. That being the consequence, a prosecution should not be launched unless that is the real intent. Prosecutions are not a mere slap on the wrist – reminding an owner of his responsibilities. In an appropriate case, a decision to prosecute or warn of prosecution might be subject to judicial review in the absence of action or evidence to justify action to cancel registration.

In prosecutions, the burden of proof will lie upon the regulatory authority, as prosecutor, but not on the balance of probabilities, with a relatively relaxed approach as to the evidence that may be adduced and as to the conduct of proceedings, before the Tribunal. In a criminal court, proof must be beyond all reasonable doubt and evidence may only be adduced in accordance with the strict rules that apply in criminal cases. Those contemplating prosecution need to consider carefully whether the evidence upon which they rely will stand such tests. In particular, where evidence is to be adduced other than by officers of the regulatory authority, advisers of the regulatory authority need to assess how lay witnesses will behave in court and whether, in fact, they will attend.

Criminal courts do not look at background circumstances in the round. That said, prosecution, or the threat of prosecution, is a real regulatory tool. It is made the more so by the procedure whereby offences which arise out of day-to-day operation of the home arise largely as a result of breach of the regulations, ie the 1984 Residential Care Homes Regulations or the 1984 Nursing Homes Regulations. Most such offences either do not become offences or are not prosecutable until after the re-commission of the offence

---

28 Registered Homes Tribunal decision No 187.

following a statutory notice.[29] The service of such notice, combined with appropriate time to correct errors in practice, concentrates the minds of regulated care home owners as to the risks and often achieves the correct result – an increase in standards rather than ruin of the regulated business.

Improvements in standards to an appropriate regulatory standard should be the aim of all good regulatory action. Action which seeks to terminate the conduct of the business should be a last resort. Notices warning of prosecution (as such notices are sometimes described) should not be over used. They should never be used unless the authority has decided to prosecute if the notice is not observed. Idle threats and unfulfilled warnings of regulatory action amount to bad regulation. Persistent service of notices in an attempt to improve standards rather than as a precursor to prosecution may be seen as conduct which no reasonable authority should permit and hence be amenable to an application for judicial review. If the authority is not prepared to proceed or, worse, not able to proceed, it is better not to serve the notice.

9.9.11   Prosecution notices

The prosecution notice is peculiar to residential care homes, registered nursing homes and registered mental nursing homes. The provisions are quite different and need to be regarded separately.

9.9.12   Residential Care Home Regulations 1984, reg 20

This provides:

'(1)   Subject to paragraph 3 of this regulation, where the registration authority consider that the person registered has contravened or failed to comply with Regulation 6, 10, 11, 13, 14, 15, 16, or 19 of these Regulations, the authority may serve a notice on the person registered, specifying:
  (a)   in what respect in their opinion the person registered has failed or is failing to comply with the requirements of that Regulation;
  (b)   what action in the opinion of the registration authority, the person registered should take first to comply with that Regulation; and
  (c)   the period, not exceeding three months, within which the person registered should take action.
(2)   Where notice has been given in accordance with Paragraph 1 of this Regulation and the period specified in the notice, beginning with the date of the notice, has expired, the person registered who contravenes or fails to comply with any provision of these regulations mentioned in the notice shall be guilty of an offence against these regulations.
(3)   The provisions of this regulation shall not apply where the registration authority has applied to a justice of the peace for an order under Section 11 of the Act or while such order is in force.'

Regulation 20 provides simple instructions as to the drafting of an effective notice and needs to be studied and implemented. The last thing that is required for a regulatory authority in relation to a prosecution is an attack on the validity of the notice.

---

29   Residential Care Homes Regulations 1984, reg 20; Nursing Homes and Nursing Mental Homes Regulations 1984, reg 15.

The notice may be served where the regulatory authority considers there has been a contravention of the regulations. Under reg 20(2), if a prosecution follows failure to comply with the notice, it is not failure to comply with the provisions of the notice that constitutes an offence, but a failure to comply with the provisions of the regulations.

It is thus for the prosecutor to prove not simply that the regulated care home owner has failed to comply with that which the authority has demanded in accordance with its own views, but that those views accord with the proper standard as provided by the statute and the regulations and that the conduct contravenes those standards. Many authorities do not understand that distinction.

The author would suggest that, before serving notice (in order to protect against unwanted applications for judicial review of the notice), the authority, through its properly delegated officers, should consider the provisions and should record why it is the opinion of the authority that the regulations have been contravened.

The provisions are:

(1)   reg 6 – keeping proper records;
(2)   reg 10 – provision of proper facilities and services (quite the most important regulation). It will be remembered the universal standard required is one of adequacy (defined in the Nursing Homes and Mental Nursing Homes Regulations as sufficient and suitability);
(3)   reg 11 – suitable provision for visits by parents, guardians and friends;
(4)   reg 13 – notification of arrival of children;
(5)   reg 14 – notification of death, illness or accident;
(6)   reg 15 – notices of absence of the owner or manager;
(7)   reg 16 – notification of termination of accommodation;
(8)   reg 19 – visits by persons in control of the home.

Interestingly, many of the matters which may constitute an offence may be regarded as technical or administrative rather than substantial, in the supply of care and the performance of care practice. The provisions which do not carry a right to serve a prosecution notice or to prosecute include:

(1)   reg 8 – consultation with the fire authority;
(2)   reg 9 – conduct of the home so as to provide proper welfare care and treatment and supervision to residents;
(3)   reg 12 – ensuring facilities for religious observance;
(4)   reg 17 – information as to complaints procedures for residents.

The selection of those matters which may be the subject of a prosecution warning has been made more by chance than reason.

Having established that the notice may be served, it is important that the drafting be correct. What is required is a notice that identifies:

(1)   the respects in which the person registered has failed to comply with the requirements of the regulation. The regulation or regulations must be identified. Drafters of the notice should be careful to identify precisely and without ambiguity what is said to be wrong;
(2)   what action the authority considers that the person registered should

take. This will be the crucial issue leading to prosecution. Again, the wording must be clear and unambiguous. It is being said that if the action has not been taken, an offence will have been committed. If there is any doubt about the required action, that prosecution is likely to fail. The action must be clearly specified and the consequences of failure to comply must be made plain;

(3)   a period must be given within which the action should be taken. Curiously, there seems no suggestion that the period should be reasonable. Perhaps there is no reason for it to be so. However, authorities should not require action to be taken 'forthwith'. In the author's view, as the regulation requires specification of a period within which action should be taken, 'forthwith' is inappropriate as that specifies no period. One hour or one day would be sufficient, but 'forthwith', it is suggested, nullifies the notice. However, it might also be argued that, as the purpose of the notice is to give a chance to avoid prosecution, then the time given must be a time within which it is possible to complete the task required. An unreasonably short period of time might lead to a challenge that the notice was perverse, being inappropriately prepared to serve its true purpose. A wise authority will give good time. The offence is committed when the person registered continues to contravene the regulations after the expiry of the time specified for remedy.

Of course, the authority must prove that the regulations have been contravened. It must also prove that the notice is valid and that the time given for remedy has expired. A prudent authority will, in the author's submission, provide a reasonable time for remedy. If something required to be done, cannot be done, that is neither fair nor appropriate regulation, even though it may be strictly permitted within the wording of the regulations.

Sub-paragraph (3) appears to be a provision which has not been well thought out. Regulation 20 only deals with breaches of the regulations. Breaches of the regulations are made offences, following the expiry of the reg 20 remedial period. The effect of sub-para (3) would appear to be that no notice may be served once an application has been made to the justice of the peace for an order or while the order is in force. The period during which the application is in process will almost certainly be short. The order will be in force permanently unless and until set aside on appeal. Post-order prosecution may not be possible, for there will be no person registered. If anything is achieved, it is a curious position that prosecution cannot take place after an application has been made to a magistrate, unless the application fails.

If an authority wishes to prosecute for breach of the regulations, it should ensure that it is well-prepared before making an application for urgent regulatory action to be supported by an order of the magistrate.

Regulation 20 notices may also be appropriate to bolster evidence in support of proposals to cancel registration using the ordinary procedure. Convictions will give added reasons, within s 10 of the 1984 Act, to support cancellation, in addition to those general reasons which are available to support cancellation, just as they may support refusal of registration, ie by supporting an allegation of unfitness.

9.9.13   Nursing Homes and Mental Nursing Homes Regulations 1984, reg 15

The provision provides:

'(1)   Any person who fails without reasonable cause –
   (a)   to keep or retain any record which he is required to keep or retain under regulation 7 or Schedule 4;
   (b)   to give to a health authority any notice which he is required to give under regulation 8 or 9; or
   (c)   to furnish any information which he is required to furnish under regulation 10(2), shall be guilty of any offence under these regulations.
(2)   Any person who without reasonable cause refuses to allow a person authorised to inspect any premises or any record under regulation 10(1) shall be guilty of an offence against these regulations.
(3)   Any person who fails to comply with any provision of regulation 12 other than regulation 12(2)(c) shall be guilty of an offence against these regulations.
(4)   Subject to paragraph 5, the Secretary of State shall not bring proceedings against a person in respect of any failure referred to in paragraph 1 or 3 unless –
   (a)   he has served on that person a notice in writing specifying
      (i)   the provision of these regulations with which that person in the Secretary of State's opinion has failed or is failing to comply;
      (ii)   the respect in which in the Secretary of State's opinion that person has failed or failing to comply with that provision.
      (iii)   the action which in the Secretary of State's opinion should be taken by that person so as to comply with that provision;
      (iv)   the period within such action should be taken;
   (b)   the period referred to in sub-paragraph (a)(iv) of this paragraph has expired.
(5)   Paragraph 4 shall not apply where at the time proceedings relating a home are brought –
   (a)   the Secretary of State has applied to a justice of the peace for an order under Section 31 of the Act (urgent procedure for the cancellation of registration etc) relating to that home and that application has not yet been determined; or
   (b)   such an order is in force.
(6)   Any person who fails to comply with Regulation 13 shall be guilty of an offence against these regulations.'

Before examining this regulation, paragraph by paragraph, a fundamental difference will be noted from reg 20 of the Residential Care Homes Regulations 1984. Under the reg 20 procedure, no offence is committed until the owner has failed to comply with the requirements of the notice in the time spescified by the notice. Under reg 15, offences are committed as soon as the provisions of the appropriate regulation are broken. The offences are committed, but, curiously, the offences may not be prosecuted.

This procedure may have more logic and certainly, makes more sense of the suspensive provisions of reg 15, whilst the urgent cancellation of registration procedure pursuant to s 30 is in train or in force, ie prosecutions may be brought and prior warning by notice is not required.

An issue of interest is whether or not, an offence having been committed, the owner may be prosecuted as regards the facts which constituted the offence in respect of which a reg 15 notice was served, notwithstanding that the only evidence pre-dates the notices or expiry of the remedy period. Strict wording of sub-para (4) would seem to suggest that, the owner having committed an offence (assuming that to be established in due course), the regulatory authority may not proceed to prosecute. However, by serving a notice identifying the offence requiring remedy and specifying a time for remedy, prosecution may follow in relation to the pre-established facts. Clearly, there is no problem where remedial action has not been taken – another offence will have been committed. Save in exceptional circumstances, the offence might have attracted minimum penalties if the owner had complied with the notice.

The matter may give rise to practical significance when considering the effect of s 26(1)(e) of the National Assistance Act 1948. Conviction for an offence under reg 15 of the Nursing Homes and Mental Nursing Homes Regulations 1984 would act as a disqualification from community care contracting. Disqualification arises upon conviction of an offence, rather than upon the commission of an offence. Therefore, rather curiously, an owner who has committed an offence which may not be prosecuted, is not disqualified from community care contracting unless and until convicted.

Such an odd position might encourage curious prosecutions in respect of failures in care practice and service which have already been remedied by the date of service of notice of information in respect of the offence.

Sub-paragraph 1
This clearly identifies statutory offences in respect of record-keeping, notice giving and information supplied. Offences committed under sub-para (1) are subject to the sub-para (4) notice procedure.

Sub-paragraph 2
This provides for an offence for the obstruction of inspection of a home or records. The offence is not subject to the sub-para (4) notice procedure and is committed by anyone and is not limited to the registered owner.

Sub-paragraph 3
This is the all-important paragraph, for reg 12 is the well-known regulation identifying the standard of adequacy, in a number of respects, for the provision of facilities and services at a registered nursing home or registered mental nursing home and is the paragraph under which prosecutions are, in practice, most likely to be launched.

The sub-para (4) notice procedure applies and here the practitioner should remember that what needs to be proven beyond all reasonable doubt is the failure to meet the expectations of facilities and services to an adequate standard and not simply failure to meet that which was required under the sub-para (4) notice.

Once again, curiously, it is not an offence to fail to consult with the fire authority.

Sub-paragraph 4

This provides in detail for the nature of the prosecution warning notice. It must:

(1) identify the provision of the regulations said to be breached;
(2) identify the respect in which the regulations have been breached;
(3) identify action to be taken to remedy the breach;
(4) identify the period within which action should be taken.

Prosecutions may not be brought until the expiry of the period, although as already argued, once the period has expired there appears to be no necessity for prosecutions to be linked to subsequent contravention.

Once again, the wording for the requirements of the notice is clear and should be simple to follow. Practitioners are advised to have the words of the regulation in front of them as they draft or settle the drafting of proposed notices. It is suggested, once more, that the requirement for a period within which action should be taken is not met by provisions stating that action should be taken 'forthwith'. Some period, however short, should be specified.

Sub-paragraph 5

This provides that sub-para 4 shall not apply. What is clearly intended is that the restriction on prosecution shall not apply, for sub-para (4) starts:

'the Secretary of State shall not bring proceedings:'

Insofar as it may be relevant, therefore, in between the time of the application to the magistrate for urgent cancellation and the determination by the magistrate of that application there is no restriction on prosecution. Similarly, there is no restriction on prosecution while the order is in force, ie either permanently or from the magistrates' order until the determination of the Tribunal proceedings. However, the offences committed under reg 15(1) and (3) are offences committed by the person registered. Once the magistrates' order is in force, the prospective defendant may not be a person registered, for the registration has been cancelled or, arguably, suspended. It might be possible to prosecute in respect of offences committed prior to the order even if the notice period had not then expired.

If authorities consider it appropriate to bring prosecutions, notwithstanding that they expect to achieve cancellation by the urgent procedure, then there is clearly room for a following application to the magistrate, ie lodging the application with the magistrate, and then lodging informations alleging contravention of the regulations prior to the moment when the magistrate's order is made – possibly whilst the authority and its solicitors are waiting to be received by the magistrate. In that period, the prosecutions will not be restricted by the requirement for warning notice under sub-para (4) and may, in any event, take their course after the urgent cancellation proceedings.

As with residential care homes, the prosecution warning notice is an important tool in the process of regulation. It may be also an important tool, by securing convictions after an order cancelling registration, to ensure that owners are, in effect, restricted from ever contracting again with public authorities through the community care scheme, where registration has been subject to urgent cancellation.

Securing convictions will ensure that discredited owners do not retain any possibility of returning to a business that may be funded by public monies.

9.10   THE APPROACH TO REGULATORY ACTION

Regulatory action is the prerogative of the regulatory authority. As has been seen, there is a wide variety of types of action and a variety of ways in which those types of action may be pursued. Authorities should always consider their purpose in taking regulatory action. The aim should be to progress the purpose of regulation, ie the protection of the frail, vulnerable, sick and needy. Regulation should not be undertaken punitively or capriciously.

In exercising regulatory powers, authorities should always have in mind the needs and interests of the clients accommodated in the regulated care home. The question should be:

> 'will the action that we propose better serve the interests of the clients in care than some other action or no action?'

The preparation for regulatory action will be time-consuming, save in sudden and unexpected applications for urgent cancellation. There will be opportunity for discussion, the taking of advice from lawyers and case conferences as to the right course.

This chapter has not dwelt on non-legal regulatory action, but there are many courses that an authority can take short of formal action:

(1)   recording concerns appearing at inspection and that require rectification;
(2)   writing to owners with the results of investigations into complaints that require improvement of standards;
(3)   informal notices requiring improvements in standards, failing which regulatory action will be considered or taken.

Warnings are always sensible. It does not need statutory regulation to suggest to authorities that they should give warning indications when standards are falling or when rectification may be required.

The more preparation and the more regulatory action is followed by correspondence or if necessary, by visits or by telephone, documented by detailed and witnessed attendance notes, the more reasonable the regulatory action will be seen to be and the easier it will be to persuade authorities to endorse and Tribunals to sustain that action.

Regulatory action should be flexible. If the needs identified which have led to regulatory action are met, authorities should not be slow or shy to withdraw action. There is no shame in recognising that the aims have been met so that the process can be halted.

Clear strategic aims, effectively controlled and implemented, will present a picture which will impress both authorities and Tribunals and shorten the regulatory process, if such becomes necessary.

Chapter 10

THE REGISTERED HOMES TRIBUNAL

10.1 INTRODUCTION

The Registered Homes Tribunal was created by the 1984 Act. Those concerned with the operation of regulated care home businesses perceived that a specialised Tribunal was needed to deal with increasing issues arising out of the registration, operation and closure of care homes.

The Tribunal came into existence, with the 1984 Act, on 1 January 1985. Up until 30 November 1997, the Tribunal had published decisions in 332 cases, had pending decisions in 25 more cases and had received appeals which had been resolved without proceeding to formally published decisions in some 293 cases. A total of 566 cases had thus been before the Tribunal, of which 50% did not proceed to a full hearing.

A reasonable estimate is that, at any one time, there are some 15,000 residential care homes and 4,000 registered nursing homes in the UK. There are, perhaps not surprisingly, a very small number of children's homes registered under Pt VI of the Children's Act 1989. Some discount must be made for the fact that a number of regulated care homes are in Scotland and Northern Ireland.

The small number of cases that have been referred to the Tribunal, and the even smaller number of cases which have resulted in formal decisions, should be regarded as attributable both to the high standard of the provision of residential care in the UK and the high standard of constructive and positive regulation.

Prior to 1 January 1985, disputes in relation to registration were referred to the magistrates' court. Magistrates' courts were already over burdened with other very important business. Care homes were becoming important businesses of not insignificant value, and issues in relation to care home management and regulation required increasing professional expertise. The nature of the issues which may be debated in a regulatory dispute about a regulated care home include all the most serious allegations that may be litigated in the courts, such as unlawful homicide, theft, fraud, forgery, and major and minor assaults. It was quite clear that reference to local magistrates was not an adequate means of dealing with such difficult problems.

10.2 CONSTITUTION

The Registered Homes Tribunal is a tribunal within the meaning of the Tribunals and Enquiries Act 1971. It is this Act which governs the operation of tribunals and provides important procedures as to further appeal from tribunals, should parties be dissatisfied with their decisions. Appeals from the Registered Homes Tribunal may be made by requiring the Tribunal to state a case for an opinion on the law from the High Court, or by way of straight appeal to the High Court on issues of law.[1] The constitution of the Tribunal is governed by Pt III of the 1984 Act.

The Tribunal exists to determine regulatory issues under the 1984 Act and the 1989 Act. Section 40 of the 1984 Act provides for the individual constitution of the Tribunal. There shall be two panels:

(1)   a panel of legally qualified Chairmen (the legal panel); and
(2)   a panel of lay members (the panel of experts).

Members of the legal panel must possess such legal qualifications as the Lord Chancellor considers suitable. Members of the panel of experts must have experience in social work, medicine, nursing or midwifery, or such other experience as the President of the Council who appoints such persons shall consider suitable. No officer of a government department shall be appointed to either panel (surprisingly, a number of officers of Health Authorities, who act in the name of the Secretary of State, have been appointed to the panel).

The difficulty with the constitution of the Tribunal is that there are only a limited number of people within the UK who have the time to devote to this important work, are inclined to seek appointment and have the relevant experience. Inevitably, such persons are directly involved in regulated care home work (usually exclusively either as a regulator or a provider) or have been so involved and have retired. Securing a truly independent view for a particular case is thus difficult.

10.2.1   Independence of the Tribunal

Both regulators and owners had hoped that the Tribunal would provide independent review of authority decisions. Such is the nature of the business of care, albeit rapidly developing, that experts usually come in the form either of regulators or owners. Their approach to regulation may be influenced by those origins. Unfortunately, the approach of such experts is bound to, at least to some extent, follow their previous experience. That is the very reason why they are appointed.

Very many more experts who will have worked in and have experience of being a part of the public sector are appointed to the panel of experts than experts from the private sector. This has, unfortunately, led some amongst the private sector to doubt the true independence of the Tribunal. It is particularly unfortunate when members of the panel are currently serving officers of regulatory authorities.

Less worrying, but equally of concern to regulatory authorities, is when owners of homes currently regulated by authorities are appointed to the panel to hear disputes in other areas and jurisdictions. The author's experience is that the attitude of Chairmen of Tribunals differs widely depending upon whether the expert advice that they receive comes from a public sector or private sector point of view. The lottery that this creates is unfortunate. Appellants to Tribunals should, therefore, take trouble to identify the panel experts well in advance.

---

1   Tribunals and Enquiries Act 1992, s 11 and Sch 1.

The concern here is not with bias. The author does not know of any case where a suggestion of actual bias has been made. However, great issues are at stake. The law is concerned not with actual bias but with the possible perception of bias. If an ordinary reasonable person in the street might perceive a Tribunal or court to be biased because of its constitution, then that may be sufficient to justify an appeal against the Tribunal decision being made as a matter of law.[2] There are no cases known to the author where such an allegation has suceeded.

Success on such a point on appeal will be of no benefit to an owner. Appeals from decisions of the Registered Homes Tribunal, on points of law to the High Court, take as much as 2 years to be heard. Despite the erroneous view taken by certain authorities, registration of a regulated care home does not continue pending an appeal to the High Court. The effective decision date is the date of written publication of the decision and, thereafter, the regulated care home is no longer registered, if the decision is adverse.[3]

10.2.2   Membership of the Tribunal

Section 41 of the 1984 Act provides that a Tribunal shall consist of a Chairman and two members. Frequently, a full Tribunal may not be available. It is not open to the Tribunal or the parties to agree that any hearing of the Tribunal shall take place without a full Tribunal being convened. Any decision of such a Tribunal is invalid. Of course, such a decision may be persuasive and helpful. The point is of issue in the so-called pre-hearing reviews.

10.2.3   Pre-hearing reviews

A practice has developed whereby the parties are encouraged to meet with the Chairman of the Tribunal, or indeed the full Tribunal, in advance of the hearing in order to identify issues and agree or receive directions about procedures. It is quite clear that no decision can be made by the Tribunal unless the Tribunal is fully constituted.

The Chairman of the Tribunal may make certain procedural directions. Whilst procedural guidance and directions from the Chairman will be helpful and persuasive, there is limited authority within the Registered Homes Tribunal Rules 1984[4] for such directions. It is suggested that all decisions are required to be decisions of the Tribunal. The Tribunal must be fully constituted, and in accordance with r 7 of the Tribunal Rules, shall sit in public unless for any reason it determines that any part shall be heard in private.

This inhibits pre-hearing reviews. The only jurisdiction of the Chairman, in accordance with the Rules, arises under r 10(3) of the Rules where the Tribunal Chairman may, before the hearing, call for further information or reports and give directions as to the manner in which such material may be furnished and by whom the material shall be furnished.

Nevertheless, the parties will wish to co-operate with each other and the Tribunal will wish to co-operate with the parties so as to improve efficiency.

---

2   See *R v Mulvihill* [1990] 1 All ER 436.
3   Registered Homes Act 1984, s 15 and s 34.
4   SI 1984/1346.

It is important to differentiate between practices and procedures developed between the parties, and parties in general, and those adopted by the Tribunal for its own convenience, from those which amount to binding rules or directions. The hope was that Tribunals would be relatively informal. They are not. The Tribunal Rules are hopelessly inadequate to meet the needs of lengthy and complex examination of facts, to which must be applied relatively complex issues of law.

10.2.4 Qualifications of Tribunal members

If the appeal relates to a registered nursing home, the panel shall include a registered medical practitioner and a qualified nurse, or a registered midwife in a case relating to a maternity home. There is no indication whether or not those requirements are satisfied if the legally qualified Chairman also possesses qualifications as a medical practitioner or a nurse or midwife.

Where the home is registered both as a residential care home and a nursing home, the Tribunal shall include a qualified nurse or a midwife.[5] Quite what this achieves is difficult to see. It may have been borne out of a misunderstanding of dual registration. If the appeal relates to a dual registered home it necessarily relates to a registered nursing home.

A qualified nurse for this purpose means a person who is both registered under the Nurses, Midwives and Health Visitors Act 1979 and would have been qualified to be registered under s 21 of the Nurses Act 1957 (now repealed).

A concern about the constitution of Registered Homes Tribunals is that they are dominated by experts. However, the legal Chairman has no controlling decision on issues of law, and the experts are not kept to decisions in their own expertise.

10.2.5 Expert witnesses

The nature of such appeals is to examine substantial and difficult issues of medical and nursing practice, as well as the practice of social welfare care. In the course of the proper presentation of cases on behalf of the owners and regulatory authorities, experts will be called. The owner of the home may well be an expert. The officers of the regulatory authority and, in particular, the inspectors, will be experts. Independent experts may be called. All these experts will be subject to the normal provision that their evidence will be challenged through cross-examination.

However, there are also experts on the panel. Those experts need take no part in examination or cross-examination. They need ask no questions of advocates or witnesses. They will, however, have a significant effect on the decision by the views that they express collectively and, particularly, by way of guidance to the Chairman in private. Tribunal Chairmen have suggested that they will have the views of their own experts to rely upon, where there is divergence among the experts who appear before the Tribunal. It must be a matter for concern that important decisions will be taken, on issues where expert evidence is required, by those who will bring to bear their own

5   See Registered Homes Act 1984, s 42(3).

experience and expertise in such a way that the parties may not even know what they think and will certainly not have the opportunity to challenge it.

Practitioners can only defend against these risks by ensuring that detailed and credible expert evidence is given, so that if the decision of the Tribunal is at odds with expert evidence, an appeal may be brought on the basis of perversity, ie that no Tribunal properly constituted, having heard the evidence, could have come to such a conclusion.

Such appeals will face considerable difficulties, and the High Court will undoubtedly approach the issue upon the basis that Parliament has constituted a Tribunal of experts to try issues requiring expert opinion and it is, therefore, not for the courts to intervene.

Curiously, no specific experts are required in relation to cases involving registered children's homes.

10.3 AGAINST WHAT DOES THE APPEAL LIE?

The appeal lies against the decision of the regulatory authority or, in the case of the urgent cancellation cases, in respect of residential care homes or registered nursing homes, the order of the magistrate. That is the limited jurisdiction of the Tribunal.

10.4 WHAT DECISION CAN BE MADE?

The decision which can be made by the Tribunal is prescribed by statute. The provisions are s 15 and s 34 of the 1984 Act and para 8 of Sch 6 to the 1989 Act. The scheme is similar for each and establishes a common jurisdiction. The only variations relate to the inclusion of orders of magistrates in relation to residential care home and nursing home cases.

The relevant provisions are s 15(4) to (7) of the 1984 Act, s 33(4) to (7) of the 1989 Act, and para 8(4) to (6) of Sch 6 to the 1989 Act. Section 15 of the 1984 Act provides:

'(4) On an appeal against a decision of a Registration Authority, the Tribunal may confirm the decision or direct that it shall not have effect.

(5) On appeal against an Order made by a Justice of the Peace, the Tribunal may confirm the Order or direct that it shall cease to have effect.

(6) A Tribunal shall also have power on an appeal against a decision or an Order –
  (a) to vary any condition for the time being in force in respect of the home to which the appeal relates by virtue of this part of this Act;
  (b) to direct that any such condition shall cease to have effect; or
  (c) to direct that any such condition as it thinks fit shall have effect in respect of the home.

(7) A registration authority shall comply with any direction given by a Tribunal under this Section.'

The jurisdiction of the Tribunal is thus limited. The preliminary decision is essentially 'succeed or fail'. The Tribunal does have original jurisdiction in relation to conditions of registration, but only the same jurisdiction on conditions as was possessed by the regulatory authority. Conditions of registration may not be imposed by a Tribunal beyond the powers of the authority.[6]

Thus, if the Tribunal is minded to allow the appeal and directs that the decision shall not have effect, it may make reasonable adjustments to the conditions of registration. This will be of great significance and great use in relation to registered children's homes, where there is a limitless discretion as to conditions.

The decision in *Warwickshire County Council v McSweeney*, although undoubtedly correct, has, in practice, been extremely unhelpful in the practical and positive resolution of regulated care home disputes. Prior to that decision, Tribunals often effected very satisfactory compromises which would not now be entertained.[7]

10.5   WHEN DOES THE TRIBUNAL DECISION TAKE EFFECT?

Section 43(1) of the 1984 Act enables the Secretary of State to make rules as to the practice and procedure with respect, inter alia, to matters incidental or consequential to such proceedings.

No matter can be more important than the date when the decision takes effect. Paragraph 11(2) of the Tribunal Rules provides that the Chairman of the Tribunal shall, as soon as possible after the hearing, notify the appellant and the registration authority in writing of the decision and the reasons for the decision. The important issues are:

(1)   notification must be by the Chairman;
(2)   notification must be in writing;
(3)   notification must be accompanied by reasons.

The decision thus takes effect when it is notified. Sometimes, decisions have been communicated without reasons. An interesting question may, one day, arise as to whether the decision takes effect before or after the reasons are delivered. How can the parties decide if there is an issue of law if reasons have not been delivered?

Regrettably, the decision is only required to be made as soon as possible. There is enormous pressure of work on Tribunals and Tribunal Chairmen and, usually, there is a gap of some three to four weeks, perhaps longer after a substantial case, before the decision is notified. In one case in which the author was involved, there was a six-month delay.

Such delay is unsatisfactory. The parties need to order their affairs and there is a risk that the interests of frail and vulnerable clients will be adversely affected, given that the home is entitled to continue in operation pending the decision but must cease operation as soon as the decision is notified.

---

6   *Warwickshire County Council v McSweeney*, (unreported) 8 December 1988, Roch J.
7   See Registered Homes Tribunal decision No 75, *Uter v Bristol and Western Health Authority*; Registered Homes Tribunal decision No 60, *Evans v Mid-Staffordshire Health Authority*.

There is no further suspension of the effect of a regulatory decision pending an appeal to the High Court on a point of law. Sections 15 and 33 of the 1984 Act and para 7(3) of Sch 6 to the 1989 Act make it clear that the decision takes effect, if an appeal is brought, when the appeal is abandoned or when the appeal is determined. The appeal cannot be determined later than the date when the decision is notified.

To assist, a senior Registered Homes Tribunal Chairman has developed the very helpful practice of indicating to the parties, prior to decision, the decision that the Tribunal is minded to make. The Chairman is careful not to give such an indication in writing and to indicate that this is merely a preliminary view. In practice, of course, the decision is rarely different from the preliminary view, but regulatory authorities and owners do have a period of time within which to order their own affairs and take steps to protect the medium and long-term interests of vulnerable clients.

This course is warmly welcomed by the author as overcoming a rather unsatisfactory gap in the legislation. This could have been avoided by extending the suspension of the effect of the decision until 28 days after the decision of the Tribunal. That would, of course, be met with the criticism that it would be 28 days more care in unsatisfactory circumstances.

10.6   IS THERE A FURTHER APPEAL?

A further appeal may only be made upon issues of law. The Tribunal has clearly been established by Parliament to determine issues in relation to regulated care homes. The Tribunal is an arbiter of disputes of fact. Parties dissatisfied with the findings of fact will not be able to appeal the issue further.

This is an issue which unsuccessful parties to litigation find most difficult to accept. There must be a finality to litigation. Procedures, no matter how sophisticated, cannot possibly allow constant review of issues of fact.

Issues of law are different. An appeal lies to the High Court on a point of law. The legal authority for further appeal is contained in the Tribunals and Enquiries Act 1971. There are two alternatives:

(1)   to request the Tribunal to state a case to the High Court for determination of a point of law;
(2)   as an alternative, the appellant may appeal to the High Court on the basis that the Tribunal decision is wrong in law.[8]

An appeal lies to the Divisional Court of the Queens Bench Division of the High Court of Justice and the practice in relation to the appeal is laid out in the Rules of the Supreme Court (RSC), Ords 55 and 56.

Order 55 deals with all appeals to the High Court from the Registered Homes Tribunal, save for the hearing of an appeal by way of 'case stated', which is governed by Ord 56, rr 7–11.

Appeals must be served upon the other party (respondent) and the Chairman of the Tribunal. Appeals must be entered and served within 28 days

---

8   Tribunals and Enquiries Act 1992, s 11 and Sch 1. The Registered Homes Tribunal is under the general supervision of the Council on Tribunals.

from the date of judgment. It is not clear whether time starts to run when the decision is given or received. The court will be *very* reluctant to grant extensions, or to receive appeals out of time. Practitioners are advised to treat the 28-day period as running from the date when the Tribunal posts the decision.

Such appeals from a specialist Tribunal are not welcomed by the High Court. An appeal, apparently without merit, will not be one that the High Court is likely to indulge by the grant of a time extension.

To lodge an appeal the appellant requires:

(1)   notice of motion with grounds;
(2)   copy of decision appealed;
(3)   affidavits filed and relevant documents;
(4)   an index.

Two copies, with a fee of £100 payable to HM Paymaster General, must be lodged at the Crown Office, Royal Courts of Justice, The Strand, London WC2.

It must be remembered that, although the appeal is by way of re-hearing, it may only proceed on an issue of law. The court will not review the evidence, unless it be said that the decision is perverse on the evidence (a point of law in itself). Appeals launched upon the grounds of perversity of decision have been markedly unsuccessful. The High Court may *not* substitute its view for that of the Tribunal of first instance. On a specialist subject, the High Court will be very slow to say that a specialist Tribunal has acted perversely.

Under Ord 56, a single judge of the High Court may determine an issue of law upon a case stated by the Registered Homes Tribunal, either where the Tribunal states the case at the request of one or more of the parties, or following an order from the High Court that the Tribunal state such a case.

Such cases will obviously relate solely to issues of law and, although the High Court has power to amend the case or return it for amendment,[9] those issues will be more constrained than where the issues may arise upon an appeal under Ord 55, launched by one of the parties.

Cases stated have not occurred frequently in the Registered Homes Tribunal.[10] Cases stated are more likely to arise on preliminary issues rather than where all the issues of fact have been examined.

Such an appeal must be brought within 28 days of the decision. That is interpreted to mean 28 days from the date when the decision is communicated to the appellant. Decisions from the Tribunal are communicated by post. The 28 days will be calculated from the date when the decision would be expected to have been delivered in the ordinary course of the post. An appeal out of time can only be made with leave of the High Court. Prospective appellants are well advised not to risk being out of time. The courts do not welcome appeals from specialist Tribunals. In the author's experience, very few such appeals have produced a satisfactory result for the appellant. The courts will rightly regard themselves as reviewing the decision of a specialist Tribunal. The courts will be

---

9   RSC Ord 56, rule 11.
10   See Registered Homes Tribunal decision No 115, *Coombes v Hertfordshire County Council.*

loath to interfere with the decision of a specialist Tribunal unless a manifest error of law appears.

An error of law can be argued on the basis that the decision made by the Tribunal is a decision that no reasonable Tribunal could have reached upon the facts before it, ie a perverse decision. Such is a difficult course. The more specialist the Tribunal, the more reluctant are the courts to interfere with their findings. In the author's experience, there have been a number of appeals to the High Court making such allegations and none of them have been successful.

If such an appeal is to succeed, the seeds for success should have been sown during the course of the Tribunal hearing. If a Tribunal is likely to make a decision which might be characterised as perverse, it is almost inevitable that that result will become apparent to the advocates appearing at the Tribunal. The advocate for the appellant should be careful and astute to adduce all evidence in support of his client's position. The greater the detail (supported by detailed record-keeping) the more easy it will be to show, if it is so alleged, that the decision of the Tribunal is perverse.

Appellants should be encouraged to accept their fate after Tribunal hearings. The prospect of a favourable result on appeal to the High Court is extremely remote.

10.7   BURDEN OF PROOF

Tribunals are conducted upon an adversarial basis. In preparing for such a hearing, it is important to determine upon which party lies the burden of proof, ie which party has to prove the relevant issues in order to succeed. The party upon whom the burden of proof does not lie, is not obliged to take any steps until the other party has adduced material which requires to be answered.

Upon this basis, the burden of proof is said to shift during the course of the Tribunal hearing. Where the party upon whom the burden lies adduces evidence sufficient to succeed, then the onus will shift to the other party to displace that evidence. In practice, the burden may shift to and fro during the course of the hearing.

What does not shift is the ultimate and underlying role of the party who is subject to the burden of proof. That party starts with the obligation to prove the case and at the end of the day, after the shifting of the burden throughout the trial, it is that party who remains under the burden of proof and whose case will be judged by the Tribunal to see if they have discharged that burden.

The burden of proof cannot be agreed between the parties, with or without the Tribunal's consent. Nor can the burden of proof be decided by the Tribunal. The identity of the party who is subject to the burden of proof, in any proceedings, is a matter of law.

In a criminal prosecution, the prosecution are required to prove the guilt of the accused. The defence are not required to take any steps whatsoever until the prosecution have at least raised a prima facie case. The burden of proof before the Tribunal clearly rests upon the registration authority in relation to residential care homes and nursing homes. An owner is entitled to be registered unless the authority establishes reasons which entitles it to refuse registration and establishes that it is an appropriate exercise of its discretion so to refuse.[11] The registered owner, having been entitled to be registered and being registered, is entitled to remain registered unless the authority establishes permitted reasons as to why the registration should be cancelled and why it is right that the discretion to cancel registration should be exercised on those facts.[12]

The registration authority, as the party subject to the burden of proof, opens the proceedings before the Tribunal and is subject to the burden throughout.

The Registered Homes Tribunal conducts civil proceedings. The burden of proof is upon the balance of probabilities (ie is an allegation more likely to have ocurred than not?). Serious allegations have attracted various approaches. The more serious the allegation, the higher the standard of proof, the Court of Appeal rules in *Lyons*.[13] The more serious the allegation, the less likely it is to have ocurred, and thus the more cogent must be the proof.[14] In practical terms, there may be little between the two explanations.

10.7.1 Cases concerning children's homes

An interesting debate lies in relation to cases concerning registered children's homes. The position with such cases is that the applicant or registered owner is in a different position to that of such a party in respect of residential care or nursing homes.

There is no obligation to register an applicant in respect of registered children's homes. The applicant is only entitled to be registered if the local authority is satisfied that the home will comply with prescribed requirements and any other requirements that it considers to be appropriate.

In conducting such an application, the applicant cannot say that he is entitled to be registered and, accordingly, it is for him to satisfy the authority that he should be registered. The Tribunal, exercising its jurisdiction of review on appeal, cannot be in a different position to the authority determining the original application. This is consistent with and would seem to follow the decision of the High Court in *Warwickshire County Council v McSweeney*,[15] in relation to conditions of registration.

Accordingly, it is suggested that, in relation to first registration of a children's home, the burden of proof lies upon the appellant and it is for the appellant to prove his or her case.

The issues came before the Tribunal on two occasions. In *Paul Hett v Gwynedd County Council*,[16] the Tribunal, encouraged no doubt by its long and

---

11 See Registered Homes Act 1984, ss 5, 9, 23 and 25.

12 Ibid, ss 5, 9, 10, 23, 25 and 28.

13 See *Lyons & Anor v East Sussex County Council* 86 (1988) LGR 369, (1988) 152 JP 488; Registered Homes Tribunal decision No 68, *McLean v London Borough of Hillingdon*.

14 *Re H and R (Child Sexual Abuse: Standard of Proof)* [1996] 1 FLR 80, HL, adopted by the Registered Homes Tribunal in decision No 321, *Berry and Berry v Calderdale Metropolitan Borough Council*.

15 (Unreported) 8 December 1988, Roch J.

16 Tribunal decision No 214.

satisfactory practice in relation to residential care and nursing homes, held that it was right that the burden of proof should always remain on the authority and that, in effect, the authority should open the case. Such appeared to be uncontroversial.

However, in *Bryn Alyn Community Limited v Clywd County Council*,[17] counsel for the authority raised the issue of the burden of proof for the first time. Quite clearly, the issue troubled the Tribunal, particularly as the Chairman of the Tribunal was the same Tribunal Chairman who had determined the *Gwynedd* case. From reading the decision, it appears that the Tribunal rather reluctantly conceded that the decision in *Gwynedd* was wrong and accepted that it was probably right that the burden of proof lay upon the appellant. The Tribunal avoided the issue by ruling that, whether the burden of proof lay upon the appellant or the respondent, the appellant failed.

Issues of the burden of proof cannot, it is submitted, be determined with the benefit of hindsight. The parties were clearly very helpful to the Tribunal and the Tribunal had much material upon which it could make its decision. However, issues as to the burden of proof go to the central issue as to how a Tribunal hearing should be conducted. They go to issues of pleading (minimal as it is before the Tribunal) and they go crucially to questions of preparation.

The author suggests that the view propounded by counsel in *Clywd* is correct and that the decision in *Gwynedd* was wrong. The Tribunal clearly took the view that to place the burden of proof upon the appellant would make the conduct of the Tribunal extremely difficult. Neither the appellant nor the Tribunal would necessarily know the issues with which the respondent authority was concerned. In effect, the appellant would have to conduct a complete and detailed presentation of his application in all respects, save to the extent that matters were agreed (if at all) to be uncontroversial.

It is suggested that the burden of proof is plainly upon the appellant in relation to an application for registration of a children's home. The parties may agree to narrow the issues. However, if there is no such agreement, the law has provided that the appellant must satisfy the authority in the original application and, accordingly, the appellant must so satisfy the Tribunal. If that means adducing evidence upon each and every aspect of the operation of the children's home, then those are the provisions that the law has made.

Matters are complicated by the application of the Registered Homes Tribunal Rules 1984 to the conduct of appeals in relation to the registration of children's homes. The first required step of pleading (clearly designed for residential care home and nursing home cases where the burden of proof is on the respondent authority) is that the authority is required to make a statement of reasons. How can the authority make a statement of reasons if it is not subject to the burden of proof and the issue before the Tribunal is whether the Tribunal, in place of the authority, is satisfied, within a wider discretion, that the appellant should be registered?

Difficulties arise when jurisdictions are widened without sufficient attention to variations in the rules that govern proceedings. The matter may be

---

17 Tribunal decision No 231.

resolved by an authority, no doubt being considered rather unhelpful, stating that having taken into account all matters arising on the appellant's application, it was not satisfied that the appellant should be registered. That is the reason and that will be the underlying reason. A helpful authority might indicate the particular issues, in greater or lesser detail, which caused it to be so dissatisfied.

Whether or not that course was followed, it would surely only be as a guide to the Tribunal. The issue will be whether the Tribunal are satisfied. It is suggested that the issues would not be limited by pleading or even by agreement. In conducting such a Tribunal, given the requirement that the Tribunal must be satisfied by the appellant, it is for the appellant to adduce evidence on all issues and indeed for the Tribunal to challenge and probe, perhaps even over matters that are not raised by the respondent. It has to be said that this situation is highly unsatisfactory.

In both cases, the appellant failed. Had the appellant succeeded, the respondent authorities might well have taken such issue on appeal. Similar problems do not seem to arise in relation to cancellation of registration of registered children's homes.[18] Here the authority has to advance reasons to justify cancellation and the burden of proof remains with them to sustain those reasons on appeal. Where the application for registration is launched for technical reasons relating to a particular case (which is really cancellation), the Tribunal accepted that the authority could accept the evidential burden of proof.[19]

10.8   RULES FOR THE CONDUCT OF PROCEEDINGS BEFORE THE TRIBUNAL

Using the word 'rules' in its most general sense there are two types of rules:

(1)   the Tribunal Rules, ie the Registered Homes Tribunal Rules 1984;
(2)   rules of practice developed and perhaps established by the Tribunal.

Whether such rules of practice attain any force of law is an interesting question.

When the Tribunal was first established, the hope was expressed in circulars issued by the Department of Health that it would be informal, not necessarily attended by lawyers and not dogged by arcane arguments about rules of law. Such hope, similarly expressed in the 1960s by the predecessor to the Department of Employment and Education, in relation to the Industrial Tribunal, was doomed to disappointment. It is naive to consider that any process, conducted adversarially, to resolve issues between parties of any nature, let alone issues where the subject matter is of such importance as in Tribunal hearings, could ever be resolved on an informal basis or without detailed rules of procedure. The issues before Tribunals usually relate to the

---

18   See Registered Homes Tribunal decision No 293, *Amelia Sansom v London Borough of Newham.*
19   Registered Homes Tribunal decision No 321, *Berry and Berry v Calderdale Metropolitan Borough Council.*

survival of a regulated care home business. In these days, such a business is unlikely to have a value lower than £500,000 and, in most cases, it is likely that the value will be well in excess of £1 million. The business is likely to be supported by very substantial loans from third parties. The issues that arise may impugn the reputations of professional carers and, indeed, of professional regulators. The issues, which may concern the physical well being of frail and vulnerable clients, may raise matters which, in another forum, would be considered subject to the gravest criminal liability.

The Tribunal is hampered by a wholly inadequate set of rules. The Tribunal has endeavoured to assist by establishing rules of practice. Such rules of practice can never be binding, but may be a helpful guide to the parties as to how to assist the Tribunal and save time and costs.

Paragraph 4(3) of Sch 6 to the 1989 Act provides that where it appears to a responsible authority that a registered home is being carried on otherwise than in accordance with the relevant requirements, it may determine that the registration of the home should be cancelled. The burden of proof lies upon it to establish that the registration of the home should be cancelled.

If the allegations proposing cancellation rely upon convictions of the owner, under the 1984 Act the burden would be discharged in this case relatively easily as the fact of conviction will be clear. If the dispute arises out of an exercise of a discretion, the authority will have to demonstrate why it was appropriate to exercise the discretion. The Registered Homes Tribunal Rules 1984 set out the relevant rules governing the Tribunal. The practitioner will wish to study those rules. The essential rules are:

(1)   the appellant who appeals to the registration authority shall state an address for service of documents;
(2)   the registration authority shall notify the Secretary of State within 7 days of receipt of notice of appeal[20] (even where the Secretary of State is nominal regulator, the Health Authority will act in his name and thus have the requirement to notify). Notification is to the Registered Homes Tribunal Secretariat, a division of the Department of Health, whose address, telephone number and fax number are:

Registered Homes Tribunal Secretariat
Area 217
Wellington House
133–155 Waterloo Road
London SE1 8UG
Telephone: (0171) 972 4035
Fax: (0171) 972 4525

Rule 4

As soon as the notice of appeal is received, the Secretary of State arranges for the appointment of a legally qualified Chairman and expert panel members and the appointment of a Secretary. The Secretary will be one of the Tribunal staff.

---

20   Registered Homes Tribunal Rules 1984, r 3.

Rule 5

This sets out the sole rules as to pre-hearing statement of case. Within this rule are the limited and rather inadequate provisions for what litigators call pleadings. The principles are:

(1) within 28 days from appointment, the Chairman shall fix a date, time and place for the hearing;

(2) notice of that hearing shall be given to the appellant with a copy to the registration authority. The notice shall be delivered not later than 42 days before the date when the hearing is fixed;

(3) not later than 30 days before the date of the hearing, the registration authority shall send to the Tribunal, with a copy to the appellant, four copies of the statement of its reasons for the decision;

(4) where the appeal is against the order of the Justice of the Peace, all that is required to be served (or indeed permitted to be served) is a copy of the statement made to the magistrate which persuaded the magistrate to make the urgent regulatory order;

(5) within the next nine days, the appellant must serve upon the Tribunal with a copy to the registration authority, four copies of the Grounds of Appeal.

Practitioners will note with surprise the speed at which such an appeal is convened.

The time-limits appear reasonable against the background of 42 days' notice of a Tribunal hearing. The reality, for reasons of logistics and resources, is that the Tribunal hearing will almost certainly not take place for at least 3 to 4 months, and maybe longer, from the date when notice of appeal is received by the Secretariat. The longer the period from notice of appeal to hearing, the more strange seems the concertina effect of the pleadings in the pre-hearing period.

In the author's experience, authorities wait until the 31st day to deliver statements of reasons. That is perhaps the inevitable result of pressures of work on legal practitioners. It is odd that a procedure should encourage delay and then require performance in very short order.

Rule 6

Appellants may be represented by whomsoever they wish, including solicitors and counsel. Registration authorities may be represented by officers of the authority or by counsel or solicitor.

Rule 7

Tribunals shall sit and listen to the proceeding in public, unless the Tribunal shall determine otherwise. The decision is the decision of the Tribunal, not the decision of the Chairman. If the Tribunal is not properly constituted, those sitting are not sitting as a Tribunal.

Rule 8

Hearings may be adjourned at the discretion of the Tribunal. Reconvened hearings shall be on not less than 14 days' notice to both parties. If either party does not attend, the Tribunal has a discretion as to whether to proceed, or to adjourn, or to act as it sees fit.

Rule 9

The parties have full rights to address the Tribunal, give evidence, call witnesses and examine and cross-examine witnesses. The Chairman of the Tribunal may require the attendance of further witnesses. If that occurs, the question arises as to the capacity in which the witnesses are being called. The author would suggest that the witnesses are being called by the Tribunal to assist the Tribunal and should thus be examined first by the Tribunal and thereafter as may be determined or directed by the Tribunal.

The principle applicable at inquests may be suitable for application to these circumstances, in that the party whose interests are adversely affected by the evidence should have the opportunity to question the witness last. The difference from inquests would be that this questioning would truly be cross-examination. It would seem wrong that parties who have not called a witness should not have the opportunity to cross-examine.

Rule 10

This paragraph deals with evidence. Section 12(3) of the Arbitration Act 1950 applies to proceedings before the Tribunal, so that the Chairman has the powers of an arbitrator in relation to the administration of oaths, and the summoning of witnesses by subpoena.

However, any hope that the rules of arbitration might be taken to apply is dashed by reference to s 43(3) of the 1984 Act. The Arbitration Act 1950 does not apply to Tribunal proceedings, except to the extent that rules made under the 1984 Act apply such procedures, ie the arbitration rules apply only in relation to administration of oaths and summoning of witnesses.

10.9 RULES OF EVIDENCE

A wider discretion as to the admittance in evidence of documents and information than is usual in civil proceedings is provided. The wording of the rule is important. The appellant, the registration authority or any witness, may produce in evidence any document or information, notwithstanding that such document would be inadmissible in a court of law. The Tribunal may receive in evidence such document or information if the Chairman of the Tribunal is satisfied that it is desirable, in the interests of justice, to receive it. It is helpful that Tribunals are thus not restricted by legally artificial rules of evidence.

This provision has been interpreted by Chairmen of Tribunals to allow admission in evidence of a wide variety of material which may be of assistance, even if not directly probative and which would normally be excluded, for example evidence of a hearsay nature or, sometimes, evidence which is not strictly relevant to the issues. The practice that has developed is that Tribunal Chairmen will admit any evidence on the basis that the Tribunal will then decide how much weight to give to that evidence.

It is suggested that this may be over simplistic and, indeed, not a correct course.

It is beyond the scope of this book to consider in detail the law of evidence as it applies to Tribunals. However, it is suggested that the principal rule is that the rules of evidence as they apply to civil proceedings in the UK should apply to proceedings before Tribunals. If an issue then arises about admissibility of evidence, the Chairman should deal with the matter in the following way.

(1)   First determine if the material in issue is admissible or inadmissible evidence, as a matter of law.

(2)   If the evidence is admissible, the matter proceeds no further. If the evidence is inadmissible, then the Chairman should decide, as a separate issue, whether notwithstanding its inadmissibility, it is desirable for the Tribunal to receive the evidence in the interests of justice. It is suggested that it is an inappropriate practice to determine, almost as a rule, that all material will be admitted and that the Tribunal will then sift such material and determine the weight to be given during the course of its deliberations. Such a course could lead to injustice.

The parties are entitled to know whether or not evidence has been admitted and, in the author's submission, are entitled to have a decision upon whether material which would otherwise be inadmissible as a matter of law is to be admitted.

(3)   Rule 3 provides an important power for the Chairman. The Chairman of the Tribunal may, before or after the beginning of the hearing, call for such further information and reports as he thinks desirable and may give directions as to the manner in which such material shall be furnished. This provides a clear and useful power for the Tribunal, through its Chairman, to seek further information where there may be a gap in the evidence. The author's experience is that parties do not leave much opportunity for such a gap in evidence. Preparation is fulsome and evidence is detailed.

Practitioners will have noted that there is no provision for the legal procedure known as discovery in Tribunal hearings. The author would suggest that this cannot be achieved through the Chairman's orders under r 10(3). The crucial question is what is covered by the words 'information or reports'. Information is defined in the *Oxford English Dictionary*, 3rd edn, as:

> 'The action of informing; training, instruction; communication of instructive knowledge.'

It is suggested that this definition cannot extend to evidence. Information suggests to the author factual information as opposed to disclosure of evidence that may be given by particular witnesses. If facts are unknown, the Chairman may require that those facts be ascertained, as far as possible, and placed before the Tribunal. 'Reports' suggests reports from experts about issues that may arise. This important power of the Chairman seems to be rather limited in its real application. However, under r 9(2) the Chairman may require the attendance of further witnesses.

(4)   Rule 11 states that decisions for Tribunals shall be by majority. No member of the Tribunal has a casting vote. The Chairman does not even

have the right to determine legal issues, save for issues of procedure for which specific provision is made in the regulations (see r 9(2) and (3) and r 10(1), (2) and (3)).

The decision must be notified by the Chairman of the Tribunal as soon as possible, accompanied by reasons. The notification shall be in writing. Where the decision is against an order made by a magistrate, the Tribunal must also notify the magistrate of the decision and the reasons.

Rule 12

An appellant may at any time withdraw an appeal without reason and without penalty.

Rule 13

Two or more appeals may be held together, with the consent of the appellant and the Chairman of the Tribunal, where the appeals relate to different regulated care homes, provided that the appellants are the same.

Rule 14

The Chairman of the Tribunal may extend time for doing acts required by the rules upon such terms (if any) as are deemed fit.

Rule 15

Subject to the provisions of the 1984 Act and the rules, the Tribunal may regulate its own procedure. This provision appears helpful at first; further thought may suggest that it does not advance the Tribunal's position very far. If the Tribunal's discretion is limited by the Act under which it is constituted and the rules laid out by the Secretary of State, the opportunity for regulating the procedure is limited.

It will be noted that the power to regulate the procedure is a power for the Tribunal and not the Chairman. As the power is one to regulate the procedure of the Tribunal and not the conduct of cases proceeding before the Tribunal, it is suggested that this power does not entitle the Tribunal to make binding rules of practice about pre-Tribunal preparation. This is a problem and is to be regretted.

10.10   TRIBUNAL PRACTICES

Tribunals have, not surprisingly, felt restricted and to some extent frustrated by the lack of rules which enable them to provide for the most efficient determination of the issues which arise. Two steps have been taken by the Tribunal to encourage practices which will assist the resolution of cases. Neither of these practices has the force of law and, whilst sensible, practitioners will wish to consider whether, in the interests of their clients, the practices should be followed. Parties to the Tribunal are entitled to have their case conducted in accordance with the rules and are not obliged to compromise a position which may be to their advantage purely as a matter of convenience.

10.10.1   Exchange of statements, affidavits and documents

When the hearing date and place are appointed, the Tribunal issues a standard letter to the parties. That letter is reproduced below:

> 'I enclose notice of the hearing of the above Appeal in accordance with r 5(1) of the Registered Homes Tribunal Rules 1984[21] which govern the proceedings of the Tribunals.
>
> Rule 5(2) requires the registration authority to send to the Secretary, at the above address, four copies of the statement of reasons for its decision. Four copies of the authority's guidelines should be supplied with the statement. The purpose of this statement is to inform the Tribunal and the appellant of all the grounds for the authority's decision, but not the detailed evidence on which the authority relied. Each of the reasons must be clearly stated so that the appellant knows precisely the case to be met. The authority may be confined to the stated reasons. A copy of this statement must be served on the appellant at the same time.
>
> So that neither party is taken by surprise at the hearing, each party should disclose to the other all the documents upon which they intend to rely. All letters exchanged between the parties should be prepared as an agreed bundle in date order, with numbered pages, securely fastened, and four copies provided for the Tribunal at least 14 days before the hearing.
>
> Evidence is dealt with by rr 9(3) and 10, but the parties will find it convenient for the speedy resolution of the proceedings to prepare and exchange statements of the witnesses they intend to call and to provide copies for the Tribunal at least 14 days before the hearing.
>
> If it is intended to rely on affidavit evidence, copies of any affidavit should be made available to the Tribunal and to the other party at least 14 days before the hearing.
>
> Application can be made direct to the Crown Office for issue of subpoenas to compel the attendance of any witness if necessary, giving at least five working days' notice.
>
> The hearing will ordinarily be held in public (r 7) and the Press will be notified.
>
> Decisions are published and copies can be obtained from the DSS, BAPS, Storage and Publications Unit, Manchester Road, Heywood, Lancashire, OL10 2PZ, price £113.50. They are a guide to practice, procedure and points of law.
>
> The parties to an appeal have to bear their own costs.
>
> Please contact the Secretary to the Tribunal if there is any question of procedure which you wish to discuss.
>
> A letter in similar terms has been sent to the appellants' solicitors.'

The letter is a mixture of information as to the rules that do apply and practices that the Tribunals would like to see. The most important issue is the request that statements of evidence, affidavits and documents be exchanged not later than 14 days before the hearing date. Therefore, practitioners will observe that the Tribunal is suggesting, irrespective of how long a period has elapsed from notice of appeal, that:

(1)   the authority's reasons be delivered 30 days before the hearing date (a requirement);

---

21   SI 1984/1346.

(2) the appellant's grounds of appeal be delivered 22 days before the hearing date (a requirement);

(3) evidence, documents, affidavits, etc be exchanged 14 days before the hearing date.

As statements of evidence, affidavits and relevant documents cannot truly be identified until the statement of reasons and grounds of appeal have been exchanged, a period of 7 days is allowed to complete discovery and exchange of witness statements. This is an extraordinary telescoping of normal litigation or arbitration procedure.

The Tribunal has done its best, but given the extremely short period of time before a hearing at which so-called pleadings are to be delivered, the Tribunal has little option.

10.10.2 Pre-hearing meetings for directions

The Tribunal encourages a meeting between the parties with the Tribunal, or possibly just the Chairman, to see if the procedural issues can be resolved prior to the hearing. This is to be welcomed, but is not a matter upon which the Tribunal can insist. In any event, the meeting can have no force unless the whole Tribunal is present, for as a matter of law, the Tribunal will only then and under those circumstances be properly constituted.

It is always helpful to have a meeting to see if issues can be resolved or methods for smoothing determination of issues before the Tribunal can be determined. However, such meetings cost time and time costs money. With respect to the Tribunal, parties need to be advised carefully as to whether or not spending such time and, in consequence, money (which is, in any event, irrecoverable), is a right course of action to follow. Some benefit needs to be seen. The author would suggest that, unless a clear benefit can be ascertained, and in most cases any discussions at such a meeting will not be binding upon the parties, it is difficult to see how any real benefit can be achieved by attending a meeting at which decisions or directions do not have the force of law.

10.11 THE HEARING

The hearing will be organised by the Registered Homes Tribunal Secretariat in premises which will be secured for the purpose of the individual hearing. There are no permanent premises from which the Tribunal operates. In practice, the Secretariat will ask the respondent authority to provide suitable accommodation. This will be extensive. A substantial room for the hearing is required. The room must have at least two exits. There must be a substantial room to which the Tribunal may retire for deliberation, and a separate room for each of the parties to use for deliberation and consultation.

Authorities should be aware that the not insignificant costs of representation and conduct of Tribunal hearings will be increased by the direct or indirect costs of being expected to provide facilities for the hearing.

The hearing of a Registered Homes Tribunal is, in effect, a trial. It may not have the panoply of a High Court or county court trial, but, in essence, the conduct of the proceedings is similar. The party subject to the burden of proof will open the case, as in any other legal case. Evidence will be called and witnesses examined, cross-examined and re-examined, as at a trial. Advocates will make closing speeches and the Tribunal will retire to make its decision after deliberation, usually some 2 to 3 weeks after the close of the hearing.

Such hearings take considerable periods of time. The very simplest of cases are likely to take two to three days and it is never safe to estimate a case as lasting less than one full week. Cases which involve serious dispute as to issues of fact will last longer. It is not unusual for Tribunal cases to last several weeks.

10.12 PLEADINGS

There is provision for pleadings, but the requirement to plead so close to the hearing itself makes it impossible to have the usual post-pleading litigation or arbitration procedure.

If those determining the issues are not to be burdened with a mass of irrelevant material, it is impossible to prepare documents until one knows the issues that arise in the case. Those are usually defined by pleadings. Until pleadings are closed, it is not really possible to ascertain what documents will be relevant to the issues before the Tribunal. Furthermore, the preparation and exchange of witness statements cannot really be undertaken until both pleadings are closed and relevant documents have been exchanged.

The remedy to this, surely, is to set the date for pleadings within a reasonable time from the notice of appeal, rather than from the date when a hearing has been fixed. That, in the author's submission, will overcome a great many of the problems, given that the period from notice of appeal to hearing is frequently not 10 weeks, as suggested by the rules, but two or three times that period.

There is no requirement for the parties to disclose documents by way of discovery, nor is there a requirement, as a matter of law, for the parties to exchange witness statements. There is no provision for procedural matters to be dealt with by way of pre-hearing directions.

10.13 COSTS

There is no provision for ordering costs against unsuccessful parties, even to the extent that the conduct of the parties has been seen only to serve to waste the time of the Tribunal. Surely this needs to be addressed.

In the author's experience, both owners and regulatory authorities are guilty of allowing cases to go to Tribunal that should have been resolved. An owner may be more inclined to abandon an appeal or an authority be more inclined to encourage its officers to concentrate on the real issues, if in either case the consequence of losing were, in addition some loss of face and the bearing of one's own costs, the prospects of having to pay the not insubstantial costs of one's successful opponent.

There can be no good reason why the normal rule of English law that an unsuccessful party to litigation or arbitration should bear the costs of the successful party should not apply in Tribunals. The costs are very substantial. Any Tribunal hearing is likely to incur for each side, in costs, somewhere between £60,000 and £80,000. Prolonged Tribunal hearings may cost very much more.

10.14 CONCLUSIONS

The defects in procedure which have been identified in this chapter are matters which individual parties before Tribunals may seek to use to their own advantage. The absence of an obligation to discover documents or disclose witness statements may be of advantage to either party. Parties should understand the limits of the procedure and, until changes are made, are entitled to insist that the proceedings be conducted in accordance with the statutory rules and not be required to submit to voluntary disclosure or procedures possibly designed to assist their opponent.

Unless and until there are changes in the rules, practitioners should study those rules which do exist and decide how best to use them to the advantage of their clients.

Chapter 11

REGISTERED HOMES –
THE FUNDING OF RESIDENTS IN CARE

11.1   INTRODUCTION

Every business, to survive, requires a steady reliable stream of income with which to service its expenditure and, in a private venture, to produce profit.

Care homes are no different. They must attract customers who pay fees of sufficient amount regularly to exceed expenditure.

The customer or client pays a fee for the provision of serviced accommodation. The services supporting the accommodation will be tailored to meet the client's need.

However, care homes are unique in that very many of the clients are unable to pay from their own resources fees sufficient to meet proper business criteria. Such clients are largely dependent upon public funding to support their needs and care.

The special features which arise in relation to that funding do not alter the basic premise that accommodation and service provided in a care home, are provided by contract. The relationship between the client and public agencies or others who may support the client in need is a different relationship from that between the care provider and the client.

In this chapter, we shall consider the nature of the contract between care home and client and the aspirations and expectations of the parties to or associated with that contract, how that contract is affected by the source and availability of resources to meet the client's need. We shall also examine in outline the terms of a contract for residential care, an example of which is to be found in the Appendix.

Thereafter, we shall examine the system of public funding of residential care, as seen both in historical context and its current application.

11.2   NATURE OF THE CONTRACT

A contract for residential care is a contract by which the client secures the provision of serviced facilities to meet need.

As in any contractual relationship, a balance must be struck between the competing interests of those who are party to the contract.

Those parties may be identified as:

(a) the client;
(b) the client's sponsor (where applicable);
(c) the care home owner.

11.3   THE CLIENT

The client well seek to secure:

(1)   certainty as to the amount payable and times at which payment should be made;

(2)   certainty as to the scope and quality of the service to be provided, so that the client is able to judge any failure in such service (which will entitle the client to withhold payment or leave the home) but not with so much detail as to inhibit the proper development of the relationship between the care home owner and client.

The specification should be sufficiently flexible to meet the changes of every-day life and to adapt (possibly with consequent changes in price) to rises and falls in levels of dependency and the needs of care of an individual client.

11.4   THE SPONSOR

The sponsor's aims will be much the same as the client's but, since the sponsor is responsible for payment, he may wish to ensure that he is able to control and supervise the delivery of care as circumstances demand. The sponsor, in consideration of such rights of consultation and intervention, may be expected to be contracted as a primary party rather than as, for example, a guarantor. In many cases, in practice, the client himself may be incapable of understanding or intervening in the contractual relationship and may depend upon the sponsor for advocacy and support of his interests.

11.5   THE CARE HOME OWNER

The owner needs to know:

(a) to whom he must look for payment;
(b) with whom be must negotiate changes in payment levels or structures;
(c) the scope and quality of service which he must provide;
(d) how he can change service specification to meet changing client needs.

A care home owner has a restricted business. He has a limited number of sales opportunities, ie available beds, and commercial markets suggest that, in order to be viable, those beds should be filled to capacity most of the time. The care home owner requires certainty of income stream and sufficient time to manage potential changes caused by client change of mind, increase of dependency or death.

11.6   GENERAL

Common to all three is the need for certainty of contractual terms in what is an intrinsically simple contractual relationship.

The contract draughtsman should anticipate the likely changing circumstances over what may in many cases be a long-term relationship and seek to ensure simply and clearly that those circumstances are documented in advance and understood.

Those concerned with handling such contractual negotiations need to appreciate the inequality of bargaining power. The client and private sponsor are not well placed to negotiate unless there is a surplus of accommodation available in their local market. The care home owner should not seek to take advantage of this. The public authority sponsor (a common participant in such negotiations since the introduction of the 'care in the community' scheme in 1993) is a dominant purchaser. However, in purchasing, that local authority is performing a public service. The authority is charged with ensuring the proper delivery of social welfare care both in residential and non-residential settings. That authority must strike a proper balance between the needs of clients, the needs of other social services users and local tax payers as a whole. It is important that the providers of residential care in a locality should be recognised by their dominant purchaser who should ensure by open and fair contractual negotiation that a choice of such facilities remains available for those in need. Overly zealous negotiation by local authorities may lead to significant numbers of such providers being forced out of business. Political engineering through contract negotiation is inappropriate but, as a significant purchaser, the local authority should ensure value for money combined with adequate facilities to ensure that those who rely upon that authority for protection receive adequate care at all times.

That authority should:

(a) act only within its powers;
(b) not constrain or fetter its activities by preordained policy;
(c) act in accordance with proper procedures;
(d) not act irrationally.[1]

11.7 THE DIFFERENT FUNDING SCHEMES

There are three schemes which are outlined at **11.7.1–11.7.3**.

11.7.1 Entirely self-funded

Self-funding is self-explanatory. The client with sufficient means to purchase the required care enters into a contract which is funded from his own resources.

11.7.2 The client-supported scheme

In a client-supported scheme the client has insufficient personal resources to fund the care and calls upon the financial support of others. Here care home owner, client and the third party, the sponsor, need to consider carefully the contractual arrangement with the sponsor. Most clients have, historically, fallen into this group.

Within such schemes falls that administered through the Benefits Agency of the Department of Social Security by which the client receives funds to

---

1 See discussion later but, in particular, *Associated Provincial Picture Houses Ltd v Wednesbury Corporation* [1947] 2 All ER 680, *Council of Civil Service Unions v Minister for the Civil Service* [1984] 3 All ER 935 and *Bromley London Borough Council v Greater London Council* [1982] 1 All ER 129.

enable the client to meet his contractual obligations. That support may be ultimately provided by the safety net of income support but will include other means and non-means tested benefits, including State pension entitlements.

Other sponsors may be relatives and appropriate charities.

The principles of the scheme are the same. The care home owner is entitled to contract with its customers, ie the users, for payment of appropriate charge to meet need. The resources of the client or the client's sponsors are entirely available to meet the contractual obligation. Only if the contractual obligation specifies a specification for care is there a restriction in the contract on charging extra for extra service. Clients must be aware of potential extras.

Thus, for social security benefit supported clients, their personal expense allowance or so-called 'pocket money', is available to meet their contractual obligations. Such will probably not be the case with the third scheme, below.

11.7.3   Public authority funded scheme

The public authority, be it a Health Authority or a local authority, contracts with the care home owner to provide care within a particular specification. The client may or may not be party to the contract. The client may, if well advised, seek to have rights to enforce the contract but such will not be usual practice. Health Authorities, acting under delegated power from the Secretary of State, may enter into contracts for the purchase of long-term care for periods and at rates that are appropriate.[2] Those patients are and remain patients of the National Health Service and may not be charged any extra by the care home owner or provider. NHS patients are entitled to be treated free of charge.

Similarly, if a local authority undertakes responsibility, following an assessment of need, it is responsible to make arrangements for the provision of the residential accommodation and to pay for each in full.[3] Local authorities are rightly astute to negotiate detailed specifications for services. The price negotiated with and payable by the local authority is a fully inclusive price for services contracted, without any charges for extras. Therefore, there is no room for residents to be required to top up shortfalls in local authority funding. As with any other contract, the client may only be expected to pay an extra (as indeed may the local authority) if it is extra to the services contracted. Care home owners need to be sure that they are content to provide full services, as identified in the specification, for the fee contracted. They will certainly be bound until the next contracting round and probably until the client departs.

11.8   TERMS OF CONTRACT

It is invidious to generalise about contractual terms. However, the following are issues to consider in negotiations.

---

2   See National Health Service Act 1977, s 23.
3   See National Assistance Act 1948, s 21.

11.8.1 Scope of services

It is vital for the contract to define the service that will be provided in sufficient detail for the parties to know:

(a) whether the service has objectively failed;
(b) whether a service in respect of which additional payment is sought is additional to the contractual service;
(c) whether the actual service is a reduction or enhancement of that contracted, by reference to a predetermined base.

The scope of the service should be defined by reference to the requirements of the client rather than, in most cases, the method of operation of the home. (The method and adequacy of the home operation are matters for regulation and not contract.) Sufficiency and suitability of individual service are matters for contract.

Similarly, public authorities should be careful to distinguish between their roles as a purchaser of services from a home and as a regulator or accrediting body of it. Confusion may lead to suggestions that they are acting unlawfully and beyond their powers by mixing functions.

However, it is not unlawful and is perfectly proper as a contracting party that a public authority, after proper consultation, should require personal services for clients beyond or supplementary to those provided within the Registered Homes Act 1984 or other regulating legislation.[4]

11.8.2 Payment

The contract must provide clearly for the amount and timing of payment. It should state whether payment is made in advance or in arrear. It should also provide a mechanism for adjusting the payment as a consequence of a change in service specification and increases in the home's costs. Residential care contracts are likely to be long term and care home owners are unlikely to be able to hold prices to those contracted for longer than one year.

Where possible, items which may form the subject of an extra charge should be identified and a method for verification of extra changes should be established.

The contract should provide a procedure for withholding payment if a client has justifiable dissatisfaction with the service. A prudent owner may require a deposit to secure performance over a long-term contract. This will depend upon the relative negotiating strength of the owner and his judgment as to the quality of the purchaser's long-term covenant.

11.8.3 Occupation

The contract must address the basis upon which the client occupies accommodation. In most cases, the care home owner will require continuing exclusive control over the accommodation. Tenancies providing any degree of

---

4   See *R v Newcastle upon Tyne City Council, ex parte Dixon* (1993) 92 LGR 169.

security of occupation are inappropriate in long-term care establishments (unlike, say, sheltered housing). The needs of the business operation and the need to change accommodation to meet client dependency requirements will require most home owners to retain control of accommodation so that occupants occupy on a non-exclusive licence basis.

11.8.4   Termination of contract

Most contracts will be long term. Short-term respite care contracts can be predetermined by reference to a fixed period. In such cases, agreements to extend the period or an absolute requirement to depart at the conclusion of the contract period must be clearly specified.

In longer-term contracts, each party will wish to know the circumstances in which the contract may be terminated, for example, by the client, or the home owner if the clients fails to pay fees.

Owners will need to ensure that they can terminate the contract if dependency needs rise to such an extent that they are no longer able to provide the care required.

Clients will need rights to terminate the contract should they wish to move either because of dissatisfaction with the service or because their families or friends have removed elsewhere or for any reason that may occur.

Both parties will, of course, be mindful of the effect on the contract of the client's death. The client and the client's sponsor would like the contract to terminate immediately. The owner, however, will be faced with an unforeseeable vacancy and, without protection, a gap in the income stream. A balance should be struck identifying a reasonable period for the owner to seek a new client and certainty as determination of obligation from the client or the client's sponsor.

Local authorities rarely agree to continue payment beyond death. It must be noted too that in respect of those clients who are dependent upon public funding social security benefit ceases with death.

Owners may wish to take a deposit, if possible, from such clients. Unpaid care home liabilities are merely liabilities of the deceased's estate and come second to preferential claims, eg funeral expenses.

11.9   PERSONAL BELONGINGS

In a long-term contract for care, the owner welcomes the client into what will become the client's home. The client will have personal belongings, certainly money and perhaps furniture, books or other items of varying value. It is essential that the contract provides for any limitations or restrictions on personal belongings, as defined in the contract and the responsibility for insuring such belongings under particular circumstances.

Regulatory law provides for keeping of records as to money and valuables held in safe custody. The contract should take that matter further and make it clear how such items will be protected, how they will be insured and if liquid assets, how they will be invested. The client will usually have neither advisers nor technical financial ability.

11.10   GIFTS AND GRATUITIES

The offer and acceptance of unsolicited gifts is a problem in the operation of care homes and should be covered by the agreement. It should be made clear to clients by owners that they should not make gifts to owners or owner's staff under any circumstances. As between the owner and his staff, the issue will also be regulated by the contract of employment.

11.11   DISPUTES

The drafting of every contract must take into account that there may be disputes between the contracting parties. Where one of those parties is old or sick or vulnerable the efficiency of dispute resolution must be considered carefully.

The contract should provide for a clearly transparent complaints procedure.

The contract should provide identification of those who will be entrusted to resolve disputes on behalf of those clients who cannot speak or act for themselves.

The prospect of arbitration or litigation between care home owner and client is untenable. The relationship would break down. The owner does not wish to lose a client as the result of an unresolved dispute and the client does not want to feel under pressure because of fear that his home would become insecure if he disagreed with aspects of his treatment.

11.12   CHOICE OF CARE HOME

Clearly, in the first two schemes for funding care the capacity to move is both transparent and paramount. Those who seek to purchase services can choose whether or not to purchase a particular service or to continue with the purchase of that service.

The position is less clear with the third scheme, ie those who find themselves constrained to seek assistance from a public authority may feel that they should follow the suggestions and advice or even 'so-called' requirements of the local authority in selecting a particular home.

The local authority may feel that, if they are paying the price, then they should make the selection.

To meet this perceived problem, the Secretary of State made the National Assistance Act 1948 (Choice of Accommodation) Direction 1992 (as now amended). The Direction provides that:

(1)   If a resident for whom accommodation is to be provided has indicated a wish for 'preferred accommodation' then he should be accommodated in the place of his choice.[5] Clients and owners should note that that obligation arises only if a preferred choice has been indicated.

---

5   National Assistance Act 1948 (Choice of Accommodation) Direction 1992, para 2.

(2)   There are limits upon the local authority's need to accede to the client's
       choice.[6] The accommodation must appear to be suitable to the client's
       needs as assessed. The cost of making the arrangements must not require
       the authority to pay more than they would usually expect to pay having
       regard to those needs.

       The preferred accommodation must be available. The owners of the
       preferred accommodation must provide the accommodation upon the
       authority's usual terms and conditions.

       As a matter of fulfilling their public duty the authority should not
       seek to impose 'usual terms and conditions which constrain choice being
       terms and conditions which providers in the locality would not normally
       or usually accept. Such might be regarded as an unlawful fetter upon the
       authority's power to provide accommodation and an unlawful constraint
       upon the individual's right of choice.

(3)   If the charge for the preferred accommodation exceeds that which the
       authority would normally expect to pay then the authority may still be
       required to fund a placement in the preferred accommodation if a third
       party makes a contribution sufficient to make up the difference
       between:[7]

       (a) the cost which the local authority would usually expect to pay; and
       (b) the full cost of the accommodation.

The local authority are entitled to make arrangements for the provision
of accommodation anywhere, even at a cost which is above that usually
paid. The constraint is on the ability to compel the authority to purchase
such accommodation.

       The third party contribution must be demonstrably available for the
duration of the arrangements so that third parties may have to subject
themselves to significant disclosure of their long-term means if they are
to assist clients in enforcing a choice of accommodation beyond an
authority's normal budget.

       Care will have to be taken to ensure properly negotiated contracts
with the third party contributor. Owners must be careful not to find
themselves seeking payment in two parts. Failure of one paying party
could leave the owner obliged to continue the service for less than the
full charge. The third party must consider carefully his or her long-term
commitment.

       The better course is for the third party to contract with the client and
the local authority to make the contribution by way of payment to the
local authority as a part of the client's contribution under s 22 of the
National Assistance Act 1948 so that client and owner know that they may
look to the authority to meet the whole of the cost of residential care. The
third party will then face an enforceable obligation at the suit of the local
authority but the client's interest will be protected.

---

6   National Assistance Act 1948 (Choice of Accommodation) Direction 1992, para 3.
7   Ibid, para 4.

11.13   CONTRACTING WITH THE LOCAL AUTHORITY

Section 21(1) of the National Assistance Act 1948 provides as follows:

> 'Subject to and in accordance with the provisions of this part of this Act, a local authority may with the approval of the Secretary of State, and to such extent as he may direct shall, make arrangements for providing –
>
> (a)   residential accommodation for persons aged 18 or over who by reason of age, illness, disability or any other circumstances are in need of care and attention which is not otherwise available to them . . .'

This section has recently been much litigated. A little used section, it has become the focus of public attention since translated into the vehicle for operation of the 'care in the community' scheme for funding care home placements through local authorities since 1 April 1993.

An interesting amendment has been the extension of provision by local authorities of accommodation for the sick and the disabled previously considered clients of the National Health Service. For patients of the NHS, significantly, care is free whereas under the National Assistance Act 1948, care is subject to repayment to the local authority of the costs of accommodation for care, subject to means.

Such accommodation may be provided by the local authority from its own accommodation or by purchase of services from voluntary organisations or private contractors pursuant to the provisions of s 26 of the 1948 Act.

Section 26 is produced in full at **11.14**.

11.13.1   The constraints on contracting

It is important to note the constraints.

(1)   Accommodation for those in need of board and personal care must be accommodation registered under Pt I of the 1984 Act or in premises which are not required to be registered because they are for less than four persons who are also the staff or family members of the owner, or provided by bodies exempt from registration.

(2)   Premises providing nursing care must be registered under Pt II of the 1984 Act or maintained or controlled by bodies which do not fall within the definition of a nursing home in s 21 of that Act.

(3)   No admission may be made to a nursing home save in the case of emergency without the consent of the local health authority.

(4)   Arrangements may not be made for such residential accommodation with any person who has been convicted of a statutory offence under the 1984 Act or the regulations made under that Act. This is of great significance to owners. From time to time even respected owners may make a mistake, leading to a conviction. The effect of such a conviction is to make it unlawful for all time for any local authority to contract with that owner under s 26 of the 1948 Act. With the dominance of purchasing power of local authorities, such a conviction effectively drives that operator out of business.

   An offence which results in a discharge, whether absolute or conditional, will not be deemed to have resulted in a conviction.

11.13.2   Client's contribution

Pursuant to s 22 of the 1948 Act, clients accommodated in accommodation provided or purchased by the local authority are required to contribute to the costs of care either to cover the whole of that cost or to such extent as may be limited by their means assessed in accordance with the National Assistance (Assessment of Resources) Regulations 1992.[8]

Clients accommodated in accommodation operated by the private sector are obliged to refund the whole or part of the authority's cost in the same way that they are obliged to pay to the authority the cost of provision of their service in directly managed units.

Section 26(3)(a) provides that the owner, the local authority and the client may make a tripartite agreement so that the client's contribution is paid direct to the owner and to the extent that that payment is made the local authority is relieved of liability.

It must be emphasised that it is *the fact of payment* that relieves the local authority of liability. If no payment is made the local authority remains liable and retains its obligation to recover that payment from the client. The owner is not expected to look to two sources for payment.

The pre-requisite that such an arrangement should be by agreement suggests that it would be unlawful for an authority to require such an agreement as a condition of providing accommodation unless the price of the accommodation was above that which the authority would normally expect to pay.

The authority has a separate right of inspection of premises, where accommodation has been purchased by them or a client in addition to their regulatory powers of inspection under the 1984 Act, ie sponsoring local authorities have a separate right of inspection of homes which they would not normally enjoy.

11.14   SECTION 26 OF THE NATIONAL ASSISTANCE ACT 1948 (AS AMENDED)

'Provision of accommodation in premises maintained by voluntary organisations

26.[(1) Subject to subsections (1A) and (1B) below, arrangements under section 21 of this Act may include arrangements made with a voluntary organisation or with any other person who is not a local authority where:
    (a) that organisation or person manages premises which provided for reward accommodation falling within subsection (1)(a) or (aa) of that section, and
    (b) the arrangements are for the provision of such accommodation in those premises.
    (1A) Subject to subsection (1B) below, arrangements made with any voluntary organisation or other person by virtue of this section must, if they are for the provision of residential accommodation with both board and personal care for such persons as are mentioned in section

---

8   SI 1992/2977.

1(1) of the Registered Homes Act 1984 (requirement of registration), be arrangements for the provision of such accommodation in a residential care home which is managed by the organisation or person in question, being such a home in respect of which that organisation or persons:

(a) is registered under Part I of the Act, or

(b) is not required to be so registered by virtue of section 1(4)(a) or (b) of that Act (certain small homes) or by virtue of the home being managed or provided by an exempt body;

and for this purpose 'personal care' and 'residential care home' have the same meaning as in that Part of that Act.

(1B) Arrangements made with any voluntary organisation or other person by virtue of this section must, if they are for the provision of residential accommodation where nursing care is provided, be arrangements for the provision of such accommodation in premises which are managed by the organisation or person in question, being premises:

(a) in respect of which that organisation or person is registered under Part II of the Registered Homes Act 1984, or

(b) which, by reason only of being maintained or controlled by an exempt body, do not fall within the definition of a nursing home in section 21 of that Act.

(1C) Subject to subsection (1D) below, no such arrangements as are mentioned in subsection (1B) above may be made by an authority for the accommodation of any person without the consent of such [Health Authority] as may be determined in accordance with regulations.

(1D) Subsection (1C) above does not apply to the making by an authority of temporary arrangements for the accommodation of any person as a matter of urgency; but, as soon as practicable after any such temporary arrangements have been made, the authority shall seek the consent required by subsection (1C) above to the making of appropriate arrangements for the accommodation of the person concerned.

(1E) No arrangements may be made by virtue of this section with a person who has been convicted of an offence under any provision of:

(a) the Registered Homes Act 1984 (or any enactment replaced by that Act); or

(b) regulations made under section 16 or section 26 of that Act (or under any corresponding provisions of any such enactment).]

(2) Any [arrangements made by virtue of ... this section] shall provide for the making by the local authority to [the other party thereto] of payments in respect of the accommodation provided at such rates as may be determined by or under the arrangements [and subject to subsection (3A) below the local authority shall recover from each person for whom accommodation is provided under the arrangements the amount of the refund which he is liable to make in accordance with the following provisions of this section].

(3) [Subject to subsection (3A) below] a person for whom accommodation is provided under any such arrangements shall, in lieu of being liable to make payment therefor in accordance with section 22 of this Act, refund to the local authority any payments made in respect of him under the last foregoing subsection;

provided that where a person for whom accommodation is provided, or proposed to be provided, under any such arrangements satisfies the local authority that he is unable to make a refund at the full rate determined under that subsection, subsections (3) to (5) to section 22 of this Act shall, with the necessary modifications, apply as they apply where a person satisfies the local authority of his inability to pay at the standard rate as mentioned in the said subsection (3).

[(3A) Where accommodation in any premises is provided for any person under arrangements made by virtue of this section and the local authority, the person concerned and the voluntary organisation or other person managing the premises (in this subsection referred to as 'the provider') agree that this subsection shall apply:

(a) so long as the person concerned makes the payments for which he is liable under paragraph (b) below, he shall not be liable to make any refund under subsection (3) above and the local authority shall not be liable to make any payment under subsection (2) above in respect of the accommodation provided for him;

(b) the person concerned shall be liable to pay to the provider such sums as he would otherwise (under subsection (3) above) be liable to pay by way of refund to the local authority; and

(c) the local authority shall be liable to pay to the provider the difference between the sums paid by virtue of paragraph (b) above and the payments which, but for paragraph (a) above, the authority would be liable to pay under subsection (2) above.]

(4) Subsections [...] [(5A), (7) and (9) of the said section 22 shall, with the necessary modifications, apply for the purposes of the last foregoing subsection as they apply for the purposes of the said section 22.

[(4A) Section 21(5) of this Act shall have effect as respects accommodation provided under arrangements made by virtue of this section with the substitution for the reference to the authority managing the premises of a reference to the authority making the arrangements.]

(5) Where in any premises accommodation is being provided under [...] this section in accordance with arrangements made by local authority, any person authorised in that behalf by the authority may at all reasonable times enter and inspect the premises.

(6) [*Repealed by the Health Services and Public Health Act 1968, s 78(2), Sch 4.*]

(7) In this section the expression 'voluntary organisation' includes any association which is a housing association for the purposes of the Housing Act 1936, or the Housing (Scotland) Acts, 1925 to 1946 [[...] and 'exempt body' means an authority or body constituted by an Act of Parliament or incorporated by Royal Charter].

11.15   THE POSITION OF THE PUBLIC AUTHORITY

The public authority is a different category of purchaser from a private individual or company. By force of circumstances, the public authority will be a dominant purchaser and may for many homes be the sole purchaser.

The decisions as to whether or not to purchase care for a particular client, whether or not to purchase care from a particular home and the terms and conditions upon which residential care should be contracted are public decisions which should be taken in accordance with principles of public law overlaying normal contractual discretions.

11.15.1   The principles of public law

Whilst detailed consideration of public administrative law is beyond the remit of this book, an understanding of those principles is important. They are as follows:

(1)   the authority may act only within its powers;
(2)   in so acting it must act properly so as to execute those powers for a proper purpose and having followed proper procedures;
(3)   decisions at whim or by a reference to preordained policies may be unlawful;
(4)   the local authority must not act irrationally;
(5)   the local authority must not act unreasonably.

That is an outline code by which local authorities must exercise their powers.

Local authorities, which are entrusted with executive powers, are not subject to automatic review of executive decisions by the courts. The High Court does not act as a Court of Appeal for those dissatisfied with a local authority decision. However, the courts will intervene against acts of executive authorities if it is shown that those authorities have contravened the law. The judgment of Lord Green MR in *Associated Provincial Picture Houses Ltd v Wednesbury Corporation*[9] established the modern law in this area.

The court must not substitute its decision for that of the local authority. The local authority, in exercising its discretion, must have considered all these matters which it is required to consider (whether as a result of the law or policy) and not to have been influenced by irrelevant considerations. The local authority must not have acted in bad faith or dishonestly; and must not have acted in a manifestly unreasonable manner.

The rationale, according to Lord Greene, is that the local authorities are entrusted with decisions on matters in which the knowledge and experience of the authority can best be trusted to be of value.

However, an authority's decision is subject to review if it is 'so unreasonable that no reasonable authority could have come to that decision'.

Where an authority is given a discretion over an executive act it must exercise that discretion individually in each case.

Therefore, it must not fetter its ability to make a decision by reference to preordained rules or policies or election manifesto commitments (see *Bromley London Borough Council v Greater London Council*.[10] There is, however, no reason why, when authorities have to make similar decisions arising out of similar circumstances, they should not establish broad policy guidelines to assist them in reaching consistent decisions provided that such guidelines are not regarded as a constraining fetter and each case is regarded on its own merits (see, for example, *Isle of Wight County Council v Humphreys*[11]). Where an authority has competing interests of citizens or local taxpayers to take into account, it must fairly and objectively balance those competing interests so as to make a decision which is both fair and reasonable (*Bromley v Greater London Council*).

---

9   [1947] 2 All ER 680.
10   [1982] 2 WLR 62.
11   [1992] COD 308.

11.15.2   Impugning a public authority decision

In *Council of Civil Service Unions v Minister for the Civil Service* (the GCHQ case)[12] the House of Lords reviewed the law and Lord Diplock identified three grounds for impugning a public authority decision:

(1)   Illegality, ie was the public authority empowered to made the decision?
(2)   Irrationality, ie was the decision perverse?
(3)   Procedural propriety, ie was the decision (albeit lawful in principle) correctly executed?

11.15.3   Consultation

The right to or a legitimate expectation of consultation by owners or users of residential care home accommodation has come before the courts (see below). The emergence of the local authority as a dominant purchaser makes it important that the market for residential care is conducted upon fair terms subject to a degree of consensus between providers, sponsors and users.

Even where there is no duty to consult there may be a legitimate expectation of consultation. If there is such a legitimate expectation of consultation then it must be carried out effectively and in good faith with a view to reaching agreement. Such consultation must be seen to have occurred.[13] Even where there is no legitimate expectation of consultation, a local authority will be expected to act reasonably and not in a capricious or high-handed fashion as in imposing terms and conditions of trade upon care home owners which may effectively drive them from the market place.[14]

Thus, although Auld J (as he then was) held in *R v Newcastle upon Tyne City Council, ex parte Dixon*[15] that there was no reason why local authorities should not seek contractual terms which imposed standards beyond those required by the 1984 Act and that there was no constraint upon the commercial terms which an authority might legitimately seek, in the *Cleveland* case the local authority, which sought to impose conditions, which would have devastatingly adverse commercial effects upon owners was found to have acted unlawfully as it had behaved unreasonably. Instead, the authority, through consultation, should have sought to understand the needs of providers and, whilst not ultimately compromising standards of care, allowed time for enhancement of facilities; this would have been a proper exercise of the local authority's powers. A demand for impracticably higher standards, in too short a time scale with no opportunity to improve, was unlawful by reason of irrationality and unfairness of process.

Whilst such cases attracted the attention of the courts following the implementation of the 1993 (Care in the Community) Scheme they will still be subject to important consideration when owners have to consider:

(a)   sudden adverse changes in contracting terms;

---

12   [1985] AC 374.
13   See *R v Kingston and Richmond Health Authority, ex parte Paxman*, CO/2847/93 (unreported).
14   See *R v Cleveland County Council, ex parte Cleveland Care Homes Association* [1994] COD 221.
15   92 LGR 169.

(b) contract terms that inhibit the choice of residents under the Choice Direction;

(c) decisions to accredit or not accredit a particular home;

(d) decisions in relation to individual residents.

11.16 MAY THE AUTHORITY BE COMPELLED TO PROVIDE ACCOMMODATION?

An important issue of topical interest is the extent to which a client or the supporters or family of a client may require a local authority to purchase or provide residential accommodation. Is there an obligation upon a local authority to provide residential accommodation?

The power and the duty are set out in s 21 of the 1948 Act. Other relevant legislation is set out at **11.16.1–11.16.3**.

11.16.1 Chronically Sick and Disabled Persons Act 1970, s 2(1)

'Where a local authority having functions under s 29 of the National Assistance Act 1984 are *satisfied* in the case of any person to whom that section applies who is ordinarily resident in their area *that it is necessary in order to meet the needs* of that person for that authority to make arrangements for all or any of the following matters –

(a) ... (h) [a wide selection of examples of assistance] then ... subject ... (to the provisions of sections 7 (1) of the Local Authority Social Services Act 1970 (which requires local authorities in the exercise of certain functions, including functions under the said section 29, to act under the general guidance of the Secretary of State)), *it shall be the duty of that authority to make those arrangements* in exercise of their functions under the said section 29.'

(Emphasis is supplied by the author.)

Section 1 of that Act placed local authorities under a duty to inform themselves of the need for making arrangements for disabled persons within their area.

11.16.2 Disabled Persons (Services, Consultation and Representation) Act 1986, s 4

'When requested to do so by:

(a) a disabled person ... a local authority shall decide whether the needs of the disabled person call for the provision by the authority of any services in accordance with section 2(1) of the 1970 Act [ie the Chronic Sick and Disabled Persons Act].'

11.16.3   National Health Service and Community Care Act 1990, s 47

'(1) ... where it appears to a local authority that any person for whom they may provide or arrange for the provisions of community care services may be in need of any such services, the authority:

(a)   shall carry out an assessment of his needs for those services, and
(b)   having regard to the results of that assessment shall then decide whether his needs call for the provision by them of any such services.

(2)   If at any time during the assessment of the needs of any person under sub-section (1)(a) above it appears to such a local authority that he is a disabled person, the authority –

(a)   shall proceed to make such a decision as to the services he requires as is mentioned in section 4 of the Disabled Persons (Services Consultation and Representation) Act 1986 without his requesting them to do so under that section; and
(b)   shall inform him that they are doing so and of his rights under that Act.'

'Community care services' are services which a local authority provides, inter alia, under Pt III of the 1948 Act.

11.16.4   'Disabled' person

A 'disabled' person for the purposes of s 47 of the 1990 Act is defined by reference to s 16 of the 1986 Act, which itself identifies such a person in England and Wales as a person described by s 29 of the 1948 Act, ie:

'persons aged eighteen or over who are blind deaf or dumb (or who suffer from a mental disorder of any description) and other persons aged eighteen or over who are substantially and permanently handicapped by illness, injury or congenital deformity of such other disabilities as may be prescribed by the Minister.'

It is probable that all those accommodated in nursing homes or mental nursing homes, and a very large proportion of those accommodated in residential care homes, come within this definition.

11.16.5   Assessment by local authority

Those claiming local authority support or placement in a registered care home will be the subject of an assessment under s 47 of the 1990 Act and will be entitled to such an assessment if it appears to their local authority that they may need community care services.

In *R v Gloucestershire County Council, ex parte Barry*,[16] the House of Lords decided that a local authority was entitled to take into account the authority's own limited resources when determining whether or not a person had 'needs which it was necessary to meet'. The majority decided that in order to define 'necessary needs' the local authority must be the judge of eligibility criteria

---

16   [1994] 4 All ER 421.

which initially could only be judged by reference to available resources. Accordingly, Gloucestershire were held to be justified in withdrawing home help services for Mr Barry.

In *R v Sefton Metropolitan Council, ex parte Help the Aged,*[17] a similar issue fell to be determined in relation to the provision of residential accommodation under s 21 of the 1948 Act, ie may the authority take into account its own limited resources when determining whether an individual is 'in need of care and attention which is not otherwise available to them'.

Jowitt J gave judgment after the *Gloucestershire* case had been decided, but without the benefit of full argument. He held that the decision of the House of Lords was to be applied to s 21 of the 1948 Act exactly as it was to s 2 of the 1970 Act. He held that a local authority was entitled to take into account its own resources when determining whether an applicant was 'in need of care and attention'. That ruling was upheld by the Court of Appeal which, however, reversed the judge's decision upon two further grounds, one of fact and one of legal construction. Those grounds are as follows:

(1) *Fact*: the authority had not formulated a policy which defined criteria of eligibility for need and excluded the applicant because of lack of need. The authority had found that the applicant had a need for care and attention but the authority would not provide such care and attention having regard to eligibility criteria established by reference to its own resources, that was clearly unlawful.

(2) *Law*: the authority argued that the decision was lawful because the applicant's financial resources were sufficient to meet the liability, even though it was below the threshold at which a full contribution could have been demanded, if the authority was to have made the arrangements. The Court of Appeal dismissed this argument on the basis that it overrode the contribution scheme provided by s 22 of the 1948 Act and associated regulations. Lord Woolf held that the relevance of applicants' resources was exhaustively covered by s 22 and the authority were not entitled to implement a policy that excluded an applicant in need with sufficient resources, if those resources fell below the statutory threshold for full contribution.

Therefore, an authority may set a policy which sets criteria of eligibility for those in need of residential accommodation by reference to the authority's limited resources.

However, the authority may not decline to support an applicant assessed to be in need by reference to the applicant's own resources or indeed the authority's resources after the 'need' has been established.

The conclusion at this stage is that the words 'not otherwise available to them' in s 21 of the 1948 Act cannot be construed to include a reference to the applicant's financial resources but must refer to other criteria. What could these be? Perhaps they would cover an applicant who was mentally incapable or an applicant who owns a care home; or possibly an applicant where many needs are adequately met by the National Health Service.

If this is right, an applicant, with capital in excess of the statutory threshold, who is assessed in need of care and attention, may still expect the

17 (Unreported) 26 March 1997

authority to arrange residential care albeit subject to a right to recover the full cost. This would represent a high administrative burden for the Authority.

A further decision is awaited with interest.

Two further decisions assist in construing s 21 of the 1948 Act:

(1)   There is no limit on the type or source of need which may give rise to the local authority's duty to make arrangements for residential accommodation, eg a penniless but fit asylum seeker who is not allowed to work will qualify.[18] However, if the *Sefton* case is right, the poor or the incompetent who are unable to find suitable accommodation may be able to require local authority housing albeit subject to a contribution subject to means testing.

(2)   The power to provide 'residential accommodation' does not extend to the power to make cash advances to support living.[19] The rationale is that the power is to make arrangements for the provisions of accommodation, not (however administratively burdensome) to fund the applicant so that he may make his own arrangements.

For these purposes, 'accommodation' includes board and other services, amenities and requisites provided in connection with the accommodation except where in the opinion of the authority managing the premises their provision is unnecessary (s 21(5) of the 1948 Act).

The authority may also provide transport to and from the accommodation and such other services on the premises as appears to the authority to be required (s 21(7) of the 1948 Act).

11.17   PUBLIC FUNDING OF CARE

11.17.1   Background

Until the mid-1500s, the relief of poverty was largely a matter for the Church and there was little systematic provision. A more formal provision was made by the Elizabethan Poor Law with responsibility being firmly placed on local (parish) authorities. Under this legislation, the only form of relief for those unable to work was to enter the Poor House as a resident: there being no 'out relief'. The Poor Law made the relief of poverty a local authority business and Poor Houses were built, maintained and controlled by the local authority and their funding was firmly in the realm of the local authority. Since the local authority paid the whole cost, it did not matter whether they were paying for food, clothing, personal expenses, housing or personal care.

Over time, there was eventually private provision for the sick and elderly but this went largely unregulated until the Beveridge legislation at the end of World War II.

There was a major change in 1948 when the Poor Law became the National Assistance Act (1948) and the funding of it moved from local to

---

18   See *R v London Borough of Hammersmith and Fulham, ex parte M* (1997) *The Times*, 19 February. Collins J.

19   See *R v Secretary of State for Health, ex parte London Borough of Hammersmith and Fulham* (1977) *The Times*, 15 July.

central government. From 1948, all housing costs for assisted persons were met under the National Assistance scheme and later under the Supplementary Benefits Act 1976 where claimants were divided into several groups: non-householders – not liable for housing costs; householder tenants – responsible for rent; householder owners responsible for mortgage interest and boarders – 'person(s) paying an inclusive charge for board and lodging'. Residents of both public and private care homes clearly fell into this last category and the Supplementary Benefits Commission was content to pay any 'care' element of these changes. Since central government now paid the whole cost, again it really did not matter whether they were paying for food, clothing, personal expenses, housing or personal care provided that they made arrangements for provision rather than providing cash for self-provision.

The Social Security Act 1980 fundamentally reorganised supplementary benefit by starting a process of differentiation between housing and other costs. In 1985 the housing costs of tenants became the responsibility of local authorities whilst boarders and owner occupiers remained with the DHSS. By leaving boarders alone, the legislation left care home residents alone and responsibility for funding the whole of private care home fees remained with central government. There were, however, special arrangements with local authorities as to the funding of persons in National Assistance Act (Pt III) accommodation: public care homes, whereby the local authority became responsible for the 'housing' and 'personal care' elements of these charges whilst central government remained responsible for food, clothing, personal expenses etc: the items covered by the supplementary benefit ordinary scale rates albeit by funding the resident to enable payment of a contribution to the local authority to reimburse these elements of the obligations undertaken by them.

In 1986, supplementary benefit was replaced by income support and the whole benefit structure 'simplified' by the Social Security Act 1986 and it is in the regulations made under this Act that we see the first separation between 'boarders' and residents of residential care homes.

After a number of scandals in the early to mid-1980s, eg so-called 'young spongers' spending the summer as 'boarders' in holiday resorts, benefit for boarders was split into income support at the ordinary scale rates for day-to-day needs and the housing element for which housing benefit was paid by the local authority with standard deductions for the food and utilities supplied as part of the board and lodging package.

Residents of private residential care homes, however, remained where they were as part of the income support scheme, one of the 'special cases', and it was not until the commencement of the NHS and Community Care Act 1990 in April 1993 that responsibility for the 'care element' of new entrants to private residential care and nursing home fees passed from the DSS to local social services authorities.

The position now is that, subject to a means test, central government pays for day-to-day needs by way of the income support ordinary scale rates; it also pays for the 'housing' element of care home charges through income support by the addition of the 'residential allowance' to the 'need' element of income support whilst the local authority meets the 'care' element of the private care home charges. Thus the resident who cannot meet the charges receives assistance from both central and local government.

However, the local authority pays the arrangements and is then required to recover the government's share by way of a contribution under s 22 of the 1948 Act.

With the introduction of the new Act in 1993, control of who could and could not benefit from assisted accommodation in private residential care homes also passed to the local authority and, it was planned, that 'self-placement' should come to an end except for those able to pay the full cost themselves without recourse to a means tested benefit, and that there should initially be four methods of funding:

(1)   those accommodated privately who were self-funding;
(2)   those accommodated pre-April 1993 who were accommodated and supported by the local authority;
(3)   those accommodated pre-April 1993 who were accommodated privately and supported by income support;
(4)   those placed and supported post-April 1993 whose accommodation costs would be supported by income support but whose care costs would be borne by the local authority.

But it was recognised that those accommodated before April 1993 would eventually die and that there would then be only the other two groups left.

However, because of difficulties with drafting of legislation, several other groups came into existence including:

(1)   those who had placed themselves privately and were able to support their costs with the assistance of income support but without the assistance or involvement of the local authority;
(2)   those who had placed themselves privately, and were initially able to support their costs without the assistance of income support or the local authority but ran out of money;
(3)   those who were initially placed by the local authority and supported by them and income support but who acquired capital assets by one route or another, often from the sale of their home one or more years down the line;
(4)   those who were initially placed by the local authority but not supported by them because their income or capital was too high, ie the whole cost of support was recoverable through the clients' contribution.

11.18   ENTRY INTO THE CARE HOME SYSTEM BEFORE 1993

11.18.1   Local authority homes

Entry into local authority 'Part III' homes prior to 1993 was strictly controlled and financed by the local authority. The only charge they could make was the single rate of retirement pension per person per week (currently £64.25) and the resident had to be left with a weekly allowance for personal expenses (currently £14.10) per week. If the resident could not afford these charges, then income support was paid to this level and payments were made to the resident who paid the authority. These arrangements remain in force and cause little difficulty to residents but are a considerable financial drain to the authority. Not surprisingly, authorities have tried all manner of routes to avoid these arrangements and to transfer these residents to the 'post-April 1993' system. Government has, however, set its face against such avoidance measures and, whilst it has lost individual battles, seems to have won the war.

11.18.2 Private homes

Although we speak, perhaps loosely, of the 'placement' of people in private residential care homes, before 1993 there was effectively no control over who was and who was not accommodated in such establishments. People simply found a place in a home and admitted themselves and, to the extent that their resources were insufficient to meet their needs, the DSS paid the balance without question and whilst the local authority was responsible for the registration and conduct of such homes, it had no direct control (as it now does) over who was admitted to which home.

11.18.3 Preserved rights

This group of residents now have 'preserved rights', that is, they are treated by income support as a special category to whom the usual rules do not apply. They themselves made the contract with the owner of the home and are personally responsible for the costs which they pay out of their own resources topped up, where appropriate, with income support up to a ceiling defined within DSS regulations.

The theory of income support is that it provides a stream of income up to the statutorily specified level of need for the individual claimant and those deemed to be statutorily dependent on him. In the case of these residents, the level of financial need is specified in reg 19 of and Sch 4 to the Income Support (General) Regulations 1987 (as amended) (ISGR).[20] Briefly, the regulations define a residential care home as an establishment required to be registered as such under the Registered Homes Act 1984 and is so registered.

Once the adjudication officer at the DSS has satisfied himself that the resident has been continuously accommodated in a care home since before the commencement of the Act in April 1993 and that reg 19 is appropriate, the applicable amount (weekly need figure) is prescribed by Sch 4 to ISGR as 'the weekly charge for the accommodation', plus a weekly amount for personal expenses. None of the usual income support premiums are payable.

Current rates are:

Residential Homes Reason care is required	Weekly amount
Old age	£208
Past or present mental disorder but not mental handicap	£220
Past or present drug or alcohol dependence	£220

---

20 SI 1981/1967.

Mental handicap	£250
Physical disablement if under pension age or over pension age where the disablement began before pension age	£285
Physical disablement if pension age or more	£208
Very dependent elderly	£240
Any other condition	£208
Amount of increase if home is in Greater London	£41

Nursing Homes **Reason care is required**	**Weekly amount**
Past or present mental disorder but not mental handicap	£312
Past or present drug or alcohol dependence	£312
Mental handicap	£318
Physical disablement if under pension age or over pension age where the disablement began before pension age	£352
Physical disablement if pension age or more	£208
Very dependent elderly	£311
Terminal illness	£311
Any other condition (including elderly)	£311
Amount of increase if home is in Greater London	£46

Having assessed the 'applicable amount' for a resident under reg 19 and Sch 4, the adjudication officer then goes on to look at the resources of the claimant and to determine which, if any, of these resources should be taken into account as income.

11.18.4   What is income?

Generally, income is treated similarly for both income support and local authority assessment purposes but some income is wholly or partially ignored.

Income which is completely ignored is as follows:

(a)   attendance allowance (unless resident in a residential care home or nursing home before 1 April 1993);
(b)   disability living allowance care component (unless resident in a residential care home or nursing home before 1 April 1993);
(c)   disability living allowance mobility component;
(d)   housing benefit;
(e)   council tax benefit;
(f)   income from capital and savings;
(g)   pensions paid with the George Cross or Victoria Cross; special pre-1973 war widows' payments.

Income which is partially ignored is as follows:

(a)   war widow's and war disablement pensions (£10 per week);
(b)   charitable and voluntary payments (£10 per week);
(c)   student loan (£10 per week).

If the total of these three disregards comes to more than £10 per week, only £10 in total will be disregarded.

11.18.5   Earned income

Income from employment or self-employment is treated differently. Depending on who the claimant is and where the earnings come from, either £5, £10, £15 or £25 per week will be ignored.

11.18.6   Income taken into account in full

Income other than that described above is normally taken into account in full after tax has been deducted. This would include most social security benefits, and any family credit and student grants but not loans. Retirement pension, invalid care allowance, invalidity benefit and widow's pensions, maintenance and occupational pensions count in full.

As we have seen, as part of the 'special category' status of this group, attendance allowance or DLA care component remains payable to them but it is taken into account in full as a resource by the adjudication officer so it ceases to be of any benefit to them, being deducted from the final amount of income support payable.

11.18.7   The income support calculation

The present weekly allowance for personal expenses is £14.10 and a typical income support calculation for this group would be:

Applicable amount		Resources	
Accommodation		Retirement pension	£62.45
(old age)	£208.00	Attendance allowance	£49.50
Personal expenses	£14.10	Private pension	£25.00
TOTAL	£222.10	TOTAL	£136.95

Income support   **£222.10−£136.95 = £85.15**

Many residential care homes charge amounts much in excess of these ceilings which are comparatively low when compared to charges for full board and lodging without personal care at smaller seaside hotels where many elderly people choose to spend their latter years. The ceilings were set by government in 1987 to limit public spending in this area and have simply kept pace with inflation since their introduction. Unhappily, as an 'anti-avoidance' measure there is no method by which the local authority can 'top up' the money available to people with preserved rights unless they are first evicted from the home where they live, and that eviction constitutes a genuine loss of home.

On a simple transfer between homes the person transfers with preserved rights. As the fees recoverable are not the most generous, the ability to opt for a transfer may be inhibited.

Preserved rights are also lost and the resident enters the 'post-April 1993' system of funding when they are absent from the home for more than 13 weeks (4 weeks for temporary residents) or in hospital for more than 52 weeks.

11.19 ENTRY INTO THE CARE HOME SYSTEM AFTER 1993

The government's intention was that people who needed (or wanted) to live in a private care home after the introduction of the new Act would fall into one of two groups. Those who could manage to pay the fees should simply find a home, place themselves in it, make a contract with the owner and pay the fees until they died. Those who could not afford to pay the fees would present themselves to the local authority who would carry out an assessment of need. If the assessment showed that they needed to be in a care home then they would be offered a choice of home (within financial limits), some homes being local authority run and others being privately run, and the authority would make the arrangements, it would make the contract with the home, it would pay the fees and it would then recover from the resident as much as he or she could statutorily afford to pay. The resident, meanwhile, would be able to claim income support at ordinary scale rates to cover day-to-day needs and personal expenses plus an additional 'residential allowance' to cover the 'housing' element of the care home charges and in order to fund his obligations to the authority.

11.20 Local authority assessment

This scheme deserves to be investigated thoroughly by way of an example.

Mrs Jones is an 81 year old who lives alone in a council house. She has no capital but lives on her State retirement pension and a small private pension from her late husband's employment. She does not qualify for income support but she does receive about £40 per week towards her rent and council tax from the local authority. She has no children or other family but manages quite well with the help of neighbours, a home help and meals on wheels. She has a stroke which paralyses her left side but leaves her mind as sharp as ever. She is admitted to hospital and, whilst the treatment gives her some use in her side, it is clear that she cannot manage at home decides, with a social worker's encouragement, to move into a residential home, Sunnyside.

The local authority contracts with the owner of Sunnyside for Mrs Jones's accommodation there and agrees to pay £210 per week.

If Mrs Jones had been able to go home she would have received attendance allowance of about £50 and income support of about £25 per week and all her rent and council tax would have been paid. At Sunnyside, there is no rent or council tax to pay, but she is not allowed to have attendance allowance because that is a 'care' type benefit from central government and the local authority is responsible for 'care' for people in homes. Thus, the local authority must decide how much she can pay. They do this by telling her to claim income support as a care home resident under the new (April 1993) scheme which she does. The DSS assess income support as follows:

Applicable amount		Resources	
Personal allowance	£49.15	Retirement pension	£62.45
Higher pensioner premium	£26.55	Private pension	£25.00
Residential allowance	£56.00		
TOTAL	£131.70	TOTAL	£87.45

Income support   **£131.70 − £87.45 = £44.25**

Thus, she receives £44.25 per week. The local authority assesses Mrs Jones's contribution to her fees as £117.61 per week leaving her with £14.10 per week for her personal expenses such as clothes, hair dressing, newspapers, etc. The assessment is as follows:

Applicable amount		Resources	
Personal allowance	£14.10	Retirement pension	£62.45
		Private pension	£25.00
		Income support	£44.25
TOTAL	£14.10	TOTAL	£131.70

Income support   **£131.70 − £14.10 = £117.60**

The local authority is paying out £210 for Mrs Jones and recovering from her £117.60 in respect of housing and day-to-day needs. Therefore, the local authority has a net obligation of £92.40 in respect of her care.

11.21   CAPITAL

The assessment of Mrs Jones's contribution would be different if Mrs Jones had capital. Capital is the main bone of contention in the process of moving into residential care. The effect depends on the amount and type of capital.

11.21.1   Capital under £10,000

If Mrs Jones has less than £10,000, there is no effect on the amounts either paid by income support or taken by the local authority but she must make sure she spends the income from the capital as she receives it. If she does not, it becomes capital itself and is added to the original sum. If this process takes her over the limit then the next level rules apply.

11.21.2   Capital between £10,000.01 and £16,000

Tariff income is applied to the capital which lies between these limits. The rule is that actual income from the capital is ignored and income of £1 per week is 'assumed' to arise from each unit of £250 'or part thereof' between these limits. So, if she has £15,903, the first £10,000 is ignored, the balance of £5903 produces 23 whole units of £250 and one unit of £153; 24 units in all by the rule so she is assumed to have an additional weekly income of £24 and her income support claim now looks like this:

Applicable amount		Resources	
Personal allowance	£ 49.15	Retirement pension	£ 62.45
Higher pensioner premium	£ 26.55	Private pension	£ 25.00
Residential allowance	£ 56.00	Tariff income	£ 24.00
TOTAL	£131.70	TOTAL	£111.45

Income support   **£131.70−£111.45 = £20.25**

This is a substantial saving for central government, but the local authority still sends the same bill because its assessment now looks like this:

Applicable amount		Resources	
Personal allowance	£ 14.10	Retirement pension	£ 62.45
		Private pension	£ 25.00
		Income support	£ 20.25
		Tariff income	£ 24.00
TOTAL	£ 14.10	TOTAL	£131.70

Amount payable   **£131.70−£14.10 = £117.60**

One of the things that frequently goes wrong with people in this group is that income support (and technically the local authority charge) needs to be reassessed frequently. Mrs Jones, in this example, would be spending £24 per week of her capital on her local authority bill so every 7 weeks or therabouts her capital will drop by £250 and her income support should increase by £1. Since she is unlikely to know the ins and outs of the tariff income rule herself, and has no relatives to keep an eye on this, the DSS will not do anything until someone approaches them or an annual or bi-annual assessment comes round. But as it makes no difference to either the local authority or the owner of Sunnyside, who both get paid the same amount no matter what, the odds are that she will lose track of her savings and lose benefit.

Capital over £16,000

This really is nice and simple! If you have capital over £16,000, even 1p, then the local authority sends you a bill for the whole of the amount of your care, £210 per week in Mrs Jones' case, and you can't claim any income support so you just pay up. The good news is that you can claim attendance allowance and Mrs Jones could get an additional £50 per week towards the cost of her care.

11.21.3   What is 'capital'?

Capital includes any assets or savings which belong to the claimant or partner. It can be difficult to distinguish capital from income. In most cases, capital resources arise out of income resources, ie they represent savings out of past income. However, before they undergo the change from income to capital all relevant debts including, in particular, tax liabilities, are first deducted.

11.21.4   Capital which is ignored

Some capital will be ignored[21] such as:

(a) the cash or surrender value of an annuity;
(b) the value of the right to receive any income under a life interest or from a life rent or an occupational or private pension or any rent or most reversionary interests;
(c) the right to receive a capital sum by instalments;
(d) the sale value of the right to an income in another country which cannot be transferred to this country;
(e) money from social work departments for children, unless the claimant is on strike;
(f) money from the Social Fund, the Macfarlane Trust, the Macfarlane (Special Payments) Trust or the Independent Living Fund or its successors;
(g) the assets of any business, but only for 26 weeks or longer than that if reasonable where the claimant is ill, unable to work in the business because of the illness, and intends to return to it any NHS travelling expenses, welfare foods payments, prison visiting payments, or any arrears of special war widow's payments, but only for up to 52 weeks.

11.21.5   Income treated as capital

The following items are treated as capital, although they would otherwise be regarded as income:

(a) annual bounty from the fire brigade, coastguard, lifeboat, territorial or reserve forces;
(b) holiday pay payable more than 4 weeks after the end of the employment;
(c)   most income derived from capital;
(d) advances of earnings or loans from employers or income tax refunds (except to strikers);
(e) prisoners' discharge grants;
(f) arrears of custodian's payment from a local authority.

11.21.6   How to value capital

Capital is valued at its current market or surrender value, after deducting any debt or mortgage secured on it and 10 per cent for the expenses of the sale, if there will be such expenses.

Capital abroad which cannot be brought to this country is valued at the price it could be sold for in the UK.

In cases of dispute, it must be first established that the claimant owns an asset which is saleable. Assets should not be valued at a figure higher than anything a person could realise on them.

Where a claimant owns something jointly with one or more other persons they are treated as if each of them were entitled to equal shares. The cost of

---

21 Capital Disregards – Income Support (General) Regulations 1987 (ISGR), Sch 10; Local Authority National Assistance (Assessment of Resources) Regulations 1992 (NAARR), Sch 4.

converting money into sterling is deducted from the value of capital paid in any other currency.

Personal possessions will not be counted as part of capital unless it is thought that they have been acquired in order to reduce capital and increase benefit. There is no clear definition of 'personal possessions' but items in regular use would presumably count, even if they were valuable, such as an expensive car. It is less clear how stamp collections or valuable paintings are to be treated.

Capital paid to a third party on behalf of any member of the claimant's family is treated as the claimant's if the money is derived from social security, or if it is used for food, ordinary clothing or footwear (not school uniform or sports kit), household fuel, rent or rates which qualify for housing benefit, or other housing costs to the extent that they are met by income support.

11.21.7   Capital other than property

Insurance policies – Money paid to the claimant in consequence of damage or loss to the home or any personal possession is ignored for 26 weeks or longer if it is to be used for repair or replacement.

Endowment policies – The surrender value of an endowment policy is completely ignored but not money received on maturity of the policy.

Money in trust – Money in trust must be valued as any other capital or income. Money put in trust for a child after a personal injury will be ignored until the child leaves school. Payments actually made by these or other personal injury trusts will normally be treated as capital or income.

Payments of income from a discretionary trust will normally be treated as voluntary or charitable payments.

The value of a trust derived from a personal injury to the claimant is wholly ignored. However, the compensator of a personal injury victim is required to repay to the DSS all DSS benefits paid to a victim prior to final settlement, irrespective of whether such sums are withheld from the victim's compensation settlement.

Business assets – The assets of a business wholly or partly owned by the claimant will be ignored so long as he is engaged in the business, or for long enough to allow for the sale if it ceases trading. Business assets have been defined as 'part of the fund employed and risked in the business'.

If the claimant owns a business in the form of a company either alone or with partners, the capital of the business is treated as belonging to him and, accordingly, the value of the shares is ignored.

Social security payments – All social security payments are taken into account first as income, and then as capital (if not spent immediately) except arrears of DLA attendance and mobility allowance, and of any means tested benefit, all of which are ignored for 52 weeks.

Social fund payments are completely ignored.

11.21.8   The capital value of the home

The dwelling occupied as the home is ignored as are any parts of the premises which it would be impracticable to sell separately, and croft land in Scotland. The home includes the dwelling together with any garage, garden and outbuildings. Of course, people who move permanently into residential care will no longer be occupants of their former home and therefore do not come into this category.

11.21.9 The capital value of premises other than the home for income support purposes only

Any premises occupied by a partner or close relative 'as his home' who is aged over 60 or incapacitated are completely ignored.

The value of the following premises is disregarded for a period of 6 months, or longer it if it is thought reasonable:

(a) premises acquired for occupation;
(b) any premises which the claimant is taking steps to sell;
(c) any premises in respect of which the claimant has commenced legal proceedings with a view to occupation;
(d) premises which are being repaired or altered before occupation.

The following amounts of money connected with property are disregarded for a period of 6 months, or longer if it is thought reasonable:

(a) the value of capital connected with property;
(b) the proceeds of the sale of a former home if they are to be used to buy another;
(c) compensation for damage to or loss of a home, money acquired for essential repairs or improvements;
(d) money deposited with a housing association as a condition of occupation of a former matrimonial home.

Of course, the key provision is 'any premises which the claimant is taking steps to sell'. The DSS will ignore the value of the former home if it is on the market for a reasonable sum for 6 months, or longer if it is thought reasonable. If, however, the DSS does not think that the sale price is reasonable, it will regard the house as capital. In such circumstances, the resident can appeal against this decision to an independent Social Security Appeal Tribunal.

11.21.10 The capital value of the home for local authority assessments

These regulations are much tighter than the income support regulations, and the value of the home will only be ignored if it is the dwelling of a temporary resident in circumstances where he intends to return to occupy that dwelling as his home and which is still available to him or it is occupied by a partner, former partner or a relative, provided the partner or relative is aged 60 or over, or is incapacitated or is a child whom the resident is liable to maintain.

Therefore, residents find that the DSS will pay them income support because, since their house is for sale, the DSS will ignore its value. Nevertheless, the local authority still charges them for the whole amount of their care and because it does not ignore the value of the house, the resident may have only the income support to use to assist in meeting their contribution liability.

If Mrs Jones had no liquid capital but a house worth £50,000, which she put up for sale before entering residential care, her income support assessment would be as follows:

Applicable amount		Resources	
Personal allowance	£49.15	Retirement pension	£62.45
Higher pensioner premium	£26.55	Private pension	£25.00
Residential allowance	£56.00		
TOTAL	£131.70	TOTAL	£87.45

Income support   **£131.70–£87.45 = £44.25**

So her received income is £131.70 per week because the DSS ignore the value of the house. However, the local authority take account of the value of the house of £45,000. Therefore, she has to pay the full cost of £210 per week, the local authority has the discretion to take a 'charge' on the house through an administrative procedure. A 'charge' is a legally imposed mortgage and when the house is eventually sold, the local authority can recover everything that it is owed by Mrs Jones from the proceeds of the sale. There are, however, three important points to note:[22]

(1)   The power to charge is discretionary; the local authority does not have to do it and it can be petitioned throughout its formal procedures not to do so.
(2)   As with any mortgage, the local authority can apply to the courts at any time for an order to sell the property no matter who is living in it. Such an application can of course be defended.
(3)   The charge may be imposed without the consent of or notification to the resident.

As soon as the house is sold Mrs Jones becomes a 'self-funder' and is able to claim attendance allowance to help her pay the local authority's charges. In a recent case, it was held that since the resident has, in effect, had a loan from the local authority to tide her over while the house was sold, she cannot claim backdated attendance allowance.

11.21.11   Notional capital

If someone spends or gives away capital shortly before or after going into residential care, it will be assumed that the money has been spent or given away to take advantage of the system.

> 'A claimant shall be treated as possessing capital of which he has deprived himself for the purpose of securing entitlement to income support or increasing the amount of that benefit (or reducing liability to the local authority for residential care costs).'[23]

A person deprives himself of capital if he ceases to possess it, even if he receives some other resource in return. The crucial question is the *intention* of the claimant. Obtaining benefit must be a reasonably foreseeable purpose of the

---

22   Health and Social Services and Social Security Adjudications Act 1983, s 21.
23   Income Support (General) Regulations 1987, reg 51; National Assistance (Assessment of Resources) Regulations 1992, reg 25.

transaction. If it can be shown that the money has been spent on something which a prudent person would have spent it on if they had no intention of claiming any benefit then this rule should not be applied.

Only if the donee is a 'liable relative' (spouses, parents of children and those who have received the gift within 6 months prior to care home entry) may be subject to a claim from the DSS to recover the benefit received.

Gifts into trust are even more complicated. The rule of thumb is that any gift made once it is reasonably foreseeable that entitlement to income support and/or admission to a care home will arise will be ineffective insofar as it seeks to enhance entitlement to benefit or reduce liability to local authority charges. Furthermore, any gift which does not relinquish complete control of the asset such as the gift of a house with a lease back or licence to continue to occupy will also be ineffective for those purposes.

There are, however, some precautions which can and should be taken. Take, for example, Mr Kennedy. He and his wife are aged 67 and have no capital or income except for the usual State pensions, but they do live in a house which, because of the quirks of the property market, is now worth £200,000 which they own jointly. Neither of them is in particularly good health but Mrs Kennedy needs so much care that she has had to move into a care home. For income support and care in the community purposes they are no longer a couple, and Mrs Kennedy receives income support to pay a contribution towards her care home fees which the council are obliged to fund. If Mr Kennedy died, Mrs Kennedy would have to sell the house and then she would either have the money or be treated by the DSS and the local authority as having the money; her income support would stop and she would become liable for the whole of the care home fees. There would, however, seem to be nothing to prevent them giving the house away now, and retaining a beneficial life tenancy for Mr Kennedy, because that course of action would not establish or increase entitlement to income support or reduce her fees.

Of course, Mr Kennedy would have to beware of other pitfalls associated with giving away assets. Such gifts can also disrupt the donee's entitlement to benefit by putting them over the capital limit for other social security benefit claims and, however close and trusted they are, donees can go bankrupt or die or disappear removing the donated asset completely from the donor's sphere of influence.

Furthermore, once Mr Kennedy has given away the house and got a tenancy, he is stuck there. If he becomes ill and needs to move to a bungalow or sheltered accommodation, he can't just sell up and move, it's no longer his house!

Capital which is available on application will be treated as the claimant's notional capital unless it is part of a discretionary trust or a trust derived from a personal injury, or a loan which would be secured on disregarded capital.

Capital, cash or resources made available to a third party to be applied for the benefit of the claimant/resident is to be treated as notional capital of the resident. This does not apply where the capital is expressly to be used for matters other than 'ordinary income support needs'.

Example. R is the resident, D is the donor, C is a chauffeur-driven limousine supplier, and S is the shoe manufacturer. D gives S £1,000 and says please provide R with shoes while I am away in Zanzibar for the next 5 years.

That £1,000 counts as capital possessed by R in so far as it is used for shoes. He also gives £5,000 to C to deal with R's transport needs during his absence. That £5,000 is not R's capital under these rules. Therefore, 'top-up payments' from relatives or others, even if made as a lump sum of capital to the home, will not count as capital because they are not made to cover 'ordinary income support needs', they are made to cover additional costs not covered by either the income support or local authority funding schemes.

11.21.12 Couples, liable relatives and residential care

When elderly couples separate so that one can receive residential or nursing care, it is often the case that one of them, usually the man, has the bulk of the income and capital and the other has almost none. Such people are causing considerable difficulties for local authorities seeking to apply the strict regulations about charging. Where the spouse in the care home has the resources, the spouse remaining at home is often in danger of being driven into poverty by the means test.

In the reverse situation, the remaining spouse may, in certain circumstances, refuse either to give information or to enter into unreasonable voluntary arrangements.

The first problem to arise is one of information. When a person enters local authority residential care, he or she becomes a separate person from his or her spouse for financial purposes. It is clear from both the Act and the guidance that authorities have neither right nor power to require the spouse to give any financial details, although they can of course ask nicely. Some authorities are purporting to have the right to require the spouse to provide such information and their assessment forms are designed to give this impression. Such rights probably exist where a third party contribution is required as a result of a choice for superior accommodation.

Liable relatives faced with a request for information should always seek skilled advice before providing it. Before responding to such a request, they might wish to ask the authority what guidelines it has in place for determining the amount of maintenance it will seek, how it intends to apply those guidelines and what are the arrangements, if any, for negotiation and review of the amounts suggested by the authority.

However, 'liable relatives' are liable to maintain spouses and others for whom they are liable.[24] Where local authorities have made arrangements for residential accommodation they may complain to the magistrates' court against anyone liable.[25] The court will have regard to all circumstances and, in particular, the resources of the defendant before ordering such payment as they consider to be appropriate.[26]

11.21.13 How much should separated spouses pay?

If the liable relative decides to supply information, there is a clear temptation for authorities to apply the income support means test to the partner and seek

24 National Assistance Act 1948, s 42.
25 Ibid, s 43(1).
26 Ibid, s 43(2).

to get him or her to pay all income above that level thus driving him or her into poverty – such cases have been reported. Even the Child Support Act which has been described as 'punitive' and 'draconian' does not go as far as this and the Department of Health clearly disapproves of such tactics.

The partner's 'resources' should surely take into account the needs of the partner for their own personal living.

The formal place for such settlements is the magistrates' court and the authority must decide 'whether the amount being sought would be similar to that decided by the courts'. Responsible authorities will consider carefully what criteria they should use in assessing the 'appropriate' amount of maintenance and will have some flexible guidelines in place.

Where information is supplied and an authority asks for a certain sum per week from the liable relative, the amount may be challenged and the matter will be decided in the magistrates' court. The authority's only remedy is to apply to the magistrates' court.[27] The magistrates' court is a family proceedings court and has power to give directions in relation to the issues. In a case of difficulty, a direction to file evidence for means of the liable relative would seem to be appropriate although there is no express provision in the Rules.[28] If the court chooses not to do so then the liable relative can pay nothing or as much or as little as he or she considers to be appropriate. If the authority chooses to apply to the court, then the liable relative will have the assurance of knowing than an independent third party has looked at the issue and that there is a true appeal through the court system. Liable relatives should be reassured that these are not criminal proceedings, that the courts are for their benefit as much as for the authority's and that both sides will get a sympathetic hearing.

Those who withhold relevant information may well be at risk of an order for costs, which could be avoided if sensible disclosure of all 'resources' were made in advance.

11.21.14 People at home with no resources

The other side of the coin is where the resident has all the family resources and is assessed as able to pay the whole or a large part of the charge in the home leaving the spouse remaining at home at or below income support level. I came across a man a couple of years ago who had a pension of £19,000 per year and had developed Alzheimer's disease so badly that he needed to be in a nursing home at a cost of £365 per week. This leaves his wife with an income of £20 per week. This situation can no longer arise because the rules were changed in 1996 to allow him to pay half of his occupational pension to his wife without it counting as his income for either income support or the local authority assessment.

Authorities can allow a (much) larger amount for personal expenses than the amount prescribed (currently £14.10 per week). Allowing a larger allowance will enable the resident to return anything in excess of the prescribed amount to his or her spouse to meet their day-to-day living

---

27 Magistrates' Courts Act 1980, Pt II; Magistrates' Courts Rules 1981, SI 1991/552.
28 Family Proceedings Courts (Matrimonial Proceedings, etc) Rules 1991, SI 1991/1991.

expenses. The Department of Health urges authorities to do this and also urges them to resist the simplistic 'income support levels' type of means test and to take account of the remaining spouse's usual lifestyle. Responsible authorities will consider carefully how much they should return to the spouse at home and will have some flexible guidelines in place.

Again, unreasonable decisions may be challenged by an application for judicial review. Such claims should be made immediately and in any event within 3 months from the decision.

If an authority refuses to allow money for a spouse at home then he or she can use the magistrates' court to obtain a liability order of his or her own. They can also get an attachment order and take the money before it is paid to the local authority.

The rationale is that each spouse is a 'liable relative' for the other.

Capital which is available on application will be treated as the claimant's unless it is part of a discretionary trust or a trust derived from a personal injury, or a loan which would be secured on disregarded capital.

11.22   THE PRIVATE ROUTE

It is also possible for residents to preserve some capital by avoiding the local authority but still relying on income support. If Mrs Jones (who still has her house worth £50,000 which is on the market but no liquid capital) had contracted privately with Sunnyside, she would have been able to claim attendance allowance because she needs help with her bodily functions. However, attendance allowance does not count as income for income support purposes and it also is a trigger for an additional 'premium' in the needs section of the income support calculation, so her income support calculation would look like this:

Applicable amount		Resources	
Personal allowance	£56.00	Allowance not counted	£49.50
TOTAL	£168.85	TOTAL	£87.45
Income support	**£168.85 − £87.45 = £81.40**		

So her total income would be:

Retirement pension	£62.45
Private pension	£25.00
Attendance allowance	£49.50
Income support	£81.40
TOTAL	**£218.35**

She pays Sunnyside £210 per week and has £8.35 left for herself instead of the £14.10 she would have had if she had gone down the local authority route. Of course, the income support will stop when the house is sold but it would do anyway, and she will have had the benefit of attendance allowance of about £50 per week throughout all the time it takes to sell the house. There are, of course, some potential drawbacks. Some home owners charge private residents more than local authority residents and, if the differential is appreciable, the attraction of such a scheme declines dramatically. If and when her capital does decline to £16,000 and she makes a new claim for income support, or for the local authority to arrange residential accommodation for her, she should have little difficulty. On the credit side:

(a) her care needs will be very visible on assessment;
(b) she will be in a home of her choice.

BUT she must expressly make that choice when she seeks a community care assessment.

APPENDIX

SPECIMEN CONTRACT FOR RESIDENTIAL CARE HOME

THIS AGREEMENT is made on the   day of   1997

BETWEEN

(1)   ("THE CLIENT") of [   ]; and

(2)   [of ("THE HOME")

WHEREAS:

(A)   The Home carries on a number of small residential care homes for persons having various needs of care and support as a result of difficulties and disabilities in learning and daily living.

(B)   The client wishes to be accommodated in a care home operated by the Home with a view to such accommodation becoming their permanent home (subject to the provisions of this Agreement) for the rest of his/her life.

(C)   The Home have agreed to provide such accommodation and appropriate associated care and attention for the Client.

NOW IT IS HEREBY AGREED as follows:

1.
    1.1   With effect from [   ] 1997 the Home shall provide for the Client accommodation at (name of Home) (   ) a residential care home carried on by the Home or such other accommodation as may from time to time be agreed or determined as appropriate by the Home as herein provided together with board and personal care as may be appropriate to and required for the client from time to time (as hereafter defined).

    1.2   Board and Personal Care shall mean all food and drink and individual care as the Client may require from time to time so as to provide help and assistance with all her individual needs, including bathing, dressing, supervision at mealtimes, laundering of personal items, supplying of clothing so as to meet requirements of warmth decency and personal taste, needs of mobility and communication, educational improvement, leisure activities and specialist medical and therapeutic care (e.g. occupational and speech and language therapy, physiotherapy and osteopathy) provided that such care shall be in accordance with a care plan for the Client agreed between the parties prior to this agreement and annexed hereto marked A as the same may be amended on review.

1.3   Such care plan shall be reviewed as often as may be necessary and in any event at the end of each period of six months commencing upon the date hereof. The Home shall provide all such additional care as may be required as a result of such review or such further care as may apparently be required between reviews without additional charge provided that if any such additional care services increase the cost to the Home of caring for the Client by more than 5% the Home may require fees payable hereby to be so increased upon 14 days notice to the Client.

1.4   The Client is entitled to receive medical treatment provided by the United Kingdom National Health Service free of charge and will be registered with the Home's general medical practitioner .... or such other medical practitioner as the Home may decide after consultation with the Client.
If the Home shall decide after consultation with the Client that she shall receive any medical treatment or therapy from a private practitioner any fees payable in respect of such treatment shall be reimbursed by the Client to the Home within 28 days after a written request therefor provided that the Client shall have agreed that such fees be incurred.

1.5   It is intended that the Client should occupy a single room at the Home but both parties recognise that either as a result of the Client's wishes or in order more effectively to provide care and attention for the Client it may be necessary for her to move to other accommodation (such a move only to be effected after consultation with the Client and only so as to share with another or others with her written approval) and accordingly any occupation by the Client of any accommodation provided by the Home shall be upon a non-exclusive basis as a licensee and nothing shall or shall be deemed to create the legal rights and obligations of a tenancy or the relationship of the Landlord and Tenant as between the Home on the one hand and the Client on the other hand.

1.6   Accommodation and care provided to the Client under this Agreement shall be available for the Client's use, support, assistance and enjoyment upon a full time basis throughout the period of this Agreement ie throughout each of the fifty two weeks in any year. If the Client for any reason should be absent:

(a)   The Home will not make the Client's accommodation facilities and services (in so far as they may be personally individual to the Client) to any other person AND

(b)   The Client shall not be allowed any refund credit or allowance or deduction from any fees due hereunder as a result of any such non use or non-enjoyment thereof.

2.   The accommodation and services to be provided hereunder shall be

continuously available to and paid for by the Client and from [   ]
July 1997 without any limit in time unless and until this Agreement shall
have been terminated in accordance with the provisions herein
contained.

3. The Client may bring to her accommodation with the Home and retain
    with and about her such personal property as she may wish provided that
    the holding of any such items shall not contravene any law to which the
    Client or the Home may be subject and further that (in its final discretion
    but only to be exercised after consultation with the Client) the Home may
    require the Client to remove any item if the Home consider such an item
    to be unsafe or to pose a risk of accident to or adverse influence upon the
    Client or any other person at accommodation provided by the Home.

    The Home will not be liable under any circumstances (save for wilful
    default or action upon its part or the part of its staff) for loss of or damage
    to any such item (including but not limited to money) unless such items
    shall have been lodged with the Home for safekeeping and kept under the
    exclusive control of the Home.

4.
    4.1 The Home shall not under any circumstances be liable to the Client
         or any other person claiming upon either or both of their behalf or in
         trust for them or either of them or in any way so that such a claim is
         derived from rights due or alleged to be due to them or either of
         them save to the extent that such a claim is within the limits of
         insurance cover effected by the Home which cover and the limits
         thereof and thereto are as follows:

    4.2 The Home will throughout this Agreement maintain policies of
         insurance to cover the risks identified in clause 4.1 with limits of
         indemnity no less than those set out in clause 4.1.

    4.3 As full consideration for the provision of accommodation and
         services as herein provided to the Client, the Client hereby agrees to
         pay to the Home the sum of [   ]
         (   ) per annum (or such adjusted sum as may be payable
         pursuant to Clause 5.2 hereof) such sum to be exclusive of any Value
         Added Tax payable thereon which shall be payable in addition,
         payment to be made to the Home in cleared funds by equal quarterly
         instalments in advance upon 1st April, 1st July, 1st October and 1st
         January in any year the first such payment to be paid in cleared funds
         prior to the Client taking up accommodation with the Home, shall be
         a rateable proportion of one quarter's payment calculated from the
         day of commencement of provision of accommodation until 30th
         September 1997.

         4.3.1 The amount of the annual fees shall be adjusted from time to
                time in accordance with changes in the Client's requirements

for care as hereinbefore provided and changes in the costs of such care.

a)   the annual fee shall be reviewed every year so that any change will take effect from 1st April following commencement of the Review;

b)   by 1st December in any year the Home shall by written notice inform the Client of the fees proposed to be payable for the year due to commence on the following 1st April.

Any adjustments may only be made by reference either to increases or reductions (actual or reasonably anticipated) in the cost of provision of accommodation and services for the Client (including without limitation the cost of provision of working capital for the Home) AND adjustments in the requirements of the Client's care as determined in accordance with this Agreement.

For the avoidance of doubt the Home shall be obliged to reflect reductions in such costs and requirements in any such proposal as they are entitled so as to reflect any increases therein.

(c)   by no later than 15th January following such notification the Client shall by notice in writing inform the Home whether he/she accepts such proposal or not. Failure to so inform by the Client shall be deemed conclusive acceptance of such proposals by him.

(d)   if the Client shall not accept such proposals the parties shall negotiate together in an attempt to resolve any such difference. If such negotiations shall be unsuccessful by 1st February in any year either party may require the other to agree upon the appointment of an expert to resolve the dispute or in default of agreement with seven days from a written request, seek appointment of such an expert by the President for the time being of the Law Society or his Deputy if the President shall be unavailable or there be no holder of such post at that time which appointment shall be final and conclusively binding upon the parties.

(e)   any such expert shall act as an expert and not an arbitrator and shall be entitled to conduct such enquiries by such procedures as he deems fit without challenge. His power shall be to determine the issue as to fees payable hereunder from 1st April following his appointment and he shall deliver any such determination within 28 days. Any decision of such an expert shall be final and binding upon the parties.

4.3.2   In addition to fees the Client shall reimburse to the Home the cost to the Home of any extra goods or services to the Home reasonably supplied to the Client or supplied at the Client's request or with her written approval.

4.3.3 The Home shall not be responsible to supply any pocket money for the Client which shall be her sole responsibility.

4.3 If the Client shall fail to make any payment due hereunder by the due date for payment (whether or not the amount thereof shall then have been formally determined by the Expert as hereinbefore provided) he shall pay to the Home interest upon the sum outstanding from the due date for payment until actual payment calculated at a rate of 4% above the Base Lending Rate of Midland Bank Plc for the time being.

5.

5.1 Either party may terminate this Agreement by not less than six months notice in writing to expire upon only 31st March or 31st October in any year and upon expiry of any such notice this Agreement shall terminate without prejudice to the accrued rights and liabilities of the parties.

6.

6.1 If the Client shall die during the period of this Agreement the fees payable hereunder shall remain due and payable for [   ] months and thereafter until whichever shall be the earlier of [   ] and [   ] October **PROVIDED THAT** such liability shall cease forthwith upon if the Home place another client in the accommodation last occupied by the Client which the Home undertake to use reasonable endeavours to achieve.

6.2 Any notice to be given by either party to the other under this Agreement shall be in writing and may be given by hand delivery or delivering by Recorded Delivery postal service or Registered Mail or by Facsimile Transmission proof of delivery (which shall be conclusively deemed to be confirmation of delivery by postal or telecommunication services where appropriate) shall be conclusive proof of receipt.

6.3 This Agreement shall be governed by English law and the parties (save where otherwise expressly provided) agree to the submission of disputes to the exclusive jurisdiction of the English Courts.

AS WITNESS the hands of the parties hereto the day and year first before written.

INDEX

References in the right-hand column are to paragraph numbers.